Human Developme[
Freedom

C000150198

How has human development evolved during the past 150 years of globalisation and economic growth? How has human development been distributed across countries? How do developing countries compare to developed countries? Do social systems matter for well-being? Are there differences in the performance of developing regions over time? Employing a capabilities approach, *Human Development and the Path to Freedom* addresses these key questions in the context of modern economic growth and globalisation from c.1870 to the present. Leandro Prados de la Escosura shows that health, access to knowledge, standards of living, and civil and political freedom can substitute for GDP per head as more accurate measures of our well-being.

LEANDRO PRADOS DE LA ESCOSURA is Emeritus Professor of Economic History at Carlos III University. He is the author of *Spanish Economic Growth, 1850–2015* (2017). He is the editor of *Exceptionalism and Industrialisation: Britain and Its European Rivals, 1688–1815* (2004) and former editor of the journal *Revista de Historia Económica*.

New Approaches to Economic and Social History

SERIES EDITORS

Marguerite Dupree (University of Glasgow)
Debin Ma University of Oxford
Larry Neal (University of Illinois, Urbana-Champaign)

New Approaches to Economic and Social History is an important new textbook series published in association with the Economic History Society. It provides concise but authoritative surveys of major themes and issues in world economic and social history from the post-Roman recovery to the present day. Books in the series are by recognised authorities operating at the cutting edge of their field with an ability to write clearly and succinctly. The series consists principally of single-author works – academically rigorous and groundbreaking – which offer comprehensive, analytical guides at a length and level accessible to advanced school students and undergraduate historians and economists.

A full list of titles published in the series can be found at:
www.cambridge.org/newapproacheseconomicandsocialhistory

Human Development and the Path to Freedom

1870 to the Present

LEANDRO PRADOS DE LA ESCOSURA
Carlos III University

CAMBRIDGE
UNIVERSITY PRESS

CAMBRIDGE
UNIVERSITY PRESS

University Printing House, Cambridge CB2 8BS, United Kingdom

One Liberty Plaza, 20th Floor, New York, NY 10006, USA

477 Williamstown Road, Port Melbourne, VIC 3207, Australia

314–321, 3rd Floor, Plot 3, Splendor Forum, Jasola District Centre,
New Delhi – 110025, India

103 Penang Road, #05-06/07, Visioncrest Commercial, Singapore 238467

Cambridge University Press is part of the University of Cambridge.

It furthers the University's mission by disseminating knowledge in the pursuit of
education, learning, and research at the highest international levels of excellence.

www.cambridge.org
Information on this title: www.cambridge.org/9781108477345
DOI: 10.1017/9781108769655

First published 2022

A catalogue record for this publication is available from the British Library.

ISBN 978-1-108-47734-5 Hardback
ISBN 978-1-108-70858-6 Paperback

For Teresa

In the present epoch, the domination of material relations over individuals, and the suppression of individuality by fortuitous circumstances, has assumed its sharpest and most universal form, thereby setting existing individuals a very definite task (...) replacing the domination of circumstances and of chance over individuals by the domination of individuals over chance and circumstances.

Karl Marx and Friedrich Engels, *The German Ideology*, 1846

What in the future will probably appear the most significant and far-reaching effect of this success is the new sense of power over their own fate, the belief in the unbounded possibilities of improving their own lot, which the success already achieved created among men.

Friedrich Hayek, *The Road to Serfdom*, 1944

Contents

List of Figures	*page* ix
List of Tables	xiv
Preface	xvii
Introduction	1
Part I An Aggregate View	11
1 *Augmented* Human Development: What Is It? How to Measure It?	13
2 Trends in Human Development	37
3 World Distribution of Human Development	65
Part II *The* OECD *and the* Rest	97
4 Human Development in the *OECD* and the *Rest*	99
5 Human Development in Latin America	135
6 Human Development in Africa	184
Postscript	241
Appendix A The Augmented *Human Development Index: Sources and Procedures*	244
Appendix B Alternative Indices of Augmented *Human Development and Their Drivers*	259
Appendix C International Inequality	260
Appendix D Augmented Human Development Index in World Regions	267

Appendix E Latin America   286
Notes   288
References   298
Index   326

Figures

1.1 Healthy life expectancy at birth (HALE) and life
    expectancy at birth (LEB), 1990–2016   *page* 17
1.2 Quality-adjusted and raw years of schooling
    (1965–2015) (normalised)   18
1.3a *Old* Preston curve, 1870–2015   19
1.3b *Revised* Preston curve, 1870–2015   20
2.1 *AHDI* and its non-income dimensions   39
2.2 *AHDI* and real per capita GDP growth (%)   40
2.3a AHD in the world 1870   42
2.3b AHD in the world 1913   43
2.3c AHD in the world 1938   44
2.3d AHD in the world 1960   45
2.3e AHD in the world 1980   46
2.3f AHD in the world 2015   47
2.4 Kakwani index of life expectancy and social transfers
    (% GDP) in advanced countries, 1880–2013   58
3.1 AHD inequality: breakdown into dimensions'
    contributions (population-weighted MLD)   75
3.2 Relative and absolute AHD inequality, 1870–2015
    (population-weighted MLD) (2015=1)   78
3.3 Relative and absolute inequality in schooling,
    1870–2015 (population-weighted MLD)
    (2015=1)   79
3.4 Relative and absolute inequality in life expectancy,
    1870–2015 (population-weighted MLD) (2015=1)   80
3.5 Relative and absolute inequality in civil and political
    liberties, 1870–2015 (population-weighted MLD)
    (2015=1)   81
3.6 Relative and absolute inequality in real GDP per
    head, 1870–2015 (population-weighted MLD)
    (2015=1)   82

3.7a   Absolute and relative AHD growth incidence curves,
       1870–2015   82
3.7b   Relative AHD growth incidence curves: main phases
       (balanced panel 1870–2015)   83
3.8a   Absolute and relative schooling growth incidence
       curves, 1870–2015   84
3.8b   Relative schooling growth incidence curves: main
       phases (balanced panel 1870–2015)   85
3.9a   Absolute and relative life expectancy growth
       incidence curves, 1870–2015   86
3.9b   Relative life expectancy growth incidence curves:
       main phases (balanced panel 1870–2015)   87
3.10a Absolute and relative civil and political liberties
       growth incidence curves, 1870–2015   87
3.10b Relative civil and political liberties growth incidence
       curves: main phases (balanced panel 1870–2015)   88
3.11a Absolute and relative per capita GDP growth
       incidence curves, 1870–2015   89
3.11b Relative per capita GDP growth incidence curves:
       main phases (balanced panel 1870–2015)   89
3.12   Schooling distribution versus level: bivariate kernel
       linear fit (Epanechnikov, 100)   90
3.13   Life expectancy distribution versus level: bivariate
       kernel linear fit (Epanechnikov, 100)   91
3.14   Civil and political liberties distribution versus level:
       bivariate kernel linear fit (Epanechnikov, 100)   92
3.15   AHD distribution versus level: bivariate kernel
       linear fit (Epanechnikov, 100)   93
3.16   GDP per head distribution versus level (logs):
       bivariate kernel linear fit (Epanechnikov, 100)   94
4.1   *AHDI* and real GDP per head growth in the *OECD*,
       1870–2015   108
4.2   *AHDI* and real GDP per head growth in the *Rest*,
       1870–2015   108
4.3   Relative *AHDI* and Real GDP per head in the *Rest*
       (*OECD*=1)   109
4.4   *AHDI* in *OECD* regions   110
4.5   Kakwani index of schooling in *OECD* regions   117

4.6   Kakwani index of life expectancy in *OECD*
      regions   118
4.7   Index of liberal democracy in *OECD* regions   119
4.8   *AHDI* in regions of the *Rest*. (a) Latin America,
      Eastern Europe, Russia, and East Asia; (b) sub-
      Saharan Africa, north Africa, Middle East, China,
      and South Asia   120
4.9   Kakwani index of schooling in regions of the *Rest*.
      (a) Latin America, Eastern Europe, Russia, and East
      Asia; (b) sub-Saharan Africa, north Africa, Middle
      East, China, and South Asia   121
4.10 Kakwani index of life expectancy in regions of the
      Rest. (a) Latin America, Eastern Europe, Russia, and
      East Asia; (b) sub-Saharan Africa, north Africa,
      Middle East, China, and South Asia   123
4.11 Index of liberal democracy in regions of the *Rest*. (a)
      Latin America, Eastern Europe, Russia, and East
      Asia; (b) sub-Saharan Africa, north Africa, Middle
      East, China, and South Asia   124
4.12 Relative AHD in regions of the *Rest*, 1870–2015
      (*OECD*=1). (a) Latin America, Eastern Europe,
      Russia, and East Asia; (b) sub-Saharan Africa, north
      Africa, Middle East, China, and South Asia   128
4.13a AHD catching up, 1870–1913 (%)   129
4.13b AHD catching up, 1913–1950 (%)   130
4.13c AHD catching up, 1950–1970 (%)   131
4.13d AHD catching up, 1970–1990 (%)   132
4.13e AHD catching up, 1990–2015 (%)   133
5.1   *AHDI* in Latin America   147
5.2   Inter-country *AHDI* distribution in Latin America
      (MLD)   147
5.3   Real GDP per head in Latin America (G-K 1990$,
      logs)   148
5.4   *AHDI* and real GDP per head long-term growth in
      Latin America   148
5.5   *AHDI* and IER in six Latin American countries,
      1870–2010   149
5.6   Schooling in Latin America (Kakwani indices)   150

5.7   Life expectancy in Latin America (Kakwani
      indices)   151
5.8   Civil and political liberties in Latin America
      (Kakwani indices)   152
5.9   Inter-country distribution of *AHDI* and its
      dimensions in Latin America (MLD)   153
5.10 Kakwani index of schooling and public spending on
      education (% GDP) in six Latin American countries,
      1900–2010   154
5.11 Kakwani index of life expectancy and public spending
      on health (% GDP) in six Latin American countries,
      1900–2010   155
5.12 Relative *AHDI* and real GDP per head in Latin
      America (*OECD*=1)   156
5.13 Relative *AHDI* non-income dimensions in Latin
      America (*OECD*=1)   157
6.1   *AHDI* in Africa   190
6.2   Inter-country AHD distribution in Africa and sub-
      Saharan Africa (MLD)   190
6.3   *AHDI* in Africa's regions   191
6.4   Real GDP per head and *AHDI* long-term growth in
      Africa   191
6.5a Real GDP per head in Africa (G-K 1990$, logs)   192
6.5b Real GDP per head in Africa's regions (G-K 1990$,
      logs)   193
6.6   Inequality in AHD and real GDP per head in sub-
      Saharan Africa (MLD)   193
6.7a Schooling in Africa (Kakwani indices)   194
6.7b Schooling in Africa's regions (Kakwani indices)   205
6.8a Life expectancy in Africa (Kakwani indices)   205
6.8b Life expectancy in Africa's regions (Kakwani
      indices)   206
6.9a Civil and political liberties in Africa (liberal
      democracy index)   206
6.9b Civil and Political Liberties in Africa's Regions
      (liberal democracy index)   207
6.10 Relative AHD in Africa and its regions
      (*OECD*=1)   207

6.11 Relative real GDP per head in Africa and its regions
(*OECD*=1) 208
6.12 Relative AHD and its non-income dimensions in
Africa (*OECD*=1) 208
6.13 Relative AHD and its non-income dimensions in
North Africa (*OECD*=1) 211
6.14 Relative AHD and its non-income dimensions in
Central Africa (*OECD*=1) 213
6.15 Relative AHD and its non-income dimensions in
West Africa (*OECD*=1) 215
6.16 Relative AHD and its non-income dimensions in
East Africa (*OECD*=1) 217
6.17 Relative AHD and its non-income dimensions in
Southern Africa (*OECD*=1) 219
C.1 Pop-weighted inequality in schooling: Kakwani index
and original values 260
C.2 Pop-weighted inequality in life expectancy: Kakwani
index and original values 261
E.1 *AHDI* and IER in Latin American countries,
1950–2010 286
E.2 Kakwani index of schooling and public spending on
education (% GDP) in Latin American countries,
1954–2010 287

Tables

1.1 Alternative indices of years of schooling, life expectancy, per capita income, and liberal democracy, 1870–2015   *page* 21

1.2 Multiplicative and additive *augmented* human development indices   31

1.3 *Augmented* and *non-augmented* human development indices   32

1.4 Alternative *augmented* human development indices, 1870–2015   34

2.1 *AHDI* and its components in the world   38

2.2 AHD country ranking at selected benchmark years   48

3.1 International inequality in AHD and its dimensions, 1870–2015 (MLD)   72

3.2 International inequality in real per capita GDP, 1870–2015 (MLD)   76

4.1 *AHDI* across world regions, 1870–2015   100

4.2 AHD inequality within world regions, 1870–2015 (MLD)   103

4.3 *AHDI* and its components: *OECD*   104

4.4 *AHDI* and its components: the *Rest*   106

4.5 AHD catching up in the *Rest*: dimensions' contribution (%)   111

4.6 Decomposing international AHD inequality (population-weighted MLD)   112

4.7 Decomposing international inequality in schooling (population-weighted MLD) (Kakwani indices)   113

4.8 Decomposing international inequality in life expectancy (population-weighted MLD) (Kakwani indices)   114

4.9 Decomposing international inequality in civil and political liberties (population-weighted MLD)   115

4.10 Decomposing international inequality in real per
capita GDP, 1870–2015 (population-weighted
MLD) 116
5.1 *AHDI* and its components: Latin America 145
5.2 AHD catching up in Latin America: dimensions'
contribution (%) 158
5.3 AHD ranking of Latin American countries 159
5.4 AHD and its dimensions ranking of Latin American
countries 164
6.1 *AHDI* and its components: Africa 188
6.2 *AHDI* and its components: North Africa 195
6.3 *AHDI* and its components: Central Africa 197
6.4 *AHDI* and its components: West Africa 199
6.5 *AHDI* and its components: East Africa 201
6.6 *AHDI* and its components: Southern Africa 203
6.7 AHD catching up in Africa: dimensions'
contribution (%) 210
6.8 AHD catching up in North Africa: dimensions'
contribution (%) 212
6.9 AHD catching up in Central Africa: dimensions'
contribution (%) 214
6.10 AHD catching up in West Africa: dimensions'
contribution (%) 216
6.11 AHD catching up in East Africa: dimensions'
contribution (%) 218
6.12 AHD catching up in Southern Africa: dimensions'
contribution (%) 220
6.13 *AHDI* in African countries, 1950–2015 221
6.14 AHD ranking of African countries, 1950–2015 227
6.15 AHD growth and its breakdown by dimensions,
1950–2015 233
C.1 International AHD inequality, 1870–2015: the
contribution of China and India, sub-Saharan Africa,
and Russia (MLD) 262
C.2 International inequality in schooling, 1870–2015: the
contribution of China and India, sub-Saharan Africa,
and Russia (MLD) (Kakwani indices) 263

C.3   International inequality in life expectancy,
      1870–2015: the contribution of China and India,
      sub-Saharan Africa, and Russia (MLD) (Kakwani
      indices)   264
C.4   International inequality in civil and political liberties,
      1870–2015: the contribution of China and India,
      sub-Saharan Africa, and Russia (MLD)   265
C.5   International inequality in real GDP per head,
      1870–2015: the contribution of China and India,
      sub-Saharan Africa, and Russia (MLD)   266
D.1   *AHDI* and its components: Western Europe   267
D.2   *AHDI* and its components: Western offshoots   268
D.3   *AHDI* and its components: Japan   270
D.4   *AHDI* and its components: Eastern Europe   271
D.5   *AHDI* and its components: Russia   273
D.6   *AHDI* and its components: China   275
D.7   *AHDI* and its components: South Asia   277
D.8   *AHDI* and its components: East Asia   279
D.9   *AHDI* and its components: Middle East   281
D.10 *AHDI* and its components: sub-Saharan Africa   283

Preface

Economic growth has been the main topic of interest for me since my days as an Economics undergraduate. I have allocated a substantial part of my academic career to studying long-run economic perform-ance and made my own modest contribution to the reconstruction of historical national accounts. However, the use of GDP as a measure of well-being on the grounds that it was a convenient synthetic index, backed by economic theory, and presumably correlated with different social indicators of well-being, has never convinced me. That is why I became interested in human development.

The United Nations Development Programme's launch of the Human Development Index (*HDI*) in 1990 represented a major leap forward to provide a comprehensive measure of well-being. Human development, inspired by Amartya Sen's capabilities approach, puts freedom at the centre and focuses on enlarging people's choices. The new concept was most appealing to me for historical and ethical reasons, but I identified a contradiction between the habitually pessimistic narrative of the Human Development Reports and the optimistic message its numbers provided. I suspected that this had to do with the linear transformation of the non-income variables of the *HDI*, which were bounded; conse-quently, their absolute increases represented smaller relative gains, as the initial level was higher. This led to shrinkage of the variance and provoked spurious convergence between countries. More important for me was the discovery that countries where freedom was suppressed or seriously curtailed still ranked high. This was the case of my own country, Spain, in 1975, under General Franco's dictatorship.

I started investigating human development as a break from my research on long run growth. Yet again, Nick Crafts showed himself to be a pioneer of historical research, and his studies of human devel-opment indices and England's living standards, incorporating civil and political rights (Crafts, 1997a, 1997b), served as a role model for my investigation.

I was fortunate to come across a path-breaking article by Nanak Kakwani (1993). Using an axiomatic approach, he proposed a non-linear (convex) rather than a linear transformation for bounded variables. This largely solved the problem I have found in the *HDI*'s non-income dimensions. In Kakwani's alternative proposal, increases from higher initial levels implied greater achievements than the same absolute increase at lower levels. Moreover, as available non-income indicators only capture quantity changes, Kakwani's transformation provides a way of allowing for quality changes when quality and quantity improvements are associated. Kakwani's index is, to some extent, comparable to Amartya Sen's (1981) measure of the relative shortfall reduction, in which the improvement of an index is computed over the difference between the maximum potential level and the level from which the index starts. The advantage of Kakwani index is that it provides consistent comparisons between achievements from different initial levels and over different periods of time.

I wrote several articles on historical human development using Kakwani's non-linear transformation for life expectancy and education variables. However, I was still unsatisfied with the historical *HDI*, since it continued to be inconsistent with the free choice between different sets or bundles of achievements. This implied that the way in which one achieved a decent material standard of living, with access to knowledge and a healthy life, did not actually matter. It could be achieved, therefore, in an advanced country's maximum security prison, but this preposterous possibility obviously falls short of choosing the life one wants to lead.

Thus, I started looking for quantitative indicators of liberties and democracy. Vanhanen's Democratization and Polity IV's Polity indices provided a partial solution since, as Péter Földvári (2017) observed, they represent de facto and de jure measures of democratisation, that is, a collective and 'positive' freedom in Isaiah Berlin's terms. Fortunately, Ignacio Sánchez-Cuenca pointed me to the new Varieties of Democracy dataset that included the Liberal Democracy Index, a combination of civil and political rights, encompassing 'negative' and 'positive' freedoms. This index resolved the bottleneck, and I was able to construct the 'augmented' human development index on which this book is founded.

Over the years, I have incurred many intellectual debts. The works of Amartya Sen and, subsequently, Angus Deaton provided the intellectual framework for the project. Branko Milanovic's leading work on global income inequality inspired the part of this volume that deals with the international distribution of human development and its dimensions, in which I use growth incidence curves to show how the different deciles of the distribution benefit from *augmented* human development gains. Christian Morrisson's work on the international distribution of income and education was also a source of inspiration, and his advice proved most useful.

I have had long discussions with colleagues and friends about human development and its measurement and have enjoyed our disagreements. I would like to mention, in alphabetical order, Pablo Astorga, Luis Bértola, John Devereux, Ewout Frankema, Daniel Gallardo-Albarrán, Şevket Pamuk, and Giovanni Vecchi. In addition, I have taken advantage of Patrick Wallis's thorough editorial suggestions regarding a recent article of mine.

Sharing unpublished data is an altruistic part of the academic profession, and I am most grateful to Facundo Alvaredo, Alexander Apostolides, Pablo Astorga, Joerg Baten, Luis Bértola, Peter Boomgaard, Victor Bulmer-Thomas, Ewout Frankema, Mark Harrison, Alfonso Herranz-Loncán, Salomón Kalmanovitz, Bruno Seminario[+], Joaquim da Costa Leite, Christian Morrisson, Fabrice Murtin, Les Oxley, Şevket Pamuk, David Reher, Alvaro Ferreira da Silva, Jan-Pieter Smits, Socrates Petmetzas, and Marianne Ward in this respect.

Earlier versions of this volume's chapters were presented at the African Economic History Workshop, the Graduate Institute, Geneva, the Annual Economic History Society Conference (Oxford, 2012 and Cambridge, 2014), the conference 'Wellbeing and Inequality in the Long Run: Measurement, History, and Ideas', Fundación Ramón Areces-Universidad Carlos III (Madrid), the World Economic History Congress Presidential Session (Stellenbosch), the 9th BETA-Workshop in Historical Economics (Strasbourg), the 10th European Historical Economics Conference (London, 2013), the 4th World Bank-Banco de España Policy Conference (Madrid), the GGDC 25th Anniversary Conference (Groningen), the World Congress of Cliometrics (Strasbourg), the LSE-Stanford-Andes Conference (London), and CLADHE, Santiago de Chile. Parts of the book were also submitted to seminars and workshops at Chatham House, the Copenhagen Institute of Economics, the European University Institute, Florence, Oxford, the London School of Economics, Imperial College, Bar-Ilan (Tel Aviv),

NYUAD (Abu Dhabi), ANU (Canberra), Higher School of Economics and Lomonosov (Moscow), Warwick, Universidad de San Andrés, CAGE, UPF, Utrecht, and the International Macro History Online Seminar.

I am indebted to a considerable number of colleagues who gave me feedback in these seminars and conferences and in private exchanges. An incomplete list includes Bob Allen, Carlos Álvarez-Nogal, Benito Arruñada, Gareth Austin, Jutta Bolt, Leonid Borodkin, Carles Boix, Elise Brezis, Juan Carmona, Myung Soo Cha, Denis Cogneau, Nick Crafts, Angus Deaton, John Devereux, Claude Diebolt, David Edgerton, Rui P. Esteves, Giovanni Federico, James Fenske, Valpy Fitzgerald, Péter Földvári, Pedro Fraile Balbín, Ewout Frankema, Daniel Gallardo-Albarrán, Giorgia Giovannetti, Mark Harrison, Tim Hatton, Alfonso Herranz-Loncán, Carmen Herrero, Stefan Houpt, Herman de Jong, Stefan Klasen[+], Morten Jerven, Bas van Leeuwen, Jonas Ljundberg, Manuel Llorca-Jaña, Luis Felipe López-Calva, Branko Milanovic, José Miguel Martínez Carrión, Adolfo Meisel Roca, Alex Moradi, Christian Morrisson, Tommy Murphy, Cormac Ó Gráda, Avner Offer, Les Oxley, Amadeo Petitbò, Claudia Rei, Jaime Reis, Jim Riley, James Robinson, Carlos Rodríguez Braun, Joan Rosés, Blanca Sánchez-Alonso, Carlos Santiago-Caballero, Isabel Sanz-Villarroya, Max Schulze, James Simpson, Xavier Tafunell, Giovanni Vecchi, Ilya Voskoboynikov, Jeff Williamson, and Jan Luiten van Zanden.

Over the years I have received research support from the Spanish Ministry of Science and Innovation (Research Project 'Consolidating Economics', Consolider-Ingenio 2010 Programme), the EC HI-POD Project, Seventh Research Framework Programme Contract no. 225342, and the Leverhulme Trust (VP2–2012-050 Grant).

A research grant from Fundación Rafael del Pino (Cátedra Rafael del Pino) helped me to write this book and made it possible for its database to be freely available online. I gratefully acknowledge the Fundación for its generous support and, especially, Carlota Taboada, and its director, Vicente Montes Gan, for their encouragement and help.

I want to thank Juana Lamote de Grignon for her statistical advice and Mark Hounsell for his superb editing job.

At Cambridge University Press I am most grateful to Michael Watson, who has been a most supportive editor. I have tested his patience with consecutive delays in submitting the book. I deeply appreciate an anonymous reader's useful and thorough comments. At the Press, I appreciated Lisa Carter and Emily Plater's editorial support. Beth Morel has been a most meticulous and patient copyeditor.

I am indebted to Oscar Fanjul for his crucial help with the book's cover image and to my brother Luis for having suggested it.

Universidad Carlos III, my home university for the past thirty-two years, and its vibrant Department of Social Sciences have provided the stimulating environment in which to research and write the book. I owe special thanks to my economic history colleagues. A sabbatical leave at the Economic History Department of the LSE was of great help.

Lastly, I want to express special recognition to Blanca Sánchez-Alonso, companion, wife, and critic. Without her encouragement, endless patience, and sense of humour, most of my academic career, and certainly this book, would have not existed.

The book is dedicated to my daughter Teresa, who has been most supportive during its completion.

Madrid, March 2022

Introduction

The purpose of this book is to provide an account of well-being in the context of modern economic growth and globalisation over the past one and a half centuries. It is inspired by Amartya Sen's capabilities approach. Its central tenet, the enlargement of people's choices, informs the concept of human development and its reduced form, the *augmented human development index*, on which the volume rests. A long and healthy life, access to knowledge, and command of resources to enjoy a meaningful life are human development dimensions, and their achievement represents for individuals a historical path to freedom.

Well-Being beyond GDP

Human well-being is increasingly viewed as a multidimensional phenomenon, of which income is only one facet. In Angus Deaton's (2013: 24) terms, well-being includes income, health, life satisfaction, education, and participation in a democratic society under the rule of law.

Nonetheless, economists and economic historians continue to rely on GDP and economic growth to assess well-being. Empirical observations suggesting that GDP per person does provide an 'informative indicator of welfare' (Jones and Klenow, 2016) and is highly correlated with non-monetary dimensions of well-being (Oulton, 2012) lend support to this view.

In spite of its advantage as a synthetic index, and the observed association between economic growth and welfare (Lewis, 1955, Beckerman, 1993), the use of GDP per capita as a measure of welfare has been regularly challenged since the spread of national accounts after World War II (United Nations, 1954; Nordhaus and Tobin, 1972; Beckerman, 1976; Engerman, 1997; Nordhaus, 2000; Fleurbaey, 2009; Syrquin, 2016). The publication of the report from the Commission on the Measurement of Economic Performance and

1

Social Progress to France's President Sarkozy (Stiglitz, Sen, and Fitoussi, 2009) triggered a new round of criticism of GDP that questioned its ability to gauge well-being in broad terms (including social and environmental), and was accompanied by a plea for a comprehensive measure of quality of life covering health, education, non market activities, the environment, political voice, and personal security (OECD, 2011). This has led to updates of old critiques, claiming that in so far as GDP only captures market economic activity, it fails to account for non-market and informal activities, leisure, environmental damage, and inequality (Coyle, 2014; Masood, 2016).

There have been a number of attempts to provide comprehensive measures of living standards that transcend GDP and include non-income dimensions of well-being (infant mortality, life expectancy at birth, height, literacy, etc.). They are presented individually by those who favour a dashboard of indicators, or combined into a composite index by those who prefer to portray well-being as a latent, unobserved variable, so the addition of variables is more informative than each variable individually considered.[1] Examples include the Basic Needs approach and the Physical Quality of Life Index.[2]

Sen (1984: 76) made a clarifying distinction between three approaches to well-being: utility, opulence, and freedom. The utility approach uses satisfaction and intensity of desire as its criteria. Studies that weight the various non-monetary dimensions of quality of life and focus on life satisfaction exemplify this strategy.[3] The opulence approach centres on command over commodities, as is the case in income and wealth studies. Finally, the freedom approach stresses capabilities, namely, individuals' ability to choose between various combinations of functionings or achievements (i.e., a consumption bundle, a health condition, a level of education) (Alkire, 2002; Fleurbaey, 2015).[4]

The capabilities approach inspired the concept of human development. As a synthetic indicator, the Human Development Index (HDI) was launched by the United Nations Development Programme (UNDP) in 1990 and has been published annually ever since. As Sen (2020) has commented, Mahbub ul Haq, his intellectual co-author of the *HDI*, claimed that it was created 'to compete with the GDP' but containing 'more relevant information than the GDP managed to do'. In fact, the *HDI* differed from earlier attempts to capture multidimensional well-being because its aim is to track the evolution of a set of basic capabilities: longevity, education, and control of resources to achieve a decent living standard (UNDP, 1990: 1; 2020: 245) across countries and over time and, thus, to provide an 'inclusive approach to the measurement of human flourishing' (Heckman and Corbin, 2016: 342).

Purpose of the Book

This book favours the capabilities approach to well-being and places human development at its centre. How has human development evolved during the past 150 years of globalisation and economic growth? How has human development been distributed across countries? How do developing countries compare to developed countries? Have they caught up? Do social systems influence well-being? What accounts for performance differences across developing regions? These are issues at stake that this volume will address over a lengthy time span from the late nineteenth century to the aftermath of the 2008 Global Financial Crisis.

Thirty years after the launch of the *HDI*, it is time to take stock. That is why the book is grounded on a new *Augmented* Human Development Index that, while it includes achievements in longevity and education using objective measures, departs significantly from the UNDP *HDI*. Available proxies for non-income dimensions of the index (life expectancy at birth and years of schooling) only allow for quantity but not for quality changes and, unlike GDP per capita, are bounded. Unfortunately, the linear transformation introduced by the *HDI* falls short of providing a sound solution. More importantly, the *HDI* includes achievements or functionings, that is, 'the various things a person may value doing or being' but fails to allow for capabilities, namely, the freedom to choose 'alternative combinations of functionings' or, in other words, one's own life (Sen, 1999: 75). Moreover, by excluding agency and freedom, the *HDI* captures only 'basic needs', not human development. Instead, the *AHDI* makes an attempt to allow for quality changes in non-income dimensions (schooling and life expectancy at birth), as well as for its bounded nature, and, more crucially, includes civil and political liberties as an indispensable dimension of human development. Thus, the *AHDI* provides a measure of both positive and negative freedom.[5]

Overview

The volume is divided into two parts. Part I, An Aggregate View, presents the new *augmented* human development index, describes its trends, and assesses its international distribution. It consists of three chapters.

The challenge of moving from an abstract concept – human development – to an empirical measure is the focus of Chapter 1. First, it discusses the measurement of human development, examining each of its dimensions: access to knowledge, a healthy life, and other aspects of well-being, and the reduced forms of these dimensions used as proxies. It then proposes a new, *augmented* human development index (*AHDI*) that combines achievements in terms of health, education, and material welfare in a context of freedom of choice, consistent with the capabilities approach. In order to allow for its bounded nature and quality improvements, the new *AHDI*, unlike the *HDI*, derives the proxies for health and education, namely, life expectancy at birth and years of schooling, as Kakwani indices that transform them non linearly, so increases at a higher level represent higher achievements than similar increases at a lower level. Moreover, the *AHDI* adds a crucial dimension, civil and political liberties, to proxy agency and freedom. The contrast with alternative transformations of the income dimension reveals that introducing diminishing returns to per capita GDP (its log), as the *HDI* does, is warranted since it merely represents a proxy for commanding resources with which to lead a meaningful life while, from a practical perspective, preventing GDP, a non-bounded variable, from dominating the *AHDI*. As in the *HDI*, the four indices are combined using the unweighted geometric average to obtain the *AHDI*, as all of them are considered indispensable. The sample covers between 115 and 162 countries between 1870 and 2015, amounting to most of the world population.

The long-run trends for (*augmented*) human development and its dimensions and how they compare to those for GDP per head are addressed in Chapter 2, which also includes a breakdown of *AHDI* gains into their dimensions' contributions and some explanatory hypotheses.

But how has human development been distributed internationally? Chapter 3 offers an answer, first, by presenting absolute and relative inequality trends for *AHDI* and its dimensions, along with those for per capita income and then by examining absolute and relative gains across the distribution with the help of growth incidence curves.

Part II, The *OECD* and the *Rest*, examines the evolution of human development in world regions, compares present-day advanced countries and developing regions (the *OECD* and the *Rest*, for short), and pays special attention to Latin America, a region that closely matches the world average, and to Africa, the region persistently at the bottom of world distribution.

How human development evolved across world regions, whether the differences between these regions widened, and, in particular, whether the gap between the *OECD* and the *Rest* deepened are investigated in Chapter 4 by breaking down *AHDI* gains into dimensions' contributions, and assessing whether the gap between the *OECD* and the *Rest*, or the dispersion within each group, accounts for the international inequality of AHD and its dimensions. Finally, it considers regional drivers in the *Rest* that contribute to AHD catching up to the *OECD*.

Whether human development improved in Latin America and the gap with the *OECD* narrowed since 1870, and how human development has been affected by economic performance and income distribution are the issues Chapter 5 addresses.

Does the pessimistic view of Africa's performance in both the colonial and post-independence periods derived from per capita income hold water in terms of human development? Did AHD match economic performance? Chapter 6 attempts to answer these questions. It compares trends in *AHDI* and GDP per capita over the long run and investigates the drivers of AHD gains and catching up to the *OECD* at regional levels before taking a closer look at national levels since 1950.

The main findings can be summarised as follows.

Long-Run Trends

Human development has improved significantly all over the world since 1870, especially during the period 1920–1970, but significant room for improvement remains.

While *AHDI* and real per capita GDP exhibit similar progress in the long run, they behaved differently during the different phases that can be distinguished over one and a half centuries. For example, major gains in human development were achieved across the board during the economic globalisation backlash of the first half of the twentieth century.

Human development progress was driven by its non-income dimensions. Life expectancy at birth was the main contributor over time, although its principal contribution took place during 1920–1970, as the epidemiological transition that begun in north-western Europe in the late nineteenth century diffused internationally. Improvements in life expectancy depend on economic growth, which results in nutritional improvements that strengthen the immune system and reduce morbidity and in the public provision of health. In the long run, however, it was medical technological change that was the main contributor to greater longevity. Education based on new social views (including liberal ideas, redistribution of wealth, and human capital formation), industrialisation, and nation building made a steady contribution over time. Civil and political liberties led to AHD gains in the past two decades of the twentieth century as the demise of authoritarian regimes gave way to an expansion of liberal democracy.

Distribution

Relative international inequality in terms of human development declined from 1900 onwards. In the long run, countries in the middle and lower deciles obtained larger relative gains over the past century. These findings are at odds with the evolution of per capita income dispersion, which increased until the late twentieth century and only fell after 1990.

A breakdown of relative inequality of AHD into its dimensions' contributions reveals that the spread of mass (primary) education and epidemiological transition drove the decline in long-term AHD inequality from the late 1920s, while civil and political liberties only contributed to this fall from the 1970s onwards.

The uneven diffusion of new medical knowledge and health practices in the early stages of the epidemiological and in the *second* health transitions during the late nineteenth and early twentieth centuries and the late twentieth and early twentieth-first centuries, respectively, provoked increasing inequality in life expectancy.

Inequality in terms of political and civil liberties grew over time, especially between World War I and the demise of the Soviet Union, as authoritarian ideologies emerged in parallel to liberal democracy, and only fell in the late twentieth century when authoritarian regimes lost ground and liberal democracy spread.

The OECD *and the* Rest

Human development achieved substantial but unequally distributed gains across world regions in the long run. Life expectancy and schooling drove AHD in both the *OECD* and the *Rest*.

The relative gap between the *OECD* and the *Rest* shrank from the late 1920s onwards in terms of human development, but increased in terms of GDP per capita. The gap between the *OECD* and the *Rest* drove AHD international distribution until the mid-twentieth century, when the dispersion between the regions of the *Rest* took over.

Life expectancy and civil and political rights were the main drivers behind the *Rest*'s catching up to the *OECD*. There was faster catching up prior to 1970, as the epidemiological transition spread, and again in the 1990s, when liberties expanded in the *Rest*.

Latin America

Latin America presents sustained AHD gains since the late nineteenth century, especially during the 1940s and 1950s and from 1970 onwards. AHD progress was therefore not restricted to phases of economic progress, that is, the 1940–1980 phase of state-led growth, but extended to the globalisation backlash (1914–1950) and the 'lost decade' (1980s). However, extreme inequality at low-income levels, which led to a large Inequality Extraction Ratio, was inversely correlated with high AHD levels.

Schooling and life expectancy drove AHD over the long run and accounted for catching up to the *OECD* until 1960, while civil and political liberties had a similar effect in the 1980s. The rise of life expectancy before pharmaceutical drugs spread internationally from the mid-twentieth century onwards points to the diffusion of new medical knowledge that helped to eradicate communicable diseases through good hygienic practices and improvements in water supply and sanitation. In the rise of education, the diffusion of new ideas, urbanisation, and nation building played decisive roles.

Africa

Human development experienced sustained gains in Africa as of 1880, more rapidly between 1920 and 1960, under colonial rule, and at the turn of the century, but the continent remains at the bottom of the world distribution, albeit not all African regions behaved similarly, with the northern and southern regions forging ahead while the rest lagged behind.

AHD grew twice as quickly as per capita GDP, thriving at times of poor economic performance. Unlike GDP per head, which fell behind from a higher relative position, AHD catching up to the *OECD* took place in Africa from the late 1920s onwards.

A mixed picture emerges. Long-term AHD performance does not justify either the pessimistic view of the colonial era or the depiction of 'lost decades' for the post-independence era, but there still is a long way to go from a comparative perspective.

Schooling was the main driver behind AHD gains and catch-up, to which life expectancy made a significant contribution in the interwar period, during the early stage of the epidemiological transition. This confirms that, as in the case of Latin America, the diffusion of low-cost health practices reduced the spread of infectious disease and helped cut infant and maternal mortality before the introduction of modern drugs. Civil and political liberties contributed, both at the time of independence (late 1950s–early 1960s) and in the 1990s.

In Latin America and Africa (and presumably in other developing regions), gains in life expectancy at birth often paralleled those in adult height, but there are also occasions on which the rise of life expectancy is at odds with height stagnation. This may result from the exogenous improvement of infant survival rates, while adult heights are dependent on early-life nutrition, conditioned by income level and distribution.

Some Lessons

What lessons can be drawn from the experience of human development over the last one and a half centuries? In the conventional *HDI*, public policies play an important part, since education and health improvements are associated with government activism and intervention. However, this is not a sufficient condition, as there have been national experiences in which governments did not play an active role.

Moreover, in most world regions, economic performance has undergone recurrent episodes of expanding and shrinking, in which countries have failed to provide steady social spending and to raise living standards that would result in improved nutrition, health care, and education. Thus, focusing only on movements along the health or education (or, by the same token, freedoms) function, which derive from increases in average incomes, ignores shifts in the function that, in the case of health, is closely connected to the diffusion of new medical knowledge. The latter is often, but not always, accompanied by new technology (new drugs), and in the case of education and liberties, new ideas and social practices.

Moreover, the spread and contraction of civil and political liberties, an essential ingredient of human development, plays a major role, particularly in developing regions. The socialist experiments of the twentieth century provide an illustration. Despite their initial success in raising human development, they failed to sustain momentum and fell behind prior to the definitive demise of the socialist model. As was also the case with other authoritarian experiences, the suppression of agency and freedom thwarted human development.

PART I

An Aggregate View

1 | Augmented *Human Development: What Is It? How to Measure It?*

1.1 Introduction

Human development is defined as 'a process of enlarging people's choices', which includes enjoying a healthy life, acquiring knowledge, and achieving a decent standard of living (United Nations Development Programme [UNDP], 1990: 10; 1993: 105). But how can we move from an abstract concept to an empirical measure? This chapter provides an answer to this question and implements an empirical measure, the *Augmented* Human Development Index. The chapter consists of three substantive sections. Section 1.2 discusses the measurement of human development, examining each of its dimensions and exploring their proxies. Section 1.3 offers an *augmented* human development index [*AHDI*] that differs from the conventional human development index [*HDI*] by virtue of a non-linear transformation of its health and education variables and the addition of a new dimension: political and civil rights as a way of incorporating freedom of choice.[1] Section 1.4 compares the resulting *AHDI* with alternative specifications of the index. The time span covered by the *AHDI* runs from the late nineteenth century, when human welfare was being widely affected by improvements in global health and education, to the aftermath of the 2008 Great Recession.[2] Its geographical coverage ranges from 115 to 162 countries that represent most of the world population.

1.2 Human Development: From Concept to Measure

Shifting from the conceptual to the practical level when considering human development presents a challenge. In order to provide a synthetic measure of human development, proxies for its different dimensions need to be chosen from among the array of available objective measures. In the UNDP's *HDI*, a healthy and long life is proxied by life expectancy at birth; access to knowledge, by years of schooling; and

13

command over resources needed for a decent living standard, by the logarithmic transformation of per capita income.

An important distinction exists between longevity and education, on the one hand, and per capita income, on the other. The former are measures not only of achievement but also of capability: namely, avoiding premature death or ignorance. This is not true of the latter. Per capita income is not the ultimate objective for individuals; it simply represents an input that can be turned into a capability: being able to live a full, meaningful life. This implies that being able to command resources is one ingredient in an individual's ability to lead a freer life. That is why per capita income enters the index at a declining rate, since, in terms of capabilities, its return diminishes as its level rises (Anand and Sen, 2000: 100). In the *HDI*, the transformed income index is also intended to provide a surrogate for well-being dimensions aside from health and knowledge (Anand and Sen, 2000: 99).

Although conceptually unaltered, the composition of the *HDI* has varied over time. In 2010, the *Human Development Report* introduced major changes in the indicators used to represent two of the dimensions of human development (UNDP, 2010). For education, the expected years of schooling for a school-age child and the mean years of schooling among the population aged 25 and older were combined using an unweighted arithmetic average (UNDP, 2014).[3] In the case of income, purchasing-power-parity (PPP) adjusted per capita Gross National Income (GNI) replaced PPP-adjusted GDP per head. This represented an improvement, as GNI captures the income accruing to residents of a country, not just the income produced in the country irrespective of the share retained at home. In health, measured by life expectancy at birth, no changes were made.

In order to homogenise the indicators for the different dimensions, their original values (I) are transformed into an index in the form of

$$I = (x - M_o)/(M - M_o), \qquad\qquad [1.1]$$

where x is the observed value of a given dimension of welfare, and M_o and M are the minimum and maximum values, or goalposts, to facilitate comparison over time. Each dimension therefore ranges between 0 and 1.

New goalposts were introduced by the UNDP in 2014, replacing those defined in 2010.[4] For life expectancy at birth, the maximum and the minimum values were established at 85 and 20 years, respectively.

For education, maximum values were set at 15 for the mean years of schooling among the adult population and 18 for the expected years of schooling for a school-age child, with the minimum set at 0 for both indicators. For GNI per capita, the maximum and minimum were established at 75,000 and 100 purchasing-power-parity adjusted (PPP) 2011 dollars.[5]

An unweighted geometric average of all three dimensions (longevity, education, and income) is used to derive a synthetic human development index, replacing the arithmetic mean used until 2010. This approach is an attempt to reduce the substitutability between its different dimensions, to penalise low and uneven achievements, and to portray each dimension as equally indispensable. Thus, the UN index is calculated as:

$$HDI = \left(I_{Life\ Expectancy} \cdot I_{Schooling} \cdot I_{Adjusted\ Income}\right)^{1/3}. \qquad [1.2]$$

The human development index has drawn criticism since its inception (Srinivasan, 1994). The lack of foundations in welfare economics has been highlighted as its main shortcoming (Dowrick *et al.*, 2003: 502), even though the *HDI* was explicitly defined as a measure of well-being in terms of capabilities, not utility. Some of the main criticisms are addressed here.[6]

1.2.1 Longevity and Education

The transformation of the original values of social dimensions (life expectancy, height, literacy, schooling years) into index form presents a challenge. Social variables are often used in their raw form (Acemoglu and Johnson, 2007; Hatton and Brey, 2010; Lindert, 2004; Morrison and Murtin, 2009). Nevertheless, the fact that these non-income variables are bounded raises concerns about the use of their original values to make comparisons over space and time.

In the *HDI*, the linear transformation of the indicators for the social dimensions reduces the size of the denominator by introducing maximum and minimum values (goalposts) and thus widens the index's range (see equation [1.1]). However, the values assigned to the goalposts have been challenged as being discretionary. For example, Carmen Herrero et al. (2012: 54–55) reject the use of arbitrarily fixed minimum values that, they claim, penalise poorer performers and may determine countries' ranking. They instead recommend expressing each dimension x as a share of some maximum set value, M.

$$I = x/M \qquad\qquad [1.3]$$

It can be argued, nonetheless, that as a natural floor often exists, lower goalposts simply aim at capturing subsistence levels. For example, historical evidence of life expectancy at birth indicates that 20 years was most probably a floor in human societies dating back to Neolithic times (Fogel, 2009: 13; Steckel, 2009: 34). This is also the case for per capita income, as human life cannot survive below a basic level of physiological subsistence (Milanovic *et al.* 2011: 262).[7]

However, when linearly transformed social variables (as in both the UNDP's *HDI* and Herrero *et al.*'s (2012) proposal) are used to compare countries (or time periods), identical absolute changes result in a smaller proportional improvement for the country (time period) with the higher starting level (as would also be the case if we were using their original values). Consider, for example, a 10-year improvement in life expectancy at birth, in one case, from 30 to 40 years, and in another, from 70 to 80 years. Although these changes are identical in absolute terms, the second is smaller relative to the initial level. Placed in the index for health used in the 2014 UN *HDI*, the first country would see a 100 per cent improvement from 0.15 to 0.31, while the second would see a 20 per cent improvement from 0.77 to 0.92. Therefore, a linear transformation does not solve the problem of the comparability of bounded social dimensions across countries or over time.

For health, there is a further problem. In poor countries, the main reduction of mortality takes place among children, as infectious disease declines, whereas in rich countries, mortality falls among the elderly as a result of better treatment of cardiovascular and respiratory diseases. Thus, if minimum original values of life expectancy at birth are employed and absolute changes of the same magnitude therefore receive a larger weight when the starting level is lower, the index will arbitrarily give more weight to saving the lives of younger people than the lives of older people (Deaton, 2006: 9).

The limitations of linearly transformed measures become more evident when quality is taken into account. Life expectancy at birth and years of schooling are just crude proxies for the actual goals of human development: a long and healthy life and access to knowledge. Unfortunately, data on health-adjusted longevity, 'healthy life

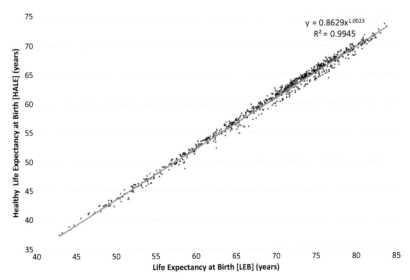

Figure 1.1 Healthy life expectancy at birth (HALE) and life expectancy at birth (LEB), 1990–2016.
Note: Pool of 1990, 2000, 2006, and 2016 benchmarks.
Sources: Global Burden of Disease Study (2016) in Murray et al. (2017).

expectancy', that is, a summary measure of health computed using age-specific death rates and years of life lived with disability per capita (Murray et al., 2017), have only existed since 1990. Reassuringly, the Global Burden of Disease Study 2016 allows us to compare healthy life expectancy at birth (HALE) with conventional life expectancy at birth (LEB) for the period 1990–2016. This shows that healthy life expectancy at birth rises with raw life expectancy at birth (Figure 1.1).[8]

The available evidence for the last three decades indicates that, although morbidity increased in absolute terms, it underwent a relative compression: the proportion of years lived in disability fell (Murray *et al.*, 2017). As life expectancy rose, disability for each age-cohort declined (Mathers *et al.*, 2001; Salomon *et al.* 2012; Murray *et al.*, 2017). More specifically, longer lives – due to a rapid decline in years of life lost – together with a more modest age-adjusted decline in years lived with disability have led to lower age-standardised disability-adjusted life years rates across the board (Murray *et al.*, 2017: 1331). In other words, the quality of life improves for each age cohort as life expectancy at birth increases.[9] Thus, the apparent ethical-measurement conflict observed by

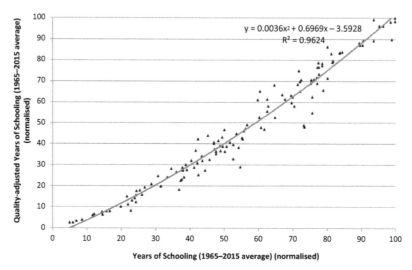

Figure 1.2 Quality-adjusted and raw years of schooling (1965–2015) (normalised).

Note: 1965–2015 average. Normalised (expressed relative to its maximum value).

Sources: Cognitive Skills, Altinok et al. (2018); years of schooling, see the text and Appendix A.

Partha Dasgupta (1990: 23) when he asserts, 'Equal increments are possibly of less and less ethical worth as life expectancy rises to 65 or 70 years and more. But we are meaning performance here. So it would seem that it becomes more and more commendable if, with increasing life expectancy, the index were to rise at the margin', fades away.

Similarly, the quality of education grows as the quantity of education increases. A comparison between quality-adjusted and quantity indices of education suggests a convex association between the two, with quality-adjusted education increasing more than proportionally at higher levels (Figure 1.2).[10]

To sum up, on the basis of the available evidence for the last decades, it can be claimed that more years of life expectancy and schooling imply higher quality of health and education, respectively, during childhood and adolescence. Hence, when transforming the original values of the health and education variables, one needs to allow for the fact that they are bounded and that their quality improves along with their quantity. The non-linear transformation proposed by Kakwani (1993) provides a means of achieving this.

Using an axiomatic approach, Kakwani constructed a normalised index from an achievement function in which an increase in the standard of living of a country at a higher level implies a greater achievement than would have been the case had it occurred at a lower level:[11]

$$I = (\log(M - Mo) - \log(M - x))/\log(M - Mo) \qquad [1.5]$$

The same notation used in equation [1.1] applies: x is an indicator of a country's standard of living; M and Mo are the maximum and minimum values, respectively; and *log* stands for the natural logarithm. The achievement function proposed by Kakwani is a convex function of x. It is equal to 0 if $x = Mo$, and equal to 1 if $x = M$, ranging, thus, between 0 and 1.

The consequences of the Kakwani transformation of an original variable can be illustrated for a well-known empirical regularity such as the Preston curve, that is, the association between life expectancy and real per capita GDP proposed by Samuel Preston (1975). Figure 1.3a shows Preston's concave relationship between the original values of life expectancy at birth and real income per head; thus, initially, proportional increases in life expectancy correspond to increases in income but soon, that is, at relatively low income

(a)

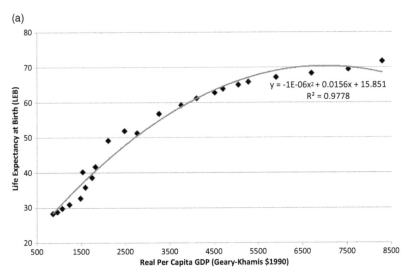

Figure 1.3a *Old* Preston curve, 1870–2015.
Sources: See the text and Appendix A

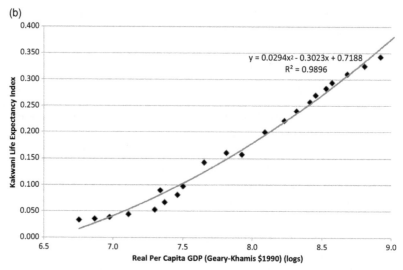

(b)

Figure 1.3b *Revised* Preston curve, 1870–2015.
Sources: See the text and Appendix A

levels – around Geary-Khamis 1990 $2,500, namely, the income per head in the UK by 1850 (Maddison Project Database, 2013) – the association flattens out, so successive increases in income imply less than proportional increases in life expectancy. Angus Deaton (2013) replicated the Preston curve, using the log of real GDP per head rather than its value to represent proportional changes, with the effect of reducing the concavity of the per capita income-life expectancy association. However, when a Kakwani convex transformation of the original values of life expectancy at birth is introduced, a linear relationship emerges between the life expectancy index and the log of real per capita GDP. This, at higher levels, shows convexity, suggesting that medical technology advances lead to more than proportional gains in health relative to income (Figure 1.3b).

How do the non-linearly transformed variables compare to their original, linearly transformed, values, or other approaches to transformation? For world average years of schooling and life expectancy at birth during 1870–2015, Table 1.1, cols. 2–6, presents, respectively, the non-linearly transformed (Kakwani) indices, alongside their conventional UNDP linearly transformed indices, and linear indices that present the share of maximum values, as suggested by Herrero,

Table 1.1. *Alternative indices of years of schooling, life expectancy, per capita income, and liberal democracy, 1870–2015*

	Years of schooling		Life expectancy at birth				Per capita income				Liberal democracy
	Kakwani	UNDP	Kakwani	UNDP	HMV	UNDP	Bértola-Vecchi	Zambrano	HMV	HMV-eei	
1870	0.032	0.084	0.033	0.128	0.334	0.350	0.016	0.094	0.018	0.010	0.093
1880	0.037	0.096	0.036	0.138	0.341	0.368	0.018	0.102	0.020	0.012	0.102
1890	0.042	0.108	0.039	0.151	0.351	0.386	0.021	0.110	0.023	0.014	0.105
1900	0.048	0.123	0.045	0.170	0.365	0.408	0.024	0.121	0.026	0.015	0.115
1913	0.055	0.138	0.053	0.198	0.387	0.438	0.029	0.138	0.031	0.017	0.137
1925	0.063	0.158	0.067	0.244	0.422	0.450	0.032	0.145	0.034	0.017	0.161
1929	0.070	0.173	0.081	0.286	0.454	0.465	0.035	0.154	0.037	0.017	0.154
1933	0.076	0.186	0.090	0.312	0.474	0.444	0.031	0.141	0.033	0.015	0.144
1938	0.081	0.198	0.098	0.335	0.492	0.471	0.037	0.158	0.039	0.018	0.143
1950	0.094	0.225	0.143	0.450	0.579	0.496	0.043	0.174	0.045	0.020	0.208
1955	0.104	0.245	0.161	0.490	0.610	0.522	0.051	0.192	0.053	0.024	0.257
1960	0.115	0.267	0.157	0.482	0.604	0.540	0.057	0.206	0.059	0.026	0.262
1965	0.127	0.291	0.200	0.565	0.668	0.566	0.067	0.228	0.069	0.031	0.265
1970	0.141	0.317	0.222	0.604	0.697	0.589	0.078	0.248	0.080	0.035	0.254
1975	0.153	0.340	0.240	0.633	0.719	0.604	0.085	0.262	0.087	0.035	0.225
1980	0.169	0.368	0.257	0.658	0.738	0.619	0.094	0.277	0.096	0.042	0.267
1985	0.184	0.392	0.271	0.677	0.753	0.626	0.098	0.283	0.100	0.045	0.277
1990	0.194	0.409	0.283	0.693	0.765	0.638	0.106	0.296	0.108	0.048	0.331
1995	0.212	0.436	0.294	0.707	0.776	0.645	0.111	0.303	0.112	0.048	0.366
2000	0.229	0.462	0.310	0.726	0.791	0.663	0.124	0.323	0.126	0.049	0.392

Table 1.1. (*cont.*)

	Years of schooling		Life expectancy at birth				Per capita income				Liberal democracy
	Kakwani	UNDP	Kakwani	UNDP	HMV	UNDP	Bértola-Vecchi	Zambrano	HMV	HMV-eei	
2005	0.244	0.483	0.325	0.742	0.803	0.683	0.141	0.347	0.143	0.058	0.390
2010	0.257	0.502	0.342	0.760	0.817	0.702	0.158	0.371	0.160	0.072	0.398
2015	0.274	0.524	0.380	0.796	0.844	0.718	0.175	0.392	0.176	0.085	0.374

Sources: See the text.

Notes:

HMV, Herrero, Martínez, and Villar (2012). HMV-eei means HMV adjusted for inequality (*egalitarian equivalent income*) In the case of years of schooling, since the minimum goalpost is 0, the results of the HMV and the UNDP transformations are identical.

Transformation of social dimensions (life expectancy, years of schooling)

-UNDP, linear transformation (expression [1]), $I = (x - M_o) / (M - M_o)$

-Kakwani, convex transformation (expression [5]) $I = (\log (M - M_o) - \log (M - x)) / \log (M - M_o)$

-HMV (Herrero, Martínez, and Villar) (expression [3]) $I = x / M$

Transformation of per capita income

-UNDP, linear transformation (expression [1]) but with values in natural logarithms (ln), $I = (\ln x - \ln M_o) / (\ln M - \ln M_o)$

-Bértola et al. and Vecchi et al. (expression [1]), $I = (x - M_o) / (M - M_o)$

-HMV (expression [3]) $I = x / M$

-HMV-eei, expression [3]) $I = x / M$ but replacing per capita income, y, with the egalitarian equivalent income, $y^e = y * (1 - G)$, where y represents per capita income and G, the Gini.

-Zambrano (expression [6]), $I = (x^r - M_o^r) / (M^r - M_o^r)$, with $r = 0.5$ r (a fraction of per capita income growth that translates into capabilities) $0 < r < 1$

Transformation of liberal democracy

-linear transformation (expression [1]), $I = (x - M_o) / (M - M_o)$

x is the observed value of a given dimension of welfare, and M_o and M are the maximum and minimum values, or goalposts

Martínez, and Villar (2012) (HMV). These indices are computed using the UNDP 2014 maximum goalposts. In the case of schooling, the HMV index is, by construction, identical to the UNDP transformation, so it is not reported separately. It can be observed that the Kakwani indices show systematically lower values, but also faster growth.

1.2.2 Income

The UNDP use of the log of per capita income to proxy a decent standard of living has been challenged since the early stages of the *HDI*. One alternative proposal has been to use a simple linear transformation without logarithms (equation [1.1]), which would arguably add another equally valuable dimension of human development and avoid underestimating per capita differences across countries as their levels increase (Bértola et al., 2011: 3–4). Another suggestion has been to express countries' real per capita income as a percentage of an established maximum level (Gormely, 1995; Herrero et al., 2012: 258). Recently, Eduardo Zambrano (2017: 535) has proposed a way to normalise per capita without using the logarithmic transformation. Unlike the social dimensions (health and education) of the *HDI*, for which a growth in the level achieved causes a proportional increase in terms of capabilities, Zambrano claims that per capita income growth translates less than proportionally in terms of capabilities; namely, in a fraction of it (r), with r varying within 0 and 1 and being the same for all income levels:

$$I = (x^r - M_o{}^r)/(M^r - M_o{}^r), \qquad\qquad [1.6]$$

In the particular case of $r = 0$, the result is the UNDP log transformation of income. However, as the value assigned to r is largely discretionary, an element of arbitrariness is introduced in the estimates.

The alternatives to the logarithmic transformation of per capita income (with the exception of Zambrano's proposal) do not address the very different nature of income compared to the other dimensions in the *HDI*, which are bounded in the cases of longevity and education, and without a known upper limit in the case of real per capita income. Although the convex transformation of the indicators of longevity and education dimensions mitigates the difference between these bounded variables and unbounded variables such as GDP per capita, it does not put them on a level playing field, and some form of compression of the income dimension of human development is required to make it comparable to its social dimensions (Sagar and Najam, 1998: 254).[12] Furthermore, the logarithmic transformation of average income may be interpreted as a multiple of the subsistence level, M_o, that is, in terms of the size of the income gap, M/M_o, to be bridged by a country whose average income is at subsistence level (Zambrano, 2014).[13] Therefore, although a logarithmic transformation of per capita income, as employed in the *HDI*, is a second-best solution, I have adopted it here in the absence of a superior alternative.[14]

Table 1.1, cols. 7–11, presents indices of real per capita income for the world between 1870 and 2015. It shows the conventional UNDP log-linear transformed index, along with four of the different alternatives that have been suggested: an index employing the linear but non-logarithmic transformation, as proposed by Bértola *et al.* (2011: 3–4) and Vecchi et al. (2017: 468) [*Bértola-Vecchi*]; an index expressing each country's average incomes as a share of an upper bound – here defined as the UNDP's 2014 maximum goalpost, 75,000 dollars – as suggested by Herrero et al. (2012) [*HMV*]; an index based on a further adjustment also proposed by Herrero *et al.* (2012) [*HMV-eei*], the *egalitarian equivalent income*, y^e, derived as $y^e = y^*(1 - G)$, where y represents per capita income and G represents the Gini;[15] and finally an index based on the non-logarithmic transformation proposed by Zambrano, here with an r value of 0.5.[16] It can be observed that compared to the UNDP logarithmic transformation, these indices exhibit much lower levels and higher growth rates, which imply larger differences across countries and over time.

1.2.3 Freedom

An objection to the choice of *HDI* components has been the absence of an equality dimension.[17] Since 2010, the *Human Development Report* has included an inequality-adjusted index, but a dearth of reliable historical data on inequality for most countries of the world precludes the use of this approach here.[18]

A more relevant issue is that, so far, attempts to portray human development in index form have only been made in terms of achievements or functionings.[19] However, the ability to choose between alternative bundles of functionings, a defining feature of human development as a measure of capabilities, is not considered in the *HDI*. But without agency – that is, the ability to pursue and realise the goals a person has reason to value – and freedom, any index falls short of being even a reduced-form measure of human development and simply becomes another 'basic needs' metric (Ivanov and Peleah, 2010: 17–18). However, attempts to incorporate agency and liberty into the *HDI* have been discouraged by threats from totalitarian countries (Klugman *et al.*, 2011: 265).

Unlike inequality, for which no comprehensive historical data are available, the inclusion of freedom into a historical human development index is feasible. Dasgupta and Weale (1992: 120–122) added civil and political rights to a set of demographic and educational indicators in order to provide a comprehensive view of well-being, and Crafts (1997b: 621–622) expanded the exercise to Britain and other Western European countries during the Industrial Revolution. More recently, Bértola *et al.* (2011: 5) and Vecchi *et al.* (2017: 475–480), respectively, have added democratisation and political and civil rights as a fourth dimension to their *HDI* historical estimates.

Agency and freedom cover a wide range of capabilities, from civil to economic and political liberties, for which unfortunately there is not enough comprehensive data at a global level over the past 150 years. A partial solution is to consider a variable representing political and civil liberties.

One practical issue is the choice of the variables that may serve to proxy political and civil liberties. *Varieties of Democracy* [*V-Dem*], the latest and most complete database encompassing 201 countries from 1789–2018, provides a *Liberal Democracy Index*, which combines electoral democracy (including free competition, extensive participation, freedom of expression, and rulers' responsiveness to citizens), a collective and positive freedom, with a 'liberal' component concerning the protection of individual and minority rights (including civil liberties, the rule of law, an independent judiciary, and effective checks and balances that place limits on government), that is, a measure of negative freedom (Coppedge *et al.*, 2018). The *Liberal Democracy Index* is more comprehensive than historical indices such as Polity IV Project's *Polity2* index and Vanhanen's *Index of Democratisation*.[20]

Table 1.1 (last column) shows the evolution of civil and political rights proxied by the population-weighted index of liberal democracy in the world since 1870.

1.2.4 A Composite Index

The decision to aggregate the different dimensions of human development into a synthetic index has provoked adverse reactions. Ravallion (2012a, 2012b) argued against the use of composite indices due to their limited theoretical underpinning and implicit trade-offs. The alternatives that have been suggested include addressing each dimension's indicator separately (Aturupane *et al.* 1994), resorting to a 'dashboard' of indicators (Ravallion, 2012a), and producing an ordinal, rather than a cardinal, measure (Dasgupta and Weale, 1992). In defence of an aggregate index of well-being, it has been argued that summarising a set of indicators into a single number avoids the risk of divergence between different well-being dimensions and offers an alternative to per capita income (Krishnakumar, 2018). Furthermore, it could be argued that in so far as human development is a latent unobservable variable, the composite index captures more information than its components individually considered.

Two aspects of the process of aggregation have also been the focus of debate. First, the equal weighting given to the dimensions in the human development index has been questioned. Why should each dimension (longevity, education, and income) receive the same weight in the index over space and time? (See Hopkins, 1991: 1471; Kelley, 1991: 319.) A substantive objection to the use of fixed weights is that the relative values of the index components are not necessarily the same across countries (or individuals) or over time (Srinivasan, 1994: 240). Moreover, it has been argued that the weights used in the *HDI* are based on judgement rather than on welfare theory (Dowrick *et al.*, 2003: 503). However, the notion that each of the dimensions is equally essential in determining the level of human development is one of the main attributes of the concept (Desai, 1991; Sagar and Najam, 1998: 251). A technical test of the validity of this approach has been developed, based on applying Principal Component Analysis (PCA) to the *HDI*. PCA estimates the optimal weights for each *HDI* component over time by weighting attributes by their variance and, thus, allows one to establish whether the human development index attributes are redundant or add information on different facets of well-being.[21] Perhaps counter-intuitively, the results obtained from using PCA suggest stable one-third weights are appropriate for each dimension of the index, offering some support for the UNDP methodology (UNDP, 1993; Ogwang, 1994; Nguefack-Tsague *et al.*, 2011).

The second substantive debate about the aggregation of the dimensions of the *HDI* centres on the shift from additivity to multiplicativity of the index's components introduced in 2010 (UNDP, 2010). The reason for the change was that the assumption of perfect substitutability between dimensions implicit in the arithmetic average was deemed to be in flagrant contradiction with the notion that each dimension was equally crucial in determining the human development index. Substitutability among the components of the index could be restricted by using their geometric average (Desai, 1991: 356; Sagar and Najam, 1998: 252). Yet, even though the geometric average favours a more balanced combination of human development dimensions, it is less intuitive than the arithmetic average (Klasen, 2018: 8).

Several harsh criticisms of the multiplicative method of aggregation have been put forward (Ravallion, 2012b; Chakravarty, 2011; Anand, 2018). Significantly, Ravallion (2012b) attacks the implicit trade-offs between the new index's dimensions, measured by their marginal rate of substitution (MRS), claiming that, in comparison with the additive method, the new multiplicative method downgrades life expectancy, penalising poor countries.[22] The 2010 *HDI*, he argues, 'generates a steep income gradient in the index's implicit valuations of life expectancy and schooling' (Ravallion, 2012b: 206). In particular, the value assigned to longevity relative to average income rises with per capita income, reaching a value 17,000 times higher for the richest countries than for the poorest ones.[23] Ravallion's bottom line is that the embodied social values of the new *HDI* imply that we value longevity (or education) more in rich countries than in poor ones.[24] Thus, he suggests, the HDI's implicit trade-offs lead to the unacceptable conclusion that 'the most promising way to promote human development in the world would be by investing in higher life expectancy in rich countries' (Ravallion, 2012b: 208). In response to Ravallion's objection, it can be argued that, for rich countries, the high value of longevity in terms of income simply means that per capita income makes a negligible contribution to increasing capabilities (Klugman et al., 2011: 278–280).[25]

The move to employing a geometric average for the *HDI* has two further consequences that should be recognised. First, the combination of the logarithmic transformation of per capita income in this multiplicative framework makes the *HDI*, according to Zambrano (2014: 864), 'very conservative in allowing income to be transformed into capabilities at high income ... and very aggressive in allowing capabilities to shrink as income losses take place at very low income levels'. In addition, the geometric mean gives the *HDI* a cardinal dimension that allows for comparison of its change over space and time (Herrero et al., 2012: 251).[26]

1.3 An *Augmented* Human Development Index

Having considered the issues at stake in the construction of a synthetic index to capture the dimensions of human development, I propose a historical index on the basis of a new world dataset of life expectancy at birth, years of schooling for population 15 and older,[27] per capita GDP,[28] plus a new dimension, political and civil liberties, represented by the *Liberal Democracy Index*, which aims to capture agency and freedom so that the resulting augmented human development index provides a crude measure of capabilities.

Gathering the best possible dataset represents a challenge, and the proxies used for a long and healthy life and access to knowledge, life expectancy at birth and years of schooling, are unavoidably crude (for details, see Appendix A). Data on life expectancy at birth for the period 1980–2015 come from the *Human Development Reports* (UNDP, 2010 and 2016), the World Bank's 'World Development Indicators for 1960–1975', and the United Nations' *Demographic Yearbook Historical Supplement* (United Nations, 2000) for the 1950s. Estimates for the pre-1950 era come mostly from Riley (2005b,c), Flora (1983), and national sources. However, for most OECD countries the Human Mortality Dataset www.mortality.org/ has been preferred, complemented with the Clio-Infra Dataset www.clio-infra.eu/, and the case of Latin America the OxLAD, now MoxLAD database (Astorga et al., 2003) has been mainly used.

Data on the average years of total schooling (primary, secondary, and tertiary) for population aged 15 and over, for 2015 and 2010, derive mostly from the *Human Development Reports* (UNDP, 2016, 2013). For 1870–2010, the Clio-Infra dataset www.clio-infra.eu/Indicators/AverageYearsofEducation.html provides the most comprehensive database that has been completed with estimates from Földvári and van Leeuwen (2014) for Europe, and Barro and Lee (2013) www.barrolee.com/ and Lee and Lee (2016) https://barrolee.github.io/BarroLeeDataSet/DataLeeLee.html

The *Liberal Democracy Index* provided by Varieties of Democracy [V-Dem] (Coppedge *et al.*, 2018) www.v-dem.net/en/ has been chosen as the best proxy for civil and political liberties. It merges the electoral democracy index that comprises freedom of association, expression, suffrage, and clean elections, and the liberal component index that includes equality before the law and individual liberty, judicial constraints on the executive, and legislative constraints on the executive.

GDP per head in 1990 Geary-Khamis dollars comes from the Maddison Project Database (2018) [MPD2018, MPD2013], completed with Maddison (2006, 2010) www.rug.nl/ggdc/historicaldeve lopment/maddison/ and CEPAL (2009, 2017) http://interwp.cepal.org/ for Latin America since 1950, plus individual countries' historical national accounts. For sub-Saharan Africa, most estimates come from Prados de la Escosura (2012). Conference Board (2016) 'alternative' series have been accepted for China since 1950.

In designing the new *augmented* human development index, I accept the goalposts (maximum and minimum values) set in the 2014 *Human Development Report*, which replaced those in place since 2010.[29] For life expectancy at birth, the maximum and the minimum values are 85 and 20 years, respectively. For education, the maximum and minimum values of average years of total schooling (primary, secondary, and tertiary) are 15 and 0, respectively. For liberal democracy, 0 and 1 are the lower and upper bounds. In addition, arbitrary 'floor' values (values closer to their actual minimum levels than the minimum goalposts, which tend to be too extreme) have been adopted in order to allow the inclusion of countries for which no data exist in earlier periods and, at the same time, to avoid zero values in the variables transformed with equations 1.1 and 1.5. Thus, 25 years of life expectancy at birth, 0.1 years of schooling, and a value of 0.01 for liberal democracy have been used as 'floor' levels. Per capita GDP is expressed in Geary-Khamis (purchasing-power-parity) 1990 dollars (G-K 1990$, hereafter) to adjust for the difference in price level across countries, and the goalposts are set at $100 and $47,000, respectively.[30] I have assumed G-K 1990$ 300 equates to a basic level of physiological subsistence and use this value as an adequate 'floor' for income.[31] In general terms, the upward bias the 'floor' introduces for the poorest countries does not vary the overall picture.

Indices for education and life expectancy are obtained following Kakwani (1993), through a convex transformation as in equation

[1.5]. In the case of political and civil liberties, a linear transformation (derived with equation [1.1]) has been adopted. The reason is that, unlike the other bounded variables considered here, the *Liberal Democracy Index* measures quality as well as quantity. Lastly, the adjusted per capita income index has been derived with equation [1.1], but with all its terms expressed in logs.

Then, following the 2014 *Human Development Report*, the indices for each dimension have been combined as an equally weighted geometric average using a modified version of equation [1.2], in which I_k represented the indices derived with Kakwani's non-linear (convex) transformation for longevity and education. The Augmented Historical Human Development Index [*AHDI*] is thus defined as:

$$AHDI = \left(I_{k\,Life\,Expectancy} \cdot I_{k\,Schooling} \cdot I_{Adjusted\,Income} \cdot I_{Liberal\,Democracy}\right)^{1/4}$$

[1.7]

Data constraints mean that the country coverage varies over the time span considered here. From 1870 onwards, 115 countries are considered, with the number rising to 121, 146, 161, and 162 countries in samples starting in 1913, 1950, 1980, and 1990, respectively. The countries in these samples represent over 90 per cent of the world population, and nearly 100 per cent since 1950 (the sources and procedures are presented in Appendix A). Regional and world averages for the original values of each variable have been transformed into indices for each dimension, and then combined to derive human development indices.

When the coverage of countries varies between the five regional and world samples, splicing was applied, using the more recent period, for which the coverage is larger, as the benchmark. Thus, the new series (Y^R) results from using the level provided by the series closer to the present (that has wider spatial coverage) at the year T in which the two series overlap (Y_T), and re-scaling the earlier series (X_t) with the ratio between the two series for the year (T) at which they overlap (Y_T/X_T):

$$Y^R_t = (Y_T/X_T)_* X_t \quad \text{for } 0 \leq t \leq T$$

[1.8]

Given that a range of researchers strongly oppose the use of a geometric average to combine the dimensions of human development in the *HDI*, it seems reasonable to compare the performance of indices obtained alternatively as arithmetic and geometric averages. Thus,

Table 1.2. *Multiplicative and additive* augmented *human development indices*

	Geometric mean	Arithmetic mean	Ratio geometric/arithmetic
1870	0.077	0.127	0.60
1880	0.084	0.136	0.62
1890	0.091	0.143	0.63
1900	0.100	0.154	0.65
1913	0.115	0.171	0.67
1925	0.132	0.185	0.71
1929	0.142	0.193	0.74
1933	0.144	0.188	0.77
1938	0.152	0.198	0.77
1950	0.193	0.235	0.82
1955	0.218	0.261	0.83
1960	0.225	0.269	0.84
1965	0.248	0.290	0.86
1970	0.262	0.302	0.87
1975	0.266	0.306	0.87
1980	0.291	0.328	0.89
1985	0.305	0.339	0.90
1990	0.328	0.361	0.91
1995	0.348	0.379	0.92
2000	0.369	0.399	0.92
2005	0.381	0.410	0.93
2010	0.396	0.425	0.93
2015	0.409	0.437	0.94

Sources: See the text.

I have also computed a version of the augmented index using an unweighted arithmetic average of its dimensions [$AHDI_a$], which implies increasing their substitutability:

$$AHDI_a = \left(I_{k\,Life\,Expectancy} + I_{k\,Schooling} + I_{Adjusted\,Income} + I_{Liberal\,Democracy} \right) / 4$$

$$[1.9]$$

The contrast between the arithmetic- and geometric-average indices for world AHD over 1870–2015 is visible in Table 1.2. Although both indices share the same trends, the geometric-average index has a lower initial level and faster growth.[32] This confirms the penalisation of low

Table 1.3. Augmented *and* non-augmented *human development indices*

	AHDI	HDI	AHDI/HDI ratio
1870	0.077	0.072	1.06
1880	0.084	0.079	1.07
1890	0.091	0.086	1.05
1900	0.100	0.096	1.05
1913	0.115	0.108	1.06
1925	0.132	0.124	1.07
1929	0.142	0.138	1.03
1933	0.144	0.145	1.00
1938	0.152	0.155	0.98
1950	0.193	0.188	1.03
1955	0.218	0.206	1.06
1960	0.225	0.214	1.05
1965	0.248	0.243	1.02
1970	0.262	0.264	0.99
1975	0.266	0.281	0.95
1980	0.291	0.300	0.97
1985	0.305	0.315	0.97
1990	0.328	0.327	1.00
1995	0.348	0.342	1.02
2000	0.369	0.361	1.02
2005	0.381	0.378	1.01
2010	0.396	0.396	1.00
2015	0.409	0.422	0.97

Sources: See the text.

and uneven levels of dimensions when the geometric formula is used, a feature that is consistent with the indispensability of each dimension to human development.

Finally, it is worth comparing the new *AHDI* with a human development index constructed with identical transformed variables but excluding the liberties dimension (*HDI*). *AHDI* and *HDI* present a similar evolution and long-run growth, as can be observed in Table 1.3, but the *AHDI* shows slower progress in the interwar years, over 1960–1980, and since 2000, with the difference being substantial in the 1930s and 1960s, and a faster pace during the 1940s and 1950s and the last two decades of the twentieth century. However, given the unequal distribution of liberties across countries over time, we should expect large differences between the AHDI and the HDI in specific countries (regions) and periods.

1.4 A Comparison with Alternative Specifications of the Index

How does this new historical index (*AHDI*) compare to alternative specifications for a multiplicative human development index that incorporates political and civil liberties alongside the standard dimensions? Table 1.4 shows the *AHDI* alongside six other possible approaches to constructing the index. The first two historical indices are derived using the UNDP (col. 2) and Zambrano (col. 3) specifications for the three conventional dimensions (longevity, education, and income) plus the addition of the fourth dimension, political and civil liberties, as incorporated in the *AHDI*; these are labelled *UNDP* and *Zambrano*, respectively.[33] It is noticeable that the *AHDI* exhibits systematically lower levels than these alternative methodologies, as a result of the Kakwani transformation of the education and health dimensions, which also translates into faster growth over time. The *Zambrano* specification produces intermediate values that fall between the *UNDP* specification and the *AHDI*.

Four other alternative specifications are also presented. The *Bértola-Vecchi* specification (col. 4) is obtained using the UNDP linear transformation of the non-income dimensions and a non-log linear transformation of per capita income, as suggested by the Bértola *et al.* (2011) and Vecchi *et al.* (2017) 'extended' human development index.[34] The *HMV* (col. 5) specification results from taking on board Herrero *et al.*'s (2012) proposal to transform the original values of the human development dimensions by computing them as shares of maximum values.[35] Counter-intuitively, these two indices are highly coincidental with the *AHDI*, as the higher values for the transformed non-income dimensions in *Bértola-Vecchi* and *HMV* specifications offset the lower value for the transformed income dimension.

The fifth alternative specification (col. 6) corresponds to Bértola *et al.*'s full proposal, with a geometric average of Kakwani indices for life expectancy and years of schooling, and linear indices for per capita income (with no log transformation) and political and civil liberties, labelled *Bértola-Kakwani*.[36] Finally, the last alternative, labelled *HMV-eei* (col. 7), includes Herrero *et al.*'s (2012) 'newer' *HDI* components, which transform the original values of the human development

Table 1.4. *Alternative augmented human development indices, 1870–2015*

	Prados de la Escosura	UNDP	Zambrano	Bértola & Vecchi	HMV	Bértola (Kakwani)	HMV-eei*
1870	0.077	0.137	0.098	0.063	0.083	0.036	0.072
1880	0.084	0.149	0.108	0.071	0.091	0.040	0.079
1890	0.091	0.160	0.117	0.077	0.098	0.044	0.086
1900	0.100	0.177	0.131	0.087	0.108	0.049	0.093
1913	0.115	0.201	0.151	0.102	0.123	0.058	0.105
1925	0.132	0.230	0.173	0.119	0.138	0.068	0.116
1929	0.142	0.244	0.185	0.128	0.146	0.074	0.120
1933	0.144	0.247	0.185	0.127	0.143	0.074	0.117
1938	0.152	0.258	0.197	0.136	0.152	0.080	0.125
1950	0.193	0.320	0.246	0.173	0.187	0.105	0.153
1955	0.218	0.356	0.278	0.199	0.212	0.122	0.173
1960	0.225	0.367	0.289	0.209	0.223	0.128	0.183
1965	0.248	0.396	0.316	0.233	0.245	0.146	0.199
1970	0.262	0.412	0.332	0.248	0.259	0.158	0.210
1975	0.266	0.414	0.335	0.254	0.263	0.163	0.209
1980	0.291	0.447	0.365	0.279	0.289	0.182	0.235
1985	0.305	0.463	0.380	0.291	0.301	0.192	0.246

34

1990	0.328	0.495	0.408	0.316	0.325	0.209	0.265
1995	0.348	0.520	0.430	0.334	0.344	0.224	0.277
2000	0.369	0.543	0.454	0.357	0.366	0.242	0.290
2005	0.381	0.556	0.469	0.375	0.383	0.257	0.306
2010	0.396	0.571	0.487	0.394	0.402	0.273	0.329
2015	0.409	0.579	0.497	0.406	0.413	0.287	0.344

Sources: See the text.

Notes:

HMV, Herrero, Martínez, and Villar (2012). HMV-eei means HMV adjusted for inequality (*egalitarian equivalent income*)

AHDI combines the social dimensions and per capita income with expression (7), $AHDI = (I_{k\ Health} \cdot I_{k\ Education} \cdot I_{Income} \cdot I_{Liberal\ Democracy})^{1/4}$

-Bértola-Vecchi and Zambrano use UNDP linear transformation of social variables (Table 1.1)

-UNDP, HMV, and HMV-eei (egalitarian equivalent income) use their own transformation of social variables and per capita income (Table 1.1)

-Bértola (Kakwani) combines the Kakwani transformation of years of schooling and life expectancy with Bértola-Vecchi transformation of per capita income (Table 1.1)

dimensions (health, education, political and civil liberties) by computing their shares of maximum values, and adjusts per capita income for inequality, using the *egalitarian equivalent income* formula $y^e = y *$ $(1 - G)$. It can be seen that my proposed *AHDI* specification produces higher values, with the absolute difference increasing as the levels get higher, even though their growth rates are similar, while the *Bértola (Kakwani)* specification presents the lowest level across time.

In conclusion, the different specifications for an augmented human development index share common trends. The *AHDI* proposed here uses a specification that results in an intermediate position among the alternative options offered for an index of augmented human development.

1.5 Conclusions

This chapter has presented an *augmented* human development index that combines achievements in terms of health, education, and material welfare in a context of freedom of choice, and therefore meets the conceptual requirements of the capabilities approach. The comparison with alternative indices shows how crucial it is from both a conceptual and an empirical perspective to introduce diminishing returns in per capita income. Moreover, it confirms that the new index of augmented human development provides a balanced intermediate position among the available alternative specifications.

2 | Trends in Human Development

2.1 Introduction

This chapter examines long-run trends in international well-being during the age of globalisation on the basis of in the new *Augmented Human Development Index (AHDI)*, looks at their different dimensions, and identifies their contribution to AHD gains across different phases.

The chapter is organised as follows. Section 2.2 presents trends in *AHDI* and compares them to those of GDP per head. Section 2.3 looks at AHD dimensions and their contribution to human development over time. Section 2.4 proposes some explanatory hypotheses. Section 2.5 concludes.

2.2 Trends in Human Development

Augmented human development (AHD, or human development, for short, hereafter) has improved substantially over the last one and a half centuries, reaching in 2015 a level 5.3-fold that of 1870, which implies a cumulative growth rate of 1.2 per cent per year (Table 2.1). Nonetheless, as the world average in 2015 remained below 0.5 (on a 0–1 scale), there is still significant room for improvement (Figure 2.1, continuous line). Different phases can be observed in world human development's long-run upward trend: mild and steady growth before World War I (0.9 per cent over 1870–1913), followed by a phase of acceleration between the 1920s and 1970s (growing at 1.4 per cent per year over 1913–1980), and a phase of more stability but slower progress since 1980 (1.0 per cent over 1980–2015), but for a spurt around 1990. The phase of intense expansion presents, however, a great variability, with fast growth in the late 1920s, the late 1940s and early 1950s, early 1960s, and late 1970s, and sharp deceleration during the Great Depression (1929–1933), the late 1950s, and the early 1970s (Table 2.1).

Table 2.1. *AHDI and its components in the world*
Panel A. *Levels*

	AHDI	Kakwani index of schooling	Kakwani index of life expectancy	UNDP index of income	Liberal democracy index
1870	0.077	0.032	0.033	0.350	0.093
1880	0.084	0.037	0.036	0.368	0.102
1890	0.091	0.042	0.039	0.386	0.105
1900	0.100	0.048	0.045	0.408	0.115
1913	0.115	0.055	0.053	0.438	0.137
1925	0.132	0.063	0.067	0.450	0.161
1929	0.142	0.070	0.081	0.465	0.154
1933	0.144	0.076	0.090	0.444	0.144
1938	0.152	0.081	0.098	0.471	0.143
1950	0.193	0.094	0.143	0.496	0.208
1955	0.218	0.104	0.161	0.522	0.257
1960	0.225	0.115	0.157	0.540	0.262
1965	0.248	0.127	0.200	0.566	0.265
1970	0.262	0.141	0.222	0.589	0.254
1975	0.266	0.153	0.240	0.604	0.225
1980	0.291	0.169	0.257	0.619	0.267
1985	0.305	0.184	0.271	0.626	0.277
1990	0.328	0.194	0.283	0.638	0.331
1995	0.348	0.212	0.294	0.645	0.366
2000	0.369	0.229	0.310	0.663	0.392
2005	0.381	0.244	0.325	0.683	0.390
2010	0.396	0.257	0.342	0.702	0.398
2015	0.409	0.274	0.380	0.718	0.374

Panel B. *AHD drivers* [*] *(%)*

	Kakwani index of schooling	Kakwani index of Life expectancy	UNDP index of income	Liberal Democracy index	AHDI
1870–1880	0.3	0.2	0.1	0.2	0.9
1880–1890	0.3	0.2	0.1	0.1	0.8
1890–1900	0.3	0.3	0.1	0.2	1.0
1900–1913	0.2	0.3	0.1	0.3	1.0
1913–1929	0.4	0.7	0.1	0.2	1.3

Table 2.1. (*cont.*)

	Kakwani index of schooling	Kakwani index of Life expectancy	UNDP index of income	Liberal Democracy index	AHDI
1929–1938	0.4	0.5	0.0	−0.2	0.8
1938–1950	0.3	0.8	0.1	0.8	2.0
1950–1960	0.5	0.2	0.2	0.6	1.5
1960–1970	0.5	0.9	0.2	−0.1	1.5
1970–1980	0.5	0.4	0.1	0.1	1.1
1980–1990	0.3	0.2	0.1	0.5	1.2
1990–2000	0.4	0.2	0.1	0.4	1.2
2000–2010	0.3	0.2	0.1	0.0	0.7
2010–2015	0.3	0.5	0.1	−0.3	0.7
1870–2015	0.4	0.4	0.1	0.2	1.2

Note: * Dimensions' contribution to *AHDI* growth

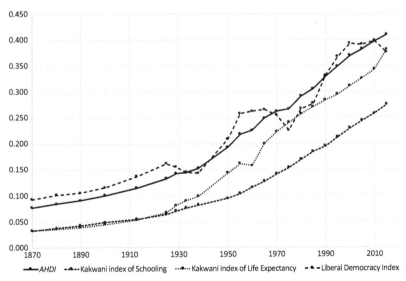

Figure 2.1 *AHDI* and its non-income dimensions.
Sources: See the text and Table 2.1.

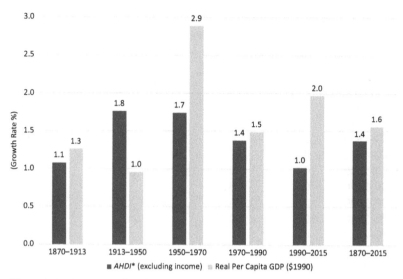

Figure 2.2 *AHDI** and real per capita GDP Growth (%).
* Excluding the income dimension.
Sources: See the text.

How does human development compare to GDP per head? It is often assumed by economists that real GDP per head adequately captures trends in welfare.[1] Does historical evidence confirm this assumption? Human development (excluding the income dimension to avoid duplication) exhibits slightly slower long-run growth than GDP per capita: 1.4 per cent per annum compared to 1.6 per cent, respectively, from 1870–2015.[2] However, a closer look reveals an apparent development puzzle: progress in economic growth and human development do not match (Figure 2.2). During the backlash against economic globalisation between 1914 and 1950, real per capita GDP growth slowed down as world commodity and factor markets disintegrated, while human development experienced major gains across the board, especially from 1938 to 1950. The paradox increases further when we consider that research on subjective well-being suggests that economic uncertainty – as would have been the case during the interwar years – hurts well-being in a broad sense (i.e., health).[3] Liberties declined during the late 1920s and 1930s, but longevity and education experienced remarkable gains (see below). However, AHD achieved smaller gains to GDP per head during the *Golden Age* (1950–early 1970s) and from 1995 onwards, but larger gains from the late 1970s to the early 1990s.

Although there has been human development progress across the board, its pace varied across the world, with differences between regions appearing to be rather persistent (Figures 2.3a–2.3f). Between 1870 and 1913, the first quartile was composed by countries of Western Europe and its offshoots plus Japan, with the addition of Latin America's Southern Cone (Uruguay, Argentina, and Chile) and members of the Austro-Hungarian Empire (Czechia, Hungary), while the bottom quartile included countries of Africa and the Middle East (Table 2.2). During the interwar period, the lower quartile's composition remained similar but for the addition of Indochina countries (Cambodia and Laos), and the top quartile added Costa Rica, in Central America, and Cuba, in the Caribbean, and Hong Kong and Sri Lanka, in Asia, to its initial group. During the Golden Age (1950–1975), the top quartile remains largely unaltered except for the addition of Israel, (non-Spanish-speaking) Caribbean countries, and small East African islands (Seychelles and Mauritius), and the exclusion of Eastern European countries while Hong Kong and Sri Lanka were in and out. At the bottom quartile, the group of countries persistently there, mostly from Africa, as most Middle East countries moved up, was joined by Haiti, in the Caribbean and South Asian countries (Afghanistan, Bangladesh, Nepal) plus Myanmar and China. Since 1980, the bottom has incorporated Middle East countries, including Saudi Arabia, and the upper quartile completed its stable composition with South Korea and Taiwan plus former socialist countries of Eastern Europe (Baltic republics, Slovakia, Poland, Croatia, and Slovenia).

2.3 Drivers of Human Development

The comparison between the historical trajectories of per capita income and human development may inform current controversies. Should policy in developing societies give priority to economic growth on the grounds that it will automatically promote access to a healthier and longer life, knowledge, and political and civil liberties? The finding that trends in GDP per capita and human development were uncorrelated for quite lengthy periods challenges this view. Exploring the specific drivers, or proximate determinants, of human development over the long run provides a more precise answer.

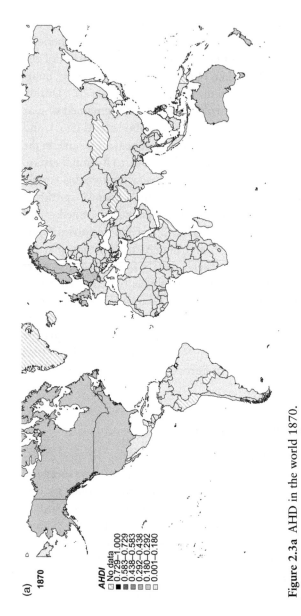

Figure 2.3a AHD in the world 1870.

Sources: Appendix A and https://frdelpino.es/investigacion/en/category/01_social-sciences/02_world-economy/03_human-development-world-economy/

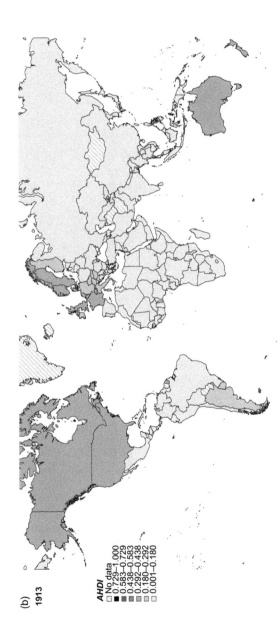

Figure 2.3b AHD in the world 1913.

Sources: Appendix A and https://frdelpino.es/investigacion/en/category/01_social-sciences/02_world-economy/03_human-development-world-economy/

44

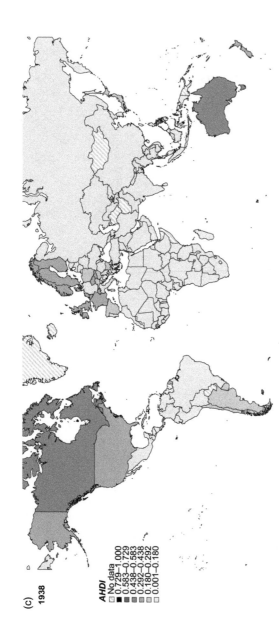

Figure 2.3c AHD in the world 1938.

Sources: Appendix A and https://frdelpino.es/investigacion/en/category/01_social-sciences/02_world-economy/03_human-development-world-economy/

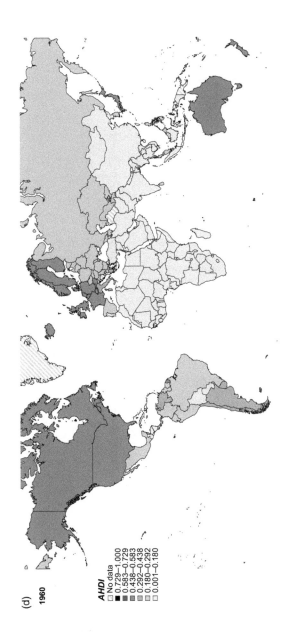

Figure 2.3d AHD in the world 1960.

Sources: Appendix A and https://frdelpino.es/investigacion/en/category/01_social-sciences/02_world-economy/03_human-development-world-economy/

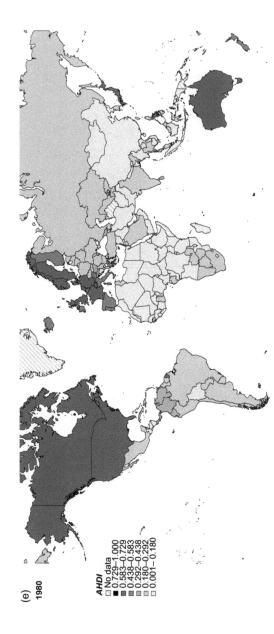

Figure 2.3e AHD in the world 1980.

Sources: Appendix A and https://frdelpino.es/investigacion/en/category/01_social-sciences/02_world-economy/03_human-development-world-economy/

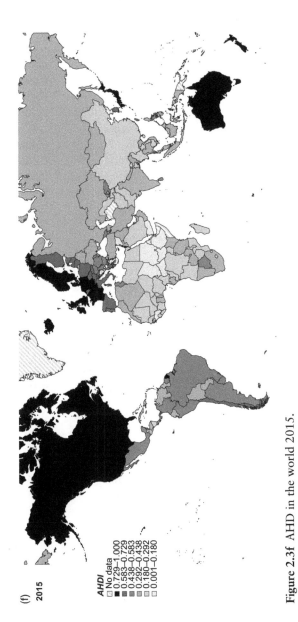

Figure 2.3f AHD in the world 2015.

Sources: Appendix A and https://frdelpino.es/investigacion/en/category/01_social-sciences/02_world-economy/03_human-development-world-economy/

47

Table 2.2. *AHD country ranking in selected benchmark years*

1870		1913		1938	
Switzerland	0.263	Australia	0.400	Australia	0.467
Canada	0.245	Canada	0.371	Canada	0.442
Norway	0.242	Switzerland	0.365	New Zealand	0.437
Australia	0.241	New Zealand	0.358	Denmark	0.429
New Zealand	0.240	Denmark	0.347	Switzerland	0.429
USA	0.237	Norway	0.325	Netherlands	0.415
Denmark	0.236	USA	0.324	Norway	0.411
Netherlands	0.221	France	0.323	USA	0.409
Belgium	0.219	Netherlands	0.322	Sweden	0.401
Sweden	0.208	UK	0.308	UK	0.396
UK	0.203	Belgium	0.298	France	0.366
Germany	0.184	Sweden	0.297	Ireland	0.364
Ireland	0.181	Ireland	0.290	Czechoslovakia	0.349
France	0.177	Germany	0.265	Belgium	0.337
Czechia	0.154	Austria	0.228	Finland	0.313
Austria	0.150	Czechia	0.214	Uruguay	0.257
Uruguay	0.148	Italy	0.208	Hungary	0.254
Hungary	0.129	Uruguay	0.203	Argentina	0.241
Finland	0.124	Finland	0.196	Japan	0.223
Argentina	0.124	Hungary	0.195	Austria	0.220
Greece	0.110	Argentina	0.188	Chile	0.209
Spain	0.105	Bulgaria	0.173	Spain	0.203
Bulgaria	0.093	Spain	0.173	Poland	0.192
Italy	0.091	Japan	0.172	Hong Kong	0.185
Japan	0.087	Greece	0.172	Costa Rica	0.183
South Africa	0.084	Portugal	0.144	Cuba	0.183
Portugal	0.081	Romania	0.138	Bulgaria	0.181
Chile	0.081	Chile	0.136	Sri Lanka	0.176
Poland	0.078	Costa Rica	0.134	Germany	0.167
Russia	0.069	Cuba	0.134	Romania	0.161
Romania	0.065	Cyprus	0.123	Lebanon	0.161
Jamaica	0.064	Jamaica	0.123	Greece	0.159
Colombia	0.064	Sri Lanka	0.117	Jamaica	0.157
Cuba	0.062	Poland	0.117	Colombia	0.154
Brazil	0.061	Serbia	0.114	Cyprus	0.151
Venezuela	0.056	South Africa	0.111	Yugoslavia	0.149
Mexico	0.055	Colombia	0.102	Italy	0.146
Sri Lanka	0.053	Hong Kong	0.101	Philippines	0.140

Table 2.2. (*cont.*)

1870		1913		1938	
Singapore	0.052	Mauritius	0.100	South Africa	0.138
Nicaragua	0.051	Russia	0.097	Portugal	0.131
Serbia	0.049	Bolivia	0.089	Mauritius	0.125
Syria	0.046	Ecuador	0.087	Bolivia	0.117
Ecuador	0.046	Philippines	0.085	Venezuela	0.117
Viet Nam	0.044	Brazil	0.084	Mexico	0.114
Turkey	0.043	Lebanon	0.081	Singapore	0.114
Korea, South	0.042	Honduras	0.079	Syria	0.105
Liberia	0.042	Singapore	0.077	Jordan	0.103
Algeria	0.042	Peru	0.075	Russia	0.102
Bolivia	0.041	El Salvador	0.075	Taiwan	0.100
Hong Kong	0.040	Venezuela	0.070	Ecuador	0.099
China	0.040	Liberia	0.070	Peru	0.099
Lebanon	0.040	Myanmar	0.067	Zambia	0.096
Egypt	0.039	Mexico	0.066	Thailand	0.096
Mauritius	0.039	Algeria	0.065	Brazil	0.094
Malaysia	0.036	Turkey	0.064	Myanmar	0.094
Kuwait	0.034	Egypt	0.063	Egypt	0.093
Tunisia	0.033	Namibia	0.062	Turkey	0.093
Iraq	0.032	Syria	0.061	Albania	0.092
India	0.032	Nicaragua	0.059	Malaysia	0.091
Albania	0.032	Guatemala	0.059	Zimbabwe	0.088
Lao PDR	0.031	Lesotho	0.057	Honduras	0.088
Jordan	0.029	China	0.056	Namibia	0.087
Cambodia	0.029	Albania	0.055	Korea, South	0.086
Taiwan	0.029	Madagascar	0.055	India	0.085
Qatar	0.029	Botswana	0.054	Liberia	0.083
Thailand	0.027	Malaysia	0.053	Viet Nam	0.083
Morocco	0.026	Mauritania	0.052	Algeria	0.079
U A Emirates	0.026	Tanzania	0.052	Lesotho	0.078
Myanmar	0.026	Taiwan	0.052	El Salvador	0.076
Madagascar	0.025	India	0.051	China	0.076
Indonesia	0.025	Jordan	0.050	Saudi Arabia	0.076
Iran	0.025	Korea, South	0.050	Tanzania	0.075
Mauritania	0.025	Thailand	0.049	Nicaragua	0.074
Malawi	0.024	Tunisia	0.048	Mauritania	0.072
Tanzania	0.024	Ghana	0.048	Guatemala	0.072
Saudi Arabia	0.023	Viet Nam	0.044	Iraq	0.070

Table 2.2. (*cont.*)

1870		1913		1938	
Nepal	0.023	Gambia	0.044	Madagascar	0.070
Kenya	0.022	Indonesia	0.043	Bahrain	0.069
Gabon	0.021	Kuwait	0.042	Kuwait	0.067
Philippines	0.021	Zambia	0.041	Ghana	0.067
Mozambique	0.021	Iraq	0.040	Indonesia	0.066
Senegal	0.021	Kenya	0.039	Botswana	0.064
Oman	0.021	Benin	0.039	Eswatini	0.063
Namibia	0.020	Zimbabwe	0.039	Tunisia	0.060
Côte d'Ivoire	0.020	Eswatini	0.038	Cambodia	0.060
Benin	0.020	Congo	0.037	Qatar	0.060
Congo	0.020	Morocco	0.037	Uganda	0.059
Bahrain	0.020	Côte d'Ivoire	0.036	Iran	0.054
Yemen	0.020	Senegal	0.036	Kenya	0.053
CAR	0.019	Qatar	0.036	Congo	0.053
Angola	0.019	Sierra Leone	0.035	Senegal	0.052
Nigeria	0.019	Iran	0.034	Nigeria	0.052
Cameroon	0.019	Malawi	0.034	Gambia	0.049
Niger	0.019	Congo DR	0.034	Morocco	0.049
Togo	0.019	Gabon	0.033	Congo DR	0.048
Ghana	0.019	Cambodia	0.033	Gabon	0.046
Uganda	0.019	Saudi Arabia	0.032	Lao PDR	0.046
Gambia	0.018	Sudan	0.032	Malawi	0.045
Sudan	0.018	Nigeria	0.031	Benin	0.045
Sierra Leone	0.018	Rwanda	0.030	U A Emirates	0.045
Burkina Faso	0.018	Uganda	0.030	Burundi	0.043
Chad	0.018	Lao PDR	0.030	Côte d'Ivoire	0.042
Mali	0.018	U A Emirates	0.028	Sierra Leone	0.042
Congo DR	0.018	Mozambique	0.028	Niger	0.041
Botswana	0.017	Angola	0.027	Rwanda	0.040
Burundi	0.017	Guinea	0.026	Mozambique	0.039
Eswatini	0.017	Togo	0.025	CAR	0.039
Ethiopia	0.017	Mali	0.024	Sudan	0.039
Guinea	0.017	Oman	0.022	Burkina Faso	0.038
Guinea-Bissau	0.017	Bahrain	0.022	Cameroon	0.038
Lesotho	0.017	Yemen	0.022	Mali	0.033
Rwanda	0.017	Cameroon	0.022	Oman	0.032
Zambia	0.017	Burundi	0.021	Angola	0.031
Zimbabwe	0.017	Nepal	0.021	Libya	0.030

Table 2.2. (*cont.*)

1870		1913		1938	
Libya	0.016	Burkina Faso	0.021	Nepal	0.029
		Ethiopia	0.021	Chad	0.027
		Libya	0.021	Togo	0.026
		Guinea-Bissau	0.021	Guinea	0.026
		CAR	0.019	Ethiopia	0.025
		Niger	0.019	Yemen	0.022
		Chad	0.018	Guinea-Bissau	0.021

1960		1980		2015	
Australia	0.538	Switzerland	0.663	Switzerland	0.861
Denmark	0.535	Germany	0.643	Australia	0.826
Norway	0.525	Australia	0.643	Canada	0.810
Canada	0.522	Norway	0.640	Japan	0.803
Germany	0.515	USA	0.636	Norway	0.800
Switzerland	0.510	Sweden	0.631	Sweden	0.784
Sweden	0.507	Canada	0.620	UK	0.779
UK	0.504	Denmark	0.614	Germany	0.776
New Zealand	0.504	Japan	0.610	Denmark	0.771
USA	0.503	France	0.608	USA	0.771
Netherlands	0.503	Netherlands	0.598	Iceland	0.768
France	0.478	UK	0.594	New Zealand	0.761
Japan	0.465	New Zealand	0.576	Ireland	0.751
Austria	0.458	Austria	0.566	Netherlands	0.747
Iceland	0.444	Finland	0.552	France	0.743
Ireland	0.444	Iceland	0.547	Israel	0.735
Finland	0.443	Belgium	0.539	Hong Kong	0.734
Belgium	0.438	Israel	0.515	Italy	0.720
Italy	0.402	Ireland	0.509	Slovenia	0.719
Israel	0.399	Italy	0.506	Estonia	0.709
Uruguay	0.393	Spain	0.505	Austria	0.707
Bahamas, The	0.367	Greece	0.499	Belgium	0.705
Trinidad-Tobago	0.347	Barbados	0.470	Finland	0.705
Barbados	0.347	Trinidad-Tobago	0.451	Korea, South	0.699
Argentina	0.338	Portugal	0.438	Czechia	0.679
Greece	0.327	Bahamas, The	0.434	Cyprus	0.678

Table 2.2. (*cont.*)

1960		1980		2015	
Belize	0.321	Cyprus	0.420	Spain	0.668
Chile	0.311	Costa Rica	0.411	Chile	0.662
St. Kitts and Nevis	0.311	Malta	0.410	Slovak Rep	0.662
Costa Rica	0.309	Venezuela	0.404	Poland	0.661
Venezuela	0.308	St. Kitts and Nevis	0.392	Lithuania	0.660
St. Vincent & Gr.	0.302	St. Vincent & Gr.	0.389	Taiwan	0.655
Jamaica	0.300	Belize	0.386	Greece	0.648
Suriname	0.290	Jamaica	0.376	Malta	0.632
Seychelles	0.282	Mauritius	0.374	Latvia	0.623
Cyprus	0.269	Georgia	0.367	Portugal	0.619
Sri Lanka	0.266	St. Lucia	0.347	Singapore	0.615
Hong Kong	0.258	Ecuador	0.344	Croatia	0.608
Czechoslovakia	0.255	Singapore	0.340	Bahamas, The	0.592
Hungary	0.250	Slovenia	0.339	Costa Rica	0.581
Singapore	0.249	Brunei Darussalam	0.333	Hungary	0.574
Panama	0.246	Croatia	0.314	Barbados	0.564
St. Lucia	0.245	Sri Lanka	0.310	Panama	0.560
Malta	0.244	Seychelles	0.310	Uruguay	0.559
Mauritius	0.237	Hungary	0.301	Trinidad-Tobago	0.554
Guyana	0.234	Colombia	0.297	Bulgaria	0.551
Poland	0.233	Poland	0.287	Mauritius	0.547
Colombia	0.232	Serbia & Montenegro	0.285	Argentina	0.545
Brunei Darussalam	0.229	Malaysia	0.284	Romania	0.538
Bulgaria	0.226	Korea, South	0.282	Jamaica	0.526
Lebanon	0.225	Lebanon	0.281	Belize	0.519
Philippines	0.221	Czechoslovakia	0.280	Moldova	0.510
Spain	0.220	Suriname	0.274	St. Lucia	0.507
Brazil	0.219	Bulgaria	0.267	St. Kitts and Nevis	0.505
Ecuador	0.213	Taiwan	0.264	Peru	0.504

Table 2.2. (*cont.*)

1960		1980		2015	
Peru	0.205	Botswana	0.263	Georgia	0.502
Yugoslavia	0.205	Dominican R	0.262	Brazil	0.501
Kuwait	0.199	Kuwait	0.262	St. Vincent & Gr.	0.491
Korea, South	0.198	Guyana	0.260	Albania	0.489
Mexico	0.185	Mexico	0.257	Sri Lanka	0.484
Malaysia	0.182	Panama	0.250	Mexico	0.476
Romania	0.182	Ghana	0.249	Serbia & Montenegro	0.464
Russia	0.181	Argentina	0.239	Seychelles	0.459
Portugal	0.180	Thailand	0.239	Suriname	0.458
South Africa	0.177	Brazil	0.239	Tunisia	0.457
Jordan	0.174	Chile	0.238	Armenia	0.455
Taiwan	0.169	Uruguay	0.237	Colombia	0.447
Cuba	0.166	Romania	0.231	Botswana	0.443
India	0.163	Hong Kong	0.230	Kyrgyzstan	0.438
Ghana	0.163	Jordan	0.229	Mongolia	0.436
Qatar	0.161	Armenia	0.228	South Africa	0.430
Cambodia	0.159	Qatar	0.227	Lebanon	0.429
Viet Nam	0.155	India	0.224	Indonesia	0.429
Myanmar	0.153	Latvia	0.221	Philippines	0.423
Bolivia	0.153	Estonia	0.221	Paraguay	0.422
Turkey	0.147	Peru	0.221	Malaysia	0.417
Zimbabwe	0.147	Turkey	0.217	Ecuador	0.411
Albania	0.145	Albania	0.217	Brunei Darussalam	0.404
Paraguay	0.142	Russia	0.216	Turkey	0.402
Thailand	0.139	Belarus	0.216	Ukraine	0.399
Syria	0.131	Lithuania	0.216	Jordan	0.397
Zambia	0.131	Ukraine	0.213	Bolivia	0.394
Gabon	0.129	Tunisia	0.210	Dominican R	0.393
Namibia	0.129	South Africa	0.210	Namibia	0.390
Egypt	0.129	Kazakhstan	0.209	Kuwait	0.387
Honduras	0.127	Uzbekistan	0.208	El Salvador	0.387
U A Emirates	0.126	U A Emirates	0.206	Guyana	0.385
El Salvador	0.125	Azerbaijan	0.205	Guatemala	0.382
Tunisia	0.124	Cuba	0.203	Belarus	0.380
Congo	0.122	Zimbabwe	0.202	Kazakhstan	0.378

Table 2.2. (*cont.*)

1960		1980		2015	
Guatemala	0.119	Moldova	0.199	India	0.377
Saudi Arabia	0.119	Kyrgyzstan	0.197	Russia	0.373
Bahrain	0.117	Paraguay	0.193	Cuba	0.367
Lesotho	0.116	Tajikistan	0.193	Iran	0.364
Dominican R	0.116	Bahrain	0.192	Ghana	0.361
Uganda	0.114	Philippines	0.190	Qatar	0.361
Tanzania	0.112	Namibia	0.188	Viet Nam	0.350
Mongolia	0.112	Gabon	0.188	São Tomé & Principe	0.349
Indonesia	0.112	Eswatini	0.188	Venezuela	0.348
Lao PDR	0.112	Zambia	0.185	Gabon	0.343
Nicaragua	0.111	Saudi Arabia	0.184	U A Emirates	0.340
Mauritania	0.111	Mongolia	0.180	Oman	0.334
Nigeria	0.111	Nicaragua	0.179	Algeria	0.327
Madagascar	0.108	Algeria	0.178	Morocco	0.322
Iraq	0.107	Kenya	0.177	Honduras	0.318
Kenya	0.106	Egypt	0.176	Thailand	0.309
Pakistan	0.101	Honduras	0.174	Nepal	0.308
Libya	0.099	Lesotho	0.172	Iraq	0.304
Botswana	0.098	Syria	0.169	Tanzania	0.304
Liberia	0.098	Iran	0.167	Zambia	0.299
Eswatini	0.096	São Tomé & Principe	0.167	Azerbaijan	0.297
Senegal	0.094	China	0.165	Kenya	0.293
Iran	0.094	Oman	0.164	Libya	0.290
Congo DR	0.092	Viet Nam	0.164	Nicaragua	0.289
Bangladesh	0.090	Iraq	0.163	Pakistan	0.288
Morocco	0.089	Morocco	0.161	Lesotho	0.288
Algeria	0.089	Libya	0.156	Nigeria	0.286
Benin	0.088	Tanzania	0.156	Liberia	0.283
Cameroon	0.087	Guatemala	0.154	Senegal	0.282
Equat. Guinea	0.086	Senegal	0.154	Uzbekistan	0.276
Rwanda	0.080	Bolivia	0.152	Benin	0.275
Haiti	0.080	Indonesia	0.152	Malawi	0.270
Sierra Leone	0.078	Côte d'Ivoire	0.150	Egypt	0.264
China	0.077	Bangladesh	0.146	Saudi Arabia	0.263
CAR	0.076	Nigeria	0.145	Madagascar	0.262
Gambia	0.076	Congo	0.142	Uganda	0.257
Côte d'Ivoire	0.076	El Salvador	0.141	Tajikistan	0.256

Table 2.2. (*cont.*)

1960		1980		2015	
Togo	0.074	Gambia	0.139	Zimbabwe	0.256
São Tomé & Principe	0.071	Cameroon	0.138	Cambodia	0.256
Nepal	0.069	Pakistan	0.133	Bahrain	0.256
Burundi	0.069	Madagascar	0.132	Bangladesh	0.251
Eritrea	0.068	Myanmar	0.128	China	0.250
Oman	0.068	Togo	0.127	Côte d'Ivoire	0.244
Mali	0.067	Rwanda	0.123	Mozambique	0.242
Sudan	0.066	Lao PDR	0.119	Haiti	0.242
Malawi	0.065	Mauritania	0.115	Myanmar	0.236
Afghanistan	0.061	Liberia	0.112	Congo	0.230
Burkina Faso	0.056	Sierra Leone	0.111	Togo	0.226
Mozambique	0.052	Malawi	0.109	Rwanda	0.224
Niger	0.052	Benin	0.108	Mauritania	0.223
Chad	0.047	Sudan	0.107	Cameroon	0.222
Guinea	0.044	Haiti	0.106	Lao PDR	0.220
Ethiopia	0.043	CAR	0.104	Mali	0.210
Angola	0.041	Cambodia	0.103	Angola	0.210
Yemen	0.036	Equatorial Guinea	0.102	Eswatini	0.207
Guinea-Bissau	0.029	Nepal	0.102	Sierra Leone	0.206
		Uganda	0.102	Afghanistan	0.205
		Burundi	0.095	Guinea-Bissau	0.203
		Congo DR	0.091	Niger	0.197
		Mali	0.090	Equatorial Guinea	0.196
		Mozambique	0.086	Burkina Faso	0.184
		Angola	0.082	Congo DR	0.181
		Afghanistan	0.079	Gambia	0.179
		Guinea	0.078	Syria	0.177
		Guinea-Bissau	0.078	Sudan	0.176
		Niger	0.073	Guinea	0.174
		Yemen	0.072	Ethiopia	0.170
		Burkina Faso	0.069	CAR	0.161
		Chad	0.060	Yemen	0.161
		Eritrea	0.060	Chad	0.144
		Ethiopia	0.056	Burundi	0.129
				Eritrea	0.107

Trends in non-income dimensions of human development are most informative. The Kakwani index of schooling offers distinctive phases, with 1925, 1950, and 1980 as break points, and faster growth during the late 1920s and early 1930s and 1950–1980, reaching in 2015 a level 8.5-fold that of 1870 (Figure 2.1). The Kakwani index of life expectancy also presents three phases in its evolution with 1920 and 1970 as divides (but for a setback due to China's mortality during the Great Leap Forward, 1958–1961, and its recovery in the early 1960s), with its fastest progress achieved over 1920–1970, resulting in a level 11.5 times higher in 2015 than in 1870. Civil and political liberties, proxied by the index of liberal democracy, show a mild improvement since the late nineteenth century, accelerating in the first quarter of the twentieth century, and partially reversed in the late 1920s and 1930s. This was followed by a spurt in the aftermath of World War II before these freedoms faded in the 1960s, and experienced another surge during the last quarter of the century, particularly in the 1990s, following the collapse of socialism in Russia and Eastern Europe and the spread of democratisation. Over 1870–2015, the index multiplied by 4.

Given the *AHDI*'s multiplicative structure, in which dimensions enter with equal weights, *AHDI* growth equals the weighted sum of each dimension's growth rate, with the weights set at one-fourth for each dimension. Thus, using the lower case for rates of variation:

$$ahdi = \tfrac{1}{4} i_{k\ Life\ Expectancy} + \tfrac{1}{4} i_{kSchooling} + \tfrac{1}{4} i_{Adjusted\ Income} \qquad [2.1]$$
$$+ \tfrac{1}{4} i_{Liberal\ Democracy}$$

Non-income dimensions have driven most of the world's human development gains over time (Table 2.1, Panel B). Life expectancy was the main contributor to progress in human development through the one and a half centuries considered (37 per cent), closely followed by education (32 per cent). Specifically, life expectancy's contribution was largely concentrated in the 1920–50 period and in the 1960s, when it provided about half of the gains in human development. Education led the late-nineteenth-century advance and was a steady contributor to human development over the entire time span considered. Political and civil liberties made substantial contributions to AHD growth in the late 1940s and early 1950s and during the late 1980s and early 1990s.[4]

2.4 Ultimate Determinants of Human Development

What explains the timing and depth of life expectancy and schooling contributions to human development? It is commonly assumed that economic progress largely explains this, as higher levels of income per capita facilitate the allocation of more resources to social services that improve people's health and education. It has been suggested, for example, that increases in social sharing and public support for social services explain the paradox in the case of Britain during the war decades (Sen, 1999: 51). It has also been argued that during the regulated phase of capitalism the success in improving well-being was largely due to public intervention, as markets alone would not have contributed to universal provision of health services or stimulated medical research (Easterlin, 1999). Has government intervention and, in particular, the expansion of social spending, played such a decisive role? For a group of today's advanced countries, a positive non-linear association may be observed between social transfers – that is, all social spending except investment in education – expressed as a share of GDP, and the Kakwani index of life expectancy at birth, with larger longevity gains corresponding to increases in social transfers at low levels but the association gradually flattening as the share of social transfers in GDP rises (Figure 2.4).[5] Thus, social spending appears to have contributed to improving life expectancy only up to a point. In fact, over the past one hundred years, education and health improved across the board, including countries in which social spending did not expand at times of sluggish economic growth (Benavot and Riddle, 1988; Riley, 2001). A global explanation seems to be required.

Another stylised fact that is often found in the literature is that global health improvements only occurred in the era following World War II, when, with the help of international institutions, new drugs from the West reached the rest of the world (Acemoglu and Johnson, 2007: 935–936; Cardona and Bishai, 2018; Klasing and Milionis, 2020). However, life expectancy provided half the gains in human development in the world between 1920 and 1950 (Table 2.1). This suggests that improvements in life expectancy took place across the board and, therefore, that the epidemiological transition spread beyond advanced countries much earlier than has been presumed, and also requires an explanation.

Health improvements can be depicted in terms of a health function (Preston, 1975; Easterlin, 1999). Movements along the function

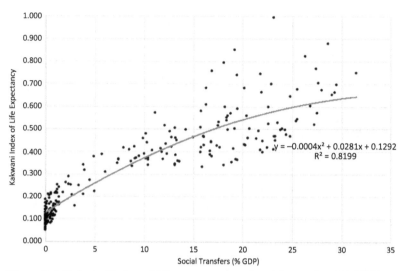

Figure 2.4 Kakwani index of life expectancy and social transfers (% GDP) in advanced countries, 1880–2013.

Sources: Social transfers (% GDP), 1880–1900, Lindert (1994); 1910–2013, Lindert (2017); Kakwani index of life expectancy, see the text.

represent gains attributable to economic growth and result in improved nutrition – which strengthens the immune system and reduces morbidity (Stolnitz, 1955; McKeown *et al.* 1962, 1975; Fogel, 2004) – and increased public provision of health (Loudon, 2000; Cutler and Miller, 2005). This has often been the focus of studies by country. However, we also need to consider shifts in the position of the health function.

Outward shifts in the health function that derive from improvements in medical knowledge have been the main cause of the sustained increase in life expectancy since the late nineteenth century (Riley, 2001; Cutler et al., 2006). The major improvement in longevity between 1920 and 1970 originated in the diffusion of the germ theory of disease, for which supportive evidence had been found in north-western Europe during the 1870s and 1880s (Riley, 2001), which led to the epidemiological or health transition.[6] Persistent gains in lower mortality and higher survival rates were achieved throughout the epidemiological transition, as infectious disease gave way to chronic disease as a major cause of death (Omran, 1971, 1998).[7] Two main consequences resulted from the diffusion of the germ theory of disease. On the one hand, the germ theory triggered medical technological progress that resulted in new drugs to cure infectious diseases and spread the health transition: new vaccines (since the 1890s) and drugs to cure infectious diseases, sulphonamides since the late 1930s, and antibiotics since the 1950s, along with chemicals such as DDT, which is instrumental in battling malaria (Desowitz, 1991; Easterlin, 1999; Jayachandran *et al.*, 2010; Lindgren, 2016). On the other hand, a less obvious result of the epidemiological transition consisted of improvements in public health – often at low cost, because low incomes prevented the purchase of the new drugs – and the diffusion of preventive methods of disease transmission and knowledge dissemination through school education. The latter factors contributed to reducing mortality throughout the life course, particularly infant mortality and maternal death, two major determinants of the increase in life expectancy at birth in developing regions (Riley, 2001).[8] This helps explain why the epidemiological transition in developing countries began in the first half of the twentieth century, at a time when a large proportion of the *Rest* was still under colonial rule and the new drugs were largely unaffordable for the population.

Although a second episode in which longevity, along with education, made a massive contribution to human development took place in the 1960s, a decade of governmental activism in the developing world, by 1970, the diffusion of the epidemiological transition was largely exhausted. This helps explain the weaker contribution of life expectancy to improving human development after 1970.

The renewed contribution of life expectancy to human development since 1990, largely restricted to the currently developed countries, is associated with a *second health transition* in which mortality and morbidity fall among the elderly as a result of new medical knowledge that permits better treatment of respiratory and cardiovascular disease and vision problems (particularly cataract surgery) (Cutler et al., 2006; Eggleston and Fuchs, 2012; Deaton, 2013; Chernew et al., 2016). The diffusion of new technologies, combined with better nutrition in early years of life, has resulted in longer and healthier lives (Murray and Lopez, 1997; Mathers *et al.*, 2001; Salomon et al., 2012; Murray *et al.*, 2017). The fact that the developing countries have not participated so far in the *second* health transition, along with the AIDS-HIV pandemic in sub-Saharan Africa and the collapse of socialism in large areas of the world, help explain life expectancy's negative contribution to the *Rest*'s catch-up to the *OECD* during the period 1995–2010. Politics may have also contributed. It has been argued that autocracies successfully fought mortality through government intervention during the first health transition, but democracies facilitated the new health transition with fewer constraints on medical innovation, so gains in life expectancy have been larger in democratic than in authoritarian countries since the late twentieth century (Mackenbach, 2013).

In the case of schooling, it is worth recalling that mass primary education began in Europe and its offshoots during the 1870s. In Europe, there was a shift from private and decentralised (local or religious) to compulsory and centralised schooling, as a result of public intervention, although the speed and breadth of the process varied substantially across countries during the late nineteenth and early twentieth centuries (Ansell and Lindvall, 2013).

But why did such a change occur? John Meyer et al. (1992: 129, 132) claimed that mass education was at the core of the nation-state model and represented a project of the elites involving socialisation of individuals, extension of citizenship, and a secular vision of progress. Schooling was, thus, an instrument with which to spread the values of the elite to the rest of the population (Alesina, Giuliano, and Reich, 2020).

Centralisation and secularisation, undertaken in both democracies and dictatorships, played a major role in the expansion of mass primary education (Ansell and Lindvall, 2013: 506). The tension between central and local governments, secular and religious authorities conditioned the pace at which mass primary education spread.

The diffusion of mass education to the rest of the world would have resulted from 'the spread of the Western system, with its joined principles of national citizenship and state authority' (Meyer et al. (1992: 146). After World War II, the newly independent countries in Asia and Africa would adopt the education policies previously implemented in the mother country. The Cold War and international cooperation contributed to accelerating the spread of mass primary and secondary schooling. This acceleration is clearly noticeable in the Kakwani index of schooling (Table 2.1).

A number of non-excluding elements account for the spread of schooling: industrialisation (that required skills), war (helped by indoctrination and mass provision of public goods to motivate conscripted armies), and redistribution (Gellner, 1983; Darden and Mylonas, 2015; Manzano, 2017; Aghion et al., 2019; Alesina, Reich, and Riboni, 2020).

Homogenising the population to forge a national identity through a common national language and mass public instruction, often imposed on the population and helped by compulsory military conscription, appears as a distinctive driving force behind mass schooling (Alesina, Giuliano, and Reich, 2020). In immigration and newly independent countries, schooling was crucial for the task of nation-building. Oriana Bandiera *et al.* (2018: 66) show that U.S. schooling laws were designed 'to instil civic values to the culturally diverse migrants' during the Age of Mass Migration (1850–1914). Similarly, in Argentina, public primary schooling in Spanish was a tool for nation-building during the massive Italian immigration (Botana and Gallo, 1997).

Democratisation has been considered responsible for the spread of education. Peter Lindert (2004), for example, established a connection between the expansion of primary mass schooling and democratisation on the basis of the experience of some Western countries. Agustina Paglayan (2021) qualifies this argument by pointing out that democratisation only promotes the expansion of primary schooling when a majority of the population lacked access to primary schooling before democracy emerged, an infrequent historical situation. Most state education systems were established ahead of democracy to homogenise the population. This motivation was shared by governments in early twentieth-century Portugal, in which the success in spreading mass primary schooling corresponded to the authoritarian *Estado Novo* (1933–1974) and not to the Republic (1910–1926), a limited democracy, with the former receiving support from Roman Catholic families who opposed the liberal regime (Palma and Reis, 2021). In fact, elites perceived democratisation as a threat to their power (Alesina, Giulano, and Reich, 2020). The discrepancies observed in the international distribution of schooling and liberal democracy over the long run, declining steadily in the case of schooling and rising in the case of liberal democracy until the late twentieth century, contradict the hypothesis of a connection between the spread of democratisation and schooling.

Other external developments affected the spread of mass education. Mariko Klasing and Petros Milionis (2020) claim that the epidemiological transition, by improving relative female life expectancy, due to the better response of the female immune system to vaccination against infectious diseases, contributed to rising female education and reducing the education gender gap.[9] Thus, it can be hypothesised that, as longer and healthier lives prompt individuals to invest in their education (Hansen, 2013) and female life expectancy improved relatively, women's higher education attainment may have contributed to raising the average level of schooling. Furthermore, the second health transition, with increases in life expectancy as a result of major improvements in the treatment of cardiovascular and respiratory diseases, also had the consequence of increasing enrolment in higher education (Hansen and Strulik, 2017).

In terms of liberties, it is worth asking what drives the spread of civil and political rights. Over the past sixty years, Seymour Lipset's theory of political modernisation – namely, that economic development is accompanied by democracy – has been at the centre of the debate about democratic transitions and stability.[10] For example, Daron Acemoglu *et al.* (2008, 2009) accepted the income–democratisation correlation but reject a causal effect of income on democracy. While Carles Boix (2011) proposed a conditional version of Lipset's theory in which the association between democratisation and GDP per head exhibits diminishing returns to income. Moreover, the relationship shifts outwards over time.

Different explanations have been put forward for the introduction and spread of democracy in a country. Ruth Collier (1999) stressed the role played by the elite in the first democratisation wave up to the early twentieth century. Acemoglu and James Robinson (2006: 27) considered, instead, that the threat of a revolution in a context of high inequality stimulates democratisation, which implies 'a commitment to future pro-majority policies by the elites'. Boix (2003) claimed, however, that only in a context of declining inequality and economic diversification would the elite accept democratisation, as the redistribution threat diminishes. The spread of democracy is also associated with international conflict and exposure to war (Knutsen et al., 2019). For example, a trade-off has been suggested between the extension of suffrage and mass conscription (Ticchi and Vindigni, 2008).

Sharun Mukand and Dani Rodrik (2020) trace a sequence in which the three dimensions of liberal democracy – property, political, and civil rights – interplay, from autocracy, under which only property rights were respected, to liberal democracy, in which the three types of rights are recognised, usually in a context of mild inequality and social homogeneity. There are also intermediate stages of liberal autocracy, in which property and civil rights, but not electoral rights, were acknowledged, and illiberal democracy, in which civil rights are absent.[11] How this sequence evolves has differed over space and time and accounts for the level of liberal democracy and its distribution over the past one and a half centuries.

The time dimension of democratisation defines another stream of the literature that approaches the spread of liberal democracy as a global process that transcends national boundaries and is subjected to geopolitical events. The world trends observed in liberal democracy, with three expansion phases – up to the early 1920s, during the aftermath of World War II and until the early 1960s, and from the late 1980s onwards – and their reversals (Figure 2.1), closely resemble the evolution of the proportion of democratic countries in the world (Boix, 2011: 810) and broadly conform to Samuel Huntington's (1991) waves of democratisation. The swift diffusion of democracy in the early 1920s, late 1940s and early 1950s, and the 1990s, and its setbacks, closely match major international events.[12] Such coincidence suggests the decisive role of the major powers in shaping the international order and interfering with countries' internal politics (Boix, 2011; Narizny, 2012). Although the diffusion of ideas (liberalism, equality, human rights) also played a significant part in the spread of democratisation from the early nineteenth century (Collier, 1999; Mukand and Rodrik, 2020).

2.5 Conclusions

This chapter has presented a long-run view of human development, defined with a capability measure of well-being, over the past one and a half centuries on the basis of a new index that, in order to incorporate freedom of choice, adds political and civil liberties to the UNDP's *HDI* conventional dimensions of longevity, education, and living standard, and transforms non-linearly the non-income dimensions.

The main findings are that, on average, human development grew substantially around the world from 1870 onwards, particularly from 1920–1980, but significant room for improvement still exists, and although world regions improved at a different pace, significant differences between them persisted over time.

GDP per person and human development do not always go hand in hand, even if increases in income per head may contribute to better health and education and to expanding liberties. More specifically, human development experienced major gains across the board during the backlash against economic globalisation that occurred in the first half of the twentieth century, resulting from the advance in longevity and education in this period. The spread of new medical knowledge, new educational practices, public policies, the diffusion of new ideas, and the demand of civil and political freedoms account for the mismatch between average incomes and human development behaviour.

Life expectancy was the main contributor to human development progress over the one and half centuries considered here, although its greatest contribution was concentrated between 1920 and 1970, as the epidemiological transition took place, largely before the international diffusion of modern drugs. Education – stimulated by industrialisation, income redistribution, and nation-building – was a steady contributor to human development over the entire time span considered. Political and civil liberties, in turn, added substantially to *AHD* throughout the twentieth century, especially during its last two decades, as authoritarian rule gave way to liberal democracy.

3 | *World Distribution of Human Development*

3.1 Introduction

In the past one and a half centuries, substantial gains in well-being have been achieved in human development. But were these gains evenly distributed? The results presented so far are based on the population-weighted average of countries' mean levels, but just as the pace of AHD progress varied through time, its distribution presumably did so too.

This raises some questions. How have the gains from human development and its dimensions been distributed? Did relative and absolute inequality move together? What drove relative inequality? Which parts of the distribution achieved larger gains over time in relative and absolute terms?

This chapter contributes to the study of international well-being distribution from a *capabilities* perspective in two ways.[1] First, it offers long-run trends in relative and absolute inequality for human development and its dimensions – schooling, life expectancy, political and civil liberties – which are contrasted with those for per capita income.[2] Second, it shows the distribution of relative and absolute well-being gains by deciles, using growth incidence curves.

The chapter is organised as follows. Section 3.2 provides an overview of the empirical literature on multidimensional international inequality. Section 3.3 offers long-run trends in inequality for human development and its dimensions. Section 3.4 portrays relative and absolute gains across the distribution on the basis of growth incidence curves. Section 3.5 looks at the behaviour of well-being dimensions to account for the disparities in their distribution over time. Section 3.6 concludes.

3.2 Debating Well-Being Inequality

Earlier quantitative assessments of international inequality were carried out on the basis of per capita GDP, focusing almost exclusively on the late twentieth century. A long-term deterioration in world distribution of income, resulting from the widening gap between developed and developing countries, was the prevailing consensus up to the 1980s (Theil 1979, 1989). Albert Berry, François Bourguignon, and Christian Morrisson (1983) challenged this view by pointing out that large countries were the main determinants of the exhibited trends.[3] Later, Branko Milanovic (2005, 2016) showed that while unweighted international inequality (labelled 'Inequality 1') experienced a sustained increase until 2000 and then declined, population-weighted inequality (labelled 'Inequality 2') fell from the mid-twentieth century onwards.

In recent decades, as data on household surveys became widely available, research shifted the focus to 'global' economic inequality, that is, world income distribution among individuals ('Inequality 3' in Milanovic's typology). The results of the new approach initially supported the view of a substantial increase in global inequality, as widening inter-country income differentials more than offset the decline in within-country inequality (Korzeniewicz and Moran, 1997). The consensus was broken when Paul Schultz (1998) showed that inequality had fallen since the mid-1970s, since the contraction in inequality across countries cancelled out any increases in within-country inequality. Schultz's findings led to a new, less pessimistic consensus that challenged the view of a widening gap between the world rich and poor in the late twentieth century. Glenn Firebaugh (1999) also noticed a remarkable stability in world income distribution between 1960 and 1989, since the divergence in income growth favourable to rich countries was offset by the faster population growth in poor countries. For the post-1980 era, Christoph Lakner and Milanovic (2016) indicate that the level of global inequality remained stable and high, and only declined mildly as of the early 2000s, including the period of the Great Recession, with China's contribution playing a decisive role (Milanovic, 2020).[4]

The discussion has been conducted, so far, in terms of relative inequality, which depends on the ratio of countries to the mean, and little emphasis has been placed on absolute inequality, that is, absolute differences between countries and regions. In fact, the difference between relative and absolute inequality helps explain the contradiction often highlighted between the evolution of aggregate measures of inequality, most often, the Gini coefficient, and the gap between the top and the bottom.[5] For example, Miguel Niño-Zarazúa *et al.* (2017)

identified a decline in global inequality between 1975 and 2010 in relative terms, but an increase when measured in absolute terms.

Long-run inequality received little quantitative attention until recent decades due to data constraints. Bourguignon and Morrisson (2002), on the basis of 33 'trans-national' units, concluded that world inequality was much higher in 1992 than in 1820. This resulted from a rise in inequality between the early nineteenth and mid-twentieth centuries that tended to stabilise during the second half of the century. The main element behind long-run world income inequality was the disparity between countries. Nonetheless, within-country income distribution dominated world inequality during the nineteenth century, while in the twentieth century cross-country income distribution prevailed. Refined estimates by Jan-Luiten van Zanden et al. (2014) tend to confirm Bourguignon and Morrisson's findings. Driven by between-country inequality, the dispersion of global income distribution increased over the long run, mostly up to 1950, stabilising thereafter, and experiencing a moderate rise from 1980 onwards. When, alternatively, absolute inequality is considered, Thomas Goda and Alejandro Torres García (2017) find a sustained rise since 1850 (declining only in the 2000s), in which within-country inequality represented the driving force before 1929 and after 1985, while between-country inequality prevailed from 1929–1950.

However, per capita income is just one dimension of well-being. Inequality in access to education and health has also attracted the interest of social scientists. In the case of civil and political rights, however, although their advances and setbacks across countries have attracted much attention, no quantitative assessments of their international distribution seem to exist (cf. Noble, 2016).

Morrisson and Fabrice Murtin (2013) provided a long-run view of global education inequality on the basis of average years of schooling, finding a long-term reduction, mostly attributable to the diffusion of literacy.[6] Brian Goesling and David Baker (2008) observed a declining dispersion of schooling years since 1980 and attributed it to the globalisation of primary education.

The long-run evolution of life expectancy inequality has been addressed by Bourguignon and Morrisson (2002), who, on the basis of cross-country data for life expectancy at birth at benchmark years, found a sustained increase in inequality between 1820 and 1910, which stabilised up to 1929, and then declined sharply until

1970, remaining unaltered until 1990. An update of the estimates shows a further decline in the 1990s (Morrisson and Murtin, 2005). Thus, the levels of inequality in the late twentieth and early nineteenth centuries were similar. Rob Clark (2011) also finds that the international dispersion of life expectancy declined between 1955 and 1990 but then rose until 2005. He claims an inverted U relationship existed between life expectancy dispersion and the level of per capita GDP, and depicted it as a 'welfare Kuznets curve'. Goesling and Glenn Firebaugh (2004) identified a decline in the 1980s that was reverted during the 1990s, and which they largely attributed to the different pace at which life expectancy evolved across countries, particularly in sub-Saharan Africa.[7] Rati Ram (2006) concurred, pointing out the contrast between the pre- and post-1990 periods and attributing the divergence in the 1990s to the role of HIV/AIDS. Goesling and Baker (2008) stressed the uneven diffusion of health knowledge, practice, and technology across countries that, as Ryan Edwards (2011) observes, translated into steady, or even growing, international inequality in adult longevity between 1970 and 2000.

Whether to look at different dimensions of well-being individually or to resort to multidimensional indices poses a dilemma. On the one hand, the interpretation of individual indices is straightforward. On the other, if individual indices show conflicting tendencies, drawing general conclusions regarding its evolution becomes impossible (Decancq et al., 2009). This has led to the construction of composite indicators.

The pioneer in addressing international well-being inequality within a capabilities framework was Ram (1992), who noticed a discrepancy between the high level of income inequality and the low level of human development inequality. Earlier, using the Physical Quality of Life Index, Ram (1980) had observed a sustained decline in well-being inequality over 1950–1970, at odds with the simultaneous rising trend observed for income. Later, Farhad Noorbakhsh (2006) pointed out a slow inequality reduction in human development during the last quarter of the twentieth century, and Ricardo Martínez (2012) found a decline in the international dispersion of human development between 1980 and 2010. In the only long-run perspective on human development, Morrisson and Murtin (2005) observed that the evolution of inequality had an inverted U-shape, with a turning point in 1930.[8]

Also inspired by Amartya Sen's capabilities approach, and on the basis of 'achievement indices' (see next section) for different social indicators (infant mortality rate, life expectancy at birth, and daily calorie and protein supply), Bart Hobijn and Philip Hans Franses (2001) disputed the view that standards of living converged in the late twentieth century, and suggested an increase in unweighted inequality resulting from a widening gap between developed and developing countries since the 1960s.[9]

The main conclusion that derives from the surveyed literature is that (non-income) well-being inequality experienced a long-term rise that peaked by the early twentieth century before giving way to a sustained decline. This is at odds with the evolution of international income distribution, in which dispersion rose over time to decline only in the early 2000s. Can this depiction of the trends in well-being inequality be confirmed using a more rigorous conceptual approach and a more comprehensive database?

It is also worth mentioning the driving role played by between-country inequality in global interpersonal income and education inequality. Between-country inequality not only represented the main component of global inequality, but their trends were also largely coincidental (Bourguignon and Morrisson, 2002; Morrisson and Murtin, 2013; van Zanden et al., 2014; Lakner and Milanovic, 2016). This finding lends support to the approach that, in the absence of within-country information, is presented here: namely, studying population-weighted inequality across countries (Milanovic's Inequality 2).

3.3 Trends in Human Development Inequality

Is well-being inequality higher in the world today than it was in the late nineteenth century? Can we distinguish different phases in its evolution? How does the inequality of different well-being dimensions compare? These are the questions addressed in the section.

Alternative inequality measures, which differ in their sensitivity to different parts of the distribution, can be adopted. Among the entropy indices $G(\alpha)$, for which the more positive (negative) the α, the more sensitive the index to differences at the top (bottom) of the distribution, I have chosen $G(0)$, which corresponds to Henri Theil's (1967) population-weighted index, also known as Theil L or Mean Logarithmic Deviation (MLD), and is more sensitive to the bottom of the distribution. Entropy indices have the additional advantage of being perfectly decomposable into between- and within-group inequality.

Two types of inequality estimates are presented here: inequality between country averages in which all countries are given the same weight, regardless of size, that is, Milanovic's (2005) Inequality 1; and inequality between country averages but weighted by countries' size, so a large country counts more than a small one, namely, Milanovic's Inequality 2. The unweighted measure of inequality (Inequality 1) allows for the fact that policies are implemented at the country level and impact on its citizens' well-being. Besides, weighted measures (Inequality 2) are very sensitive to the performance of highly populated countries. However, Inequality 2, although implicitly assuming perfectly equal within-country distribution, does get us closer to a measure of world distribution by assigning higher value to more populated countries (Milanovic, 2005: 7–8). Unfortunately, no data on within-country distribution of social dimensions of well-being are available for such a large sample and long time span.[10]

Does population-weighted international inequality (Inequality 2) provide a good proxy for global inequality, that is, inequality among world inhabitants (Inequality 3)? This would be the case if between-country inequality, rather than within-country inequality, drives global inequality.[11] Evidence on global inequality estimates for both per capita income and education supports this hypothesis (see Section 3.2). The assumption here is, then, that inter-country dispersion provides a lower-bound measure of global inequality.[12]

Different country samples have been used in the alternative inequality estimates, for which the longer the time span, the narrower the spatial coverage. Thus, over the entire time span, 1870–2015, 115 countries are considered, with the number rising up to 121, 146, 161, and 162 countries for the samples starting in 1913, 1950, 1980, and 1990, respectively.[13] The country samples represent over 90 per cent of the world population. The results of these samples are very similar, so there has been no need to splice them.

The overview of the literature has shown that most studies address inequality in social dimensions of well-being using their original values (and, occasionally, their linear transformation), but this approach tends to bias the results favouring convergence. Such spurious tendency is mitigated here, if not totally suppressed, by resorting to Kakwani's non-linear transformation of health and education dimensions (Hobijn and Franses, 2001). Therefore, the results presented in this section should provide a more accurate picture of trends in well-being inequality.

Let us now look at the international distribution of human development and its dimensions over time and compare it with that of per capita income.

3.3.1 Trends in Inequality 1 and 2

Unweighted inequality in terms of human development increased up to 1890 and was followed, then, by a steady long-run decline, except for a reversal in the aftermath of World War I and stagnation in the early 1970s (Table 3.1). If we now turn to population-weighted inequality, we find a declining trend that was reversed in the aftermath of the world wars.

Let us now look at AHD dimensions. How is access to knowledge, proxied by the Kakwani index of schooling, distributed internationally? High initial levels of inequality are observed for both unweighted and population-weighted measures in the late nineteenth and early twentieth centuries, prior to the diffusion of mass primary education (Benavot and Riddle, 1988; Lindert, 2004). Inequality fell steadily after 1900, but its level was still high in the third quarter of the twentieth century.

Do the trends in schooling inequality obtained with the Kakwani transformation match those derived on the basis of the original values by Morrisson and Murtin (2013)? Inequality fell over time in Morrisson and Murtin's estimates (as occurs when I replicate the measurement of inequality using original values of years of schooling (see Figure C.1 in Appendix C)), and, as expected, the level of inequality is systematically lower because bounded variables, when transformed linearly, exhibit a spurious tendency towards convergence.

Living a long and healthy life is an essential dimension of well-being, and how it is distributed is important. Main phases can be observed in the evolution of life expectancy inequality: a rise from 1870 to 1925, followed by a sustained fall until the early 1980s, partially recovering between 1990 and 2010, before returning to a declining trend. When we compare Inequality 1 and 2, we find that, for population-weighted inequality, the rise up to the mid-1920s and the long-run contraction to 1980 was sharper, unlike the post-2010 rebound. Also noticeable is a sharp and temporary reversal in 1960 that captures the impact of the increase in mortality in China during the Great Leap Forward famine (Meng et al., 2015). This hints at the importance of large countries, as illustrated by the upsurge of Inequality 2 in 1960, not observable in Inequality 1.

Table 3.1 *International inequality in AHD and its dimensions,*
1870–2015 (MLD)
Panel A. Unweighted

	AHDI	Life expectancy	Schooling	Adjusted income	Civil and political liberties
1870	0.41	0.25	1.25	0.05	0.79
1880	0.44	0.27	1.28	0.05	0.82
1890	0.46	0.30	1.29	0.05	0.85
1900	0.42	0.33	1.27	0.05	0.62
1913	0.39	0.35	1.08	0.05	0.52
1925	0.40	0.39	1.03	0.05	0.57
1929	0.37	0.33	0.95	0.06	0.57
1933	0.35	0.32	0.89	0.06	0.54
1938	0.32	0.26	0.85	0.06	0.56
1950	0.26	0.18	0.69	0.06	0.50
1955	0.24	0.17	0.64	0.06	0.50
1960	0.23	0.17	0.59	0.05	0.46
1965	0.21	0.15	0.54	0.05	0.46
1970	0.21	0.13	0.49	0.05	0.56
1975	0.20	0.12	0.43	0.05	0.60
1980	0.17	0.10	0.36	0.05	0.63
1985	0.16	0.09	0.31	0.05	0.59
1990	0.15	0.09	0.28	0.05	0.43
1995	0.14	0.10	0.25	0.06	0.35
2000	0.13	0.11	0.23	0.06	0.34
2005	0.12	0.11	0.22	0.06	0.31
2010	0.11	0.11	0.20	0.05	0.29
2015	0.11	0.09	0.19	0.05	0.28

Panel B. Population weighted

	AHDI	Life expectancy	Schooling	Adjusted income	Civil and political liberties
1870	0.27	0.21	0.88	0.03	0.47
1880	0.30	0.23	0.85	0.04	0.54
1890	0.33	0.29	0.84	0.04	0.58
1900	0.34	0.34	0.77	0.05	0.58
1913	0.29	0.40	0.65	0.05	0.33
1925	0.34	0.42	0.69	0.06	0.55

Table 3.1 (*cont.*)

	AHDI	Life expectancy	Schooling	Adjusted income	Civil and political liberties
1929	0.28	0.25	0.60	0.06	0.56
1933	0.25	0.23	0.57	0.05	0.52
1938	0.22	0.20	0.54	0.06	0.54
1950	0.25	0.15	0.52	0.09	0.68
1955	0.22	0.15	0.49	0.07	0.68
1960	0.24	0.21	0.45	0.07	0.71
1965	0.19	0.11	0.42	0.06	0.72
1970	0.19	0.09	0.38	0.06	0.80
1975	0.18	0.08	0.35	0.06	0.77
1980	0.15	0.07	0.31	0.06	0.66
1985	0.14	0.06	0.28	0.05	0.63
1990	0.14	0.06	0.27	0.05	0.54
1995	0.12	0.06	0.24	0.05	0.48
2000	0.11	0.07	0.21	0.04	0.42
2005	0.10	0.07	0.20	0.04	0.39
2010	0.09	0.08	0.20	0.03	0.35
2015	0.09	0.06	0.15	0.03	0.41

How do inequality trends in life expectancy compare to those obtained by previous studies? Bourguignon and Morrisson (2002) computed Inequality 2 on the basis of the original values of life expectancy at birth. However, as the comparison with the Kakwani index shows, the level of inequality is underestimated and does not capture the post-1990 reversal (see Figure C.2 in Appendix C).

Thus, the substantial increases in longevity during the epidemiological transition were not distributed equally throughout the world. Lack of economic means and basic scientific knowledge prevented a fast and wide diffusion of new medical technology and health practice across countries. In the late nineteenth and early twentieth centuries, the increase in life expectancy inequality can be associated with the fact that the first health transition was unevenly distributed and initially restricted to advanced Western countries. The gradual international diffusion of the health transition favoured the reduction in life expectancy inequality between the late 1920s and 1980. The inequality contraction was particularly intense during the 1930s and 1940s, when life expectancy improved in countries of low per capita income levels as a consequence of the epidemiological transition, coinciding with stagnant or declining average incomes and growing income disparities across countries resulting from the Great Depression and World War II. The reversal in life expectancy inequality, with an increase after 1990, may be associated not only with the impact of HIV-AIDS in sub-Saharan Africa, or the demise of socialism in Eastern Europe, but also with a second health transition that has thus far been restricted to advanced countries.

Unweighted and population-weighted inequality in political and civil liberties exhibit different trends. In the case of Inequality 1, after increasing in the late nineteenth century, a long-run decline took place from 1900 onwards, punctuated by reversals in the interwar years and, more intensively, in the 1970s and early 1980s. If we turn now to Inequality 2, between 1870 and 1970, a rising trend is observed and, then, a fall took place between 1970 and 2010, followed by a mild reversal in the 2010s.

Once inequality of non-income dimensions of human development has been examined, we can assess how these contributed to AHD distribution. Given the multiplicative composition of the human development index (Chapter 1, equation 1.7), when measured with an entropy index, a breakdown of human development inequality can be conducted into the inequality of its dimensions. Namely, the equally weighted sum of each component's inequality – life expectancy (E), years of schooling (S), adjusted income (Y), political and civil liberties, proxied by the index of liberal democracy (L) – plus a residual (R), which accounts for the disparities between AHD dimensions (Martínez, 2016: 417–418).

$$MLD_{ahd} = 1/4MLD_E + 1/4MLD_S + 1/4MLD_Y + 1/4MLD_L + R$$
$$[3.1]$$

It can be observed that the level of human development inequality depended chiefly on the distribution of education up to World War II, and on that of civil and political liberties thereafter, while longevity contributed to raising inequality up to the mid-1920s (Figure 3.1).[14]

But how do international inequality trends in well-being compare to those in GDP per capita for the same country sample? If we first explore the unweighted measure, a long-run increase in per capita income

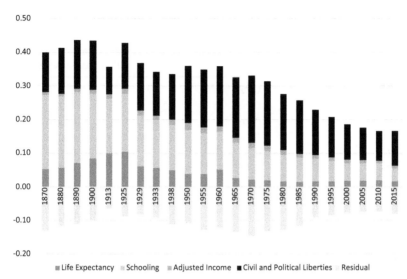

Figure 3.1 AHD inequality: breakdown into dimensions' contributions (MLD) (population-weighted).
Source: See the text.

inequality took place up to 2000 (Table 3.2). The sharp increase in inequality between the end of the Great Depression and 1950 reflects the uneven impact of World War II across countries. A contraction occurred after 2000. In the case of population-weighted inequality, a sustained rise up to the early 1970s took place, punctuated only by a severe contraction during the Great Depression. Inequality has declined since the late twentieth century. Thus, distinctive patterns of international distribution emerge for human development and GDP per capita.

3.3.2 *The Role of Large Countries*

How much do large countries condition the level and trends of population-weighted inequality? For each well-being dimension, I have simulated inequality in the absence of China and India, then Russia, and, finally, sub-Saharan Africa; that is, I have estimated inequality assuming that these regions would have behaved as the average. If, in the absence of a given region, inequality is higher (or lower) than when all regions are considered, we can claim that this region contributed to reducing (or increasing) the level of inequality.

Table 3.2 *International inequality in real per capita GDP,*
1870–2015 (MLD)

	Unweighted	Population-weighted
1870	0.22	0.18
1880	0.24	0.22
1890	0.26	0.25
1900	0.28	0.30
1913	0.30	0.36
1925	0.31	0.39
1929	0.34	0.41
1933	0.31	0.34
1938	0.34	0.42
1950	0.54	0.57
1955	0.53	0.55
1960	0.52	0.57
1965	0.51	0.58
1970	0.52	0.62
1975	0.51	0.63
1980	0.49	0.62
1985	0.48	0.60
1990	0.51	0.62
1995	0.57	0.58
2000	0.59	0.57
2005	0.58	0.50
2010	0.54	0.42
2015	0.52	0.39

In terms of human development, China and India contributed to raising the level of inequality in the early twentieth century and to reducing it from the 1970s onwards. Conversely, Russia mitigated inequality up to the early 1970s, especially until the 1920s (see Table C.1 in Appendix C). Sub-Saharan Africa, meanwhile, contributed to increasing inequality in the long run.

If we now turn to its dimensions, it appears that, in terms of schooling, China and India contributed to lower world inequality levels around 1900 and from 1970 onwards (see Table C.2 in Appendix C). Russia helped to reduce inequality until the 1960s. Sub-Saharan Africa contributed to a higher level of inequality over time, especially during the first half of the twentieth century, as post-independence education policies mitigated the schooling gap with the rest of the world.

Up to the 1920s, India and China made a significant contribution to the rise of life expectancy inequality, while Russia mitigated it (see Table C.3 in Appendix C). The high mortality in China during Mao's Great Leap Forward accounts for the dramatic increase in inequality in 1960. Since 1970, however, China and India have contributed to reducing inequality. Conversely, sub-Saharan Africa increased it from the mid-1960s onwards.

India and China contributed to raising inequality in the distribution of civil and political liberties during the late nineteenth century and after 1950, apart from the early 1980s, while helping to reducing it in the interwar years (see Table C.4 in Appendix C). Russia contributed to increasing inequality during the Soviet era (1917–1989). Sub-Saharan Africa had no influence on either the level or trend of inequality.

If we now turn to the international distribution of per capita income, China and India contributed significantly to a higher level of inequality until 1990 and to its reduction thereafter. Conversely, Russia helped to reduce inequality until the 1990s, and sub-Saharan Africa has played a part in raising inequality since the mid-1980s (see Table C.5 in Appendix C). Again, substantial discrepancies are found in the contribution of large countries or regions to inequality between human development and GDP per head.

3.3.3 Relative and Absolute Inequality

This account of the distribution of human development and its dimensions focuses on inequality measured in relative terms. That is, it depends on countries' ratios to the international mean, meaning inequality does not alter if, for example, the number of years of schooling changes by the same proportion around the globe. However, if such a global change does occur, it could widen absolute differences. For this reason, absolute inequality, which depends on the distance between countries' levels, is often preferred.[15]

Figure 3.2 allows us to compare relative and absolute inequality (the dotted line) of human development. Absolute inequality rose until 1960 and then declined, unlike the long-run contraction since the late 1920s, in relative terms.

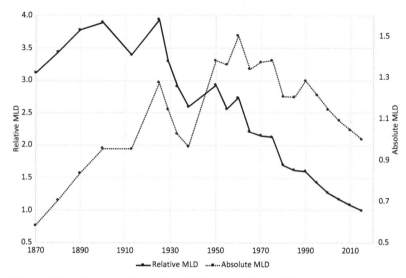

Figure 3.2 Relative and absolute AHD inequality, 1870–2015 (population-weighted MLD) (2015=1).

Note: Absolute inequality is the mean value of the variable times its relative inequality.

Source: See the text and Table 3.1, Panel B.

When AHD dimensions are considered, we observe that, in terms of schooling, while relative inequality declined steadily except for the post–World War I reversal, in absolute terms, inequality rose up to 1970 and only fell from the 1980s onwards (Figure 3.3).

In the case of life expectancy, absolute inequality rose substantially in three different periods: up to the mid-1920s; during the 1950s to peak in 1960; and between 1990 and 2010. There were episodes of decline in the late 1920s and 1930s and from 1960–1980. As a result, the level of absolute inequality in the 2010s was comparable to that of the mid-1920s. Relative inequality increased up to the mid-1920s and declined until the early 1980s, only bouncing back in 1960, remaining and remained stable thereafter but for a minor recovery during the period 1990–2010 (Figure 3.4).

In terms of political and civil liberties, the rising trends in relative and absolute inequality are very similar until 1970, but stronger in absolute terms (Figure 3.5). However, while inequality contracted in relative terms during the past half a century, in absolute terms, after a small reduction in the early 1970s, it flattened and only fell between the mid-1990s and 2010.

Figure 3.3 Relative and absolute inequality in schooling, 1870–2015 (population-weighted MLD) (2015=1).
Note: Absolute inequality is the mean value of the variable times its relative inequality.
Source: See the text and Table 3.1, Panel B.

Relative and absolute inequality in per capita GDP increased in the long run, but while the rise of relative inequality peaked by the mid-1970s and fell as of 1990, absolute inequality kept rising until 2000 and then stabilised at a high level (Figure 3.6).

Once more, discrepancies emerge between multidimensional well-being and GDP per capita. Both in relative and absolute terms, per capita inequality was higher in 2015 than in 1870, but in terms of human development, only absolute inequality was higher.

3.4 The Distribution of Human Development Gains

So much for the aggregate evolution of inequality, but how much did human development and its dimensions vary across the distribution over time? The annual cumulative growth rate by country deciles, from bottom to top, the so-called Growth Incidence Curve (GIC), provides a more nuanced picture of the distribution of gains for each well-being dimension over 1870–2015.

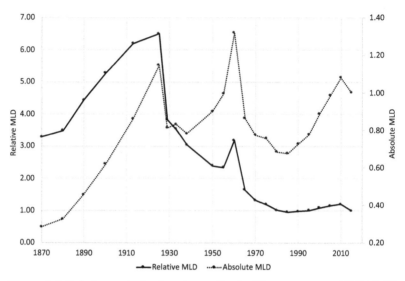

Figure 3.4 Relative and absolute inequality in life expectancy, 1870–2015 (population-weighted MLD) (2015=1).
Note: Absolute inequality is the mean value of the variable times its relative inequality.
Source: See the text and Table 3.1, Panel B.

How did countries behave across the distribution over the long run in terms of human development? The main relative gains accrued to the middle deciles (45th–60th) (the continuous line) and then to the lower quartile of the distribution (Figure 3.7a). However, a glance at the absolute gain in human development achieved by each decile between 1870 and 2015 (the dotted line) indicates that the absolute size of the increase was directly related to the initial level at which countries began. Deciles in the middle of the distribution achieved higher absolute gains than those at the bottom, but still saw lower absolute gains than the top deciles. In other words, the gap or distance between high and low *AHD* countries widened over this period. In particular, absolute gains were significantly larger for countries in the top 10 per cent. Thus, while the disproportionate improvement in the middle deciles, which grew at double the pace of those in the top decile, is consistent with the reduction in relative *AHD* inequality, the distance between high and low *AHD* countries widened over this period, and the top 10 per cent absolute level gain was nearly 0.6 against less than 0.2 for the bottom decile.

Figure 3.5 Relative and absolute inequality in civil and political liberties, 1870–2015 (population-weighted MLD) (2015=1).
Note: Absolute inequality is the mean value of the variable times its relative inequality.
Source: See the text and Table 3.1, Panel B.

A glance at the GICs for different periods reveals that middle-upper part of the distribution (60th–80th percentiles) achieved the main relative gains during the period 1870–1913, a feature that matches the rising aggregate inequality (Figure 3.7b). The early twentieth century witnessed the success of the 'middle class' (40th–55th percentiles). Although the largest relative gains went to the lower part of the distribution (10th–25th percentiles), the 'middle class' was also reinforced during the Golden Age (1950–1970). In the post–Golden Age decades, more than proportional improvements for the lower deciles were paralleled by gains in the upper-middle deciles. Differences across the distribution were reduced from 1990 onwards, although the middle deciles were the main achievers. Thus, the inverse association between relative gains and initial *AHD* levels observed for all phases, apart from the first one (1870–1913), is consistent with the sustained decline in aggregate relative inequality since the 1920s.

Let us look now at its dimensions. In the case of schooling, it can be observed (Figure 3.8a) that, in the long run, the lower deciles 10th–25th

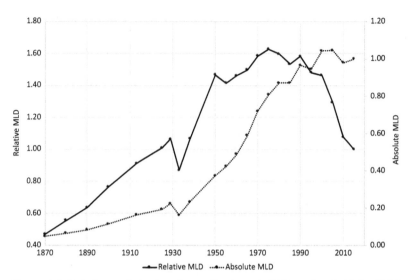

Figure 3.6 Relative and absolute inequality in real GDP per head, 1870–2015 (population-weighted MLD) (2015=1).

Note: Absolute inequality is the mean value of the variable times its relative inequality.

Source: See the text and Table 3.2.

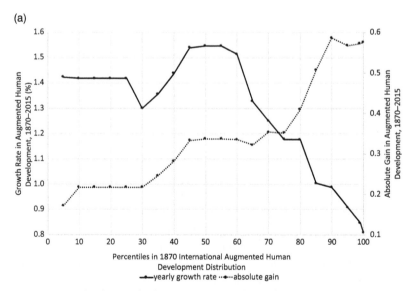

Figure 3.7a Absolute and relative AHD growth incidence curves, 1870–2015.
Source: See the text.

(b)

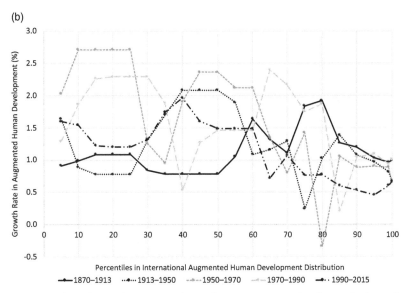

Figure 3.7b Relative AHD growth incidence curves: main phases (balanced panel 1870–2015).
Source: See the text.

(percentiles) experienced the main relative gains (the continuous line), while those above the 85th percentile received the smallest gains. The more than proportional improvement over time in low schooling countries is consistent with the reduction in relative inequality discussed above. However, a glance at the absolute gain achieved by each decile (the dotted line) offers the mirror image, and the gap or distance between high and low schooling countries widened over time. In particular, absolute gains were significantly larger for countries in the top 5 per cent. Between 1870 and 2015, low-level countries in terms of schooling (those in the 10th–25th percentiles) grew above 3 per cent per year, while those in the top 5 per cent did so at 1 per cent; however, the absolute level gain of the bottom countries was 0.2, while the top 10 per cent secured 0.6.

A look at the growth incidence curves for the main phases in the evolution of well-being reveals which parts of the distribution experienced larger relative gains in schooling (measured as annual cumulative growth rates over each of the five periods distinguished). Thus, the lower part of the distribution (more specifically, countries below the 25th percentile) achieved the largest relative gains during 1870–1913, a

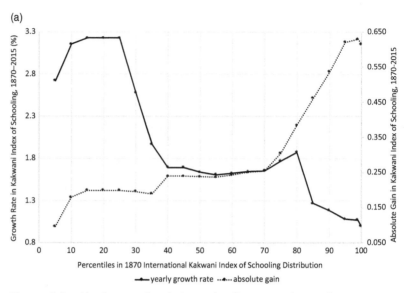

Figure 3.8a Absolute and relative schooling growth incidence curves, 1870–2015.
Source: See the text.

feature consistent with a contraction from a high initial level of inequality (Figure 3.8b). The early twentieth century (1913–1950) reinforced this tendency. The Golden Age (1950–1970) represented major gains for the lower part of the distribution, especially the lower middle deciles and the 5th percentile. In the post–oil crisis decades (1970–1990), the main gains went to the lower and middle deciles. Lastly, during 1990–2015, the main gains were attributed to the lower part of the distribution (10th–25th percentiles). In a nutshell, relative gains were larger at the bottom and, then, in the middle classes, a result that matches the long-run contraction in schooling inequality across countries.

The progress of life expectancy across the distribution shows (Figure 3.9a) that, from 1870–2015, the middle class (45th–60th percentiles) experienced the main relative gains (continuous line), followed by the lower-middle deciles, and the smallest gains accrued to those above the 80th percentile. However, in absolute terms, the largest gain went to countries in the top 20 per cent, especially those in the top 1 per cent. The upper middle deciles were next, and those below the 40th percentile experienced the smallest gains. As in the case

(b)

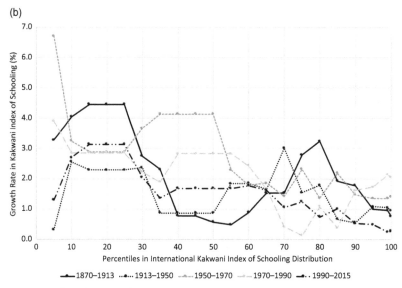

Figure 3.8b Relative schooling growth incidence curves: main phases (balanced panel 1870–2015).
Source: See the text.

of schooling, the distance broadened increased between high- and low-level countries. Thus, in the long run, middle countries (those in the 45th–60th percentiles) grew above 2 per cent per year and those in the top two deciles below 1.5 per cent; but the absolute level gain for the bottom countries was below 0.3 and above 0.8 for the top 1 per cent.

A closer look at the GICs of the main phases indicates that the upper half of the distribution achieved the main relative gains during 1870–1913, a feature consistent with the persistence of high inequality (Figure 3.9b). The early twentieth century upturned the tendency, with the main gains accruing to the lower part of the distribution, followed by the upper middle deciles. The Golden Age (1950–1970) witnessed a major increase in middle class (35th–55th percentiles) gains. After the Golden Age, relative gains were more moderate and more evenly distributed. In the period 1970–1990, the largest gains corresponded to the lower part of the distribution and, from 1990 onwards, gains were fairly evenly distributed, with the top 5 per cent improving comparatively. To sum up, relatively large gains took place at the bottom and the middle of the distribution between the 1920s and 1970.

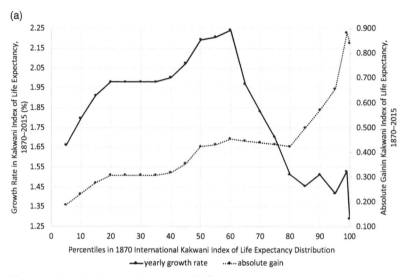

Figure 3.9a Absolute and relative life expectancy growth incidence curves, 1870–2015.
Source: See the text.

In the case of political and civil liberties, relative gains over the long run were concentrated in the broad middle part of the distribution (25th–75th percentiles) at the expense of those countries at the bottom and the top of the distribution (Figure 3.10a). In absolute terms, however, the largest gains went to the upper part of the distribution, especially accruing to the top two deciles. Thus, absolute differences widened across the distribution.

Turning now to the GICs for the main phases, we observe that countries in the lower middle deciles achieved the largest relative gains during the first globalisation during 1870–1913 (Figure 3.10b). This trend was inverted in the early twentieth century, and the upper half of the distribution, in particular, the upper middle deciles, saw the largest improvement. The gains of the upper middle class were reinforced during the Golden Age (1950–1970). In the following two decades, however, the middle and lower sections of the distribution achieved larger gains, and the post-1990 era made a major leap forward for the lower middle deciles. Hence, a process of catching up appears to have occurred in the lower half of the distribution since 1970.

(b)

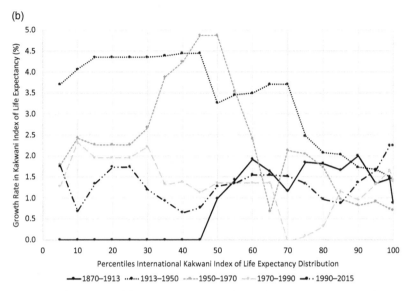

Figure 3.9b Relative life expectancy growth incidence curves: main phases (balanced panel 1870–2015).

Source: See the text.

(a)

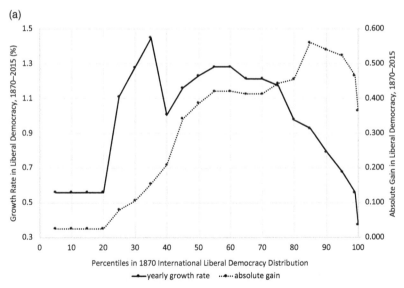

Figure 3.10a Absolute and relative civil and political liberties growth incidence curves, 1870–2015.

Source: See the text.

(b)

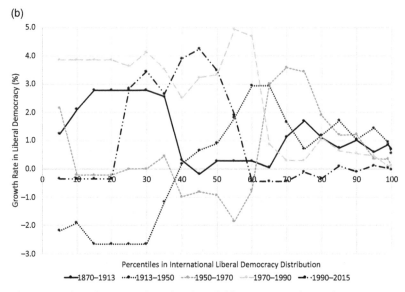

Figure 3.10b Relative civil and political liberties growth incidence curves: main phases (balanced panel 1870–2015).
Source: See the text.

How were gains spread across the distribution for GDP per head? As for life expectancy and liberal democracy, the bottom two deciles also achieved the lowest relative gains. The middle (45th–65th percentiles) and the top of the distribution (90th–95th percentiles) experienced the main relative gains (the continuous line) (Figure 3.11a). The distribution was similar in absolute terms (dotted line) but for the fact that the largest gains went to the top 10 per cent decile.

If the GICs for the main phases are considered, one finds that the upper part of the distribution achieved the main relative gains during 1870–1913 (Figure 3.11b). The early twentieth century reinforced this tendency, but gains were larger for the top 10 per cent. After a relatively even distribution of relative gains, substantial differences across deciles emerged from 1950 onwards. During the Golden Age, the bottom and the upper middle deciles were the main achievers. In the years 1970–1990, the largest relative gains were achieved by the lower part of the distribution, followed by the top 15 per cent. Lastly, over 1990–2015, major gains accrued to the middle and, then, the lower middle deciles.

(a)

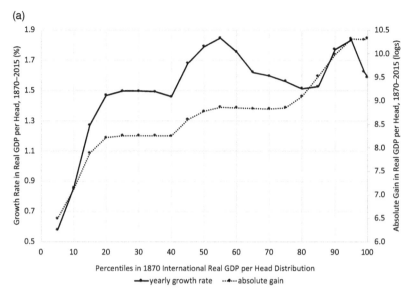

Figure 3.11a Absolute and relative per capita GDP growth incidence curves, 1870–2015.

Source: See the text.

(b)

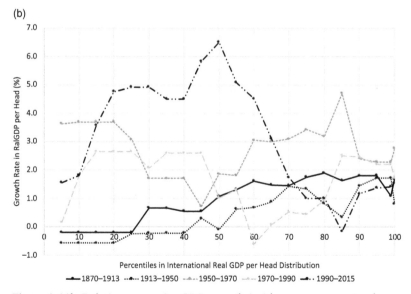

Figure 3.11b Relative per capita GDP growth incidence curves: main phases (balanced panel 1870–2015).

Source: See the text.

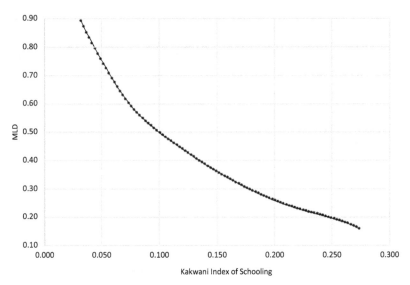

Figure 3.12 Schooling distribution versus level: bivariate kernel linear fit (Epanechnikov, 100).
Source: See the text.

A substantial difference between human development and its dimensions and per capita GDP growth incidence curves is that, in the former, relative gains over the 150 years considered corresponded to the middle and lower deciles of the distribution, and to the middle and top deciles in the latter. Discrepancies also emerge for the main phases considered; specifically, the skewed distribution of per capita income gains towards the upper part of the distribution during 1914–1970, although matching that of civil and political liberties, is at odds with schooling and life expectancy, as well as with human development, in which the middle and lower deciles enjoyed the largest gains.

3.5 Well-Being Levels and Distribution

But how does the distribution of well-being dimensions compare to their levels? I have plotted scattered diagrams, using a bivariate kernel linear fit, of inequality (MLD) against levels for each dimension. In schooling, the fit is a convex line with negative slope, which implies that the improvement in education was gradually shared by the world population (Figure 3.12).

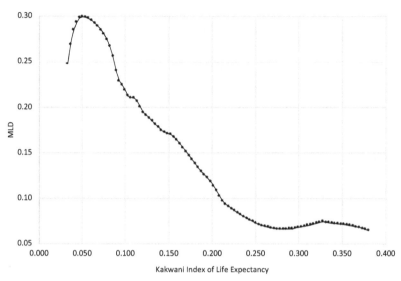

Figure 3.13 Life expectancy distribution versus level: bivariate kernel linear fit (Epanechnikov, 100).

Source: See the text.

In the case of life expectancy, the fit represents an inverted U-shape at low levels, which peaked at MLD 0.30 and corresponded to a Kakwani index of 0.05, that is, 32.3 years of life expectancy at birth, giving way to a long downside until a low inequality level (MLD 0.066) at a Kakwani index of 0.275, equivalent to 64.4 years of life expectancy at birth (Figure 3.13). Hereafter, inequality fluctuated without any trend, but for a minor rebound, as life expectancy continued to rise. The uneven diffusion of the epidemiological or first transition would account for the initial rise of inequality, and its gradual diffusion across the globe would explain its decline. Furthermore, one could suggest that the rebound in the right tail of the curve (at a value of 0.328 for the Kakwani index) corresponds to the uneven diffusion of the second health transition (Cutler et al. 2006) as well as to the effects of HIV-AIDS in sub-Saharan Africa and the demise of socialism in Eastern Europe. However, this seems to have been a short-lived episode, offset by the recovery of life expectancy in sub-Saharan Africa and former socialist Europe.

As regards political and civil liberties, the association follows an inverted U-shape, with an upside starting from a low level (0.150)

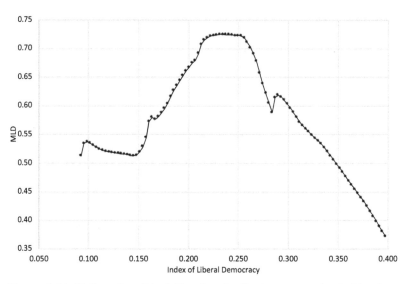

Figure 3.14 Civil and political liberties distribution versus level: bivariate kernel linear fit (Epanechnikov, 100).

Source: See the text.

but relatively high inequality (MLD 0.5) before peaking and stabilising in a high inequality plateau (MLD 0.72), associated with a 0.225–0.255 range of the index of liberal democracy, followed by a sharp downside (MLD 0.37) and an index level of 0.4 (Figure 3.14). Inequality increased as civil and political rights spread in parallel to the emergence of authoritarian and totalitarian ideologies. The downside matches the collapse of the Soviet Union and the retreat of socialism and the decline of right-wing authoritarian regimes in the world.

If we look now at well-being in aggregate terms, that is, human development, an inverted hockey stick shape, defined by a long declining straight line, after a short upward trend, represents the association between inequality and the level of human development, moving from high inequality at low AHD level and to low inequality at high AHD level Figure 3.15).

How do these results compare to those for GDP per capita? The relation between inequality and the log of per capita income (to account for its unbound nature) shows a long upside until inequality peaks at MLD 0.61, which corresponds to Geary-Khamis 1990 $4,570 per capita GDP, and a short but sharp downside with inequality still high

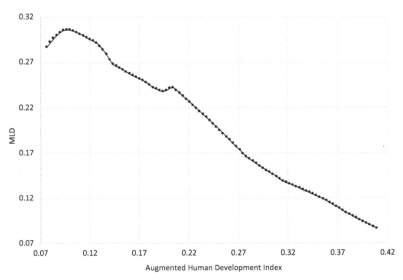

Figure 3.15 AHD distribution versus level: bivariate kernel linear fit (Epanechnikov, 100).
Source: See the text.

(MLD 0.38) at the maximum average income level of the considered time span (1990 $8,287) (Figure 3.16). These findings suggest that, while for human development, or its health and education dimensions, improvements in average levels were increasingly shared by the world population, in the case of GDP per capita, material progress was not easily disseminated across world distribution. The analogy with the case of civil and political liberties, which also exhibits a Kuznets curve, presents, nonetheless, a significant difference: the downside begins at middle levels and reaches the lowest inequality, but in terms of per capita GDP, the downside only takes place at relatively high levels and the inequality reversal is far from complete.

3.6 Concluding Remarks

Although it is often assumed that improvements in life expectancy, schooling, and civil and political rights are associated, either as a cause or as a consequence of rising average incomes, they evolve differently, as did their inequality trends. In fact, each AHD dimension presents a different distribution pattern over time.

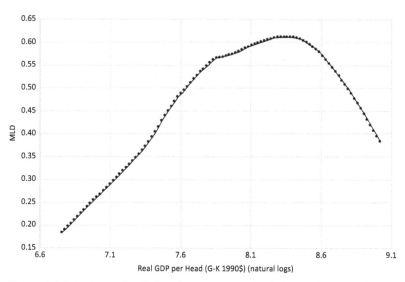

Figure 3.16 GDP per head distribution versus level (logs): bivariate kernel linear fit (Epanechnikov, 100).
Source: See the text.

The chapter's main results challenge the view of well-being distribution across countries and over time that derives from GDP per capita. While the international dispersion of per capita income increased until the late twentieth century and only fell as of 1990, relative inequality in human development declined from 1900 onwards. A look at the long-run distribution of human development and its dimensions reveals larger relative gains for those countries in the middle and lower deciles over the past century. Nonetheless, relative and absolute well-being distributions behaved differently. For most of the time span considered, the relative distance across countries shrank, but the absolute distance increased.

A breakdown of relative inequality in human development into the contribution of its dimensions reveals that schooling and political and civil liberties are the main contributors to the level of inequality, although longevity played a distinctive part up to the 1920s. However, if we turn to inequality reduction, it was mainly driven by the globalisation of primary and secondary schooling and the epidemiological transition from the late 1920s onwards, with civil and political liberties only contributing from the late twentieth century.

Episodes of rising international inequality in life expectancy in the late nineteenth and early twentieth centuries and, then, in the late twentieth and early twenty-first centuries coincided with the initial stages of two health transitions and result from the uneven diffusion of new medical knowledge and technology and health practices. Meanwhile, the inequality decline was concentrated between the late 1920s and the early 1980s, when the epidemiological transition spread across the board. In terms of political and civil liberties, population-weighted inequality grew over time, especially between the end of World War I and the collapse of the Soviet Union, when authoritarian and totalitarian ideologies emerged in parallel to the expansion of liberal democracy, only dropping from the 1970s onwards, as authoritarian regimes (socialists and non-socialists) lost ground and liberal democracy spread as of the late 1980s.

PART II

The *OECD* and the *Rest*

4 | *Human Development in the* OECD *and the* Rest

4.1 Introduction

How did Human Development evolve across world regions? Was there a persistent or a widening gap between advanced and developing regions? This chapter examines AHD long-run trends, pays particular attention to the differences between advanced countries today and the rest of the world, and examines whether and why such differences have been narrowed over time.

The chapter is organised as follows. Section 4.2 presents AHD trends across world regions and looks at the gap between Western Europe and its offshoots plus Japan (the *OECD*,[1] in other words) and the rest of the world (the *Rest* hereafter). A closer look at the *OECD* and the *Rest* follows. Section 4.3 examines their drivers, that is, the contribution of each dimension to AHD gains, and Section 4.4 addresses the extent to which the gap between the *OECD* and the *Rest*, or the dispersion within each of group, accounts for the world distribution of AHD and its dimensions over time. Going one step further, Section 4.5 considers the drivers of AHD in the world's main regions and Section 4.6 discusses catching up to the *OECD* in the regions of the *Rest*. Section 4.7 concludes.

4.2 Trends in Human Development in the *OECD* and the *Rest*

As we have seen in Chapter 3, gains in human development spread unevenly across the world. When and to what extent did different world regions share AHD gains? AHD world regional levels for the one and a half centuries are presented in Table 4.1. A cursory glance reveals that two sets of regions emerge over time: on the one hand, Western Europe and its offshoots – that is, Australia, Canada, New Zealand, the United States – and Japan – and, on the other hand, the rest of the world regions. The absolute differences between these two groups widened over time.

Table 4.1. *AHDI across world regions, 1870–2015*

						Levels						
	Latin America	East Europe	Russia	SS Africa	North Africa	Middle East	China	East Asia	South Asia	Japan	West offshoots	West Europe
1870	0.063	0.103	0.069	0.027	0.038	0.038	0.040	0.035	0.030	0.087	0.239	0.168
1880	0.067	0.108	0.066	0.028	0.038	0.037	0.041	0.036	0.032	0.095	0.238	0.194
1890	0.075	0.115	0.066	0.029	0.045	0.038	0.041	0.036	0.035	0.116	0.265	0.213
1900	0.081	0.130	0.070	0.035	0.052	0.041	0.041	0.041	0.042	0.139	0.301	0.232
1913	0.100	0.151	0.097	0.041	0.056	0.051	0.056	0.048	0.045	0.172	0.331	0.260
1925	0.122	0.219	0.084	0.047	0.067	0.060	0.049	0.064	0.060	0.191	0.382	0.301
1929	0.127	0.212	0.089	0.051	0.071	0.068	0.067	0.070	0.066	0.209	0.387	0.308
1933	0.125	0.213	0.094	0.054	0.074	0.074	0.074	0.079	0.071	0.216	0.398	0.301
1938	0.133	0.223	0.102	0.061	0.079	0.084	0.076	0.091	0.082	0.223	0.415	0.300
1950	0.192	0.192	0.127	0.077	0.109	0.124	0.068	0.127	0.118	0.304	0.469	0.399
1955	0.202	0.212	0.161	0.089	0.103	0.140	0.084	0.149	0.143	0.419	0.490	0.422
1960	0.230	0.237	0.181	0.104	0.116	0.132	0.077	0.154	0.153	0.465	0.507	0.448
1965	0.224	0.256	0.189	0.116	0.131	0.166	0.108	0.158	0.169	0.498	0.530	0.472
1970	0.222	0.265	0.195	0.117	0.138	0.198	0.117	0.176	0.183	0.546	0.556	0.497
1975	0.240	0.281	0.200	0.121	0.154	0.221	0.125	0.185	0.176	0.575	0.598	0.526
1980	0.263	0.292	0.216	0.143	0.178	0.200	0.165	0.193	0.211	0.610	0.634	0.569
1985	0.316	0.302	0.228	0.139	0.212	0.238	0.179	0.211	0.227	0.656	0.660	0.596
1990	0.382	0.410	0.316	0.153	0.234	0.263	0.185	0.270	0.249	0.675	0.692	0.622
1995	0.405	0.461	0.377	0.186	0.250	0.289	0.212	0.295	0.270	0.719	0.712	0.647
2000	0.433	0.481	0.358	0.202	0.273	0.319	0.229	0.370	0.292	0.749	0.731	0.673
2005	0.458	0.513	0.352	0.214	0.289	0.342	0.245	0.392	0.305	0.779	0.748	0.696
2010	0.471	0.539	0.385	0.230	0.305	0.337	0.268	0.389	0.313	0.815	0.793	0.727
2015	0.480	0.545	0.373	0.266	0.313	0.354	0.250	0.415	0.323	0.803	0.776	0.729

Growth rate (%)

	Latin America	East Europe	Russia	SS Africa	North Africa	Middle East	China	East Asia	South Asia	Japan	West Offshoots	West Europe
1870–1880	0.7	0.5	-0.4	0.3	0.0	-0.1	0.2	0.3	0.6	0.9	0.0	1.5
1880–1890	1.1	0.6	0.1	0.3	1.8	0.1	0.0	0.0	0.7	2.0	1.0	0.9
1890–1900	0.8	1.3	0.5	2.0	1.4	0.7	0.2	1.2	1.8	1.8	1.3	0.9
1900–1913	1.6	1.1	2.5	1.2	0.7	1.7	2.4	1.2	0.6	1.6	0.7	0.9
1913–1929	1.5	2.1	-0.6	1.4	1.5	1.8	1.1	2.4	2.4	1.2	1.0	1.1
1929–1938	0.5	0.5	1.5	2.0	1.2	2.3	1.3	2.9	2.5	0.7	0.8	-0.3
1938–1950	3.1	-1.2	1.9	1.9	2.6	3.3	-0.9	2.8	3.0	2.6	1.0	2.4
1950–1960	1.8	2.1	3.5	3.0	0.6	0.6	1.2	1.9	2.6	4.3	0.8	1.2
1960–1970	-0.4	1.1	0.8	1.2	1.8	4.1	4.2	1.3	1.8	1.6	0.9	1.1
1970–1980	1.7	1.0	1.0	2.0	2.6	0.1	3.4	0.9	1.5	1.1	1.3	1.4
1980–1990	3.7	3.4	3.8	0.7	2.7	2.7	1.2	3.4	1.6	1.0	0.9	0.9
1990–2000	1.3	1.6	1.3	2.8	1.5	1.9	2.1	3.2	1.6	1.0	0.5	0.8
2000–2010	0.8	1.1	0.7	1.3	1.1	0.5	1.6	0.5	0.7	0.8	0.8	0.8
2010–2015	0.4	0.2	-0.6	2.9	0.5	1.0	-1.4	1.3	0.6	-0.3	-0.4	0.0
1870–2015	1.4	1.2	1.2	1.6	1.5	1.5	1.3	1.7	1.6	1.5	0.8	1.0

But how representative is this regional breakdown of the world? A glance at its internal dispersion suggests a positive answer, as inequality levels within each region were initially low and declined over time (Table 4.2).

Let us now consider AHD evolution in the OECD and the Rest. In the OECD, a phase of sustained progress between 1870 and the mid-1920s gave way to deceleration until World War II (Table 4.3). A short phase of accelerated growth in the aftermath of the war initiated a period of sustained progress from the mid-1950s to 1980 and a gradual slowdown thereafter. If we now turn to the Rest, their evolution differs significantly from that of the OECD. Starting at a slower pace, the Rest grew in similar fashion to the OECD between 1890 and the mid-1920s but, unlike the OECD, AHD gains intensified in the Rest during the late 1920s and maintained a good pace until 1950, when they experienced a short, sharp surge, followed by a sharp deceleration at the end of the 1950s. AHD then bounced back to a robust trend growth until the end of the century, apart from another episode of shrinkage in the early 1970s, followed by steady progress below the historical trend in the new century (Table 4.4). In the Rest, the period between the late 1920s and 1980 emerges as that of major progress in AHD, while in the OECD the phase of acceleration was concentrated between the 1940s and 1970s.

How do AHD and GDP per capita trends compare? In the OECD, GDP per head grew faster than AHD, particularly in the second half of the twentieth century, and AHD only outstripped economic growth from 1913–25 and 1938–50, and in the 2000s (Figure 4.1). In the Rest, AHD improved faster than GDP per head between 1890 and the mid-1950s and during the period 1975–95, even though GDP per person grew slightly faster than AHD over the entire time span (Figure 4.2).

If AHD in the Rest is compared with the OECD, we notice that, in relative terms, their gap decreased from the late 1920s onwards, especially in its central decades of the century and, again, from 1990 onwards (Figure 4.3, continuous line). As a result, by 2015, the level of human development in the Rest represented half the level of the OECD, a ratio double that of a century earlier. This partial catching up in terms of human development is at odds with the Rest's sustained falling behind in terms of per capita income, aside for reversals in the 1930s and since 2000 (Figure 4.3, dotted line). Per capita income in the Rest equalled nearly one-third of the OECD level in 1870, but fell to less than 15 per cent of the OECD level in 2000, and was slightly above one-fifth in 2015.

Table 4.2. *AHD inequality within world regions, 1870–2015 (MLD)*

	Latin America	West Europe	East Europe	Sub-Saharan Africa	East Asia	MENA	West offshoots	South Asia
1870	0.03	0.05	0.04	0.12	0.04	0.04	0.00	0.00
1880	0.04	0.04	0.05	0.13	0.04	0.03	0.00	0.00
1890	0.04	0.04	0.05	0.14	0.07	0.05	0.00	0.01
1900	0.05	0.03	0.06	0.14	0.09	0.06	0.00	0.01
1913	0.06	0.02	0.03	0.12	0.08	0.05	0.00	0.01
1925	0.07	0.06	0.11	0.12	0.11	0.06	0.00	0.01
1929	0.07	0.07	0.09	0.12	0.08	0.06	0.00	0.01
1933	0.07	0.06	0.08	0.11	0.07	0.06	0.00	0.01
1938	0.07	0.09	0.07	0.11	0.07	0.06	0.00	0.01
1950	0.04	0.04	0.02	0.10	0.14	0.07	0.00	0.02
1955	0.03	0.04	0.01	0.09	0.16	0.08	0.00	0.02
1960	0.04	0.03	0.01	0.09	0.21	0.06	0.00	0.03
1965	0.06	0.03	0.01	0.08	0.14	0.07	0.00	0.02
1970	0.04	0.03	0.01	0.08	0.14	0.07	0.00	0.03
1975	0.04	0.03	0.01	0.08	0.13	0.07	0.00	0.02
1980	0.02	0.01	0.01	0.08	0.09	0.03	0.00	0.02
1985	0.03	0.01	0.01	0.07	0.09	0.03	0.00	0.02
1990	0.02	0.01	0.01	0.07	0.10	0.03	0.00	0.01
1995	0.02	0.00	0.01	0.09	0.09	0.03	0.00	0.01
2000	0.01	0.01	0.02	0.07	0.08	0.03	0.00	0.02
2005	0.02	0.01	0.02	0.05	0.08	0.02	0.00	0.01
2010	0.01	0.01	0.02	0.04	0.07	0.02	0.00	0.01
2015	0.01	0.01	0.03	0.04	0.07	0.04	0.00	0.01

Table 4.3. *AHDI and its components: OECD*
Panel A. Levels

	AHDI	Kakwani index of schooling	Kakwani index of life expectancy	UNDP index of income	Liberal democracy index
1870	0.171	0.097	0.079	0.478	0.233
1880	0.192	0.115	0.085	0.502	0.278
1890	0.213	0.135	0.101	0.523	0.289
1900	0.237	0.154	0.118	0.549	0.317
1913	0.266	0.176	0.147	0.584	0.334
1925	0.310	0.206	0.181	0.603	0.408
1929	0.318	0.218	0.188	0.619	0.404
1933	0.318	0.229	0.208	0.590	0.364
1938	0.324	0.240	0.218	0.622	0.337
1950	0.409	0.268	0.295	0.655	0.540
1955	0.447	0.292	0.329	0.686	0.602
1960	0.472	0.322	0.345	0.708	0.630
1965	0.496	0.353	0.362	0.742	0.640
1970	0.525	0.395	0.376	0.773	0.663
1975	0.558	0.435	0.403	0.791	0.701
1980	0.598	0.477	0.432	0.814	0.762
1985	0.627	0.518	0.460	0.829	0.785
1990	0.655	0.561	0.486	0.851	0.790
1995	0.680	0.606	0.509	0.861	0.805
2000	0.704	0.629	0.549	0.882	0.807
2005	0.726	0.663	0.589	0.894	0.794
2010	0.761	0.699	0.643	0.895	0.834
2015	0.753	0.661	0.675	0.903	0.796

Panel B. AHD drivers [*] *(%)*

	Kakwani index of schooling	Kakwani index of life expectancy	UNDP index of income	Liberal democracy index	AHDI
1870–1880	0.4	0.2	0.1	0.4	1.2
1880–1890	0.4	0.4	0.1	0.1	1.0
1890–1900	0.3	0.4	0.1	0.2	1.1
1900–1913	0.2	0.4	0.1	0.1	0.9
1913–1929	0.3	0.4	0.1	0.3	1.1

Table 4.3. (*cont.*)

	Kakwani index of schooling	Kakwani index of life expectancy	UNDP index of income	Liberal democracy index	AHDI
1929–1938	0.3	0.4	0.0	−0.5	0.2
1938–1950	0.2	0.6	0.1	1.0	2.0
1950–1960	0.5	0.4	0.2	0.4	1.4
1960–1970	0.5	0.2	0.2	0.1	1.1
1970–1980	0.5	0.4	0.1	0.3	1.3
1980–1990	0.4	0.3	0.1	0.1	0.9
1990–2000	0.3	0.3	0.1	0.1	0.7
2000–2010	0.3	0.4	0.0	0.1	0.8
2010–2015	−0.3	0.2	0.0	−0.2	−0.2
1870–2015	0.3	0.4	0.1	0.2	1.0

* Dimensions' contribution to *AHDI* growth

4.3 Drivers of Human Development in the OECD and the *Rest*

It is time now to examine trends in non-income dimensions of AHD in the OECD and the *Rest*. In the case of schooling, two main phases of steady growth are discernible in the OECD (Table 4.3): an initial, slower phase, up to 1950, which decelerated in the 1930s and 1940s, and a second, more accelerated phase, between 1950 and the mid-1990s. From the late 1990s onwards, progress slowed down. As for the *Rest*, the spread of schooling intensified between the mid-1920s and the 1970s, except for the World War II years, slowing down as of 1980 (Table 4.4).

Longevity presents distinct phases of expansion in the OECD: a sustained advance between 1880 and the mid-1920s, an acceleration from the 1930s to the mid-1950s and then, after slower growth, another spurt from 1995 onwards. The first two phases correspond to the epidemiological transition and the last one, at the turn of the century, to the *second* health transition.

In the *Rest*, the major improvement in life expectancy occurred between 1920 and 1970, with two main spurts in the late 1920s and in the early 1960s, following China's catastrophic mortality during the Great Leap Forward famine (1958–1961). This is the period in which the epidemiological transition spread across developing regions. The increase in life expectancy slowed down as of the 1970s once the epidemiological

Table 4.4. *AHDI and its components: the Rest*
Panel A. Levels

	AHDI	Kakwani index of schooling	Kakwani index of life expectancy	UNDP index of income	Liberal democracy Index
1870	0.049	0.016	0.022	0.293	0.056
1880	0.051	0.018	0.023	0.301	0.053
1890	0.053	0.019	0.024	0.314	0.053
1900	0.057	0.022	0.027	0.328	0.056
1913	0.067	0.024	0.030	0.349	0.080
1925	0.078	0.029	0.041	0.350	0.089
1929	0.087	0.035	0.056	0.364	0.081
1933	0.093	0.040	0.063	0.359	0.081
1938	0.103	0.046	0.072	0.381	0.089
1950	0.130	0.056	0.113	0.392	0.115
1955	0.155	0.065	0.130	0.417	0.165
1960	0.162	0.075	0.126	0.437	0.167
1965	0.186	0.087	0.172	0.461	0.174
1970	0.199	0.101	0.197	0.484	0.161
1975	0.198	0.113	0.216	0.504	0.124
1980	0.227	0.130	0.233	0.521	0.169
1985	0.243	0.146	0.248	0.527	0.184
1990	0.269	0.155	0.260	0.529	0.248
1995	0.293	0.172	0.271	0.540	0.292
2000	0.316	0.191	0.287	0.560	0.324
2005	0.331	0.206	0.301	0.595	0.326
2010	0.348	0.220	0.317	0.633	0.331
2015	0.364	0.241	0.357	0.657	0.313

Panel B. AHD drivers[*] *(%)*

	Kakwani index of schooling	Kakwani index of life expectancy	UNDP index of income	Liberal democracy Index	AHDI
1870–1880	0.2	0.1	0.1	−0.1	0.3
1880–1890	0.2	0.1	0.1	0.0	0.4
1890–1900	0.3	0.2	0.1	0.1	0.8
1900–1913	0.2	0.2	0.1	0.7	1.2
1913–1929	0.6	1.0	0.1	0.0	1.6

Table 4.4. (*cont.*)

	Kakwani index of schooling	Kakwani index of life expectancy	UNDP index of income	Liberal democracy Index	AHDI
1929–1938	0.7	0.7	0.1	0.2	1.8
1938–1950	0.4	0.9	0.1	0.5	1.9
1950–1960	0.8	0.3	0.3	0.9	2.2
1960–1970	0.7	1.1	0.3	−0.1	2.0
1970–1980	0.6	0.4	0.2	0.1	1.4
1980–1990	0.4	0.3	0.0	1.0	1.7
1990–2000	0.5	0.2	0.1	0.7	1.6
2000–2010	0.4	0.3	0.3	0.1	1.0
2010–2015	0.4	0.6	0.2	−0.3	0.9
1870–2015	0.5	0.5	0.1	0.3	1.4

* Dimensions' contribution to *AHDI* growth

transition had already spread across most of the world, and even more so from the late 1980s onwards after the demise of socialism in Eastern Europe and the HIV-AIDS pandemic in sub-Saharan Africa.

Lastly, there was an increase in civil and political liberties in the *OECD* between 1870 and the mid-1980s, more intense after the world wars but reversed in the late 1920s and 1930s by the emergence of authoritarian regimes. Since the early 1980s, liberties have stabilised at a high level. In the *Rest*, three phases of expansion of civil and political rights can be observed: in the early twentieth century, cut short by World War I; from the late 1940s to the early 1950s; and, especially, during the last quarter of the century, with the rise of authoritarian regimes accounting for the backlash in the 1920s and early 1930s and from the late 1950s to the early 1970s.

A closer look at the drivers of human development in the *OECD* and the *Rest* may help to explain their differences. *AHDI*'s multiplicative structure allows us to decompose AHD growth into the contribution of its dimensions (see Chapter 2, equation 2.1).

Longevity has been the main driver of human development in the *OECD* during the last 150 years, contributing 36 per cent of its gains, closely followed by education (32 per cent) (see Table 4.3, Panel B). Improvements in life expectancy drove advances in human

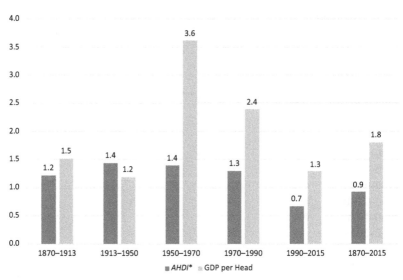

Figure 4.1 *AHDI** and real GDP per head growth in the *OECD*, 1870–2015.
Note: * Excluding the income dimension.
Sources: See the text.

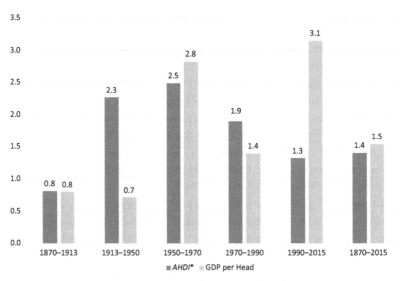

Figure 4.2 *AHDI** and real GDP per head growth in the *Rest*, 1870–2015.
Note: * Excluding the income dimension.
Sources: See the text.

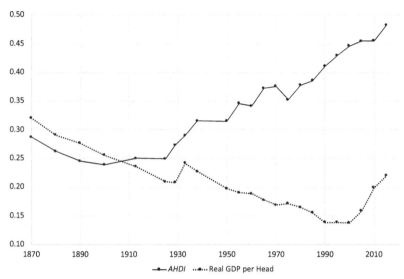

Figure 4.3 Relative *AHDI* and real GDP per head in the *Rest* (*OECD*=1).
Note: Population-weighted averages.
Sources: See the text.

development between 1880 and the early 1950s, although freedoms took over after World War II. From the late 1950s to the early 1990s, advances in education made the leading contribution to human development. Life expectancy again led the moderate gains in human development at the turn of the century.

In the *Rest*, life expectancy was also the leading contributor over time (35 per cent), although closely followed by schooling (34 per cent). However, the contribution of each dimension to human development progress differed in the *Rest* from that of the OECD (see Figure 4.4, Panel B). Between 1914 and 1950, longevity accounted for half the gains in human development. A second episode of longevity making a massive contribution to human development occurred in the 1960s, a decade of governmental activism in the developing world, including many newly independent countries. However, unlike in the OECD, longevity did not play a leading role at the turn of the century. Schooling contributed regularly to human development, becoming its main driver during the late 1960s and early 1970s. Civil and political liberties led human development gains in the 'long' decade up to World War I, the early 1950s, and during the last quarter of the twentieth century.

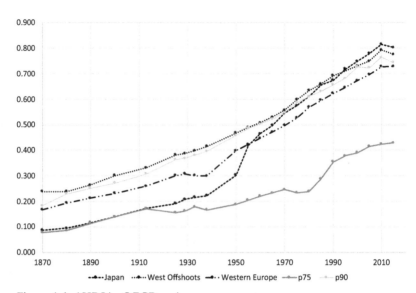

Figure 4.4 *AHDI* in *OECD* regions.
Sources: See the text and Appendix D, Tables D.1–D.3, Panel A.

The observed reduction in the gap between advanced and developing countries (Figure 4.3) highlights a process of catching up, but what were the drivers? In the *Rest*, catching up to the *OECD* in terms of human development – as measured by their differential growth rate – has taken place since the early twentieth century, especially, during the interwar period, the early 1950s and 1960s, and the last quarter of the century (Table 4.5). If we now examine the different phases of catching up, we find that longevity emerges as the main factor behind the latter in the 1920s, when a large proportion of the *Rest* was still under colonial rule, and then, more intensively, in the 1960s, a time of active public policies across the board and coinciding with China's recovery from the Great Leap Forward debacle. Civil and political freedoms led catching up in the 1930s and early 1950s, and through 1975–2000. Schooling has emerged as the dominant force behind catching up in recent times.

4.4 The OECD and the Rest in World AHD Distribution

Chapter 3 examined inequality trends in human development and their dimensions, but what drove these trends? Was it the gap

Table 4.5. *AHD catching up in the Rest: dimensions' contribution (%)*

	Kakwani index of schooling	Kakwani index of life expectancy	UNDP index of income	Liberal democracy index	Total
1870–1880	–0.2	–0.1	–0.1	–0.6	–0.9
1880–1890	–0.2	–0.3	0.0	–0.1	–0.7
1890–1900	0.0	–0.1	0.0	–0.1	–0.3
1900–1913	0.0	–0.2	0.0	0.6	0.4
1913–1929	0.2	0.6	0.0	–0.3	0.5
1929–1938	0.5	0.3	0.1	0.7	1.6
1938–1950	0.2	0.3	–0.1	–0.4	0.0
1950–1960	0.3	–0.1	0.1	0.6	0.8
1960–1970	0.2	0.9	0.0	–0.2	1.0
1970–1980	0.2	0.1	0.1	–0.2	0.1
1980–1990	0.0	0.0	–0.1	0.9	0.8
1990–2000	0.2	–0.1	0.1	0.6	0.8
2000–2010	0.1	–0.1	0.3	0.0	0.2
2010–2015	0.7	0.3	0.1	0.0	1.2
1870–2015	0.1	0.1	0.0	0.1	0.4

between the OECD and the *Rest*, or the dispersion within each of these two groups? The Theil L measure, or MLD, a decomposable entropy index, enables us to carry out a breakdown of aggregate inequality 2.

The OECD–*Rest* gap (between-group column in Table 4.6) made the largest contribution to international inequality in human development, in terms of both level and trend, up to the early 1980s, when within-group inequality, mostly in the *Rest*, took over. A closer look reveals that within-group inequality results from the differences between the regions of the *Rest* (Table 4.6, last column), since inequality within regions of the *Rest* regions was minor and decreased over time (with non-negligible inequality figures only for East Asia and sub-Saharan Africa) (Table 4.2).

If we focus now on AHD dimensions, we observe that, in the case of schooling, the level of inequality depended to a larger extent on the gap between the OECD and the *Rest* up to 1930, and the dispersion within each group dominated thereafter (Table 4.7). However, inequality

Table 4.6. *Decomposing international AHD inequality (population-weighted MLD)*

	Within-group	Between-group	TOTAL	OECD	The Rest
1870	0.08	0.19	0.27	0.05	0.08
1880	0.07	0.22	0.30	0.04	0.08
1890	0.08	0.24	0.33	0.03	0.10
1900	0.09	0.25	0.34	0.03	0.11
1913	0.09	0.21	0.29	0.02	0.10
1925	0.12	0.22	0.34	0.05	0.14
1929	0.10	0.19	0.28	0.05	0.11
1933	0.09	0.16	0.25	0.05	0.10
1938	0.09	0.14	0.22	0.08	0.09
1950	0.09	0.16	0.25	0.03	0.11
1955	0.09	0.13	0.22	0.03	0.11
1960	0.11	0.12	0.24	0.02	0.13
1965	0.08	0.11	0.19	0.02	0.10
1970	0.08	0.10	0.19	0.02	0.09
1975	0.08	0.10	0.18	0.02	0.09
1980	0.06	0.09	0.15	0.01	0.07
1985	0.06	0.08	0.14	0.01	0.07
1990	0.07	0.06	0.14	0.00	0.08
1995	0.07	0.05	0.12	0.00	0.08
2000	0.06	0.05	0.11	0.00	0.07
2005	0.06	0.04	0.10	0.00	0.07
2010	0.05	0.04	0.09	0.00	0.06
2015	0.05	0.04	0.09	0.00	0.06

trends were driven by the dispersion within the OECD and the *Rest* and, more specifically, by between-region inequality in the *Rest* (Table 4.7, last column).

Similarly, in terms of life expectancy, the gap between the OECD and the *Rest* made the largest contribution to total inequality up to 1950; within-group inequality became the main contributor thereafter (Table 4.8). Nonetheless, the dispersion within the OECD and the *Rest* drove rising inequality trends up to the 1920s and from 1990 onwards (mostly in the *Rest*, due to disparities between regions), while the reduction in the gap between the *West* and the *Rest* drove the decline in inequality between the late 1920s and 1970.

Table 4.7. *Decomposing international inequality in schooling (population-weighted MLD) (Kakwani indices)*

	Within-group	Between-group	TOTAL	OECD	The Rest
1870	0.50	0.38	0.88	0.20	0.57
1880	0.43	0.42	0.85	0.15	0.50
1890	0.39	0.45	0.84	0.12	0.46
1900	0.33	0.44	0.77	0.09	0.39
1913	0.26	0.38	0.65	0.07	0.32
1925	0.29	0.40	0.69	0.07	0.35
1929	0.27	0.33	0.60	0.07	0.33
1933	0.28	0.29	0.57	0.07	0.33
1938	0.28	0.26	0.54	0.06	0.34
1950	0.29	0.23	0.52	0.06	0.35
1955	0.29	0.20	0.49	0.06	0.34
1960	0.28	0.17	0.45	0.06	0.32
1965	0.26	0.16	0.42	0.05	0.30
1970	0.24	0.14	0.38	0.05	0.27
1975	0.21	0.14	0.35	0.05	0.24
1980	0.20	0.11	0.31	0.05	0.23
1985	0.18	0.10	0.28	0.04	0.20
1990	0.16	0.11	0.27	0.04	0.17
1995	0.14	0.10	0.24	0.04	0.16
2000	0.12	0.09	0.21	0.03	0.14
2005	0.12	0.08	0.20	0.03	0.14
2010	0.12	0.08	0.20	0.03	0.13
2015	0.10	0.06	0.15	0.03	0.10

When we turn to political and civil liberties, it is the gap between the OECD and the *Rest* that accounts for most inequality until World War I, and the dispersion within groups, in particular, within the *Rest*, explains inequality levels from 1930 onwards (Table 4.9). Nonetheless, within-group dispersion, specifically between regions of the *Rest*, drives inequality trends.

Lastly, the gap between the OECD and the *Rest* was the main contributor to the aggregate level of inequality in terms of GDP per head until 1950, when within-group dispersion took over (Table 4.10). The dispersion within the two groups, OECD and the *Rest*, mainly the latter, accounts for inequality trends over 1930–2000.

Table 4.8. *Decomposing international inequality in life expectancy*
(population-weighted MLD) (Kakwani indices)

	Within-group	Between-group	TOTAL	OECD	The Rest
1870	0.07	0.14	0.21	0.04	0.08
1880	0.07	0.15	0.23	0.04	0.08
1890	0.09	0.20	0.29	0.02	0.11
1900	0.12	0.22	0.34	0.02	0.15
1913	0.15	0.25	0.40	0.01	0.18
1925	0.20	0.22	0.42	0.02	0.25
1929	0.10	0.14	0.25	0.01	0.13
1933	0.09	0.14	0.23	0.01	0.11
1938	0.07	0.12	0.20	0.02	0.09
1950	0.07	0.08	0.15	0.00	0.09
1955	0.09	0.06	0.15	0.00	0.11
1960	0.14	0.07	0.21	0.00	0.17
1965	0.07	0.04	0.11	0.00	0.08
1970	0.06	0.02	0.09	0.00	0.07
1975	0.06	0.02	0.08	0.00	0.07
1980	0.05	0.02	0.07	0.00	0.05
1985	0.04	0.02	0.06	0.00	0.05
1990	0.04	0.02	0.06	0.00	0.05
1995	0.05	0.02	0.06	0.00	0.05
2000	0.05	0.02	0.07	0.00	0.06
2005	0.06	0.02	0.07	0.00	0.06
2010	0.06	0.02	0.08	0.01	0.06
2015	0.05	0.02	0.06	0.01	0.05

Thus, the OECD–*Rest* gap as the driver of the level of inequality up
to the early twentieth century appears as a common feature of both
human development and per capita GDP, but no such a coincidence
exists with regard to the driver of inequality trends.

4.5 AHD Drivers in World Regions

A clearer perception of human development results from comparison
of performance across regions. Let us begin with the advanced

Table 4.9. *Decomposing international inequality in civil and political liberties (population-weighted MLD)*

	Within-group	Between-group	TOTAL	OECD	The Rest
1870	0.25	0.22	0.47	0.06	0.29
1880	0.24	0.31	0.54	0.06	0.28
1890	0.27	0.31	0.58	0.06	0.33
1900	0.28	0.31	0.58	0.06	0.33
1913	0.11	0.22	0.33	0.05	0.13
1925	0.29	0.25	0.55	0.21	0.32
1929	0.28	0.28	0.56	0.25	0.29
1933	0.28	0.24	0.52	0.32	0.27
1938	0.35	0.19	0.54	0.60	0.29
1950	0.45	0.23	0.68	0.11	0.53
1955	0.57	0.12	0.68	0.11	0.67
1960	0.58	0.12	0.71	0.11	0.69
1965	0.60	0.12	0.72	0.10	0.70
1970	0.65	0.14	0.80	0.12	0.76
1975	0.55	0.22	0.77	0.09	0.63
1980	0.50	0.16	0.66	0.04	0.57
1985	0.49	0.15	0.63	0.03	0.55
1990	0.45	0.09	0.54	0.00	0.51
1995	0.41	0.07	0.48	0.00	0.47
2000	0.37	0.05	0.42	0.02	0.42
2005	0.34	0.05	0.39	0.02	0.38
2010	0.30	0.05	0.35	0.02	0.34
2015	0.36	0.05	0.41	0.02	0.40

countries. Although the three regions that compose the OECD have achieved high AHD levels, above the 90th of the distribution, their pace has been different, with AHD in Japan starting at the 75th percentile and growing nearly twice as fast as the Western offshoots, and one-third faster than Western Europe, largely as the result of more intense gains during 1870–1913 and the *Golden Age* (1950–70) (Table 4.1 and Figure 4.4). The progress across AHD dimensions also differed. Schooling achieved higher levels in the Western offshoots, but grew faster in Japan, which moved up from the 75th to the 90th

Table 4.10. *Decomposing international inequality in real per capita GDP, 1870–2015 (population-weighted MLD)*

	Within-group	Between-group	TOTAL	OECD	The Rest
1870	0.03	0.15	0.18	0.05	0.03
1880	0.04	0.18	0.22	0.05	0.04
1890	0.06	0.19	0.25	0.05	0.06
1900	0.08	0.22	0.30	0.05	0.09
1913	0.11	0.25	0.36	0.05	0.13
1925	0.12	0.27	0.39	0.06	0.13
1929	0.14	0.28	0.41	0.05	0.16
1933	0.12	0.22	0.34	0.03	0.14
1938	0.18	0.24	0.42	0.06	0.21
1950	0.26	0.31	0.57	0.11	0.30
1955	0.24	0.31	0.55	0.08	0.28
1960	0.27	0.29	0.57	0.06	0.32
1965	0.29	0.30	0.58	0.05	0.34
1970	0.34	0.28	0.62	0.03	0.40
1975	0.37	0.26	0.63	0.02	0.43
1980	0.38	0.25	0.62	0.02	0.43
1985	0.35	0.25	0.60	0.03	0.39
1990	0.34	0.28	0.62	0.02	0.39
1995	0.30	0.27	0.58	0.02	0.34
2000	0.29	0.28	0.57	0.02	0.32
2005	0.26	0.24	0.50	0.03	0.29
2010	0.24	0.18	0.42	0.02	0.27
2015	0.24	0.15	0.39	0.03	0.26

percentile (Figure 4.5). In terms of longevity, a reversal of fortune occurred, with Japan, the laggard, pulling ahead and reaching the top, and the Western offshoots, with a higher initial level, falling behind (Figure 4.6). In terms of civil and political liberties, Western Europe and Japan, starting from lower levels and suffering a contraction of liberties during the interwar period, caught up to the Western offshoots after 1950 (Figure 4.7).

If we now look at the drivers of human development, it appears that, in both Western Europe and its offshoots, life expectancy led AHD growth until the early 1950s, with the exception of the post–World

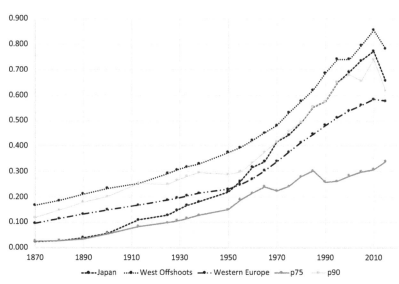

Figure 4.5 Kakwani index of schooling in *OECD* regions.
Sources: See the text and Appendix D, Tables D.1–D.3, Panel A.

War II increase in freedoms in Europe following their contraction during the late 1920s and 1930s (see Appendix D, Tables D.1-D.2, Panel B). Education led AHD advancement through most of the second half of the twentieth century, and longevity took over, again, from the late 1990s onwards. The case of Japan differs, as schooling led AHD gains until World War II, apart from the late 1920s and in the 1960s (see Appendix D, Table D.3, Panel B). Life expectancy drove AHD gains in the late 1920s and the 1950s (during this decade, second to freedoms), and along with schooling, led AHD during the rest of the century, becoming the single driving force from the mid-1990s onwards.

The *Rest* encompasses regions of distinctive behaviour in terms of human development and its dimensions. Let us begin by addressing trends in human development. Eastern Europe leads the *Rest*, followed by Latin America, both around and recently above, the 75th percentile of the world distribution, and Russia and East Asia around the 50th percentile but converging towards the 75th percentile at the turn of the century (Figure 4.8, Panel A). Next, the Middle East and South Asia fluctuate around the 50th percentile, and North Africa moves away from the 25th percentile and towards the middle of the distribution. Finally, at the bottom, China matches the 25th percentile, and sub-Saharan Africa

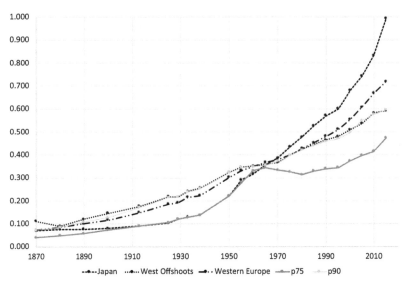

Figure 4.6 Kakwani index of life expectancy in *OECD* regions.
Sources: See the text and Appendix D, Tables D.1–D.3, Panel A.

fluctuates around the latter (Figure 4.8, Panel B). The regions' ranking has
been fairly stable over time, although Eastern Europe and Russia present
more marked fluctuations, associated with political regime changes.

A glance at the evolution of AHD dimensions reveals different
regional patterns. In terms of schooling, Russia and Eastern Europe
have been ahead of the other regions in the *Rest*, with the gap widening
from the 1930s and 1950 onwards, and moving away from the 75th
percentile since 1970 and 1990, respectively. They are followed by
Latin America, lagging somewhere between the 50th and 75th percentiles, with East Asia and China, matching the 50th percentile, kept at
distance (Figure 4.9, Panels A and B). The Middle East and North
Africa moved up from the 25th percentile in the last quarter of the
twentieth century, while South Asia matched this position and sub-
Saharan Africa remained below.

Eastern Europe, around the 75th percentile, except for a short move
upwards over 1970–90, led life expectancy in the *Rest*. Russia matched
this percentile until 1990, when it fell below the 50th percentile, while
Latin America followed an inverse path, moving upwards from the
50th percentile to reach the 75th percentile in the 1990s. China
remained at the 50th percentile, as did East Asia; the Middle East

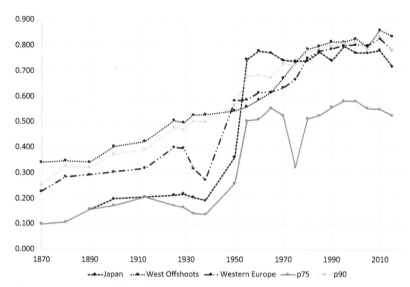

Figure 4.7 Index of liberal democracy in *OECD* regions.
Sources: See the text and Appendix D, Tables D.1–D.3, Panel A.

and North Africa fell behind, however, between the late 1960s and the early 1990s. South Asia matched the 25th percentile, and sub-Saharan Africa fell steadily behind as of the 1960s, in particular between 1985 and 2005, when life expectancy stagnated as a result of HIV-AIDS (see Chapter 6).

As we have seen, longevity presents a narrower dispersion (Table 4.8). This was helped by Eastern Europe's life expectancy stagnation from the mid-1970s to 1990 and decline in the early 1990s, and the contraction in Russia from 1965 to 1980, and even more so in the early 1990s, followed by a decade of stagnation (Figure 4.10, Panels A and B). It is worth noting that the demise of socialism in these regions only intensified the deterioration of life expectancy. Conversely, life expectancy thrived in China under social-ism after the mid-1960s, after recovering from the huge mortality rates caused by the Great Leap Forward famine, overtaking Russia in 1995. Furthermore, major gains in East Asia, North Africa, and the Middle East allowed them to catch up to Eastern Europe and overtake Russia in 1995. Since 2010, there has been evidence of a sharp and promising recovery throughout the regions of the *Rest*.

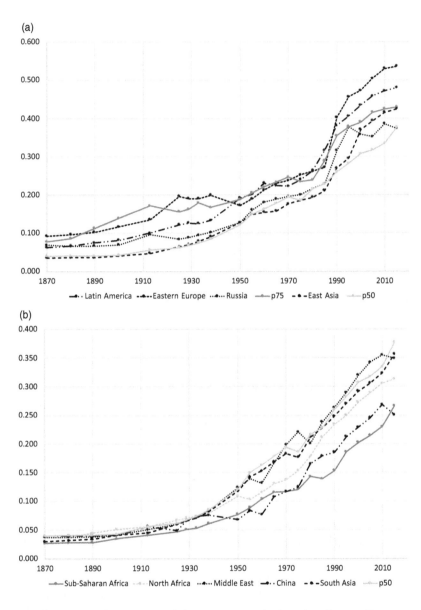

Figure 4.8 *AHDI* in regions of the *Rest*. (a) Latin America, Eastern Europe, Russia, and East Asia; (b) sub-Saharan Africa, North Africa, Middle East, China, and South Asia.

Sources: See the text and Table 4.1.

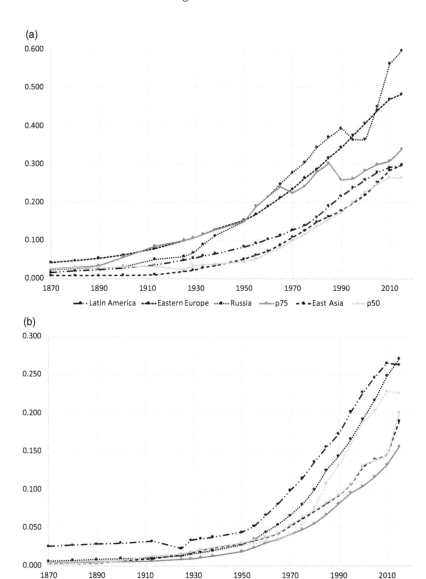

Figure 4.9 Kakwani index of schooling in regions of the *Rest*. (a) Latin America, Eastern Europe, Russia, and East Asia; (b) sub-Saharan Africa, North Africa, Middle East, China, and South Asia.

Sources: See the text, Chapter 5, Table 5.1, Chapter 6, Table 6.3, and Appendix D, Tables D.4–D.10.

The main dispersion of AHD dimensions has occurred in terms of political and civil liberties since the mid-twentieth century (Table 4.9). Prior to 1950, only Eastern Europe and Latin America distinguished themselves from the other regions, staying above the 50th percentile and with episodes of democratisation in the 1920s (Eastern Europe) and 1950s (Latin America). As of the mid-1980s, Latin America, then Eastern Europe, from 1990 onwards, converged at the 75th percentile (Figure 4.11, Panel A). From the mid-twentieth century, South Asia was an outlier in terms of freedoms, moving away from the 50th and towards the 75th percentile. In East Asia, civil and political rights remained at the 50th percentile, showing a major improvement from 2000. Sub-Saharan Africa pulled ahead of North Africa and the Middle East. In Russia, the 1917 Revolution brought wholescale violation of freedoms, leaving the region at the 25th percentile henceforth, but for a spell in the early 1990s. China's liberties declined after the 1949 Revolution, briefly and slightly in the late 1970s, and have remained practically stagnant since 1980, occupying the bottom position at the 25th percentile (Figure 4.11, Panel B).

A glance at the drivers of AHD progress in the regions of the *Rest* confirms the differences between them. Latin America's AHD gains were mostly driven by longevity and education over the long run, although life expectancy's contribution was larger during the 'long' decade up to World War I, the 1940s, and the early 1950s. Civil and political liberties drove AHD progress in the 1980s, while hindering it in the 1930s and 1960s (see Chapter 5, Table 5.1).

In Eastern Europe, life expectancy led AHD gains between 1890 and the early 1950s, but these were largely offset by the contraction of civil and political rights between the late 1920s and 1950, after a spell of freedom following World War I (Bunce, 1990). After a brief increase in liberties in the late 1950s, schooling took over until the mid-1980s. Civil and political liberties led AHD gains during the 1990s. Over the long run, schooling and life expectancy were the main drivers of AHD (see Table D.4 in Appendix D).

In Russia, AHD gains from 1870–1938, resulting from life expectancy, especially in the early 1920s, and schooling, particularly in the late 1920s and 1930s, were largely offset by the shrinking of liberties until 1900 and, above all, during the interwar period. However, the major AHD gains were achieved in the

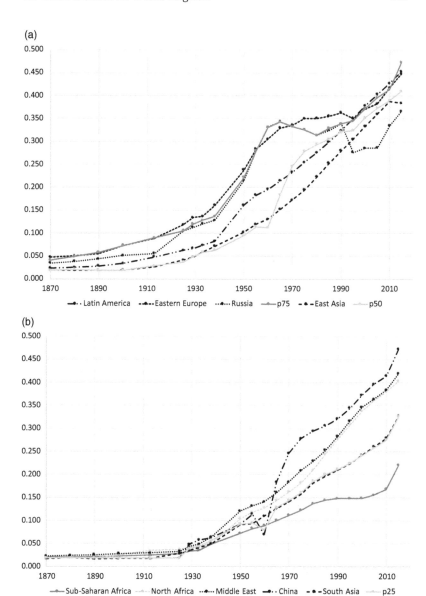

Figure 4.10 Kakwani index of life expectancy in regions of the *Rest*. (a) Latin America, Eastern Europe, Russia, and East Asia; (b) sub-Saharan Africa, North Africa, Middle East, China, and South Asia.

Sources: See the text, Chapter 5, Table 5.1, Chapter 6, Table 6.3, and Appendix D, Tables D.4–D.10.

(a)

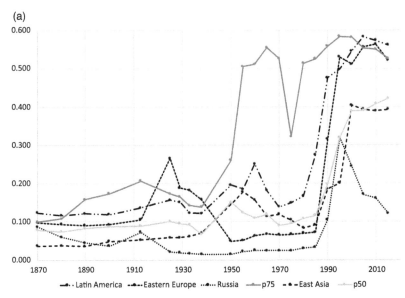

(b)

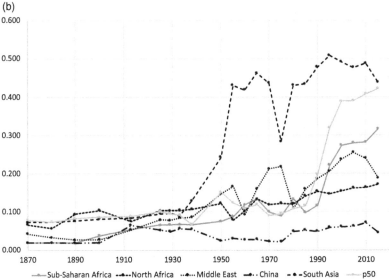

Figure 4.11 Index of liberal democracy in regions of the *Rest*. (a) Latin America, Eastern Europe, Russia, and East Asia; (b) sub-Saharan Africa, North Africa, Middle East, China, and South Asia.

Sources: See the text, Chapter 5, Table 5.1, Chapter 6, Table 6.3, and Appendix D, Tables D.4–D.10.

1950s, mainly driven by the improvement in longevity – as the expansion of health care succeeded in combatting infectious disease and child mortality (Brainerd and Cutler, 2005; Brainerd, 2010a) – and in liberties, as a result of de-Stalinisation. AHD progress, largely driven by education, slowed down between 1960 and the mid-1980s, while longevity decreased. Gains in civil and political rights since the late 1980 led to a spurt in AHD until the mid-1990s, despite the dramatic fall in life expectancy and, to a lesser extent, in schooling. After 2000, gains in education and health were largely cancelled out by the contraction in liberties. In the long run, schooling was the leading contributor to AHD progress (see Appendix D, Table D.5).

Prior to the 1949 Revolution, liberties drove AHD gains in China during the long decade up to World War I, and life expectancy was the driver in the interwar years. From 1950 to the mid-1970s, longevity led the evolution of AHD, both its gains and its sharp contraction (with extraordinary rates of mortality during the Great Leap Forward famine in the late 1950s and early 1960s), followed by education. After the 1978 economic reforms, civil and political liberties lent momentum to AHD and, henceforth, improvements in material well-being and education drove AHD gains. Nonetheless, over time, longevity made the largest contribution to gains in AHD (see Appendix D, Table D.6).

South Asia shows comparatively steady AHD progress. It is worth noting that life expectancy led AHD gains between 1913 and 1950, when the region was still under colonial rule and had very limited access to modern medicine (drugs in particular), and continued contributing significantly to advances in AHD until 1980. Civil and political liberties, which shared the leading role with longevity from the mid-1930s onwards, drove AHD gains in the late 1940s and early 1950s. Schooling made the largest contribution throughout the entire time span considered, becoming the driving force in the late nineteenth century and during the last third of the twentieth century (see Appendix D, Table D.7).

In East Asia, schooling, closely followed by life expectancy, was the leading force in AHD progress over time. This joint contribution can be observed during the phase of faster AHD gains between 1920 and the 1950s, completed with improvements in civil and political rights during the late 1940s and early 1950s. However, the contraction in civil and political liberties detracted from AHD gains between the mid-1950s and 1980. Conversely, the expansion of liberties drove AHD's intense progress in the last two decades of the century (see Appendix D, Table D.8).

In the Middle East, schooling was the main AHD driver over time and during most phases of AHD evolution, except from the mid-1920s to the early 1950s, when life expectancy became the driving force, and in the 1980s, when freedoms, which had made a substantial contribution during the 1950s and 1960s, took over (see Appendix D, Table D.9).

North Africa's AHD gains are mainly driven by schooling in the long run, which predominated in the interwar period and from 1960 onwards, although the contribution of life expectancy prevailed from 1890–1913 and, in particular, 1938–1950. Freedoms made a markedly negative contribution in the early 1950s, reversed over 1955–1965, and then, again, in the late 1960s (see Chapter 6, Table 6.3).

Lastly, the long-run progress of AHD in sub-Saharan Africa was mainly driven by schooling, which was also the main contributor to AHD gains during the early 1920s and between 1950 and the mid-1960s. Life expectancy was the driving force behind AHD between the mid-1920s and 1950 and after 2010. Civil and political rights conditioned AHD performance, both hindering its progress from 1965–1975 and, again, in the early 1980s, and driving it in the late 1970s and the 1990s (see Appendix D, Table D.10; see also Chapter 6).

4.6 AHD Catching Up to the OECD in Regions of the *Rest*

Let us finally consider the experience of the regions of the *Rest* vis-à-vis the OECD. Eastern Europe exhibited strong catching up in the interwar period, fell behind after World War II, remaining at this lower level during its socialist phase, before recovering and improving its pre-war position relative to the OECD from 1990 onwards (Figure 4.12, Panel A). Russia, however, fell behind in the late nineteenth century and, after a brief reversal in the 'long' decade up to World War I, slipped back again after the Soviet Revolution. There followed two periods of stability at a low level, split by a catching-up episode in the 1950s. A major upwards push in the late 1980s and early 1990s, at the time of the collapse of the USSR, gave way to stability at a higher level. Latin America caught up steadily to the OECD between 1900 and 1960, fell behind in the 1960s, and exhibited strong catching up in the 1980s that continued at a slower pace thereafter. In East Asia, human development improved faster than in the other developing regions, catching up between the 1920s and early 1950s and, again, from the mid-1980s onwards, overtaking Russia's relative position as of 2000. In the Middle East and South Asia, long-run catching up has taken place since the late 1920s, with short reversal episodes, while in North Africa catching up took place in the 1930s and 1940s, and after a reversal in the early 1950s followed by slow recovery, the region forged ahead again, from the late 1970s onwards (Figure 4.12, Panel B). In sub-Saharan Africa, a moderate catching up between the late 1920s and early 1960s gave way to stagnation, before catching up resumed in the 1990s. Lastly, China did not experience a long-run trend until the late 1970s, as a late nineteenth-century decline was followed by catching up in the 1920s and 1930s and another fall after the 1949 Revolution, with steady catching up evident only as of 1980.

Thus, different convergence clusters or 'clubs' have emerged within the world's developing regions, with Eastern Europe and Latin America, at the top, and China and sub-Saharan Africa, at the bottom. Less neatly defined, East Asia, Russia, and the Middle East have been in the second tier, and South Asia and North Africa in the third tier. By 2015, levels of human development in Eastern Europe and Latin America reached those of the OECD in the early 1970s and 1960s, respectively. In East Asia, Russia, and the Middle East, levels were similar to those in the OECD in 1950. Levels in South Asia and North Africa were close to those achieved by the OECD in 1929, while sub-Saharan Africa matched OECD levels prior to World War I, an unenviable position shared by China. On average, by 2015, the *Rest* was still below the level of human development in the OECD in 1950.

A more nuanced perception of human development across the *Rest* derives from consideration of the drivers of catching up in developing regions. A breakdown of catching up into its sources across the *Rest*'s regions can be provided for each of the main phases of human development performance.

Between the late nineteenth century and World War I, with the exception of Latin America, the relative position of regions in the

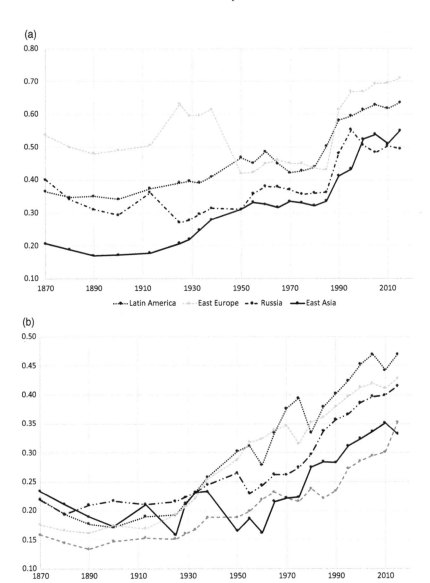

Figure 4.12 Relative AHD in regions of the *Rest*, 1870–2015 (OECD=1). (a) Latin America, Eastern Europe, Russia, and East Asia; (b) sub-Saharan Africa, North Africa, Middle East, China, and South Asia.

Sources: See the text and Tables 4.1 and 4.3.

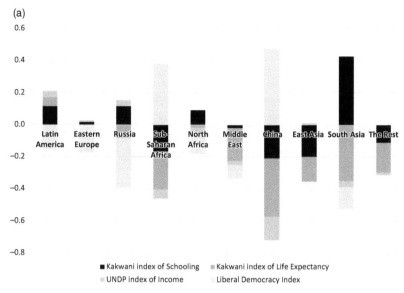

Figure 4.13a AHD catching up, 1870–1913 (%).
Sources: See the text, Chapter 5, Table 5.2, Chapter 6, Table 6.9, and Appendix D, Tables D.4–D.10.

Rest vis-à-vis the OECD deteriorated for various reasons: poorer performance in terms of civil and political liberties (Eastern Europe and Russia – despite improvement over 1900–1913 – North Africa, the Middle East, and South Asia), life expectancy (all Asian regions and sub-Saharan Africa), and schooling (China, East Asia, and sub-Saharan Africa) (Figure 4.13a).

The period 1913–1950 represented, on average, a first phase of widespread catching up in the *Rest* except for Russia and, from the late 1940s onwards, for Eastern Europe and China, which fell behind as civil and political freedoms were eroded under socialism (Figure 4.13b). Life expectancy, as a result of the spread of the epidemiological transition (Latin America, North and sub-Saharan Africa, Middle East, China, East and South Asia), and schooling, due to the expansion of mass primary education (Latin America, Russia, East and South Asia, Middle East, North and sub-Saharan Africa), were the main drivers of regional catching up, and also mitigated falling behind in China, Eastern Europe, and Russia. East and South Asia and the Middle East, aided by gains in political and civil rights, excelled in terms of catching up during this period.

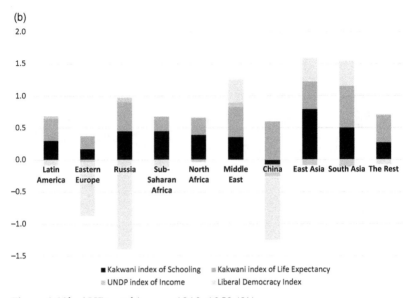

Figure 4.13b AHD catching up, 1913–1950 (%).
Sources: See the text, Chapter 5, Table 5.2, Chapter 6, Table 6.9, and Appendix D, Tables D.4–D.10.

Catching up intensified across the board during the *Golden Age* (1950–1970), with the exceptions of Latin America and North Africa, due to their decline in terms of freedoms, even though relative gains in longevity and education prevented North Africa from falling behind (Figure 4.13c). Non-income dimensions drove catching up. Gains in education were the main drivers except in China and Eastern Europe, where life expectancy led the way, and in South Asia, where civil and political rights did so. Lower restrictions of civil and political liberties in Russia, as a consequence of de-Stalinisation, also stimulated catching up. The modest contribution made by life expectancy to catching up in Russia conceals an early phase of robust catching up in the 1950s, so by the mid-1960s, life expectancy at birth had practically reached Western European levels. However, life expectancy fell since 1965 as a result of the increase in male adult mortality, largely a consequence of cardiovascular diseases, death by accident, suicide, poisoning, and alcoholism (Mazur, 1969; Dutton, 1979). In the rest of socialist Europe, life expectancy also stagnated from the mid-1960s onwards.

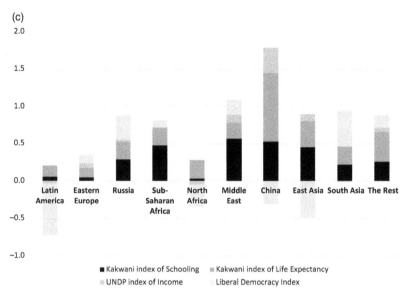

Figure 4.13c AHD catching up, 1950–1970 (%).
Sources: See the text, Chapter 5, Table 5.2, Chapter 6, Table 6.9, and Appendix D, Tables D.4–D.10.

Between the end of the *Golden Age* and the collapse of the Soviet Union, catching up took place, though unevenly, across the board (Figure 4.13d). Schooling and liberties were the main drivers of catching up. The spread of mass schooling largely accounts for catching up in North and sub-Saharan Africa, the Middle East, and South Asia. Civil and political liberties represented the largest single contribution to catching up in Latin America during the 1980s, in China, after the 1978 reforms, and, from the late 1980s onwards, in Eastern Europe and Russia too. It is worth stressing that rather than catch up, life expectancy fell behind in Russia and Eastern Europe prior to the demise of socialism, and that only in the Middle East and South Asia did liberties decline in comparison with the OECD.

In the post-1990 era, stronger catching up has taken place in the *Rest*, mainly on the basis of education, although the gains in civil and political freedoms made the largest contribution, mostly concentrated in the 1990s, in Eastern Europe, East Asia, and sub-Saharan Africa. Advances in material well-being played a leading role in China and, to a lesser extent, East and South Asia (from the 1980s), largely a

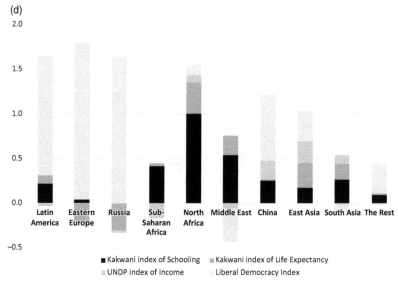

Figure 4.13d AHD catching up, 1970–1990 (%).
Sources: See the text, Chapter 5, Table 5.2, Chapter 6, Table 6.9, and Appendix D, Tables D.4–D.10.

consequence of the pro-market reforms, while social components – life expectancy, in particular – played a minor role. The slowdown in health improvements has been regarded as a direct consequence of the new economic policies (Dréze and Sen, 2002; Cutler et al., 2006) (Figure 4.13e). In Russia and Eastern Europe, life expectancy continued falling behind after the demise of socialism (Brainerd and Cutler, 2005; Brainerd, 2010b), although uneven recovery and episodes of catching up occurred in Central and Eastern Europe, especially in Czechia, Poland, and Hungary after 2000 (Stillman, 2006; Gerry et al., 2018). Alcohol consumption and stress from the transition to the market economy (unemployment uncertainty for middle-aged workers, rising inequality), along with worsening of diets and health and material deprivation, appear to be largely responsible for the increase in mortality and help to explain the severity and persistence of the decline in life expectancy in the former Soviet Union and to a lesser extent in former socialist Eastern Europe (Shkolnikov et al., 2001; Cutler and Brainerd, 2005; Brainerd, 2010a).

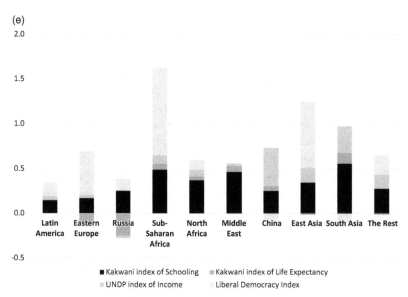

Figure 4.13e AHD catching up, 1990–2015 (%).
Sources: See the text, Chapter 5, Table 5.2, Chapter 6, Table 6.9, and Appendix D, Tables D.4–D.10.

4.7 Conclusions

This chapter has presented a long-run view of human development in today's developed and developing regions, and explored catching up to the *OECD* in the *Rest*.

The main findings are that human development achieved substantial but unevenly spread gains across world regions. Life expectancy and schooling were the main long-run drivers of AHD in both the *OECD* and the *Rest*. The absolute gap between the *OECD* and the *Rest* widened over time, although in relative terms the gap narrowed from the late 1920s onwards, driven by longevity and civil and political rights. Catching up was more intense until 1970, when the contribution of life expectancy faded as the epidemiological or health transition was being achieved, and in the 1990s, with the spread of freedoms in the *Rest*.

This finding is at odds with the widening relative gap in average incomes between the *OECD* and the *Rest* until the end of the twentieth century. The gap between the *OECD* and the *Rest* dominated AHD international distribution until the mid-twentieth century, when the dispersion within each group, the *Rest* in particular, provided increasing momentum.

The choice of economic and social system has had a far from negligible influence upon human development across countries. Socialist and capitalist models implied very different health and education policies, as well as contrasting economic policies. Despite their initial success as providers of 'basic needs', countries that embarked on socialist experiments failed to sustain momentum and fell behind the *OECD*. Moreover, as in other authoritarian experiences, the suppression of individual agency and freedom prevented real achievements in human development.

Although an overview of the performance across the *Rest* has been presented in this chapter, a more careful examination of some of the cases considered is warranted, specifically, that of Latin America, the region that most closely matches the world average in terms of human development, and Africa, and in particular the region south of the Sahara, which systematically appears at the bottom in terms of AHD and its dimensions. The next two chapters are dedicated to these two regions.

5 | Human Development in Latin America

5.1 Introduction

How has Latin America performed over time? How have the fruits of growth been distributed? How does Latin America compare to the United States or to Western Europe? These are questions repeatedly raised by social scientists and historians.[1] However, much less attention has been paid to well-being beyond material living standards.

Trends in well-being have been inferred on the basis of GDP per head (Bulmer-Thomas, 2003; Coatsworth, 2005). Modern economic growth can be traced back to the mid-nineteenth century. Two phases of moderate but sustained growth, 1870–1929 and 1938–1979, can be distinguished. Faltering growth during the 1930s and 1980s plus moderate expansion since the 1990s complete the picture (Hofman and Valderrama, 2021).

The idea of long-run relative decline in Latin America since independence has been favoured in the literature (Bulmer-Thomas, 2003). It is widely accepted that the origins of modern retardation are located in the nineteenth century (Haber, 1997). John Coatsworth (2008) emphasised that falling behind took place between 1750 and 1850, while the gap with the United States remained unchanged during the twentieth century (Astorga and Fitzgerald, 1998: 353). The fact that Latin America's position relative to the United States remained mostly unaltered during the twentieth century is, however, at odds with the catching-up experience in large areas of the Periphery (southern and Eastern Europe, Southeast Asia), which significantly reduced the income per head gap with the United States after 1950. Furthermore, Latin America kept pace with the advanced nations' club, the OECD, from 1870–1929, but experienced the paradox of achieving its fastest growth while falling behind from 1938–1980 (Prados de la Escosura, 2007b). The 1980s debt crisis heralded an unenviable situation of sluggish growth and retardation that lasted until the beginnings of the new century (Bértola and Ocampo, 2012; Astorga and Herranz-Loncán, 2021).

Were the fruits of growth shared, though? High and persistent inequality has been stressed in the literature. Some authors date its beginnings as early as the pre-colonial and colonial eras and associate it with the unequal distribution of wealth and power that was perpetuated through time by endogenously designed extractive institutions (Engerman and Sokoloff, 1997; Acemoglu et al., 2002). A second school of thought locates the beginning of persistent inequality in the post-colonial era (Williamson, 2010). Historical evidence suggests that inequality grew during the late nineteenth and early twentieth centuries, reaching a high plateau by the mid-twentieth century, where it has remained ever since except for trendless fluctuations (Prados de la Escosura, 2007a; Székely and Mendoza, 2015; Astorga, 2017). From a comparative perspective, inequality in Latin America was among the highest in the world and, if normalised by the level of average incomes, probably unparalleled during the last one and a half centuries (Prados de la Escosura and Cha, 2021).

The persistence of high inequality has been attributed to alternative, but not mutually exclusive, hypotheses: (a) the evolution of the terms of trade would have caused either de-industrialisation, by shifting the comparative advantage towards primary production (Singer, 1950), or immiserising growth (Prebisch, 1950); (b) the Stolper and Samuelson (1941) effect of opening up on income distribution, over-proportionally rewarding abundant resources (natural resources), used more intensively in exportable production and ownership of which was largely concentrated (Williamson, 1997); and (c) the elastic labour supply that broke the link between changes in average incomes and unskilled wages, so while GDP per head or per worker grew, returns to unskilled labour remained unaltered (Lewis, 1954; Astorga and Herranz-Loncán, 2021; Bleynat, Challú, and Segal, 2021).

But what would have been the impact of such an unequal income distribution on well-being? Branko Milanovic's inequality extraction ratio (IER) compares the actual level of inequality to the maximum potential inequality. Its rationale is that the closer a country's inequality gets to its potential maximum, the deeper the impact of inequality on well-being.[2] In Latin America, the actual level of inequality has represented a high proportion of the maximum potential inequality (Prados de la Escosura and Cha, 2021). This implies that in Latin America, high inequality has taken a heavy toll in terms of well-being. A more conventional way of assessing the impact of inequality on well-being is computing the absolute poverty headcount – that is, those living below a pre-determined poverty line (initially, $1 a day per person in 1985 U.S. relative prices). In Latin America, the proportion of people living in absolute poverty declined between 1900 and 1980 and, again, after 2000, but has remained high relative to OECD countries. The contraction in absolute poverty was mainly a consequence of changes in per capita income rather than in its distribution (Prados de la Escosura, 2007a; Ferreira and Robalino, 2011; Ravallion and Chen, 2017; Székely and Mendoza, 2017).

However, from this chapter's perspective the relevant question is, to what extent has sustained though unevenly distributed economic growth affected multidimensional well-being over time? We know that during the economic expansion between the 1940s and the 1970s, under 'state-led industrialisation', a 'segmented' welfare state was introduced that promoted public health and education, while during the post-1980 phase of sluggish growth, under 'market-led development', fewer demands were placed on social spending (Ocampo and Ros, 2011: 8). But did the different dimensions of well-being evolve similarly to per capita income? Or were they impervious to GDP growth and income distribution changes? More specifically, this chapter asks how much multidimensional well-being has improved in Latin America during the last one and a half centuries. What has driven changes in AHD? How does Latin America compare to the advanced nations in AHD terms? Has the gap widened? Why? These are no easy answers to these questions, but the policy implications are far reaching.

This chapter is organised as follows: Section 5.2 reviews the historical literature on Latin American well-being. Section 5.3 discusses the long-run evolution of human development in Latin America from a world perspective. How its dimensions contributed to the aggregate performance of the *AHDI* over time is examined in Section 5.4, and what explains the observed differences between Latin America and the *OECD* in Section 5.5. Next, Section 5.6 takes a closer look at level by country. Section 5.7 concludes.

5.2 Well-Being in Latin America: A Review of the Literature

Fortunately, recent literature on Latin American history has increasingly focused on well-being beyond income. Anthropometric and education research deserve to be highlighted. In the first case, adult stature is used to proxy net biological well-being, as it provides a measure of cumulative net nutrition, which is conditioned not only by food availability and disease incidence but also by genetic factors (Franken, 2019; Borrescio-Higa et al., 2019). Although improvements over the long run are confirmed in most historical cases investigated, economic distress, social differences, and non-inclusive growth are found to affect increases in average height. On the basis of a sample of prisoners, Ricardo Salvatore (2019) reports scant gains among unskilled workers in Argentina prior to World War I. Prisoners' heights increased, however, during the Great Depression, a puzzling finding that can be attributed to the increase in per capita caloric intake resulting from a decline in the relative price of food (Salvatore, 2010: 97). In the case of Chile, Manuel Llorca-Jaña et al. (2020) find that the late-nineteenth-century nitrate boom in economic growth did not percolate down into living standards. In fact, declining nutritional intake, a deteriorating disease environment, and increasing income inequality resulted in height stagnation. Between the 1930s and 1960s, sustained height increases were associated with the rise in the consumption of dairy products and meat and, as of 1990, also with an improvement in public health resulting from better health care and sewerage and drinking water facilities (Llorca-Jaña et al., 2021). With regard to height distribution, inequality increased between 1880 and the 1940s, as is evidenced by comparison of the heights of boys from lower and upper socio-economic groups. Inequality declined, however, during the second half of the twentieth century. Public policies, including housing programs and urban infrastructure (sewage and potable water), accounted for this reduction, as they enhanced nutrition, health, and living standards in a context of economic growth but persistent unequal income distribution (Núñez and Pérez, 2015: 108–109).

In Brazil, Daniel Franken (2019) finds no correlation between economic growth and height changes from 1880–1910, and attributes height gains in the 1940s and 1950s to improvements in public health, but not to the increase in average incomes. This was because, although economic growth accelerated during Getulio Vargas's *Estado Novo* (1930–1945) and, especially, after World War II, income inequality increased (Gómez-León, 2021).

As for Mexico, Moramay López-Alonso and Roberto Vélez-Grajales (2017) trace the evolution of heights on the basis of military conscripts. They find a decline in heights during 1850–1890 and stagnation in the

1890s, but a rebound in the early twentieth century that was cut short by consequences of the Revolution. During the 1930s, heights increased, an achievement the authors attribute to public health campaigns and the introduction of the welfare state during Lázaro Cardenas's presidency (1934–1940) and one that coincided with an increase in unskilled workers' wages, attributed land reform, and pro-labour policies (Bleynat, Challú, and Segal, 2021). After stagnating in the 1950s and 1960s, height began to increase again (López-Alonso and Vélez-Grajales, 2017: 83–85).

In Colombia, Adolfo Meisel-Roca et al. (2019: 330–331) observe sustained improvements in average male and female heights, accompanied by a decline in regional dispersion, over 1920–1990, which they attribute to better nutrition and public services, including education.

Lastly, heights remained stagnant in Bolivia between the 1880s and 1929, and differences were maintained between social groups. Sluggish productivity growth in agriculture, a disease environment, and persistent income inequalities account for such a stable situation (Branisa et al., 2020).

Research on infant mortality also suggests long-run improvements. Florencia Borrescio-Higa et al. (2019) attribute the rise in the infant survival rate in Chile for cohorts born between 1960 and 1989, which led to an increase in adult height, to the long-run consequences of public health policies aimed at reducing infant mortality and malnutrition. These were accompanied by urbanisation and infrastructure (sewage and drinking water supply), rather than GDP per head growth. They point out that even though health spending shrank under General Pinochet's dictatorship (1973–1990), policies fostering infant and maternal health care and nutrition were maintained (Borreschio-Higa et al., 2019: 141). Thus, public health achievements cannot easily be attributed to any single period or government. Moreover, starting from much lower health spending and higher mortality rates in the mid-twentieth century, Chile has managed to reduce infant mortality and maternal death to lower levels than Argentina. According to Daniel Brieba (2018), this achievement was possible thanks to Chile's investment in the provision of unified and higher-quality health services with better planning and coordination, territorial coverage, and standardisation.

In the Caribbean, disease prevention measures at a relatively low cost, such as 'building latrines, isolating the sick, fighting housefly and mosquito breeding, recognizing tuberculosis symptoms and learning how to reduce the chances of infection' (Riley, 2005a: 131) reduced infant mortality and raised life expectancy at birth in the case of Jamaica. In Guyana, too, public health improvements rather than increases in average incomes accounted for a decline in mortality during the period 1911–1960. Specifically, these were improvements in health provision (water supply, knowledge dissemination regarding pre- and post-natal care, waste disposal, and medical facilities) helped by advances in educational attainment up to World War II, and especially the use of DDT to fight malaria in the post-war era (Mandle, 1970). In Cuba, the decline in mortality during the American occupation (1898–1902) and the early phase of independence resulted from sanitary and public health innovations triggered by the germ theory of disease rather than from economic progress (Díaz-Brisquets, 1981: 410). In the 1930s and 1940s, nutrition and sanitation improvements and better public understanding of infectious and communicable diseases, in addition to, since the late 1930s, sulphonamides, contributed to the fall in mortality. After World War II, antibiotics made a major contribution to reduced mortality (Díaz-Brisquets, 1981: 407–411).

Thus, it can be concluded that no significant change in human stature seems to have occurred prior to World War I, as economic growth, when it took place, was paralleled by increasing income inequality, so social differences persisted and the nutrition intake of lower social groups declined or stagnated. From the late 1920s onwards, and, especially during the central decades of the twentieth century, net nutrition, which resulted in gains in adult height, improved across the board in Latin America. The experiences of infant mortality and life expectancy also follow a similar pattern. These achievements took place under distinct political regimes driven by the largely public provision of health care and water and sanitation infrastructure, often in a context of economic growth and income inequality. As Chile's experience shows, inequality in health can be reduced even at high and persistent income inequality levels (Brieba (2018: 50). Nonetheless, the extent to which inequality prevented a more intense effect of economic growth on net nutrition gains is an unknown that merits exploration.

Education is another dimension of well-being that has attracted research in Latin American economic history. Carlos Newland (1991, 1994) has described the transition from a decentralised schooling system under municipalities and private control to a centralised, state-run system financed through tax revenues. Nation-building appears as a major driving force, leading to the eradication of cultural diversity, the imposition of Spanish at the expense of the vernacular, and homogenisation of the population. Urbanisation was another major determinant. Liberal ideology led to the introduction of a literacy requirement for suffrage. Education was also enhanced to attract immigrants and by urbanisation. However, no association appears to exist between the rise of education and democratisation (Engerman et al., 2009). As of 1950, under state-led industrialisation, in addition to urbanisation and the creation of a national identity (in which the universal use of Spanish played a major role), the drivers of mass schooling expanded to include global forces (with international organisations providing an important stimulus), encouraging social mobility and fostering human capital (Reimers, 2006).

Inequality also conditioned the pace at which education spread. Stanley Engerman, Elisa Mariscal, and Kenneth Sokoloff (2009) entertain the hypothesis that inequality in income and political power led to lower levels of schooling. Broader access to primary schooling and higher literacy were associated with lower inequality and heterogeneity of the population and the extension of the franchise. Leticia Arroyo Abad (2015: 106) highlights the unequal provision of education by social and ethnic groups and the literacy constraint to suffrage that marginalised the indigenous population's political participation in Peru between the 1870s and 1940. Yue Teng (2019: 434) notices that 'state-led' industrialisation failed to mitigate the unequal distribution of education, which has its roots in inequality in terms of political rights and assets. Under-funding of public education is highlighted as a major cause of unequal access to education. María José Fuentes-Vásquez (2019), for example, finds a correlation between enrolment and the education budget at the regional level. Peter Lindert (2010: 402) stresses the political failure to support primary and secondary education in relatively rich countries such as Argentina and Venezuela, and Ewout Frankema (2009: 387) points out the heavy bias towards tertiary education, which represents a regressive redistribution towards the affluent groups. Finally, Reimers (2006: 428) blames the elites' failure to 'reach consensus on the need to provide poor children with real learning chance'.

The historical outcome has been a comparatively low level of educational attainment for a given per capita income level. Luis Bértola and

José Antonio Ocampo (2012: 36–39) hypothesise that the fact that natural resources are the abundant factor, rather than human capital, helps explain sustained economic growth at low education levels. Furthermore, social disparities in access to quality education have persisted over time (Urquiola, 2011). In fact, cognitive skills have been low relative to years of schooling in Latin America during the last half a century, by international standards (Hanushek and Woessmann, 2012).

A more comprehensive approach to living standards has been proposed by authors who looked at multidimensional well-being with adaptations of the UN Human Development Index for Latin America. Pablo Astorga, Ame Bergés, and Valpy Fitzgerald (2005) constructed a Historical Living Standard Index (HLSI) of welfare for the twentieth century on the basis of life expectancy at birth, literacy, and GDP per head, according to the pre-2010 UNDP *HDI* (in other words, the variables are linearly transformed, using logs for per capita income, and all combined as an unweighted arithmetic average) for six major countries (Argentina, Brazil, Chile, Colombia, Mexico, and Venezuela) for 1900–1950 and thirteen countries from 1950 onwards. The index shows sustained gains over time, though stronger in the central decades of the twentieth century and slowing down after 1980, a result, the authors argue, that lends support to a positive assessment of the state-led industrialisation years (1940–1980) and not to the post-1980 phase of liberalisation. Social spending and urbanisation appear to have facilitated gains in longevity and education, which, more than economic growth, were the drivers of sustained progress in living standards. From a comparative perspective, the authors find that Latin America partially converged to the United States and other developed countries, but a widening gap opened in absolute terms.

Bértola and Ocampo (2012: 33–43 and Table A.4) offer three alternative human development indices for Latin America for the period 1900–2010 (only for seven countries during the entire time span) on the basis of a geometric average of life expectancy, years of schooling, and per capita income indices. In two of them, GDP per head is not transformed into logs, and non-income dimensions are alternatively transformed linearly and with a Kakwani convex transformation (RI1 and RI2, respectively). The third index (RI3) replicates the UNDP *HDI* with the long transformation of per capita income and linear transformation of the variables. While RI3 shows a sustained improvement over time, RI1 and RI2 peaked in 1980, fluctuating around a flat trend thereafter.

In an unpublished contribution, Bértola et al. (2011) provide, for a sample of sixteen countries (four of them in Latin America: Argentina, Brazil, Chile, and Uruguay) for 1900–2000, a new measure for human development, the Historical Human Development Index (HHDI). The latter combines, with a geometric mean, life expectancy at birth, years of education, and GDP per head, with non-income variables transformed non-linearly (using the Kakwani transformation) but the actual values of GDP, not its log, linearly transformed. To this is added an index of democratisation (obtained as a geometric average of political participation, competition, and stability, transformed linearly). In addition, an inequality adjusted human development index (IAHHDI) is derived (for Latin American countries only since 1950), taking into account the distribution for its different dimensions. Bértola et al. (2011) conclude that human development in Latin American countries improved over time, except for a phase of decline in the 1970s and 1980s, converging with the most advanced nations over time despite an episode of divergence (1970–1990). The relative performance of Latin American countries worsens when the inequality-adjusted index is considered. Reducing inequality appears to be prerequisite for Latin America's convergence in terms of well-being.

There are also two investigations into national experiences. In the case of Colombia, Juliana Jaramillo-Echeverri et al. (2019) provide human development estimates for the period 1838–2013, following the approach in Prados de la Escosura (2015a). They show that the historical index of human development (HIHD) improved over time, but especially during the twentieth century, largely due to health and education contributions, with life expectancy as its main driver. They attribute the decline in mortality, underlying the rise in life expectancy from the 1930s onwards, to preventive medicine and hygiene and social spending and, during the period 1950–1980, to public health policies and the provision of public utilities, including water supply (aqueducts) and sanitation (sewerage).

Finally, in a study of the case of Cuba, John Devereux (2021) constructs a human development index for a sample of 38 countries in 1955 and 2011, 20 corresponding to Latin America, along the pre-2010 UNDP *HDI*.[3] In relation to Cuba, he observes a lack of connection between gains in health and education, which place this country near the top of the Latin America *HDI* rankings in 2011, behind Puerto Rico and Chile (a position similar to the one it occupied in

1955, after Argentina and Uruguay), although its economic performance appears sluggish. He attributes the remarkable health achievements to the coercive power of the Socialist state. Devereux also points
out the suspicion of overstated life expectancy at birth. Berdine,
Geloso, and Powell (2018: 756) attribute Cuba's success in terms of
life expectancy to the government's allocation of resources to health
care at the expense of other industries. This interpretation finds support in Devereux's extended *HDI*, which includes a freedom dimension, as Cuba appears at the bottom of the Latin America table in
2011, falling from the top position in the lower quartile in 1955.

5.3 Human Development Trends

Let us begin by addressing how much human development improved in
Latin America over the past one and a half centuries. A long-run
upward trend is apparent, reaching in 2015 a level 7.7 times higher
than in 1870, which equates to 1.4 per cent annual growth (Table 5.1).
Progress in AHD was sustained over time, and only interrupted by
episodes of mild decline during the Great Depression and the 1960s.
Several phases can be differentiated in AHD evolution: moderate progress up to 1900, which intensified until 1929, acceleration between
1938 and 1960, and sustained and fast improvement as of 1970,
especially from 1980–1990. AHD progress beyond 1980 is, no doubt,
a counter-intuitive finding, as this has been deemed a lost decade in
economic terms in Latin America. Moreover, these trends are discrep-
ant with those from previous studies. Contrary to what Astorga et al.
(2005) and Bértola and Ocampo (2012) report, *AHDI* progress neither
slows down nor stagnates after 1980, nor declines from 1970–1990, as
Bértola et al. (2011) posit.

When placed in the international distribution of human development, Latin America fluctuated around the 70th percentile until 1950,
and between then and 1990 closely matched the 75th percentile,
moving upwards thereafter. This implies a remarkably stable position
from a global perspective (Figure 5.1). In terms of the world average,
from representing four-fifths up to 1900, Latin America reached the
mean level in 1950 and one-fifth above this from 1990 onwards.

Moreover, these results are representative, since the distribution of
AHD across Latin American countries presents a low dispersion.
However, we observe a sustained increase in dispersion between

Table 5.1. *AHDI and its components: Latin America*
Panel A. Levels

	AHDI	Kakwani index of schooling	Kakwani index of Life expectancy	UNDP index of income	Liberal democracy index
1870	0.063	0.016	0.023	0.338	0.123
1880	0.067	0.020	0.025	0.346	0.116
1890	0.075	0.024	0.029	0.384	0.121
1900	0.081	0.028	0.034	0.384	0.119
1913	0.100	0.035	0.048	0.441	0.136
1925	0.122	0.048	0.063	0.465	0.157
1929	0.127	0.053	0.067	0.481	0.151
1933	0.125	0.059	0.073	0.454	0.122
1938	0.133	0.065	0.082	0.481	0.121
1950	0.192	0.083	0.162	0.518	0.196
1955	0.202	0.092	0.183	0.536	0.185
1960	0.230	0.103	0.196	0.554	0.251
1965	0.224	0.113	0.214	0.573	0.182
1970	0.222	0.127	0.233	0.596	0.138
1975	0.240	0.138	0.255	0.624	0.150
1980	0.263	0.162	0.276	0.648	0.166
1985	0.316	0.190	0.299	0.637	0.275
1990	0.382	0.216	0.324	0.637	0.475
1995	0.405	0.238	0.351	0.650	0.498
2000	0.433	0.259	0.379	0.661	0.545
2005	0.458	0.278	0.403	0.672	0.583
2010	0.471	0.291	0.427	0.692	0.573
2015	0.480	0.296	0.453	0.702	0.561

Panel B. AHD drivers [*] *(%)*

	Kakwani index of schooling	Kakwani index of life expectancy	UNDP index of income	Liberal democracy index	AHDI
1870–1880	0.6	0.2	0.1	−0.2	0.7
1880–1890	0.5	0.3	0.3	0.1	1.1
1890–1900	0.5	0.4	0.0	0.0	0.8
1900–1913	0.4	0.7	0.3	0.3	1.6
1913–1929	0.7	0.5	0.1	0.2	1.5
1929–1938	0.6	0.6	0.0	−0.6	0.5

Table 5.1. (*cont.*)

	Kakwani index of schooling	Kakwani index of life expectancy	UNDP index of income	Liberal democracy index	AHDI
1938–1950	0.5	1.4	0.2	1.0	3.1
1950–1960	0.6	0.5	0.2	0.6	1.8
1960–1970	0.5	0.4	0.2	−1.5	−0.4
1970–1980	0.6	0.4	0.2	0.5	1.7
1980–1990	0.7	0.4	0.0	2.6	3.7
1990–2000	0.4	0.4	0.1	0.3	1.3
2000–2010	0.3	0.3	0.1	0.1	0.8
2010–2015	0.1	0.3	0.1	−0.1	0.4
1870–2015	0.5	0.5	0.1	0.3	1.4

* Dimensions' contribution to AHD growth.

1870 and 1929 and a decline thereafter, only interrupted by a reversal during the 1960s and early 1970s (Figure 5.2).

Do phases in the evolution of human development match those of real per capita income? Real GDP per head evolved close to the 75th percentile of world distribution (Figure 5.3), growing at 1.5 per cent over time, slightly above the *ADHI* growth (1.4%). GDP per head exhibits higher dispersion than the *AHDI* but follows similar trends. If we compare the *AHDI** (*AHDI* excluding the income dimension) to GDP per head, we observe that, although they show similar rates of growth in the long run (slightly higher, 1.7%, in the case of *AHDI**) their pace varies over different phases. AHD* grows substantially faster than GDP per head during the 1890s, 1913–1950, and the so-called lost decade (the 1980s), but more slowly during the 1880s, the 'long' decade to World War I, 1960–1980, and since the 2000s (Figure 5.4).

Thus, during the globalisation backlash of the 1930s and 1940s, clear discrepancies emerged. Real GDP per head slowed down as world commodity and factor markets disintegrated, but AHD non-income dimensions, health and education, in particular, thrived, and human development progressed steadily. Since 1960, the pace of AHD advancement has not matched that of economic growth, except in the 1980s, when the collapse in per capita incomes paralleled impressive gains in well-being.

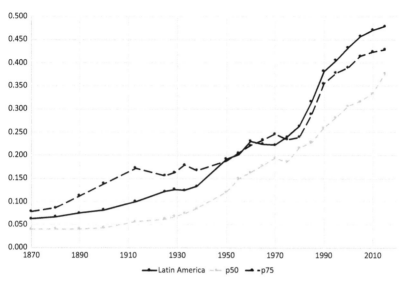

Figure 5.1 *AHDI* in Latin America.
Sources: See the text and Table 5.1.

Figure 5.2 Inter-country AHD distribution in Latin America (MLD).
Sources: See the text and Chapter 4, Table 4.2.

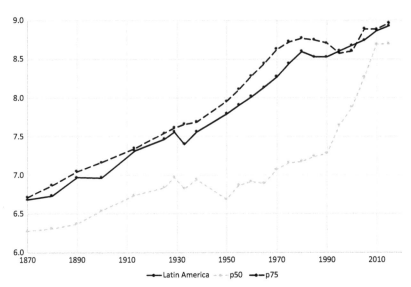

Figure 5.3 Real GDP per head in Latin America (G-K 1990$, logs).
Sources: See the text.

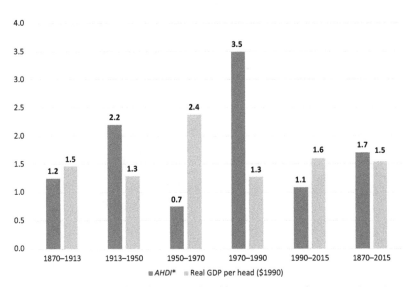

Figure 5.4 *AHDI** and real GDP per head long-term growth in Latin America.
*Excluding adjusted income.
Sources: See the text.

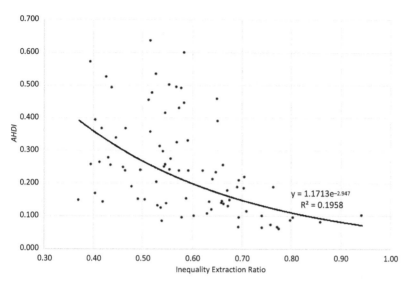

Figure 5.5 *AHDI* and IER in six Latin American countries, 1870–2010.
Note: Countries considered are Argentina, Brazil, Chile, Colombia, Peru, and Uruguay.
Sources: IER, Prados de la Escosura (2007a), updated with estimates by Castañeda and Bengtsson (2020) for Mexico, 1895–1940, and Rodríguez Weber (2016) for Chile, 1870–1950; *AHDI*, see the text.

As we saw in Section 5.2, Latin America experienced high income inequality from the mid-twentieth century onwards in a context of comparatively low per capita income levels. This implies a negative impact on welfare levels, as captured by Milanovic's inequality extraction ratio (namely, the ratio of actual inequality to maximum potential inequality) (Section 5.2, fn. 2). How does the *AHDI* compare to the IER? The intuition is that the two measures are inversely correlated, so the higher the level of human development, the lower the IER and, hence, the lesser the harm inequality causes to well-being. A negative association between AHD and IER emerges when we compare the *AHDI* and the IER for a sample of 18 Latin American countries over 1950–2010 (Figure E.1 in Appendix E). The result is confirmed when the exercise is replicated for a group of six countries for which data start before World War I (Figure 5.5). This finding supports the view that unequal developing societies have low levels of human development, and is consistent with the depiction of human development as a measure of achievement, that is, the inverse of a measure of poverty (Grynspan and López-Calva, 2011: 721).

5.4 AHD Drivers

Why do performance disparities exist between AHD and GDP per head? Let us take a look at AHD non-income dimensions.

Schooling experienced a sustained rise over time, from 0.6 years of schooling per person above 15 in 1870 to 8.3 in 2015, which in terms of the Kakwani index represents multiplying the initial level by 18.8. Distinctive phases can be defined: moderate growth over 1870–1913; acceleration between World War I and the Great Depression; slower but steady pace until the mid-1970s; another fast growth episode over 1975–1990; and a gradual slowdown henceforth (Table 5.1). In terms of international distribution, Latin America improved its position over time, from being around the 40th percentile until 1900, to moving upwards, then, to the 60th percentile, where it remained up to 1980, and moving up next to the 70th percentile for the rest of the period under consideration (Figure 5.6).

Life expectancy at birth also improved remarkably over time, nearly trebling, from 26 years in 1870 to 75 years in 2015. In terms of the Kakwani index, it multiplied 19.3 times over the one and a half centuries

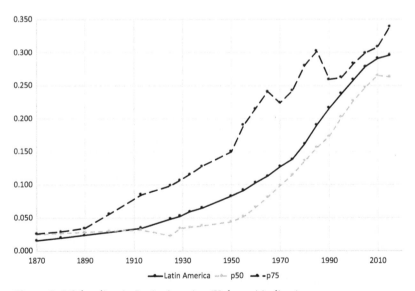

Figure 5.6 Schooling in Latin America (Kakwani indices).
Sources: See the text and Table 5.1.

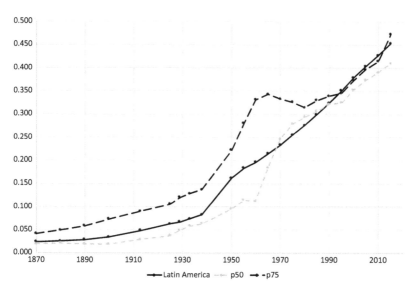

Figure 5.7 Life expectancy in Latin America (Kakwani indices).
Sources: See the text and Table 5.1.

studied. Main phases can be observed in its evolution, moderate but progressive advance until 1900, which sped up until World War II, followed by an episode of fast acceleration until the mid-1950s, and then a sustained though slower pace up to the present, fading away since 2000 (Figure 5.7). From an international perspective, after ranging between the 60th and 65th percentiles over 1870–1970, Latin America's longevity moved upwards, matching the 75th percentile from 1995.

Liberties, civil and political, proxied by the liberal democracy index, improved 4.6 times over 1870–2015 but did not follow a linear path. A moderate improvement took place between 1900 and 1929, reversed during the 1930s, followed by a major spurt between 1938 and 1960, which was upturned in the 1960s, so, by 1970, the level of freedoms had regressed to that of 1913. A dramatic upward shift after 1980 multiplied the level 3.5 times by 2005, with a slight decline thereafter. Latin America was around the 75th percentile, at both the beginning and end of the considered time span, but fell below the 60th percentile from 1938–1970, recovering moderately from 1980 onwards, and returning to the 75th percentile in the mid-2000s (Figure 5.8).

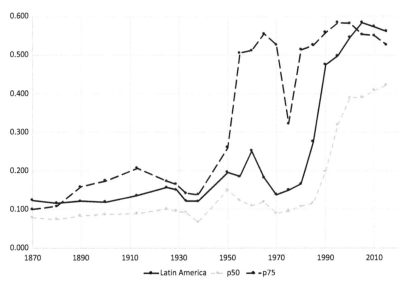

Figure 5.8 Civil and political liberties in Latin America (Kakwani indices).
Sources: See the text and Table 5.1.

The heterogenous behaviour across Latin America's countries means caution is necessary when evaluating the representativeness of the aggregate results, but the distribution of each AHD dimension over time suggests that they are increasingly representative, as the dispersion declined after 1900 in the case of longevity and from the late 1930s in the case of schooling, but only from the late 1970s for civil and political rights (Figure 5.9).

The *AHDI* multiplicative structure, with its dimensions assigned equal weights, allows a breakdown of AHD growth, as it amounts to the sum of each dimension's growth rate with equal weight (0.25) each (Chapter 2, equation 2.1). Life expectancy and schooling shared the main contribution to human development in the long run, between them accounting for nearly three-quarters of its growth (see Table 5.1, Panel B). A closer look reveals the dominant contribution of schooling to AHD progress during the late nineteenth century, between World War I and the Great Depression, and in the 1970s. Life expectancy led AHD gains in the 'long' decade prior to World War I, and prevailed from World War II to the mid-1950s. Civil and political liberties contributed above other dimensions in the late 1950s and in the 1980s in particular, but also impeded AHD advancement during the Great Depression and the 1960s.

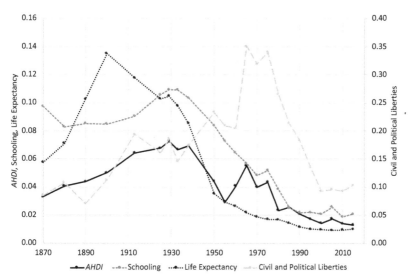

Figure 5.9 Inter-country distribution of AHD and its dimensions in Latin America (MLD).
Sources: See the text.

Interestingly, the main contribution of life expectancy to AHD improvement in Latin America took place in the first half of the twentieth century, that is, prior to the spread of modern medicine (antibiotics, in particular). This tells us about the importance of the spread of measures to prevent infectious diseases (low-cost public health measures and hygienic practices) associated with the diffusion of the germ theory of disease.

Improvements in schooling and longevity have been attributed to public intervention, specifically to spending on education, health, and social services (see Section 5.2). When the Kakwani index of schooling is plotted against public spending on education, expressed as a proportion of GDP, for Latin American countries between the 1950s and 2010, a positive association is found, although there is deceleration as levels of public spending rise (Figure E.2 in Appendix E). If the exercise is replicated for six countries for which data on education exist as of 1900, we find a positive non-linear association between *AHDI* and public spending in the case of education, which is more intense at a lower level (Figure 5.10). A similar result is obtained in the case of health, but the association flattens out as the share of GDP allocated to

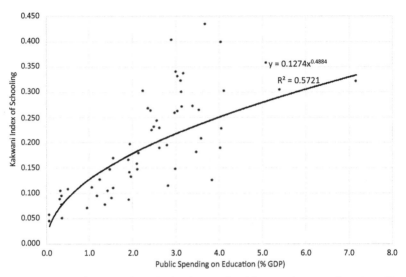

Figure 5.10 Kakwani index of schooling and public spending on education (% GDP) in six Latin American countries, 1900–2010.

Note: Countries considered are Argentina, Chile, Colombia, Costa Rica, Peru, and Uruguay.

Source: Public spending, Arroyo Abad and Lindert (2017); Kakwani index of schooling, see the text.

social spending rises, which is not the case for education (Figure 5.11). Thus, increases in social spending account, but only partially, for improvement in the levels of education and health. It can be hypothesised that, in addition to the movements along the health or education function, linked to higher average income levels and public spending, global forces in medicine and education and new social values shift the function upwards.

5.5 Catching Up to the OECD?

Has the gap between the advanced countries, the OECD, and Latin America closed or deepened over time? During the one and a half centuries studied, AHD in Latin America grew faster than in the OECD and, hence, shortened distances in relative terms. This was not a steady process, though. After falling behind slightly until 1900, catching up took place until 1960, more intensely from 1938 to 1950 and punctuated by short reversal episodes during the Great Depression and

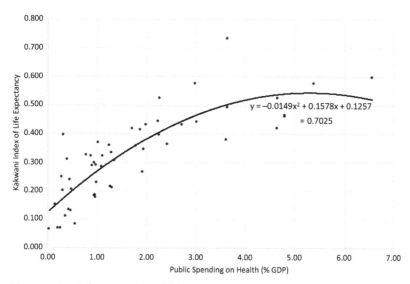

Figure 5.11 Kakwani index of life expectancy and public spending on health (% GDP) in six Latin American countries, 1900–2010.
Note: Countries considered are Argentina, Chile, Colombia, Costa Rica, Peru, and Uruguay.
Source: Public spending, Arroyo Abad and Lindert (2017); Kakwani index of schooling, see the text.

the early 1950s. Falling behind in the 1960s was followed by a weak recovery in the 1970s. Catching up resumed strongly in the 1980s and continued at a slower pace thereafter (Figure 5.12, continuous line).

It is worth stressing how different Latin America's position is relative to the OECD in terms of human development and in terms of GDP per head. While catching up in terms of AHD, Latin America fell behind in per capita income terms in the 1950s and especially during 1980–2005 (Figure 5.12, dotted line). In fact, while AHD and GDP per head represented 41 per cent and 42 per cent, respectively, of the OECD average in 1938, AHD jumped to represent 64 per cent in 2015 and per capita GDP fell to 29 per cent in 2015.

Why such a different relative performance? A glance at Figure 5.13 shows schooling caught up slowly but steadily until the 1950s and more vigorously from 1980 onwards. Starting from a mere 16 per cent of the OECD level in 1870, schooling in Latin America reached 45 per cent in 2015. Life expectancy caught up gradually between 1900 and the early 1990s, except for a major spurt from 1938 to 1950, although

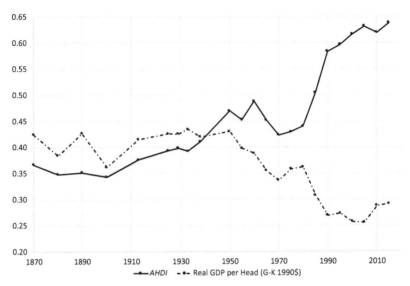

Figure 5.12 Relative AHD and real GDP per head in Latin America (*OECD*=1).
Sources: See the text and Table 5.1 and Chapter 4, Table 4.3.

it declined slightly thereafter. Thus, life expectancy moved up from below one-third of the *OECD* average in 1870 to above two-thirds in 2015. Civil and political liberties fell behind rather than catching up until 1980, with a dramatic contraction during the 1960s. However, the trend reverted after 1980 and distances shortened strongly thereafter. As a result, the level of freedoms in Latin America improved from about half the *OECD* figure in 1870 to 70 per cent in 2015.

But how much did each dimension contribute to AHD gains? The *AHDI* multiplicative structure facilitates a breakdown of AHD catch-up into the contributions of its dimensions, namely, a quarter of each dimension's differential growth between Latin America and the *OECD* (See Chapter 2, equation 2.1). Education appears as the main driving force behind Latin America's catching up over time, accounting for nearly half of the latter, closely followed by life expectancy, together amounting together to more than 80 per cent of AHD relative gains (Table 5.2). A closer look reveals that schooling was the main contributor to AHD catching up during the Interwar period, and life expectancy made a substantial contribution in the 'long' decade leading up to World War I, and from 1938–1950. Civil and political liberties led

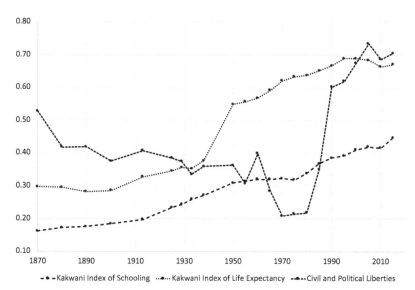

Figure 5.13 Relative AHD non-income dimensions in Latin America (*OECD*=1).
Sources: See the text and Table 5.1 and Chapter 4, Table 4.3.

catching up during the last two decades of the twentieth century, the 1980s in particular, but were also responsible for AHD falling behind before 1900 and during the 1960s. Nation-building lies behind schooling's contribution to catching up in the early twentieth century. Longevity gains slowed down as the early-life, *first* health transition spread, and in so far as Latin America was absent in the *second* health transition, did not play a part in the late twentieth-century catching up.

5.6 A Closer Look at Performance by Country

Let us begin by looking at the country ranking in terms of human development (Table 5.3). In the 12-country sample up to 1900, the Southern Cone countries, Argentina, Chile, and Uruguay, composed the top quartile, while Nicaragua, Bolivia, and Mexico, and, occasionally, Ecuador and Venezuela, occupied the bottom quartile. In the interwar years, a larger 17-country sample confirms the supremacy of Uruguay and Argentina plus Costa Rica, with Chile and Cuba completing the top quartile, while Central American countries (Guatemala, Nicaragua, El Salvador) and Venezuela constituted the bottom

Table 5.2. *AHD catching up in Latin America: dimensions'*
contribution (%)

	Kakwani index of schooling	Kakwani index of life expectancy	UNDP index of income	Liberal democracy index	AHDI
1870–1880	0.2	0.0	–0.1	–0.6	–0.5
1880–1890	0.1	–0.1	0.2	0.0	0.1
1890–1900	0.1	0.0	–0.1	–0.3	–0.2
1900–1913	0.1	0.3	0.1	0.2	0.7
1913–1929	0.3	0.1	0.0	–0.1	0.4
1929–1938	0.3	0.2	0.0	–0.1	0.4
1938–1950	0.3	0.8	0.0	0.0	1.1
1950–1960	0.1	0.1	0.0	0.2	0.4
1960–1970	0.0	0.2	0.0	–1.6	–1.4
1970–1980	0.1	0.1	0.1	0.1	0.4
1980–1990	0.3	0.1	–0.2	2.6	2.8
1990–2000	0.2	0.1	0.0	0.3	0.5
2000–2010	0.0	–0.1	0.1	0.0	0.1
2010–2015	0.4	0.1	0.0	0.1	0.6
1870–2015	0.2	0.1	0.0	0.0	0.4

quartile. From 1950 onwards, the coverage rises to 30 countries. The English-speaking Caribbean is well represented in the first quartile and the Southern Cone too: Uruguay (until 1970 and, again, from 1985), Argentina (on and off, falling off in 1955, 1970, and 1980), and Chile (but for 1975–1985), which has been the top country since 1995. Costa Rica, a Central American country, completed the top group. In the lowest quartile, the remaining Central American republics (El Salvador, Guatemala, Honduras, and Nicaragua) and Haiti dominate, with the occasional addition of Guyana, Bolivia, and Peru, plus Cuba, since 1985, and Venezuela, from 2005 onwards.

The contrast between the *AHDI* ranking and its dimensions is most informative (Table 5.4). For example, in the late nineteenth and first third of the twentieth centuries, Jamaica joined the top quartile in terms of life expectancy but belonged to the bottom quartile in terms of per capita income. The contrast is accentuated after 1950. Venezuela, a country in the first quartile in terms of GDP per head,

Table 5.3. AHD ranking of Latin American countries

1870		1880		1890		1900	
Uruguay	0.148	Uruguay	0.143	Uruguay	0.169	Uruguay	0.190
Argentina	0.124	Argentina	0.131	Argentina	0.149	Argentina	0.151
Chile	0.081	Chile	0.086	Chile	0.106	Chile	0.119
Jamaica	0.064	Colombia	0.073	Jamaica	0.095	Jamaica	0.113
Colombia	0.064	Jamaica	0.072	Cuba	0.082	Cuba	0.091
Cuba	0.062	Cuba	0.068	Colombia	0.075	Ecuador	0.084
Brazil	0.061	Brazil	0.064	Venezuela	0.071	Brazil	0.073
Venezuela	0.056	Venezuela	0.060	Ecuador	0.068	Colombia	0.069
Mexico	0.055	Ecuador	0.059	Brazil	0.065	Bolivia	0.068
Peru	0.048	Mexico	0.056	Mexico	0.062	Venezuela	0.064
Ecuador	0.046	Bolivia	0.054	Bolivia	0.060	Mexico	0.061
Bolivia	0.041	Peru	0.041	Peru	0.058	Peru	0.058

1913		1929		1938	
Uruguay	0.203	Uruguay	0.264	Uruguay	0.257
Argentina	0.188	Argentina	0.250	Argentina	0.241
Chile	0.136	Costa Rica	0.161	Chile	0.209
Costa Rica	0.134	Cuba	0.158	Costa Rica	0.183
Cuba	0.134	Chile	0.145	Cuba	0.183
Jamaica	0.123	Jamaica	0.142	Jamaica	0.157

Table 5.3. (cont.)

1913		1929		1938	
Colombia	0.102	Colombia	0.137	Colombia	0.154
Bolivia	0.089	Bolivia	0.114	Bolivia	0.117
Ecuador	0.087	Brazil	0.099	Venezuela	0.117
Brazil	0.084	Ecuador	0.099	Mexico	0.114
Honduras	0.079	Mexico	0.094	Ecuador	0.099
El Salvador	0.075	*Honduras*	0.090	Peru	0.099
Venezuela	0.070	Peru	0.088	Brazil	0.094
Peru	0.069	*El Salvador*	0.082	*Honduras*	0.088
Mexico	0.066	Venezuela	0.074	*El Salvador*	0.076
Nicaragua	0.059	*Nicaragua*	0.070	*Nicaragua*	0.074
Guatemala	0.059	*Guatemala*	0.065	*Guatemala*	0.072

1950		1960		1970		1980	
Uruguay	0.367	Uruguay	0.393	Barbados	0.433	Barbados	0.470
Bahamas, The	0.304	Bahamas, The	0.367	Bahamas, The	0.409	Trinidad-Tobago	0.451
Trinidad-Tobago	0.282	Trinidad-Tobago	0.347	Trinidad-Tobago	0.402	Bahamas, The	0.434
Argentina	0.277	Barbados	0.347	Uruguay	0.367	*Costa Rica*	0.411
Chile	0.274	Argentina	0.338	Venezuela	0.363	Venezuela	0.404
Belize	0.271	Belize	0.321	St. Kitts and Nevis	0.360	St. Kitts and Nevis	0.392
Suriname	0.262	Chile	0.311	Chile	0.357	St. Vincent & Grenadines	0.389

Costa Rica	0.256	St. Kitts and Nevis	0.311	St. Vincent & Grenadines	0.353	Belize	0.386
Barbados	0.252	*Costa Rica*	0.309	Jamaica	0.343	Jamaica	0.376
Cuba	0.245	Venezuela	0.308	Belize	0.342	St. Lucia	0.347
St. Kitts and Nevis	0.228	St. Vincent & Grenadines	0.302	*Costa Rica*	0.340	Ecuador	0.344
St. Vincent & Grenadines	0.215	Jamaica	0.300	Suriname	0.315	Colombia	0.297
Jamaica	0.203	Suriname	0.290	St. Lucia	0.296	Suriname	0.274
Panama	0.202	Panama	0.246	Colombia	0.256	Dominican R	0.262
Guyana	0.200	St. Lucia	0.245	Guyana	0.255	Guyana	0.260
Brazil	0.188	Guyana	0.234	Argentina	0.254	*Mexico*	0.257
St. Lucia	0.185	Colombia	0.232	Panama	0.212	Panama	0.250
Ecuador	0.183	Brazil	0.219	*Mexico*	0.212	Argentina	0.239
Paraguay	0.158	Ecuador	0.213	Ecuador	0.196	Brazil	0.239
Venezuela	0.150	Peru	0.205	Brazil	0.177	Chile	0.238
Mexico	0.149	Mexico	0.185	Dominican R	0.173	Uruguay	0.237
Guatemala	0.147	Cuba	0.166	Cuba	0.170	Peru	0.221
Colombia	0.142	Bolivia	0.153	Paraguay	0.168	Cuba	0.203
Bolivia	0.134	Paraguay	0.142	Peru	0.151	Paraguay	0.193
Honduras	0.123	*Honduras*	0.127	*El Salvador*	0.150	*Nicaragua*	0.179

Table 5.3. (*cont.*)

Peru	0.113	*El Salvador*	0.125	*Honduras*	0.146	*Honduras*	0.174
El Salvador	0.110	*Guatemala*	0.119	*Guatemala*	0.136	*Guatemala*	0.154
Dominican R	0.096	Dominican R	0.116	*Nicaragua*	0.129	**Bolivia**	0.152
Nicaragua	0.091	*Nicaragua*	0.111	**Bolivia**	0.126	*El Salvador*	0.141
haiti	0.080	haiti	0.080	haiti	0.088	haiti	0.106

1990		2005		2015	
Barbados	0.510	Chile	0.624	Chile	0.662
Uruguay	0.491	Bahamas, The	0.574	Bahamas, The	0.592
Chile	0.489	Barbados	0.549	*Costa Rica*	0.581
Bahamas, The	0.488	Belize	0.547	Barbados	0.564
Trinidad-Tobago	0.482	*Costa Rica*	0.546	Panama	0.560
Costa Rica	0.462	Uruguay	0.540	Uruguay	0.559
Argentina	0.453	Argentina	0.514	Trinidad-Tobago	0.554
St. Vincent & Grenadines	0.437	Trinidad-Tobago	0.505	Argentina	0.545
Belize	0.437	Panama	0.501	Jamaica	0.526
St. Kitts and Nevis	0.436	St. Kitts and Nevis	0.487	Belize	0.519
Jamaica	0.419	**Peru**	0.482	St. Lucia	0.507
St. Lucia	0.417	Mexico	0.482	St. Kitts and Nevis	0.505
Brazil	0.413	**Brazil**	0.481	**Peru**	0.504
Venezuela	0.412	St. Vincent & Grenadines	0.475	**Brazil**	0.501
Ecuador	0.396	Jamaica	0.467	St. Vincent & Grenadines	0.491

Table 5.3. (cont.)

1990		2005		2015	
Panama	0.372	St. Lucia	0.465	Mexico	0.476
Peru	0.349	Ecuador	0.451	Suriname	0.458
Bolivia	0.329	Suriname	0.414	Colombia	0.447
Colombia	0.328	Paraguay	0.393	Paraguay	0.422
Mexico	0.324	Bolivia	0.388	Ecuador	0.411
Paraguay	0.302	Colombia	0.381	Bolivia	0.394
Suriname	0.295	Dominican R	0.368	Dominican R	0.393
Nicaragua	0.290	Guyana	0.364	El Salvador	0.387
Dominican R	0.284	Nicaragua	0.362	Guyana	0.385
Guyana	0.282	Venezuela	0.344	Guatemala	0.382
Honduras	0.266	El Salvador	0.340	Cuba	0.367
Guatemala	0.242	Guatemala	0.330	Venezuela	0.348
Cuba	0.228	Honduras	0.324	Honduras	0.318
El Salvador	0.211	Cuba	0.281	Nicaragua	0.289
haiti	0.147	haiti	0.169	haiti	0.242

Sources: See the text.

Note: coverage, **bold**, 1870–2015; ***bold italics***, 1913–2015; small caps, 1950–2015.

Table 5.4 *AHD and its dimensions ranking of Latin American countries*

1870

AHDI		Schooling		Life expectancy		Civil and political liberties		Income	
Uruguay	0.148	Uruguay	0.042	Uruguay	0.089	Argentina	0.279	Uruguay	2107
Argentina	0.124	Argentina	0.039	Jamaica	0.053	Uruguay	0.264	Argentina	1560
Chile	0.081	Venezuela	0.028	Argentina	0.048	Chile	0.223	Chile	1266
Jamaica	0.064	Chile	0.024	Cuba	0.032	Colombia	0.154	Cuba	1186
Colombia	0.064	Ecuador	0.022	Brazil	0.028	Brazil	0.131	Peru	1137
Cuba	0.062	Cuba	0.021	Colombia	0.021	Peru	0.120	Bolivia	858
Brazil	0.061	Colombia	0.017	Bolivia	0.019	Mexico	0.116	Brazil	738
Venezuela	0.056	Mexico	0.014	Chile	0.019	Jamaica	0.093	Colombia	663
Mexico	0.055	Jamaica	0.013	Ecuador	0.019	Venezuela	0.067	Mexico	604
Peru	0.048	Brazil	0.012	Mexico	0.019	Cuba	0.055	Jamaica	513
Ecuador	0.046	Bolivia	0.008	Peru	0.019	Bolivia	0.052	Venezuela	504
Bolivia	0.041	Peru	0.007	Venezuela	0.019	Ecuador	0.044	Ecuador	414

1900

AHDI		Schooling		Life expectancy		Civil and political liberties		Income	
Uruguay	0.190	Uruguay	0.059	Uruguay	0.142	Uruguay	0.308	Argentina	2877
Argentina	0.151	Argentina	0.056	Argentina	0.083	Chile	0.242	Uruguay	2144
Chile	0.119	Chile	0.045	Jamaica	0.077	Argentina	0.205	Chile	2110

Jamaica	0.113	Ecuador	0.045	Cuba	0.050	Ecuador	0.198	Cuba	1458
Cuba	0.091	Jamaica	0.043	Chile	0.037	Jamaica	0.174	Mexico	1073
Ecuador	0.084	Venezuela	0.036	Brazil	0.036	Peru	0.164	Bolivia	993
Brazil	0.073	Colombia	0.033	Colombia	0.036	Brazil	0.133	Peru	785
Colombia	0.069	Bolivia	0.032	Venezuela	0.031	Cuba	0.103	Venezuela	728
Bolivia	0.068	Cuba	0.031	Bolivia	0.019	Bolivia	0.092	Brazil	700
Venezuela	0.064	Mexico	0.028	Mexico	0.019	Mexico	0.068	Colombia	630
Mexico	0.061	Brazil	0.019	Ecuador	0.019	Colombia	0.065	Ecuador	598
Peru	0.058	Peru	0.012	Peru	0.019	Venezuela	0.045	Jamaica	562

1929

AHDI		Schooling		Life expectancy		Civil and political liberties		Income	
Uruguay	0.264	Chile	0.111	Uruguay	0.184	Uruguay	0.477	Argentina	4558
Argentina	0.250	Argentina	0.105	Argentina	0.156	Argentina	0.387	Uruguay	3716
Costa Rica	0.161	Uruguay	0.094	Jamaica	0.105	*Costa Rica*	0.250	Chile	3540
Cuba	0.158	Colombia	0.076	Cuba	0.098	Colombia	0.186	Venezuela	3014
Chile	0.145	Bolivia	0.074	*Costa Rica*	0.095	Jamaica	0.181	Cuba	2096
Jamaica	0.142	Cuba	0.072	Chile	0.064	Cuba	0.177	Peru	2050
Colombia	0.137	Jamaica	0.069	Bolivia	0.058	Brazil	0.135	Bolivia	1648
Bolivia	0.114	*Costa Rica*	0.064	Mexico	0.056	Ecuador	0.120	*Nicaragua*	1632
Brazil	0.099	Ecuador	0.060	*Honduras*	0.056	Chile	0.108	Colombia	1589
Ecuador	0.099	Peru	0.044	Colombia	0.056	*El Salvador*	0.097	*Guatemala*	1566
Mexico	0.094	Venezuela	0.043	Brazil	0.056	Bolivia	0.088	*Costa Rica*	1555

Table 5.4 (*cont.*)

1929

AHDI		Schooling		Life expectancy		Civil and political liberties		Income	
Peru	0.088	Honduras	0.041	Peru	0.052	Mexico	0.081	Honduras	1539
Honduras	0.090	Mexico	0.039	Venezuela	0.045	Guatemala	0.069	Mexico	1455
El Salvador	0.082	El Salvador	0.035	Ecuador	0.035	Peru	0.066	Brazil	1171
Venezuela	0.074	Nicaragua	0.033	El Salvador	0.034	Honduras	0.065	El Salvador	1165
Nicaragua	0.070	Brazil	0.033	Nicaragua	0.028	Nicaragua	0.055	Ecuador	1060
Guatemala	0.065	Guatemala	0.031	Guatemala	0.019	Venezuela	0.027	Jamaica	677

1950

AHDI		Schooling		Life expectancy		Civil and political liberties		Income	
Uruguay	0.367	Belize	0.243	Uruguay	0.298	Uruguay	0.671	Bahamas, The	10800
Bahamas, The	0.304	Bahamas, The	0.211	Paraguay	0.255	Costa Rica	0.483	Venezuela	5310
Trinidad-Tobago	0.282	Barbados	0.183	Argentina	0.254	Suriname	0.439	Argentina	5204
Argentina	0.277	Trinidad-Tobago	0.175	Bahamas, The	0.227	Chile	0.331	Uruguay	4501
Chile	0.274	Argentina	0.165	Cuba	0.224	Cuba	0.304	trinidad-tobago	3790

Belize	0.271	Chile	0.157	Trinidad-Tobago	0.220	Brazil	0.287	Chile	3755
Suriname	0.262	St. Vincent & Gr	0.154	Belize	0.208	Trinidad-Tobago	0.277	Cuba	2639
Costa Rica	0.256	St. Kitts and Nevis	0.149	Costa Rica	0.204	Bahamas, The	0.235	Peru	2289
Barbados	0.252	Uruguay	0.146	Barbados	0.204	Belize	0.235	Mexico	2283
Cuba	0.245	Guyana	0.129	Jamaica	0.201	Jamaica	0.235	Colombia	2161
St. Kitts and Nevis	0.228	Suriname	0.126	Guatemala	0.195	Guatemala	0.222	Barbados	2123
St. Vincent & Gr	0.215	Paraguay	0.106	Suriname	0.193	Barbados	0.220	Bolivia	2045
Jamaica	0.203	Cuba	0.099	Panama	0.188	St. Kitts and Nevis	0.220	Guatemala	1955
Panama	0.202	Ecuador	0.095	Venezuela	0.187	St. Lucia	0.220	Costa Rica	1930
Guyana	0.200	Panama	0.095	Chile	0.184	St. Vincent & Gr	0.220	Panama	1854
Brazil	0.188	Colombia	0.095	St. Lucia	0.178	Argentina	0.219	El Salvador	1739
St. Lucia	0.185	Bolivia	0.091	Guyana	0.165	Guyana	0.197	Belize	1667
Ecuador	0.183	St. Lucia	0.090	St. Vincent & Gr	0.156	Panama	0.197	Ecuador	1616
Paraguay	0.158	Costa Rica	0.090	Brazil	0.155	Ecuador	0.189	Nicaragua	1564
Venezuela	0.150	Jamaica	0.086	Mexico	0.153	Honduras	0.128	Brazil	1544
Mexico	0.149	Peru	0.070	Colombia	0.152	Mexico	0.092	Suriname	1514
Guatemala	0.147	Mexico	0.069	Ecuador	0.138	Bolivia	0.081	Paraguay	1419
Colombia	0.142	Venezuela	0.068	Dominican R	0.122	El Salvador	0.064	St. Kitts and Nevis	1386

167

Table 5.4 (*cont.*)

1950

AHDI		Schooling		Life expectancy		Civil and political liberties		Income	
Bolivia	0.134	Brazil	0.063	*El Salvador*	0.117	**Venezuela**	0.061	*Honduras*	1353
Honduras	0.123	Dominican R	0.053	Peru	0.110	Haiti	0.060	Jamaica	1283
Peru	0.113	*Nicaragua*	0.047	*Nicaragua*	0.101	**Colombia**	0.057	St. Vincent & Gr	1197
El Salvador	0.110	*Guatemala*	0.044	*Guatemala*	0.099	Paraguay	0.054	Haiti	1126
Dominican R	0.096	*Honduras*	0.044	*Honduras*	0.098	Peru	0.042	Guyana	1079
Nicaragua	0.091	*El Salvador*	0.042	Bolivia	0.090	Dominican R	0.034	Dominican R	1071
Haiti	0.080	Haiti	0.023	Haiti	0.076	*Nicaragua*	0.033	St. Lucia	772

1960

AHDI		Schooling		Life expectancy		Civil and political liberties		Income	
Uruguay	0.393	Belize	0.255	Uruguay	0.321	Uruguay	0.697	Bahamas, The	8516
Bahamas, The	0.367	Bahamas, The	0.245	Argentina	0.284	*Costa Rica*	0.658	Venezuela	7601
Trinidad-Tobago	0.347	Trinidad-Tobago	0.213	Barbados	0.277	Venezuela	0.560	Trinidad-Tobago	6448
Barbados	0.347	Barbados	0.210	Jamaica	0.275	Suriname	0.461	Argentina	5803
Argentina	0.338	Argentina	0.196	Cuba	0.273	Barbados	0.437	Uruguay	4849

Belize	0.321	St. Vincent & Gr	0.186	Paraguay	0.270	St. Kitts and Nevis	0.437	Chile	4253
Chile	0.311	St. Kitts and Nevis	0.179	Trinidad-Tobago	0.267	St. Lucia	0.437	Barbados	3335
St. Kitts and Nevis	0.311	Chile	0.179	Bahamas, The	0.263	St. Vincent & Gr	0.437	Peru	3058
Costa Rica	0.309	Uruguay	0.169	Costa Rica	0.247	Chile	0.409	Mexico	3021
Venezuela	0.308	Guyana	0.152	Belize	0.246	Bahamas, The	0.391	Cuba	3003
St. Vincent & Gr	0.302	Suriname	0.150	Panama	0.238	Belize	0.391	Costa Rica	2783
Jamaica	0.300	Jamaica	0.143	St. Kitts and Nevis	0.229	Jamaica	0.391	Jamaica	2567
Suriname	0.290	Panama	0.139	Venezuela	0.227	Trinidad-Tobago	0.379	Colombia	2539
Panama	0.246	Ecuador	0.125	Suriname	0.227	Argentina	0.356	St. Kitts and Nevis	2477
St. Lucia	0.245	Paraguay	0.118	St. Vincent & Gr	0.220	Brazil	0.296	Panama	2272
Guyana	0.234	Cuba	0.111	Chile	0.211	Peru	0.276	Brazil	2199
Colombia	0.232	Colombia	0.108	Mexico	0.205	Colombia	0.258	Guatemala	2158
Brazil	0.219	St. Lucia	0.107	Colombia	0.200	Guyana	0.224	Ecuador	2026
Ecuador	0.213	Costa Rica	0.104	St. Lucia	0.200	Panama	0.219	El Salvador	2015
Peru	0.205	Venezuela	0.100	Guyana	0.196	Ecuador	0.194	Nicaragua	1916
Mexico	0.185	Bolivia	0.100	Brazil	0.184	Bolivia	0.115	St. Vincent & Gr	1766

Table 5.4 (cont.)

1960

AHDI		Schooling		Life expectancy		Civil and political liberties		Income	
Cuba	0.166	Mexico	0.096	Ecuador	0.173	Mexico	0.107	Bolivia	1721
Bolivia	0.153	Peru	0.086	Dominican R	0.163	Honduras	0.096	Suriname	1618
Paraguay	0.142	Brazil	0.085	El Salvador	0.154	Guatemala	0.069	Guyana	1600
Honduras	0.127	Dominican R	0.069	Peru	0.135	El Salvador	0.061	Paraguay	1463
El Salvador	0.125	Nicaragua	0.061	Nicaragua	0.131	Cuba	0.046	Belize	1413
Guatemala	0.119	El Salvador	0.053	Honduras	0.126	Nicaragua	0.040	Honduras	1359
Dominican R	0.116	Honduras	0.050	Guatemala	0.122	Dominican R	0.038	Dominican R	1304
Nicaragua	0.111	Guatemala	0.048	Bolivia	0.104	Haiti	0.037	Haiti	1109
Haiti	0.080	Haiti	0.028	Haiti	0.101	Paraguay	0.029	St. Lucia	1061

1990

AHDI		Schooling		Life expectancy		Civil and political liberties		Income	
Barbados	0.510	Bahamas, The	0.404	Costa Rica	0.461	Costa Rica	0.836	Bahamas, The	15354
Uruguay	0.491	Trinidad-Tobago	0.338	Barbados	0.440	Uruguay	0.812	Trinidad-Tobago	8853
Chile	0.489	Chile	0.336	Cuba	0.440	Brazil	0.717	Venezuela	8313
Bahamas, The	0.488	Barbados	0.335	Chile	0.432	Venezuela	0.654	Barbados	8152

Trinidad-Tobago	0.482	Belize	0.324	Uruguay	0.396	Trinidad-Tobago	0.653	Uruguay	6465
Costa Rica	0.462	St. Vincent & Gr	0.287	Belize	0.389	Barbados	0.640	Argentina	6433
Argentina	0.453	Jamaica	0.287	Panama	0.389	St. Kitts and Nevis	0.640	Chile	6401
St. Vincent & Gr	0.437	Panama	0.280	Argentina	0.378	St. Lucia	0.640	Mexico	6085
Belize	0.437	St. Kitts and Nevis	0.276	St. Lucia	0.372	St. Vincent & Gr	0.640	St. Kitts and Nevis	5683
St. Kitts and Nevis	0.436	Argentina	0.271	Jamaica	0.371	Argentina	0.609	Brazil	4920
Jamaica	0.419	Uruguay	0.267	Venezuela	0.370	Chile	0.582	Colombia	4826
St. Lucia	0.417	Cuba	0.259	Mexico	0.364	Ecuador	0.518	Costa Rica	4747
Brazil	0.413	Guyana	0.251	Bahamas, The	0.351	Bahamas, The	0.489	Cuba	4728
Venezuela	0.412	Peru	0.242	St. Vincent & Gr	0.340	Belize	0.489	Panama	4466
Ecuador	0.396	Ecuador	0.239	Trinidad-Tobago	0.335	Jamaica	0.489	Ecuador	3903
Panama	0.372	Bolivia	0.234	Ecuador	0.334	Bolivia	0.458	Belize	3848
Peru	0.349	Mexico	0.228	Colombia	0.325	Peru	0.383	Jamaica	3786

Table 5.4 (*cont.*)

1990

AHDI		Schooling		Life expectancy		Civil and political liberties		Income	
Bolivia	0.329	Suriname	0.226	Paraguay	0.322	*Nicaragua*	0.363	St. Vincent & Gr	3664
Colombia	0.328	St. Lucia	0.224	Dominican R	0.316	Colombia	0.302	Paraguay	3281
Mexico	0.324	Brazil	0.216	Suriname	0.312	Panama	0.285	St. Lucia	3264
Paraguay	0.302	Paraguay	0.192	St. Kitts and Nevis	0.312	Dominican R	0.262	*Guatemala*	3240
Suriname	0.295	*Costa Rica*	0.189	*Honduras*	0.299	*Honduras*	0.245	Peru	3008
Nicaragua	0.290	Colombia	0.188	Brazil	0.298	Paraguay	0.237	Suriname	2770
Dominican R	0.284	Venezuela	0.167	*El Salvador*	0.294	Guyana	0.226	Dominican R	2471
Guyana	0.282	*Nicaragua*	0.165	Peru	0.289	*Guatemala*	0.209	Bolivia	2197
Honduras	0.266	Dominican R	0.152	*Nicaragua*	0.272	Suriname	0.199	*El Salvador*	2119
Guatemala	0.242	El Salvador	0.144	*Guatemala*	0.251	Mexico	0.198	*Honduras*	1857
Cuba	0.228	Honduras	0.144	Guyana	0.250	*El Salvador*	0.094	Guyana	1562
El Salvador	0.211	Guatemala	0.115	Bolivia	0.218	Haiti	0.080	*Nicaragua*	1437
Haiti	0.147	Haiti	0.083	Haiti	0.185	Cuba	0.038	Haiti	1005

AHDI		Schooling		Life expectancy		Civil and political liberties		Y Income	
Chile	0.662	Cuba	0.565	Chile	0.733	Costa Rica	0.818	Trinidad-Tobago	22632
Bahamas, The	0.592	Trinidad-Tobago	0.477	Costa Rica	0.597	Chile	0.807	Chile	15288
Costa Rica	0.581	Bahamas, The	0.476	Cuba	0.595	Uruguay	0.770	Bahamas, The	13666
Barbados	0.564	Belize	0.442	Panama	0.526	Brazil	0.769	Uruguay	13033
Panama	0.560	Barbados	0.441	Uruguay	0.513	Bahamas, The	0.699	Panama	11790
Uruguay	0.559	Chile	0.398	Mexico	0.501	Belize	0.699	Argentina	10915
Trinidad-Tobago	0.554	Panama	0.395	Argentina	0.486	Jamaica	0.699	St. Kitts and Nevis	10709
Argentina	0.545	Argentina	0.395	Ecuador	0.477	Suriname	0.669	Barbados	9481
Jamaica	0.526	Jamaica	0.380	Jamaica	0.469	Barbados	0.664	Venezuela	9091
Belize	0.519	Venezuela	0.364	Barbados	0.468	St. Kitts and Nevis	0.664	Costa Rica	8944
St. Lucia	0.507	St. Lucia	0.360	Bahamas, The	0.462	St. Lucia	0.664	Colombia	8365
St. Kitts and Nevis	0.505	Peru	0.339	Nicaragua	0.454	St. Vincent & Gr	0.664	Mexico	7807
Peru	0.504	Costa Rica	0.321	St. Lucia	0.453	Peru	0.629	Cuba	7233
Brazil	0.501	St. Vincent & Gr	0.315	Peru	0.444	Trinidad-Tobago	0.622	Brazil	6990
St. Vincent & Gr	0.491	Uruguay	0.313	Brazil	0.442	Panama	0.611	St. Vincent & Gr	6876
Mexico	0.476	Mexico	0.312	Venezuela	0.434	Argentina	0.602	Peru	6711
Suriname	0.458	Guyana	0.304	Colombia	0.431	Colombia	0.500	Dominican R	6258

Table 5.4 (*cont.*)

AHDI		Schooling		Life expectancy		Civil and political liberties		Y Income	
Colombia	0.447	St. Kitts and Nevis	0.303	St. Kitts and Nevis	0.425	Mexico	0.465	Belize	6109
Paraguay	0.422	Suriname	0.298	**Dominican R**	0.418	***El Salvador***	0.441	**Ecuador**	5629
Ecuador	0.411	**Ecuador**	0.296	***Honduras***	0.411	***Guatemala***	0.441	Paraguay	4649
Bolivia	0.394	**Bolivia**	0.292	***El Salvador***	0.410	Paraguay	0.433	***Guatemala***	4544
Dominican R	0.393	Paraguay	0.289	St. Vincent & Gr	0.406	**Bolivia**	0.418	Jamaica	4395
El Salvador	0.387	**Brazil**	0.269	Paraguay	0.405	Guyana	0.407	St. Lucia	4223
Guyana	0.385	**Dominican R**	0.265	***Guatemala***	0.387	Dominican R	0.320	Suriname	3866
Guatemala	0.382	Colombia	0.259	Suriname	0.373	**Bolivia**	0.310	**Bolivia**	3832
Cuba	0.367	***Nicaragua***	0.212	Trinidad-Tobago	0.360	Ecuador	0.251	Guyana	3730
Venezuela	0.348	***El Salvador***	0.211	Belize	0.352	Haiti	0.235	***El Salvador***	3700
Honduras	0.318	***Guatemala***	0.201	**Bolivia**	0.332	***Honduras***	0.141	***Honduras***	2771
Nicaragua	0.289	***Honduras***	0.196	Guyana	0.301	***Nicaragua***	0.126	***Nicaragua***	2373
Haiti	0.242	Haiti	0.156	Haiti	0.261	Cuba	0.078	Haiti	790

Sources: See the text.

Note: coverage, **bold**, 1870–2015; ***bold italics***, 1913–2015; small caps, 1950–2015.

often appears in the fourth quartile in terms of education. Jamaica remains an outlier, belonging to the first quartile in terms of longevity but frequenting the lowest quartile in terms of average incomes. Cuba is, perhaps, the most significant outlier. In 1950, the country featured in the first quartile in every dimension but schooling. However, after the 1959 Revolution, while retaining a top position in terms of life expectancy, a circumstance that dates back to the pre-independence era, Cuba dropped to the lowest quartile in terms of civil and political liberties. As a result, Cuba dropped from the 10th position in 1950 to 25th in 2015 in terms of human development, confirming Devereux's (2021) findings. Thus, it can be concluded that there is a low and declining rank correlation between dimensions. For example, the coefficient of correlation between country rankings in life expectancy and in civil and political rights fell from 0.63 in 1950 to 0.26 in 2015.

These findings raise the question, what were the dimensions that actually drove changes in human development? Let us begin with the Southern Cone countries that belong to the first quartile throughout the entire time span. AHD improved until the mid-1960s in Argentina and Uruguay and until the early 1970s in Chile, accelerating during the 1930s and 1940s, and suffering reversal episodes during the Great Depression in Uruguay and in Argentina, where this also occurred in the early 1950s. Later, a period of dramatic decline, which in Argentina and Uruguay lasted until the mid-1980s and in Chile until 1990, was followed by a strong recovery, in which Chile achieved the highest level ever in Latin America.

A breakdown of the *AHDI* rate of change within each dimension's contribution is enlightening. In the case of Argentina, civil and political liberties represent the most volatile dimension that largely conditioned AHD performance, rising in the first quarter of the twentieth century and declining sharply until the mid-1950s, with a seesaw evolution over the next three decades, before a major improvement from the mid-1980s onwards. Civil and political rights made the largest contribution to AHD gains between the mid-1950s and mid-1960s and in the 1980s, but also predominated during its contraction in the 1930s and the late 1960s and 1970s. Other non-income dimensions also contributed to AHD gains. Schooling drove AHD progress in the interwar years, with nation-building as a major incentive (Botana and Gallo, 1997), and from 2000 onwards. Life expectancy led AHD growth in the 1880s, the 'long' decade prior to World War I, and the 1940s, as a result of the epidemiological transition, matching the increase in height during the 1930s but at odds with its stagnation prior to World War II (Salvatore, 2019). If we now look at Argentine's AHD position relative to the OECD, catching-up episodes took place in the first quarter of the twentieth century, the late 1950s, and the 1980s, largely fuelled by civil and political rights, a dimension that was also responsible for falling behind episodes in the 1890s, 1930s, and 1940s, and during the late 1960s and 1970s, which largely offset previous achievements. Life expectancy also contributed to catching up from 1900–1913, while schooling prevented AHD from falling behind from 1929–1950 and led catching up in the new century.

In the case of Uruguay, AHD evolution is also affected by shifts in civil and political liberties, which made the largest contribution to human development gains in the 1920s, 1940s, and 1980s, but also to its contraction in the 1930s and the late 1960s and 1970s. Education contributed steadily over time to AHD advancement, and longevity did the same in the 1880s and 1940s. As in the case of Argentina, nation-building and the epidemiological transition were the ultimate drivers of schooling and life expectancy. Moderate catching up to the OECD was restricted to the 1880s, the 1920s, the 1940s, and, in particular the 1980s, driven by liberties, which also offset progress when they fell behind in the 1930s and during 1950–1980. Only from 1913 to 1950 did another dimension, schooling, play a part in reducing differences vis-à-vis the OECD.

The case of Chile confirms the profound impact of civil and political rights on AHD performance in the Southern Cone, particularly in the late twentieth century, altering an otherwise long-term progress across other AHD dimensions. Although significant changes in freedoms occurred prior to 1970 (contracting in the first third of the twentieth century and rising in the early 1960s), they did not reverse the AHD trend resulting from the evolution of other dimensions. However, in the 1970s and 1980s, the dramatic contraction in freedoms had an extremely detrimental effect upon the *AHDI*.

If we now turn to the specific contributions made by AHD dimensions to human development gains, it emerges that civil and political rights drove AHD progress in the 1930s, late 1950s, and the late 1980s and 1990s but, as in Argentina and Uruguay, also caused AHD to decline between the early 1970s and mid-1980s and partly offset AHD gains in the 1920s. Schooling was the driving force behind AHD during the 1880s and 1920s, and life expectancy during 1890–1913 and the 1940s, and since 2010. The improvement in longevity up to 1913 is not matched by the evolution of height, which stagnated, while, between the 1930s and 1960s, height increases associated with improvements in nutrition and health care and infrastructure (Llorca-Jaña et al., 2020, 2021) match gains in life expectancy at birth. The mismatch up to the early twentieth century may be due to preventive measures of disease transmission – a result of the diffusion of new medical knowledge – which reduced infant mortality, while undernutrition remained unaltered, as shown by the stagnation of adult height. Later, the improvement in the disease environment helped to increase infant survival and average height.[4] However, rising height inequality up to 1950 (Núñez and Pérez, 2015) reveals unequal access to health services that may have, in turn, prevented a larger increase in longevity. Chile was the Southern Cone country the caught up most with the OECD, starting from a much lower relative position (27%) in 1870 and reaching a higher one (82%). Although civil and political liberties drove the main episodes of catching up, in the 1930s and late 1980s and 1990s, they also played a leading role in Chile's falling behind during the 1920s and 1970s. However, other non-income dimensions also contributed. Education led catching up in the 1880s and helped mitigate falling behind in the 1920s, and longevity also contributed to catching up in the 1880s and drove it in the 1940s and from 2010 onwards. While the epidemiological transition explains life expectancy's contribution to AHD catching up in the 1940s, its vigorous post-2010 contribution confirms Chile's long-run improvement in health services (Brieba, 2018; Borreschio-Higa et al., 2019).

Apart from small English-speaking Caribbean countries (the Bahamas, Barbados, Trinidad-Tobago, and Belize), Costa Rica completes the successful experiences in Latin America. Unlike the Southern Cone countries, no major interruptions in civil and political liberties have taken place in Costa Rica, except for a major spurt between 1938 and 1955. A glance at the drivers of human development reveals the momentum provided by life expectancy until 1980, driving AHD growth during the interwar period and the 1960s, even though achievements in civil and political rights led AHD gains in the 1940s and 1950s. Schooling, having shared the leadership with longevity in the 1970s, predominated for the rest of the considered time span. Relative to the OECD, Costa Rica shortened distances during the last century, more intensively from 1929 to 1950, although the 1950s and 1970s and the post-2000 years were also phases of catching up. Longevity during the 1930s and 1970s, civil and political liberties in the 1940s and 1950s, and education as of 2000 made the largest contributions.

Along with Costa Rica, Cuba achieved a high level of multidimensional well-being largely unrelated to its economic progress. In 1938, AHD levels were identical in both countries, as were their liberties. In 1950, Costa Rica was slightly ahead of Cuba in AHD terms, mostly due to a higher level of civil and political rights. In Cuba, the deterioration of liberties in the 1950s reached a trough with the 1959 Revolution, which pushed human development down to a lower level, where it remained despite the fact that education and health continued to thrive. Improvements in life expectancy made a substantial contribution to AHD advancement in the 'long' decade prior to World War I, just after emancipation from Spain, second only to freedoms, but the main leap forward occurred during the 1940s, when life expectancy accounted for two-thirds of AHD growth. Schooling played the leading role in the 1920s. After the 1959 Revolution, gains in longevity mitigated the contraction in AHD from 1950 to 1970, and schooling became its main driver as of 1970. In terms of catching up to the OECD, freedoms contributed in the 1900s and 1930s, while longevity and education led the way in the 1940s and 1970s, respectively, and education largely offset falling behind resulting from a reduction in freedoms in the 1920s.

It is worthwhile comparing Jamaica with Cuba. Both Caribbean islands exhibited similar levels and tendencies until 1950, with Cuba slightly ahead. The evolution of their epidemiological transition was largely independent of their level of economic development (Diaz-Brisquets, 1981; Riley, 2005a). In Jamaica, life expectancy played a leading role in AHD progress during 1913 to 1950, as mortality declined sharply at a time of sluggish economic performance, which was also the case in Guyana (Mandle 1970). Their destinies diverged between 1950 and 1965, when a large gap emerged in Jamaica's favour, driven by schooling and liberties and, although the two countries resumed a similar trend, they never converged in levels. However, Cuba already enjoyed a comparatively high position at the time of independence from Spain (1898). Since the Revolution, there has been a further improvement in life expectancy, as a result of the success in combatting and eradicating infant mortality, in striking contrast with the country's sluggish economic performance and poor record in terms of civil and political rights.

The case of post-1959 Cuba presents, therefore, an extreme contrast between the relative success in schooling and life expectancy at birth and the failure to enlarge people's choices – the core of human development – with agency and freedom curtailed by the political regime. Restrictions of individual choice in Cuba – as collectivisation, forced industrialisation, and political repression exemplify – suggest that achievements in health and education could be, strictly speaking, depicted as 'basic needs' rather than as human development (Ivanov and Peleah 2010). In fact, achievements in health have been attributed to the coercive power of the socialist state (Mesa-Lago 2005; Devereux 2010; Berdine et al., 2018). The same caveat applies to other capitalist totalitarian regimes that curtailed freedom and agency across Latin America, but did not exhibit such an acute contrast between the behaviour of their dimensions.

If we now turn to countries persistently in the lower quartile, Nicaragua, in Central America, provides a good example. Low levels of schooling and civil and political rights, improvement of which was delayed until the 1970s and 1980s, respectively, appear responsible for Nicaragua's poor AHD performance. Life expectancy was the main AHD driver from 1913 to 1970, and freedoms in the 1980s and early 1990s. In terms of catching up to the *OECD*, life expectancy drove it from the 1920s to the 1940s, while civil and political rights made the largest contribution in the 1980s, but also accounted for its falling behind during 1900 to 1913 and from 2000 onwards, cancelling out any catching up in the 1940s.

Andean countries (with the exception of Chile) also belong to the lower part of AHD distribution over time, although Ecuador and Peru escaped this zone after the 1970s and 1980s, respectively. The case of Bolivia illustrates the contribution of life expectancy to AHD gains during the period 1900 to 1938, long before the diffusion of modern medical drugs, but at odds with height stagnation (Branisa et al., 2020) and, again, from 1970 to 1990. Civil and political liberties conditioned AHD evolution, decreasing from 1960 to the mid-1970s and rebounding in the 1980s. These results translate in terms of the position relative to the *OECD*, with liberties driving both catching up in the 1980s and lagging behind in the 1940s, 1960s, and early 1970s. The picture is completed with longevity contributing to catching up during the first quarter of the twentieth century.

In the case of Peru, schooling in the 1920s and life expectancy in the 1930s and 1940s led AHD gains as well as catching up to the *OECD*, which were, however, largely offset by falling behind in terms of civil and political liberties. Since the early 1950s, a seesaw evolution of political and civil liberties has driven AHD. Episodes of strong AHD gains and catching up to the OECD from the mid-1950s to the mid-1960s, and in the early 1980s and 2000s, alternated with dramatic contraction and falling behind in the late 1960s and early 1990s.

Ecuador followed a more stable AHD evolution than Peru. Nevertheless, dramatic changes in civil and political liberties conditioned AHD evolution. Civil and political rights provided the main contribution to AHD gains prior to 1900 and in the late 1970s, but were reduced in the interwar years and in the 1960s and early 1970s. Life expectancy drove AHD growth between 1914 and 1950, especially in the 1940s, and also became the leading force in the last two decades of the twentieth century, while schooling did so during the 1950s. Catching up to the OECD took place in the 1940s, led by longevity, and the 1970s, by liberties, while the drop in liberties accounted for falling behind in the interwar period and the 1960s.

Colombia, along with Mexico and Costa Rica, is a relatively stable country from a formal political perspective. However, political events also had a deep impact on the country's AHD, as was the case at the beginning and in the middle of the twentieth century, during a long-lasting civil war, *La Violencia* (1948–1958) (Booth, 1974; Palacios, 1995). Thus, the contraction in liberties from 1890–1900, in the late 1940s and early 1950s, and in the 1980s, and the subsequent recovery between 1900 and 1913, in the late 1950s, and the early 1990s, drove AHD. In addition, advances in schooling in the 1920s and 1980s, and life expectancy in the 1930s and, in particular, the 1940s, that were attributed to improvements in water supply and sewerage (Jaramillo-Echeverri et al. 2019), led AHD gains, though these were partly offset by the collapse of civil and political rights. The same pattern dominated by liberties is observed in catching up and falling behind with respect to the OECD, with the exception of the contributions of schooling and life expectancy in the 1920s and 1940s, respectively.

Countries falling from middle or top positions to the bottom also merit consideration. Venezuela is a good example. This country reached the top quartile in the third quarter of the twentieth century and fell to the bottom in the early twentieth-first century. The overwhelming reason was the deterioration of political and civil rights. Liberties drove AHD in the late 1930s and 1950s and attained high levels between 1960 and 1990. Conversely, the contraction in liberties in the 1920s, early 1950s, and from the 1990s onwards prompted a fall in human development. Schooling, in turn, drove AHD gains during the 1960s and 1970s and helped mitigate its contraction after 1990, while life expectancy did so in the 1940s. Episodes of catching up to the OECD took place in the late 1930s and 1950s, while contributions by longevity in the 1940s and education from 1990 were offset by limitation of freedoms.

Most of Latin America's population is concentrated in Mexico and Brazil. Mexico is one of the few Latin American countries in which changes in civil and political liberties did not cause major shifts in the AHDI evolution. AHD progressed steadily from 1900, accelerating between 1980 and 2005. Analysis of its drivers reveals the leading contribution of life expectancy in the first half of the twentieth century, mitigating the impact of the reduction of liberties during the 1910 Revolution, and prevailing during the 1940s. The rise of life expectancy matches the increase in heights and can be attributed to the dissemination of health practices and the introduction of welfare state policies during the Cárdenas presidency (1934–1940) (López-Alonso and Vélez-Grajales, 2017), as well as to higher living standards after unskilled wages increased after the land reform and pro-labour policies were implemented (Bleynat, Challú, and Segal, 2021). Schooling's steady contribution to AHD progress after 1929 drove gains between 1950 and 1980, and civil and political rights played a leading role in the 1920s and over 1980 to 2005, but also accounted for the regression in AHD prior to World War I. Catching up to the OECD in the interwar years and the last two decades of the twentieth century was driven by civil and political rights. However, the reduction in freedoms was responsible for falling behind before 1913 and largely offset catching up in the 1940s. Longevity's contribution is spread over the period 1900–1970, but only became the principal AHD driver in the 1940s.

Conversely, Brazil's AHD performance was seriously conditioned by the erosion of civil and political freedoms resulting from autocratic rule during the late 1930s and early 1940s, under Getulio Vargas' *Estado Novo* (1930–1945), and in the late 1960s and 1970s, following the 1964 coup d'état against President Joan Goulart. Consequently, the recovery of civil and political rights not only led AHD gains in the late 1940s and in the 1980s, but also dragged down AHD in the 1930s and late 1960s. Life expectancy made a major contribution to AHD improvements in the 1940s, attributable to public health improvements (Franken, 2019), while schooling drove AHD gains in the interwar period and made a steady contribution between the 1920s and 1980s. Relative to the *OECD*, liberties dominated both catching up during late 1940s and the 1980s and falling behind in the 1930s and late 1960s, while life expectancy contributed significantly in the 1940s.

5.7 Conclusions

Latin America experienced substantial gains in human development from the late nineteenth century onwards, which intensified over 1938–1960 and after 1970, particularly in the 1980s. When compared to GDP per head, substantial discrepancies emerge, especially from 1914 to 1950, as the globalisation backlash negatively affected per capita income, and in the 1980s, the so-called lost decade. Thus, AHD progress corresponds not only to phases of faster economic growth such the state-led industrialisation era, as is usually presumed, but also to those of less-intensive growth such as the post-1980 era. This is due to the fact that the main drivers of human development over the long run were life expectancy and schooling, stimulated by the epidemiological transition and nation-building and urbanisation, respectively, and only partially by increased social spending. Catching up to the *OECD* was moderate during 1900–1960 and intensified after 1980. Education and, to a lesser extent, life expectancy at birth drove Latin America's limited AHD catching up until 1960, while civil and political liberties led the way in the 1980s. Moreover, freedoms often had a major impact on AHD trends at country level, driving episodes of both catching up and falling behind.

The historical experience of Latin American reinforces the idea of an early rise of life expectancy at birth prior to 1950, before modern drugs started being distributed to the population. This was the result of the epidemiological transition that facilitated the diffusion of new knowledge to prevent the spread of infectious disease. Life expectancy gains during the early twentieth century mainly derived from reductions in infant mortality and maternal death, and often occurred in societies that could not afford expensive modern medicine, as a consequence of the diffusion of low-cost health practices. Although gains in life expectancy generally paralleled those in height, as the disease environment improved, the rise of life expectancy at birth was occasionally at odds with the stagnation of adult heights. This may have resulted from the impact of health knowledge on infant survival rates through prevention of the spread of infectious disease by following basic hygienic practices, while adult heights are dependent on early-life nutrition, largely conditioned by the level of income and its distribution. Moreover, when longevity gains resulted from improvements in water supply and sanitation, it was also new scientific knowledge that stimulated investment in the latter.

6 | Human Development in Africa

6.1 Introduction

Assessments of long-run performance in Africa have been recurrently negative. The expression 'lost decades' was introduced by William Easterly (2001) to describe the mystifying scenario of faltering economic growth despite substantial policy reforms during 1980–2000, in which sub-Saharan Africa stood out. Akbar Noman and Joseph Stiglitz (2015) extended the pessimistic assessment to the 'lost quarter century' of 1980–2005, with Africa's real GDP per head falling between 1980 and 1995 and only recovering its initial level in 2005. This was, according to these authors, a period of de-industrialisation for which the so-called structural adjustment, that is, the liberalisation policies spearheaded by the Washington Consensus, should be blamed. Robert Bates, John Coatsworth, and Jeffrey Williamson (2007) broaden the concept of 'lost decades' and depict a post-independence Africa that would represent, in their view, half-a-century of instability, violence, balkanisation, and anti-market policies leading to economic stagnation. If we now turn to the pre-1960 colonial era, the conventional view of Africa is deeply pessimistic and stresses stagnation and exploitation by the motherland with immiserating effects across the board, a reflection of the lack of major health improvements (Moradi, 2008: 1117; 2009: 745).

Until recently, economists studying Africa had focused on recent decades and only occasionally ventured into the half-century following independence (Collier and Gunning, 1999a, 1999b; Ndulu *et al.* 2008). However, the dearth of data has not discouraged a new generation of economists from investigating African long-run performance and offering explicit hypotheses regarding its causes on the basis of new sources and methods (Nunn 2008; Acemoglu and Robinson, 2010; Nunn and Wantchekon, 2011; Akyeampong et al., 2014; Heldring and Robinson, 2018; Michalopoulos and Papaioannou,

2020). In parallel, economic historians have provided long-run insights based on path-breaking research. A comprehensive research agenda has now emerged that includes health and nutrition (Moradi 2008, 2010; Akachi and Canning, 2010; Fosu and Mwabu, 2010; Moradi, Austin, and Baten, 2013; Cogneau and Rouanet, 2011; Lowes and Montero, 2021), education (Cogneau and Moradi, 2014; Frankema 2012), inequality and living standards (Moradi and Baten, 2005; Bowden *et al.*, 2008; de Zwart, 2011a, 2011b; Bowden and Mosley, 2012; Frankema and van Waijenburg, 2012; Juif and Frankema, 2018;), and institutions (Fenske, 2013; Broadberry and Gardner, 2016; Bolt and Gardner, 2021).

Moreover, new assessments of economic performance depict the post-independence era as part of a long wave of recurring growth in Africa in which phases of expansion and contraction have alternated since colonial times (Jerven, 2010; Broadberry and Wallis, 2017; Broadberry and Gardner, 2022). More recently, optimistic assessments stressing Africa's potential have been put forward (Frankema, 2021; Robinson and Henn, 2021).

The result has been a thorough revision of the state of play. With regard to human development, recent findings in anthropometric history suggest, without questioning the evils of colonialism, a very different view of colonial Africa. Substantial progress in health was achieved in countries of West and East Africa under colonial rule. In West Africa, Ghana made significant gains in average height during the long decade leading up to World War I and from World War II onwards (Moradi, 2008: 1117). Furthermore, heights for the successive cohorts born in Côte d'Ivoire and Ghana during the late colonial period (1925–1960) experienced an increase comparable to that of Britain and France from 1875 to 1975 (Cogneau and Rouanet, 2011: 79). In East Africa, Kenya experienced a sustained health improvement, measured in terms of height, from the 1920s onwards (Moradi, 2009: 721). Thus, the nutritional and health status of women born in Africa in the early 1960s, around the time of independence, compared favourably with that of other developing countries at similar per capita income levels (Moradi, 2010: 27)

Another important finding is the continuity between the colonial and early postcolonial periods that Moradi (2009: 745) extends to the late 1970s for the case of Kenya.[1]

How could living standards possibly improve under colonial rule that included land expropriations and the confinement of native populations to 'reserves' in parts of East and Southern Africa, such as Kenya and Southern Rhodesia (present-day Zimbabwe)? The ending of the slave trade in West Africa, the expansion of trade and urbanisation, and the transfer of Western knowledge and technology (medical, in particular), in a context of relative security and stability, explain the paradox. Improvements in health infrastructure, sanitation, education, immunisation, and vector control took place between 1920 and 1950, as evidenced by the case of Kenya, although priority was given to preventive rather than curative care (Moradi, 2009: 742–744), which occasionally had unintended negative effects, as documented in the case of vaccination in French Central Africa (Lowes and Montero, 2021).[2]

In post-independence Africa, a decline in health standards, evidenced by a trend reversal in mean heights, took place from the mid-1970s onwards, especially in the south west and south east (Moradi, 2010). Yoko Akachi and David Canning (2010) find that the decline in adult height across age cohorts in sub-Saharan Africa from 1961 to 1985 coincided with a fall in infant mortality. They attribute this paradox to the fact that reductions in infant mortality and morbidity did not coincide. Although infant survival rates increased, the health of surviving children remained poor, as malnutrition, malaria, acute respiratory infections, and chronic diarrhoea continued to take a toll. This was associated with stagnant protein and calorie consumption per head. Akachi and Canning (2010: 287) conclude that, in sub-Saharan Africa, 'the health transition appears to be driven by medical interventions that reduce mortality, rather than by nutrition improvements and broad based reductions in exposure to infectious diseases that would reduce morbidity'.

This chapter adopts the augmented view of human development to assess Africa's long-run performance during the past 150 years.[3] How has Africa performed in terms of AHD over the long run? Does AHD confirm the pessimistic view for both the colonial and post-independence periods or support the findings of anthropometric history? Are recurring episodes of progress and regression the same as those observed for GDP per head? What drives AHD? How has Africa performed relative to the OECD? What determines the differences between the two? are the main questions addressed.

The chapter is structured as follows: In Section 6.2, trends in human development and its dimensions are considered for Africa and its main regions. Section 6.3 compares human development and GDP per head over the long run. Next, Section 6.4 investigates the AHD drivers for Africa and its regions. Africa's catching up to the *OECD* is explored in Section 6.5. Section 6.6 takes a closer look at the behaviour of individual countries in the post-1950 era. Section 6.7 concludes.

6.2 Long-Run Trends in Human Development

We observe a sustained improvement in human development since 1880, which accelerated between the 1920s and the early 1960s, before political independence spread across Africa. AHD continued to improve thereafter at a slower pace, except for growth spurts in the late 1970s, the early 1990s, and the 2010s. Overall, the level of AHD in 2015 was 8.8 times that of 1870 (Table 6.1). From an international perspective, however, Africa belongs to the bottom 10 per cent of the world distribution over time, with slight upwards deviations in the 1950s and early 1960s and from 1995 onwards (Figure 6.1). However, as AHD world dispersion declined over time (see Chapter 3), Africa's ratio to the world average (excluding Africa) rose from around two-fifths up to the early 1950s to above half from 1995 onwards. If, alternatively, the comparison is with the *Rest* of the world, as a whole, Africa's position was rather stable over time, fluctuating around 60 per cent of the *Rest*'s average level. But to what extent are these results representative? Figure 6.2 shows the distribution over time of AHD between countries in Africa as a whole, and south of the Sahara. Inequality rose in the late nineteenth century and experienced a long falling trend from 1900 onwards. Episodes of intense decline in inequality during the long decade prior to World War I, between the onset of the Great Depression and the eve of World War II, in the 1950s and early 1960s, and from the late 1990s onwards, determined the shape of AHD distribution. Thus, even though AHD dispersion was never particularly high, a closer look at different regions of Africa is warranted.

A regional breakdown of AHD presents two different groups: one including Central and East Africa, which fell below the 10th percentile after 1950, and West Africa; and another, including North and Southern Africa, which was close to the middle of world distribution, even though it fell below the 50th percentile after 1950 but remained way above the 10th percentile (Figure 6.3).[4] Nonetheless, Central and, in particular, West and East Africa, starting from lower levels, grew

Table 6.1. *AHDI and its components: Africa*
Panel A. Levels

	AHDI	Kakwani index of schooling	Kakwani index of life expectancy	UNDP index of income	Liberal democracy Index
1870	0.031	0.005	0.020	0.294	0.034
1880	0.031	0.005	0.021	0.300	0.031
1890	0.035	0.006	0.021	0.309	0.040
1900	0.040	0.006	0.024	0.312	0.055
1913	0.045	0.007	0.028	0.328	0.060
1925	0.052	0.010	0.030	0.331	0.074
1929	0.056	0.011	0.035	0.333	0.075
1933	0.058	0.012	0.038	0.322	0.076
1938	0.066	0.014	0.049	0.341	0.076
1950	0.083	0.021	0.078	0.357	0.084
1955	0.092	0.025	0.089	0.371	0.086
1960	0.107	0.030	0.096	0.384	0.115
1965	0.119	0.035	0.108	0.399	0.133
1970	0.121	0.041	0.121	0.419	0.103
1975	0.128	0.048	0.134	0.429	0.095
1980	0.151	0.059	0.149	0.443	0.131
1985	0.154	0.075	0.161	0.435	0.107
1990	0.169	0.091	0.168	0.433	0.124
1995	0.201	0.107	0.171	0.425	0.207
2000	0.218	0.118	0.173	0.439	0.252
2005	0.230	0.130	0.180	0.460	0.260
2010	0.245	0.146	0.193	0.483	0.263
2015	0.276	0.167	0.242	0.495	0.293

Panel B. AHD drivers[*] (%)

	Kakwani index of schooling	Kakwani index of life expectancy	UNDP index of income	Liberal democracy index	AHDI
1870–1880	0.2	0.0	0.1	−0.2	0.1
1880–1890	0.2	0.1	0.1	0.7	1.0
1890–1900	0.2	0.3	0.0	0.8	1.3
1900–1913	0.3	0.3	0.1	0.2	0.9
1913–1929	0.6	0.4	0.0	0.3	1.4

Table 6.1. (*cont.*)

	Kakwani index of schooling	Kakwani index of life expectancy	UNDP index of income	Liberal democracy index	AHDI
1929–1938	0.8	0.9	0.1	0.0	1.8
1938–1950	0.8	1.0	0.1	0.2	2.0
1950–1960	1.0	0.5	0.2	0.8	2.4
1960–1970	0.8	0.6	0.2	–0.3	1.3
1970–1980	0.9	0.5	0.1	0.6	2.2
1980–1990	1.1	0.3	–0.1	–0.1	1.2
1990–2000	0.7	0.1	0.0	1.8	2.6
2000–2010	0.5	0.3	0.2	0.1	1.1
2010–2015	0.7	1.1	0.1	0.5	2.4
1870–2015	0.6	0.4	0.1	0.4	1.5

* Dimensions' contribution to AHD growth.

faster than the African average, a result consistent with the decline in dispersion between African countries.

If we now turn to the relative position of Africa regions within the world (always excluding Africa from the aggregate figures), the two 'clubs' are confirmed, as well as a generalised though partial catching up to the world average from 1960, in the cases of North and Southern Africa, and from the 1930s, in the rest of the regions. The contrast with *Rest*'s average shows a long-run falling behind in Southern and North Africa, only reversed at the turn of the century, and West Africa's catching up since the mid-twentieth century.

6.3 Human Development and GDP per Head

Does the evolution of human development match that of real GDP per head, confirming pessimistic assessments of Africa's long-run performance? Growth rates for AHD (excluding the income dimension) and real per capita GDP are compared during the last one and a half centuries (Figure 6.4). Gains in human development were much more intense, doubling those of GDP per head in the long run. This pattern prevails over each of the main phases and is particularly striking from 1913 to 1950, when most of Africa was under colonial rule, during which time

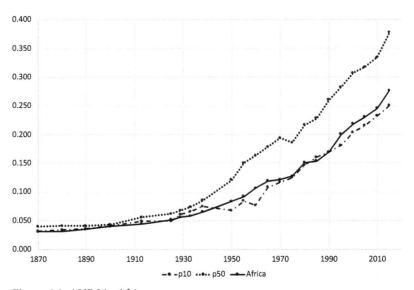

Figure 6.1 *AHDI* in Africa.
Sources: See the text and Table 6.1.

Figure 6.2 Inter-country AHD distribution in Africa and sub-Saharan Africa (MLD).
Sources: See the text and Chapter 4, Table 4.2.

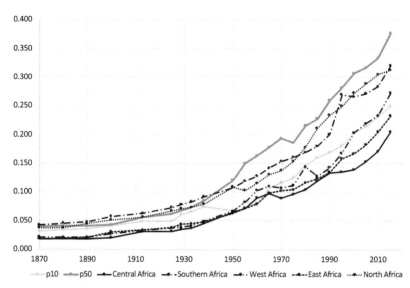

Figure 6.3 *AHDI* in Africa's regions.
Sources: See the text.

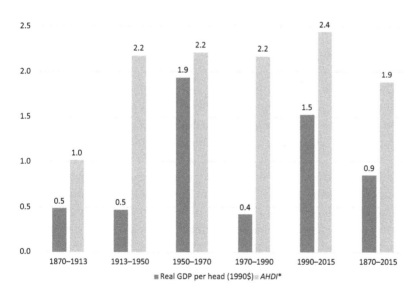

Figure 6.4 Real GDP per head and *AHDI** long-term growth in Africa.
*Excluding the income dimension.
Sources: See the text.

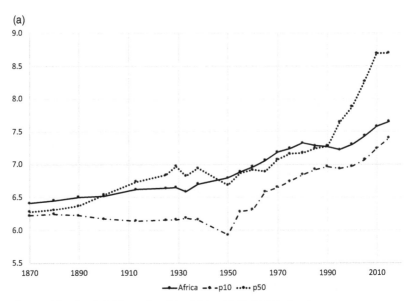

Figure 6.5a Real GDP per head in Africa (G-K 1990$, logs).
Sources: See the text.

sluggish GDP growth paralleled a sustained AHD acceleration. The last two decades of the twentieth century again witnessed a remarkable imbalance in favour of AHD, which thrived (rising more than 40 per cent) at a time of economic stagnation. Furthermore, Africa's per capita income fell between 1980 and 1995, and after fluctuating around the 50th percentile of the world's real GDP per head (though lower in the interwar years) started diverging towards the 10th percentile after 1990 (Figure 6.5a). A closer look at Africa's main regions confirms for the case of per capita income the two *clubs* distinguished for AHD, but instead of catching up to the world average, GDP per capita moved below the 10th percentile from the 1980s onwards in Central and East Africa and fell behind the 50th percentile as of 2000 in Southern Africa (Figure 6.5b). Moreover, the dispersion between countries increased in terms of per capita income while declining in terms of AHD (Figure 6.6). Nonetheless, it is worth noting that Africa's relative position within world distribution was better in terms of GDP per head (around the 50th percentile until 1990) than in terms of AHD (around the 10th percentile) (Figures 6.5a and 6.1). Thus, the evidence in terms of AHD confirms Africa's unenviable relative position in the world but reveals a slight upwards tendency.

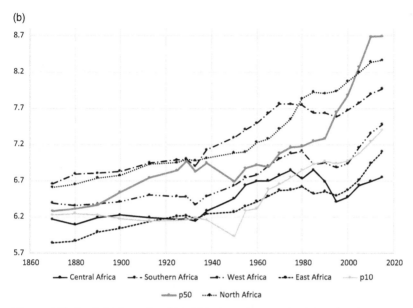

Figure 6.5b Real GDP per head in Africa's regions (G-K 1990$, logs).
Sources: See the text.

Figure 6.6 Inequality in AHD and real GDP per head in sub-Saharan Africa (MLD).
Sources: See the text and Chapter 4, Table 4.2.

(a)

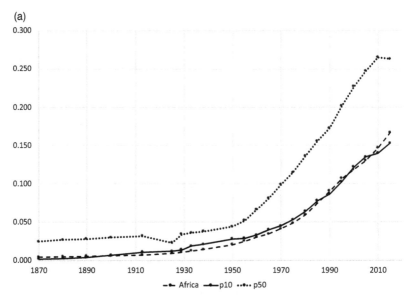

Figure 6.7a Schooling in Africa (Kakwani indices).
Sources: See the text and Table 6.1.

6.4 What Drives AHD?

But why do such disparities exist between the AHD and GDP per head?
Examination of the drivers of human development provides some answers.

Let us first take a closer look at the evolution of each the dimensions
of human development in Africa and its main regions. Schooling rose
since the early twentieth century. In terms of the Kakwani index of
schooling, this implies that the level in 2015 was 35 times that of 1870.
The pace was not steady, however, following an inverted U, accelerating up to the 1950s, keeping a high growth rate until 1990, and
slowing down thereafter (Table 6.1, Panel B). When placed in a comparative perspective, schooling in Africa adjusts to the 10th percentile
throughout the one and a half centuries considered (Figure 6.7a).
Nonetheless, significant differences are apparent across the regions of
Africa (Tables 6.2–6.6). Figure 6.7b evidences a clear difference
between Southern Africa, which fell behind the 50th percentile after
1960, but was still far away from the 10th percentile, and the
other sub-Saharan regions, which remained below this lower bound.

Table 6.2. AHDI and its components: North Africa
Panel A. Levels

	AHDI	Kakwani index of schooling	Kakwani index of life expectancy	UNDP index of income	Liberal democracy index
1870	0.038	0.005	0.019	0.325	0.067
1880	0.038	0.005	0.019	0.332	0.057
1890	0.045	0.007	0.019	0.347	0.094
1900	0.052	0.008	0.026	0.352	0.104
1913	0.056	0.010	0.035	0.377	0.076
1925	0.067	0.014	0.038	0.381	0.104
1929	0.071	0.015	0.042	0.389	0.103
1933	0.074	0.017	0.045	0.385	0.104
1938	0.079	0.019	0.050	0.391	0.107
1950	0.109	0.028	0.104	0.403	0.122
1955	0.103	0.030	0.119	0.405	0.079
1960	0.116	0.032	0.128	0.426	0.102
1965	0.131	0.035	0.144	0.434	0.133
1970	0.138	0.042	0.162	0.456	0.118
1975	0.154	0.053	0.182	0.479	0.122
1980	0.178	0.076	0.210	0.524	0.120
1985	0.212	0.108	0.245	0.539	0.141
1990	0.234	0.132	0.278	0.536	0.153
1995	0.250	0.159	0.309	0.541	0.146
2000	0.273	0.189	0.338	0.563	0.154
2005	0.289	0.203	0.361	0.583	0.162
2010	0.305	0.229	0.380	0.607	0.164
2015	0.313	0.226	0.403	0.611	0.172

Panel B. AHD drivers[*] (%)

	Kakwani index of schooling	Kakwani index of life expectancy	UNDP index of income	Liberal democracy index	AHDI
1870–1880	0.3	0.0	0.1	−0.4	0.0
1880–1890	0.5	0.0	0.1	1.2	1.8
1890–1900	0.4	0.7	0.0	0.2	1.4
1900–1913	0.5	0.6	0.1	−0.6	0.7
1913–1929	0.7	0.3	0.0	0.5	1.5

Table 6.2. (*cont.*)

	Kakwani index of schooling	Kakwani index of life expectancy	UNDP index of income	Liberal democracy index	*AHDI*
1929–1938	0.6	0.5	0.0	0.1	1.2
1938–1950	0.8	1.5	0.1	0.3	2.6
1950–1960	0.4	0.5	0.1	–0.4	0.6
1960–1970	0.6	0.6	0.2	0.4	1.8
1970–1980	1.5	0.6	0.3	0.0	2.6
1980–1990	1.4	0.7	0.1	0.6	2.7
1990–2000	0.9	0.5	0.1	0.0	1.5
2000–2010	0.5	0.3	0.2	0.2	1.1
2010–2015	–0.1	0.3	0.0	0.2	0.5
1870–2015	0.7	0.5	0.1	0.2	1.5

* Dimensions' contribution to AHD growth.

North Africa maintained an intermediate position but converged with Southern Africa from 1980 onwards.

In the case of longevity, we observe a sustained, but moderate improvement between the late 1920s and 1990 that, after stagnating, recovered from the late 2000s onwards. Life expectancy in Africa fluctuated around the 10th percentile, falling below it during the period 1970–2000 (Figure 6.8a). Expressed in terms of the Kakwani index, the level in 2015 was 11.9 times the level in 1870. The improvement in longevity did not proceed steadily in Africa: after a phase of mild growth between 1890 and the 1920s, it accelerated from 1929–1950, then slowed down, growing at a lower but steady pace from 1950 to 1980, decelerating in the 1980s and nearly stagnating in the 1990s, before recovering strongly from the early 2000s onwards. Disparities are observed between regions. North Africa grew steadily, apart from the acceleration from 1938 to 1950 and a slowdown after 2000, fluctuating around the 50th percentile, apart from 1970 to 1990. Southern Africa, however, deviated from the 50th percentile to converge to the 10th percentile in 1990, and then declined in absolute terms, falling below this percentile, only recovering the 1990 level in the 2010s (Figure 6.8b). The remaining sub-Saharan regions fell below the 10th percentile after 1970, with the gap widening between

Table 6.3. *AHDI and its components: Central Africa*
Panel A. *Levels*

	AHDI	Kakwani index of schooling	Kakwani index of life expectancy	UNDP index of income	Liberal democracy index
1870	0.019	0.002	0.020	0.254	0.010
1880	0.019	0.002	0.020	0.242	0.010
1890	0.019	0.002	0.019	0.258	0.010
1900	0.021	0.002	0.020	0.263	0.014
1913	0.031	0.004	0.023	0.258	0.036
1925	0.032	0.005	0.023	0.254	0.036
1929	0.036	0.005	0.032	0.255	0.036
1933	0.037	0.007	0.032	0.251	0.036
1938	0.045	0.009	0.050	0.273	0.036
1950	0.065	0.014	0.075	0.301	0.055
1955	0.072	0.018	0.083	0.331	0.057
1960	0.090	0.022	0.089	0.339	0.100
1965	0.098	0.026	0.099	0.340	0.103
1970	0.089	0.033	0.111	0.353	0.050
1975	0.097	0.043	0.124	0.364	0.045
1980	0.105	0.056	0.137	0.345	0.045
1985	0.119	0.074	0.148	0.365	0.051
1990	0.133	0.087	0.151	0.338	0.071
1995	0.135	0.096	0.141	0.293	0.085
2000	0.139	0.099	0.136	0.304	0.091
2005	0.153	0.105	0.139	0.330	0.113
2010	0.171	0.113	0.143	0.339	0.156
2015	0.205	0.175	0.207	0.349	0.141

Panel B. *AHD drivers* [*] *(%)*

	Kakwani index of schooling	Kakwani index of life expectancy	UNDP index of income	Liberal democracy index	AHDI
1870–1880	0.0	0.0	−0.1	0.0	−0.1
1880–1890	0.0	−0.1	0.2	0.0	0.1
1890–1900	0.0	0.1	0.1	0.9	1.0
1900–1913	1.1	0.3	0.0	1.8	3.2
1913–1929	0.3	0.5	0.0	0.0	0.8

Table 6.3. (*cont.*)

	Kakwani index of schooling	Kakwani index of life expectancy	UNDP index of income	Liberal democracy index	AHDI
1929–1938	1.3	1.2	0.2	0.0	2.6
1938–1950	1.1	0.9	0.2	0.9	3.0
1950–1960	1.1	0.4	0.3	1.5	3.3
1960–1970	1.0	0.6	0.1	−1.7	−0.1
1970–1980	1.4	0.5	−0.1	−0.3	1.6
1980–1990	1.1	0.2	−0.1	1.1	2.4
1990–2000	0.3	−0.3	−0.3	0.6	0.4
2000–2010	0.3	0.1	0.3	1.3	2.1
2010–2015	2.2	1.8	0.1	−0.5	3.7
1870–2015	0.7	0.4	0.1	0.5	1.6

* Dimensions' contribution to AHD growth.

1990 and 2010, as life expectancy at birth decelerated in East and West Africa in the 1980s and 1990s and shrank in Central Africa during the 1990s, only recovering the 1990 level after 2010.

It is worth noting the coincidence for West and East Africa during the late colonial era (1920–1950) between the improvement in life expectancy and the increase in height, observed by anthropometric historians (Moradi, 2008, 2009, 2010; Cogneau and Rouanet, 2011).

It is also relevant to observe life expectancy gains simultaneous to faltering growth of GDP per head in the 1980s, which is consistent with upward shifts in the health function triggered by medical technology improvements and absence of movements along the function as a consequence of stagnant or declining nutrition and poor provision of public services. This would explain Akachi and Canning's (2010) paradox of declining infant mortality (and rising life expectancy), presumably dependent on shifts in the health function, and height reduction, largely conditioned by movements along the function.

As nutrition and morbidity in childhood condition future health, an important long-term consequence of sub-Saharan Africa's poor economic performance from 1980 to 2000 is unhealthy adulthood. This may significantly hinder sub-Saharan Africa's prospects of joining the

Table 6.4. *AHDI and its components: West Africa*
Panel A. *Levels*

	AHDI	Kakwani index of schooling	Kakwani index of life expectancy	UNDP index of income	Liberal democracy index
1870	0.021	0.003	0.019	0.290	0.015
1880	0.021	0.003	0.019	0.285	0.015
1890	0.021	0.003	0.019	0.288	0.014
1900	0.027	0.003	0.021	0.293	0.030
1913	0.033	0.003	0.023	0.308	0.057
1925	0.038	0.003	0.025	0.305	0.078
1929	0.039	0.004	0.029	0.305	0.077
1933	0.041	0.004	0.031	0.287	0.077
1938	0.049	0.005	0.048	0.306	0.077
1950	0.067	0.010	0.066	0.330	0.095
1955	0.083	0.015	0.076	0.348	0.118
1960	0.103	0.021	0.082	0.353	0.183
1965	0.110	0.025	0.091	0.373	0.170
1970	0.108	0.030	0.101	0.390	0.114
1975	0.112	0.036	0.111	0.402	0.099
1980	0.144	0.041	0.123	0.407	0.213
1985	0.128	0.054	0.128	0.377	0.102
1990	0.143	0.068	0.132	0.380	0.122
1995	0.168	0.081	0.136	0.370	0.196
2000	0.204	0.095	0.143	0.379	0.334
2005	0.219	0.110	0.152	0.414	0.336
2010	0.234	0.126	0.162	0.447	0.326
2015	0.273	0.145	0.194	0.467	0.420

Panel B. *AHD drivers* (%)

	Kakwani index of schooling	Kakwani index of life expectancy	UNDP index of income	Liberal democracy index	AHDI
1870–1880	0.0	0.0	0.0	−0.1	−0.1
1880–1890	0.1	0.0	0.0	−0.1	0.1
1890–1900	0.2	0.2	0.0	1.9	2.3
1900–1913	0.1	0.2	0.1	1.2	1.6
1913–1929	0.2	0.3	0.0	0.5	1.0

Table 6.4. (*cont.*)

	Kakwani index of schooling	Kakwani index of life expectancy	UNDP index of income	Liberal democracy index	*AHDI*
1929–1938	1.0	1.4	0.0	0.0	2.5
1938–1950	1.3	0.7	0.2	0.4	2.5
1950–1960	2.0	0.5	0.2	1.6	4.4
1960–1970	0.9	0.5	0.2	−1.2	0.4
1970–1980	0.8	0.5	0.1	1.6	2.9
1980–1990	1.3	0.2	−0.2	−1.4	−0.1
1990–2000	0.8	0.2	0.0	2.5	3.6
2000–2010	0.7	0.3	0.4	−0.1	1.4
2010–2015	0.7	0.9	0.2	1.3	3.1
1870–2015	0.7	0.4	0.1	0.6	1.8

* Dimensions' contribution to AHD growth.

second health transition currently underway, in which increasing longevity among the elderly is the main driver.

Civil and political rights in Africa, as measured by the liberal democracy index, improved slightly during the first half of the twentieth century and enjoyed a surge around 1960 and independence, before stagnating until 1990 (Table 6.1). The 1990s witnessed a big leap forward that was renewed after 2010. From a comparative perspective, there was a long transition from the 10th to the 50th percentile between the 1920s and 1960 (Figure 6.9a). A puzzle emerges in the 1990s, when civil and political liberties improved in absolute terms but fell in relative terms, moving away from the 50th percentile. Disparities across regions are acute (Figure 6.9b). North Africa adjusted to the 50th percentile until the late 1980s, then fell behind. Central Africa improved but never, except for the early 1960s and after 2000, moved very far from the 10th percentile. East Africa matched Africa's shift from the 10th to the 50th percentile during the early twentieth century and fell behind after 1990. West and Southern Africa reached the 50th percentile in the 1930s and remained at that level.

The multiplicative structure of the *AHDI*, in which dimensions enter with equal weights, implies that growth in the *AHDI* equals the weighted sum of each dimension's growth rate (with 0.25 weight for

Table 6.5. *AHDI and its Components: East Africa*
Panel A. Levels

	AHDI	Kakwani index of schooling	Kakwani index of life expectancy	UNDP index of income	Liberal democracy index
1870	0.018	0.003	0.019	0.201	0.010
1880	0.020	0.004	0.019	0.205	0.011
1890	0.021	0.004	0.019	0.225	0.011
1900	0.030	0.005	0.019	0.234	0.036
1913	0.034	0.006	0.020	0.249	0.041
1925	0.038	0.008	0.021	0.261	0.048
1929	0.044	0.009	0.031	0.262	0.052
1933	0.045	0.010	0.031	0.255	0.053
1938	0.049	0.011	0.039	0.266	0.051
1950	0.063	0.015	0.070	0.270	0.055
1955	0.072	0.018	0.080	0.284	0.067
1960	0.080	0.022	0.087	0.294	0.071
1965	0.098	0.025	0.098	0.306	0.125
1970	0.103	0.032	0.112	0.319	0.097
1975	0.104	0.037	0.122	0.320	0.083
1980	0.116	0.045	0.140	0.327	0.089
1985	0.124	0.055	0.146	0.311	0.094
1990	0.135	0.065	0.147	0.317	0.109
1995	0.158	0.075	0.149	0.307	0.184
2000	0.167	0.083	0.156	0.320	0.189
2005	0.182	0.094	0.172	0.342	0.200
2010	0.205	0.110	0.194	0.379	0.219
2015	0.233	0.125	0.263	0.405	0.221

Panel B. AHD drivers[*] (%)

	Kakwani index of schooling	Kakwani index of life expectancy	UNDP index of income	Liberal democracy index	AHDI
1870–1880	0.5	0.0	0.1	0.2	0.7
1880–1890	0.5	0.0	0.2	–0.1	0.6
1890–1900	0.5	0.0	0.1	3.1	3.7
1900–1913	0.3	0.1	0.1	0.3	0.8
1913–1929	0.5	0.6	0.1	0.4	1.6

Table 6.5. (*cont.*)

	Kakwani index of schooling	Kakwani index of life expectancy	UNDP index of income	Liberal democracy index	*AHDI*
1929–1938	0.5	0.6	0.0	0.0	1.2
1938–1950	0.7	1.2	0.0	0.1	2.1
1950–1960	1.0	0.5	0.2	0.6	2.4
1960–1970	0.9	0.6	0.2	0.8	2.5
1970–1980	0.9	0.6	0.1	–0.2	1.3
1980–1990	0.9	0.1	–0.1	0.5	1.5
1990–2000	0.6	0.2	0.0	1.4	2.2
2000–2010	0.7	0.5	0.4	0.4	2.0
2010–2015	0.6	1.5	0.3	0.0	2.5
1870–2015	0.6	0.5	0.1	0.5	1.7

* Dimensions' contribution to AHD growth.

each dimension) (Chapter 2, equation 2.1). It is thus possible to present a breakdown of AHD growth into the contributions of each of its dimensions. Over the entire time span considered, schooling made the largest single contribution, followed by similar contributions by longevity and political and civil liberties. Nonetheless, contributions by dimensions varied over different phases (see Table 6.1, Panel B). Thus, while schooling was the main driver over most of the past hundred years, civil and political rights dominated during the time of independence (late 1950s and early 1960s) and the 1990s, and life expectancy made the largest contribution during the period 1925 to 1950 and from 2010 onwards. Therefore, non-income dimensions have driven human development. A closer look at African regions confirms these patterns. Life expectancy was the main driver of AHD in Central, West, and Southern Africa during the 1930s, in North and East Africa during the 1940s, and, since 2010, in East and Southern Africa (Tables 6.2–6.6, Panel B). Schooling dominated AHD progress between the late 1960s and 2010 in North Africa, and south of the Sahara drove AHD from 1950 to 1990, with the exception of slight variations across its regions. Civil and political rights led AHD during short periods at the time of independence (late 1950s and early 1960s), less intensely in Southern Africa, and, again, in the late twentieth century, except in North Africa.

Table 6.6. *AHDI and its components: Southern Africa*
Panel A. *Levels*

	AHDI	Kakwani index of schooling	Kakwani index of life expectancy	UNDP index of income	Liberal democracy index
1870	0.043	0.010	0.025	0.333	0.039
1880	0.046	0.011	0.026	0.355	0.041
1890	0.048	0.012	0.030	0.357	0.043
1900	0.057	0.012	0.035	0.362	0.067
1913	0.063	0.013	0.038	0.380	0.079
1925	0.073	0.021	0.043	0.387	0.083
1929	0.079	0.024	0.048	0.388	0.086
1933	0.083	0.028	0.053	0.373	0.087
1938	0.092	0.032	0.064	0.410	0.087
1950	0.108	0.045	0.084	0.437	0.084
1955	0.119	0.053	0.098	0.455	0.085
1960	0.128	0.060	0.106	0.469	0.089
1965	0.142	0.069	0.119	0.492	0.102
1970	0.154	0.079	0.131	0.513	0.106
1975	0.160	0.087	0.144	0.512	0.104
1980	0.169	0.096	0.157	0.510	0.107
1985	0.180	0.103	0.169	0.493	0.122
1990	0.201	0.127	0.179	0.492	0.145
1995	0.270	0.159	0.174	0.484	0.397
2000	0.266	0.162	0.154	0.499	0.404
2005	0.272	0.178	0.147	0.515	0.407
2010	0.284	0.198	0.161	0.534	0.384
2015	0.320	0.228	0.218	0.546	0.389

Panel B. *AHD drivers[*] (%)*

	Kakwani index of schooling	Kakwani index of life expectancy	UNDP index of income	Liberal democracy index	AHDI
1870–1880	0.2	0.2	0.2	0.1	0.6
1880–1890	0.1	0.3	0.0	0.1	0.6
1890–1900	0.1	0.4	0.0	1.1	1.7
1900–1913	0.1	0.2	0.1	0.3	0.7
1913–1929	0.9	0.3	0.0	0.1	1.4

Table 6.6. (*cont.*)

	Kakwani index of schooling	Kakwani index of life expectancy	UNDP index of income	Liberal democracy index	*AHDI*
1929–1938	0.8	0.8	0.2	0.1	1.8
1938–1950	0.7	0.6	0.1	−0.1	1.3
1950–1960	0.8	0.6	0.2	0.2	1.7
1960–1970	0.7	0.5	0.2	0.4	1.8
1970–1980	0.5	0.5	0.0	0.0	1.0
1980–1990	0.7	0.3	−0.1	0.8	1.7
1990–2000	0.6	−0.4	0.0	2.6	2.8
2000–2010	0.5	0.1	0.2	−0.1	0.7
2010–2015	0.7	1.5	0.1	0.1	2.4
1870–2015	0.5	0.4	0.1	0.4	1.4

* Dimensions' contribution to AHD growth.

6.5 Africa's AHD Catching Up to the *OECD*

How does Africa compare to the developed world? Did Africa, as a whole, or any of its regions, catch up to the *OECD*? Figure 6.10 shows that, starting from very low levels relative to the *OECD* average (below 20 per cent in 1870 for Africa as a whole, and ranging between 10 and 25 per cent for its main regions), Africa and its regions have experienced a long-run, though incomplete, catching up since the late 1920s. Thus, by 2015, Africa represented above one-third of the *OECD* level, with its regions ranging between one-quarter and two-fifths of the latter. Distinctive phases of catching up took place between the late 1920s and the eve of World War II, at the time of independence (1955–1965), in the late 1970s, and since 1990. In sub-Saharan Africa, the first catching-up episode encompassed the period between the late 1920s and the mid-1960s, except for Southern Africa. In North Africa, the early phase of catching up extended until 1950 and was followed by a sustained phase of catching up from the mid-1970s onwards.

Africa's evolution contrasts sharply in terms of human development and GDP per head. Africa and its regions started from a better relative position in terms of per capita income (over 30 per cent for the continent as a whole, and between 18 and 41 per cent for its regions) but fell

(b)

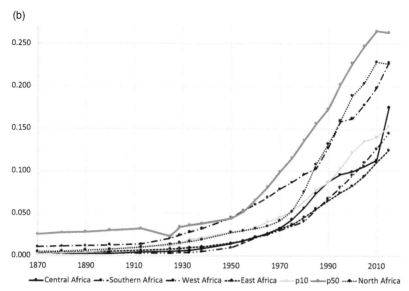

Figure 6.7b Schooling in Africa's regions (Kakwani indices).
Sources: See the text and Tables 6.2–6.6.

(a)

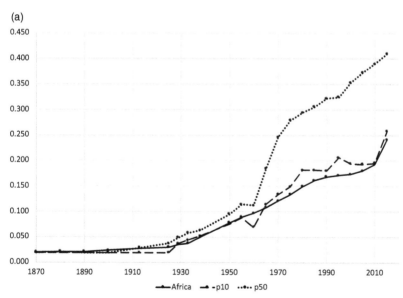

Figure 6.8a Life expectancy in Africa (Kakwani indices).
Sources: See the text and Table 6.1.

(b)

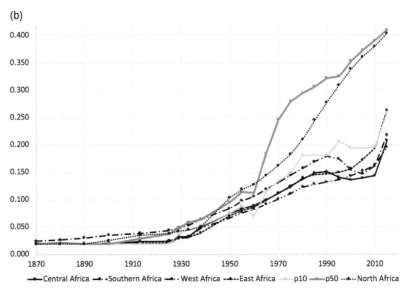

Figure 6.8b Life expectancy in Africa's regions (Kakwani indices).
Sources: See the text and Tables 6.2–6.6.

(a)

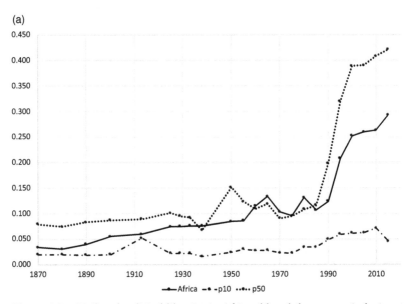

Figure 6.9a Civil and political liberties in Africa (liberal democracy index).
Sources: See the text and Table 6.1.

(b)

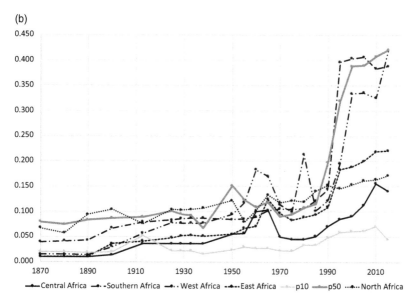

Figure 6.9b Civil and political liberties in Africa's regions (liberal democracy index).

Sources: See the text and Tables 6.2–6.6.

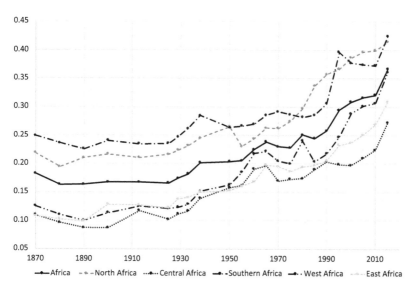

Figure 6.10 Relative AHD in Africa and its regions (*OECD*=1).

Sources: See the text and Tables 6.1–6.6 and Chapter 4, Table 4.3.

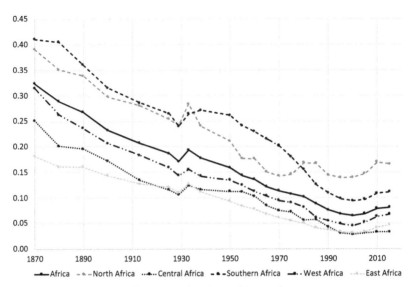

Figure 6.11 Relative real GDP per head in Africa and its regions (*OECD*=1).
Sources: See the text.

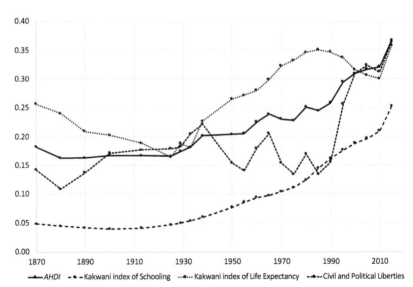

Figure 6.12 Relative AHD and its non-income dimensions in Africa (*OECD*=1).
Sources: See the text and Table 6.1 and Chapter 4, Table 4.3.

steadily behind, except during the 1930s (and North Africa in the late 1970s,) before recovering as of 2005. As a result, Africa's average income per capita relative to the OECD was only 8 per cent in 2015, and between 3 and 17 per cent for its main regions (Figure 6.11).

What drove Africa's catching up to the OECD? Figure 6.12 shows Africa's position relative to the OECD in terms of human development and its dimensions. It can be observed that within the catching up in terms of AHD exhibited by Africa since the late 1920s, each of its dimensions presents a particular behaviour. Schooling caught up in sustained fashion during the last century. In the case of longevity, after falling behind until the mid-1920s, there was significant catching up between the late 1920s and 1980, falling behind during 1990–2010, when it reached a position similar to that of 1965, and a recovery in the early 2010s. In terms of political and civil liberties, moderate catching up until World War II was followed by severe falling behind until 1990, when catching up resumed strongly. In terms of adjusted income, Africa's position differed from that of other *AHDI* dimensions by having a much higher level relative to the OECD and by falling a long way behind from 1980–1995, before recovering slightly in the 2000s. Thus, by 2015, Africa exhibited over a third of the OECD average in terms of civil and political liberties and life expectancy, and only a quarter in terms of schooling, but over a half in terms of adjusted income.

The multiplicative structure of the *AHDI* enables us to break down AHD catching up, that is, the difference between the growth rates of Africa and the OECD, into the contributions of their dimensions, namely, a quarter of each dimension's differential growth between Africa and the OECD (See Chapter 2, equation 2.1). Schooling has been the main driver of human development catching up over time, contributing a half of the latter. Life expectancy made a leading contribution in the late 1920s and 1930s and from 2010 onwards, along with schooling. Political and civil rights drove catching up in the late 1950s and early 1960s, coinciding with the independence of most African countries, and in the 1990s (Table 6.7). It is also worth pointing to the negative impact of the falling behind of dimensions upon long-run catching up. Such is the case of life expectancy in the 1990s, and civil and political rights in the aftermath of World War II, the late 1960s and early 1970s, and the early 1980s.

Given the distinctive behaviour of Africa's regions, their experience of catching up merits closer attention. In North Africa, schooling, after moderate catching during the first half of the twentieth century, caught

Table 6.7. *AHD catching up in Africa: dimensions' contribution (%)*

	Kakwani index of schooling	Kakwani index of life expectancy	UNDP index of income	Liberal democracy index	*AHDI*
1870–1880	−0.2	−0.2	−0.1	−0.7	−1.1
1880–1890	−0.2	−0.4	0.0	0.6	0.0
1890–1900	−0.1	−0.1	−0.1	0.5	0.3
1900–1913	0.1	−0.1	0.0	0.1	0.0
1913–1929	0.3	0.0	−0.1	0.1	0.3
1929–1938	0.5	0.5	0.1	0.5	1.6
1938–1950	0.5	0.3	0.0	−0.8	0.1
1950–1960	0.5	0.1	0.0	0.4	1.0
1960–1970	0.3	0.4	0.0	−0.4	0.2
1970–1980	0.4	0.2	0.0	0.2	0.9
1980–1990	0.7	0.0	−0.2	−0.2	0.3
1990–2000	0.4	−0.2	−0.1	1.7	1.8
2000–2010	0.3	−0.1	0.2	0.0	0.4
2010–2015	0.9	0.9	0.1	0.8	2.7
1870–2015	0.3	0.1	0.0	0.2	0.5

up strongly from 1970 onwards, rising from one-tenth to one-third of the *OECD* level in 2015. Life expectancy caught up strongly and steadily between 1938 and 1995 before stabilising thereafter, soaring from about 20 per cent to 60 per cent of the *OECD* level (Figure 6.13). Political and civil liberties evidence no long-term catching up and fell behind between 1938 and the early 1950s to remain unaltered henceforth, representing one-fifth of the *OECD*'s level in 2015. Adjusted income was basically trendless, fluctuating at around two-thirds of the *OECD* level, a larger share than other dimensions. Thus, if we now break down AHD catching up into the contribution of its dimensions, schooling and longevity account for all of this over time. Schooling was AHD's main driver from 1970–2000 and life expectancy from 1938–1950 and in the late 1960s, while civil and political rights drove it in the 1930s, in the early years of independence (late 1950s and early 1960s), and the 2010s (Table 6.8). The reduction of liberties also accounted for North Africa's falling behind in the early twentieth century and the early 1950s and weakened catching up from 1938 to 1950.

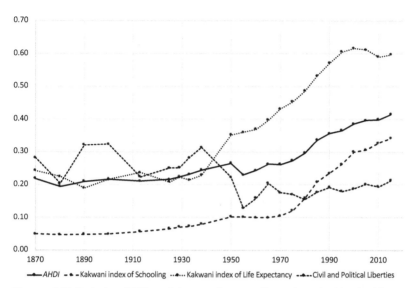

Figure 6.13 Relative AHD and its non-income dimensions in North Africa (OECD=1).

Sources: See the text and Table 6.2 and Chapter 4, Table 4.3.

In Central Africa, catching up took place in schooling between the 1930s and the 1980s and, again, in the 2010s, attaining about a quarter of the OECD level in 2015. After falling behind after 1870, life expectancy caught up between the 1930s and the early 1980s but fell behind dramatically until 2010, when it bounced back, representing over 30 per cent of the OECD level in 2015 (Figure 6.14). Civil and political rights improved relatively in the early twentieth century but stalled between World War I and independence, enjoyed a spurt of catching up in the early 1960s, and collapsed in the 1970s and 1980s, only catching up again from the 1990s onwards. Their level remained below one-fifth of the OECD's in 2015. Adjusted income fluctuated at around half the OECD level until the early 1980s, falling sharply in the 1990s and partly recovering in the late 2000s to reach about two-fifths of the OECD's level in 2015. Schooling was the main driver of AHD catching up, contributing two-thirds of the latter over the period 1870–2015, and especially during the 1940s, 1970–1985, and, again, after 2010 (Table 6.9). Life expectancy led catching up in the late 1920s and 1930s, falling behind from 1990–2005. Civil and political

Table 6.8. *AHD catching up in North Africa: dimensions'*
contribution (%)

	Kakwani index of schooling	Kakwani index of life expectancy	UNDP index of income	Liberal democracy index	*AHDI*
1870–1880	−0.1	−0.2	−0.1	−0.8	−1.2
1880–1890	0.1	−0.4	0.0	1.1	0.8
1890–1900	0.0	0.3	−0.1	0.0	0.3
1900–1913	0.3	0.2	0.0	−0.7	−0.2
1913–1929	0.3	−0.1	0.0	0.2	0.4
1929–1938	0.3	0.1	0.0	0.6	1.0
1938–1950	0.5	0.9	0.0	−0.7	0.7
1950–1960	−0.1	0.1	−0.1	−0.8	−0.8
1960–1970	0.1	0.4	0.0	0.2	0.7
1970–1980	1.0	0.3	0.2	−0.3	1.3
1980–1990	1.0	0.4	−0.1	0.5	1.8
1990–2000	0.6	0.2	0.0	0.0	0.8
2000–2010	0.2	−0.1	0.2	0.1	0.3
2010–2015	0.2	0.1	0.0	0.5	0.8
1870–2015	0.3	0.2	0.0	0.0	0.4

liberties drove catching up during the late 1950s and 1990–2010, but entirely accounted for AHD falling behind in the late 1960s.

In West Africa, sustained catching up took place in schooling from the 1930s onwards, although very moderately until 1950 and, in the case of life expectancy, limited to the central decades of the twentieth century, 1930–1980. Life expectancy fell behind, however, between 1870 and the early 1920s and from 1980 to 2010. Schooling and longevity represented 22 and 29 per cent, respectively, of the *OECD* level in 2015 (Figure 6.15). Civil and political liberties that had improved relative to the *OECD* in the first third of the twentieth century experienced strong trendless fluctuations between 1950 and 1990, except for a spurt at the time of independence and in the late 1970s. From the 1990s onwards, liberties improved, gaining ground on the *OECD* and representing over a half of its level in 2015. Adjusted income per head fell behind over time and, above all, in the 1980s and 1990s, to partially recover thereafter, reaching about a half

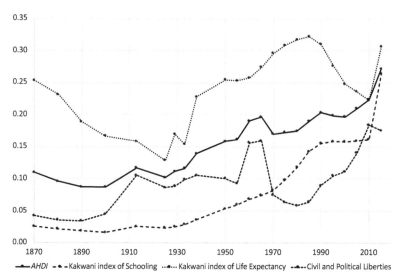

Figure 6.14 Relative AHD and its non-income dimensions in Central Africa (*OECD*=1).
Sources: See the text and Table 6.3 and Chapter 4, Table 4.3.

of the *OECD* level in 2015. Human development catching up was equally divided between education and political and civil liberties over the one and half centuries considered. A closer look reveals that schooling was AHD's main driver during the 1940s and early 1950s. Civil and political rights constituted the leading force in AHD catching up during the late 1950s and 1970s, in the 1990s, and, again, in the 2010s, but accounted for AHD falling behind between 1960 and 1975 and during the early 1980s. Life expectancy only drove AHD catching up in the late 1920s and 1930s (Table 6.10).

In East Africa, schooling caught up from the late 1920s onwards, reaching about one-fifth of the *OECD* level in 2015 (Figure 6.16). Life expectancy presents distinctive phases, falling behind between 1870 and the early 1920s, catching up strongly until 1980, and falling behind from 1980 to 2000, before recovering after 2010, representing two-fifths of the *OECD* level in 2015. Political and civil liberties experienced catching up between the late 1920s and the eve of World War II, subsequently stagnating, except for a brief catching-up spell in the early 1960s, until 1990, when strong catching up took place, reaching 28 per cent of the *OECD* level in 2015. Once again, adjusted

Table 6.9. *AHD catching up in Central Africa: dimensions'*
contribution (%)

	Kakwani index of schooling	Kakwani index of life expectancy	UNDP index of income	Liberal democracy index	AHDI
1870–1880	–0.4	–0.2	–0.2	–0.4	–1.3
1880–1890	–0.4	–0.5	0.1	–0.1	–1.0
1890–1900	–0.3	–0.3	–0.1	0.7	0.0
1900–1913	0.9	–0.1	–0.2	1.7	2.3
1913–1929	0.0	0.1	–0.1	–0.3	–0.3
1929–1938	1.0	0.8	0.2	0.5	2.5
1938–1950	0.8	0.2	0.1	–0.1	1.1
1950–1960	0.6	0.0	0.1	1.1	1.9
1960–1970	0.5	0.4	–0.1	–1.8	–1.1
1970–1980	0.9	0.2	–0.2	–0.6	0.3
1980–1990	0.7	–0.1	–0.2	1.0	1.5
1990–2000	0.0	–0.6	–0.4	0.6	–0.3
2000–2010	0.1	–0.3	0.2	1.3	1.3
2010–2015	2.5	1.6	0.1	–0.2	3.9
1870–2015	0.4	0.0	–0.1	0.2	0.6

income presents a flat trend until 1980, when it fell behind, to recover from the late 2000s onwards, representing 45 per cent of the OECD level in 2015. Breakdown of AHD catching up shows that it was equally distributed between education and civil and political liberties over the long run. A look at different phases shows that schooling was the main driver of AHD catching up in the 1950s, early 1980s, and 2000s. Civil and political liberties drove AHD catching up in the early 1960s, at the time of independence, and the 1990s, but dragged it down in the late 1960s and early 1970s. Life expectancy was the main contributor from 1925 to 1950 and in the 2010s (Table 6.11).

Southern Africa started from a better position relative to the OECD, compared to other African regions, but presents a flatter trend of catching up. Schooling shortened distances relative to the OECD between the 1920s and 1960s and only resumed catching up as of 1990. Life expectancy, after falling behind in the first quarter of the

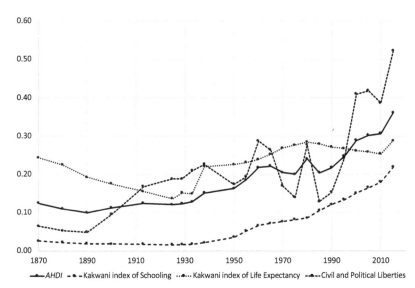

Figure 6.15 Relative AHD and its non-income dimensions in West Africa (*OECD*=1).

Sources: See the text and Table 6.4 and Chapter 4, Table 4.3.

twentieth century, bounced back until World War II, and experienced catching up between 1950 and 1980, before falling dramatically behind from 1990–2005 and recovering partially from 2010 onwards. Both longevity and education represented about one-third of the OECD level in 2015 (Figure 6.17). Civil and political liberties, which had improved relative to the OECD during the early twentieth century, fell to a lower plateau after World War II, where they remained between 1950 and 1990, and experienced a spectacular spurt in the 1990s, reaching half of the OECD level in 2015. Conversely, adjusted income did not catch up, but stagnated around two-thirds of the OECD figure until 1970 and then fell behind, representing 60 per cent of the OECD's level in 2015. Over the long run, schooling and civil and political liberties accounted equally for AHD catching up (Table 6.12). When we look at specific periods, schooling drove catching up in the 1920s. Life expectancy was the main contributor to catching up in the 1930s, and from the 2010s onwards, but caused AHD to fall behind from 1995 to 2005. Civil and political rights drove catching up in the early 1960s and, in particular, the 1990s.

Table 6.10. *AHD catching up in West Africa: dimensions'*
contribution (%)

	Kakwani index of schooling	Kakwani index of life expectancy	UNDP index of income	Liberal democracy index	AHDI
1870–1880	–0.4	–0.2	–0.2	–0.5	–1.3
1880–1890	–0.3	–0.4	–0.1	–0.2	–1.0
1890–1900	–0.1	–0.2	–0.1	1.7	1.3
1900–1913	–0.1	–0.2	0.0	1.1	0.7
1913–1929	–0.1	0.0	–0.1	0.2	–0.1
1929–1938	0.8	1.0	0.0	0.5	2.3
1938–1950	1.0	0.1	0.0	–0.5	0.6
1950–1960	1.5	0.1	0.0	1.3	2.9
1960–1970	0.4	0.3	0.0	–1.3	–0.6
1970–1980	0.3	0.1	0.0	1.2	1.6
1980–1990	0.9	–0.1	–0.3	–1.5	–1.0
1990–2000	0.6	–0.1	–0.1	2.5	2.8
2000–2010	0.4	–0.1	0.4	–0.1	0.6
2010–2015	1.0	0.7	0.2	1.5	3.3
1870–2015	0.4	0.0	0.0	0.4	0.7

6.6 A Closer Look: Human Development in Post-1950s Africa

Data reliability only allows a breakdown of AHD at country level from 1950 onwards. In most cases, individual country estimates for earlier periods should be taken as explicit quantitative conjectures.[5]

Success in raising human development in Africa can be depicted, in Paul Collier and Stephen O'Connell's (2008) words, as the interaction of opportunities and choices. This interaction is conditioned by geography (location and endowments) and institutions and policies. Often, geographic traits, in particular, being coastal or landlocked, and resource rich or poor, are assigned a defining role in countries' success or failure in the developing world, especially Africa. Alternatively, the decisive role has been accorded to institutional constraints and policies (for a discussion, cf. Easterly and Levine, 1997; Sachs and Warner, 1997; Faye et al., 2004). Collier and O'Connell (2008: 89) have emphasised the negative role played in this interaction

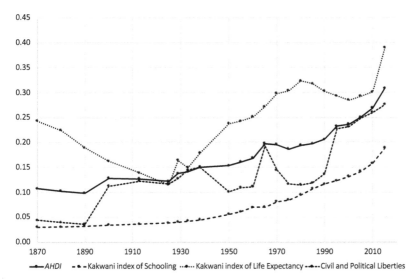

Figure 6.16 Relative AHD and its non-income dimensions in East Africa (*OECD*=1).

Sources: See the text and Table 6.5 and Chapter 4, Table 4.3.

by 'syndromes' defined as 'salient episodes of purposive failure attributable to human agency within the society'.[6] Syndromes are defined by the choices made and may be classified into four categories: regulatory – implying the regulation of economic activity, state ownership of productive resources and firms, and state-led industrialisation[7] – redistributive – that is, income redistribution between (ethnic, regional, political) groups[8] – inter-temporal – anticipated redistribution and unsustainable spending[9] – and state breakdown – when the state is unable to maintain internal security. These symptoms – presumably negatively correlated with civil and political rights – together with geographic endowments will be considered in the discussion of the performance of individual countries after World War II.

Let us look at countries in each region. In North Africa, Egypt took turns with Tunisia at the top of the AHD rankings, falling behind from 1990 to the early 2000s. Tunisia emerged as the top country in 2015, recovering the position it had occupied between the mid-1960s and mid-1980s. At the bottom appears Libya, close to Morocco until 1980 but falling behind thereafter (Table 6.13). The fact that resource-rich countries appear at the top, but Libya, also resource-

Table 6.11. *AHD catching up in East Africa: dimensions'*
contribution (%)

	Kakwani index of schooling	Kakwani index of life expectancy	UNDP index of income	Liberal democracy index	*AHDI*
1870–1880	0.0	–0.2	–0.1	–0.3	–0.5
1880–1890	0.1	–0.4	0.1	–0.2	–0.4
1890–1900	0.2	–0.4	0.0	2.9	2.6
1900–1913	0.1	–0.3	0.0	0.2	–0.1
1913–1929	0.2	0.3	0.0	0.1	0.5
1929–1938	0.3	0.2	0.0	0.5	1.0
1938–1950	0.5	0.6	–0.1	–0.8	0.2
1950–1960	0.6	0.1	0.0	0.3	1.0
1960–1970	0.4	0.4	0.0	0.6	1.5
1970–1980	0.4	0.2	–0.1	–0.6	–0.1
1980–1990	0.5	–0.2	–0.2	0.4	0.6
1990–2000	0.3	–0.1	–0.1	1.3	1.4
2000–2010	0.5	0.1	0.4	0.3	1.3
2010–2015	0.9	1.3	0.3	0.3	2.8
1870–2015	0.3	0.1	0.0	0.3	0.7

abundant, remained at the bottom therefore precludes any exclusive
hypothesis about the advantage of resource abundance. If we now
consider AHD dimensions, we find that, in terms of schooling,
Algeria, Libya, and Egypt have been at the top, after Egypt's sole
leadership until 1970, with Morocco at the bottom and lagging behind
over time. Tunisia led life expectancy, closely followed by Libya, which
sank to the bottom in the 2010s, a position held by Egypt since 1950.
In 2015, civil and political liberties were led by Tunisia, which had
occupied the first position from 1960 until its decline the mid-1980s.
Morocco, with Egypt as its close follower, took over between
1990 and 2010. Libya was at the bottom from 1970 to 2010, when
Egypt assumed this unenviable position. Lastly, in terms of adjusted
income, Tunisia led the ranking from 1990 onwards, taking over from
Libya, which had led the field by some distance after replacing Algeria
in the early 1960s. Thus, for Tunisia, leadership in terms of human
development was strongly anchored in its superior life expectancy, civil

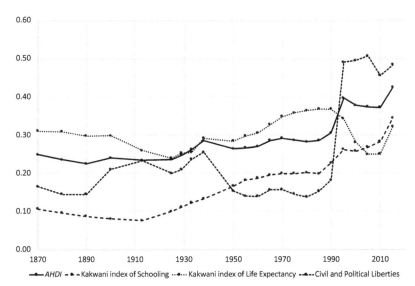

Figure 6.17 Relative AHD and its non-income dimensions in Southern Africa (*OECD*=1).
Sources: See the text and Table 6.6 and Chapter 4, Table 4.3.

and political liberties, and material well-being, while Egypt owed its lofty position to schooling and civil and political rights. At the bottom, Libya's position is closely related to its record in civil and political liberties, exacerbated by post-2010 economic collapse, which offset a distinguished long-term performance in schooling and longevity.

South of the Sahara, a clear divide appears to have existed in Central Africa, between Gabon and São Tomé and Principe, and the other countries, with Central African Republic (CAR), Democratic Republic of Congo (DR Congo), and Chad at the bottom, and Cameroon and Congo (except for a spurt in the mid-1990s) in the middle, to which Equatorial Guinea has joint in recent decades. A preliminary glance at their geographic traits suggests an opposition between coastal (and resource-rich, in the case of Gabon) countries at the top, and the landlocked, resource-poor nations (CAR, Chad, and DR Congo) at the bottom.[10] State breakdown, including civil conflict and looting, are distinctive institutional features of these three countries, DR Congo in particular. If we analyse AHD dimensions, the divide between Gabon and, on a second level, Cameroon and Congo, at the top, and DR Congo (except after 2010), CAR, and Chad is

Table 6.12. *AHD catching up in Southern Africa: dimensions'*
contribution (%)

	Kakwani index of schooling	Kakwani index of life expectancy	UNDP index of income	Liberal democracy index	AHDI
1870–1880	–0.3	0.0	0.0	–0.3	–0.5
1880–1890	–0.3	–0.1	–0.1	0.0	–0.5
1890–1900	–0.2	0.0	–0.1	0.9	0.6
1900–1913	–0.1	–0.3	0.0	0.2	–0.2
1913–1929	0.6	0.0	–0.1	–0.2	0.3
1929–1938	0.5	0.4	0.1	0.6	1.6
1938–1950	0.5	–0.1	0.0	–1.1	–0.6
1950–1960	0.3	0.2	0.0	–0.2	0.2
1960–1970	0.2	0.3	0.0	0.3	0.8
1970–1980	0.0	0.1	–0.1	–0.3	–0.3
1980–1990	0.3	0.0	–0.2	0.7	0.8
1990–2000	0.3	–0.7	–0.1	2.5	2.1
2000–2010	0.2	–0.3	0.1	–0.2	–0.1
2010–2015	1.0	1.3	0.1	0.3	2.6
1870–2015	0.2	0.0	0.0	0.2	0.4

confirmed by schooling and – adding São Tomé and Principe to the top – by life expectancy and civil and political rights. When freedoms are considered, Equatorial Guinea, the best performer in terms of adjusted income, and Congo, a country that also ranks high in terms of material welfare, join Chad and DR Congo, which also appear at the lowest levels in adjusted income (as does CAR), at the bottom. There is noticeable contraction across the board in life expectancy during the 1990s, associated with HIV/AIDS (except for São Tomé and Principe), which percolated through to material well-being.

In West Africa, a well-defined pattern emerges. Ghana appears as the highest-ranking AHD country since 1950, closely dependent on its schooling advantage, in addition to life expectancy and civil and political liberties between 1950 and 1970, and civil and political liberties and material well-being as of 2000, as life expectancy fell between the mid-1990s and 2010 as a result of HIV/AIDS (Agyei-Mensah, 2001). Benin and Senegal appear in distant second and third place to

Table 6.13. *AHDI in African countries, 1950–2015*

	1950	1955	1960	1965	1970	1975	1980	1985	1990	1995	2000	2005	2010	2015
North Africa	*0.109*	*0.103*	*0.116*	*0.131*	*0.138*	*0.154*	*0.178*	*0.212*	*0.234*	*0.250*	*0.273*	*0.289*	*0.305*	*0.313*
Algeria	0.101	0.102	0.089	0.112	0.127	0.144	0.178	0.207	0.246	0.249	0.271	0.285	0.301	0.327
Egypt	0.129	0.117	0.129	0.140	0.144	0.159	0.176	0.222	0.242	0.258	0.283	0.295	0.309	0.264
Libya	0.066	0.084	0.099	0.126	0.102	0.117	0.156	0.173	0.185	0.203	0.217	0.229	0.249	0.290
Morocco	0.065	0.071	0.089	0.113	0.121	0.128	0.161	0.180	0.203	0.228	0.251	0.273	0.293	0.322
Tunisia	0.074	0.081	0.124	0.140	0.158	0.184	0.210	0.228	0.218	0.234	0.251	0.267	0.285	0.457
Central Africa	*0.065*	*0.072*	*0.090*	*0.098*	*0.089*	*0.097*	*0.105*	*0.119*	*0.133*	*0.135*	*0.139*	*0.153*	*0.171*	*0.205*
Cameroon	0.067	0.080	0.087	0.099	0.108	0.121	0.138	0.167	0.183	0.188	0.196	0.199	0.212	0.222
CAR	0.069	0.075	0.076	0.085	0.071	0.075	0.104	0.110	0.131	0.156	0.158	0.151	0.158	0.161
Chad	0.039	0.041	0.047	0.055	0.062	0.062	0.060	0.064	0.073	0.086	0.095	0.104	0.116	0.144
Congo	0.089	0.099	0.122	0.116	0.092	0.117	0.142	0.154	0.188	0.267	0.182	0.199	0.197	0.230
Congo DR	0.063	0.068	0.092	0.099	0.082	0.088	0.091	0.100	0.112	0.094	0.102	0.122	0.141	0.181
Equatorial Guinea	0.052	0.064	0.086	0.103	0.086	0.080	0.102	0.130	0.141	0.154	0.167	0.179	0.180	0.196
Gabon	0.090	0.108	0.129	0.132	0.142	0.164	0.188	0.201	0.235	0.261	0.260	0.275	0.305	0.343
São Tomé & Principe	0.055	0.061	0.071	0.089	0.103	0.143	0.167	0.186	0.210	0.281	0.295	0.307	0.323	0.349
West Africa	*0.067*	*0.083*	*0.103*	*0.110*	*0.108*	*0.112*	*0.144*	*0.128*	*0.143*	*0.168*	*0.204*	*0.219*	*0.234*	*0.273*
Benin	0.052	0.064	0.088	0.086	0.091	0.092	0.108	0.121	0.155	0.219	0.229	0.251	0.269	0.275
Burkina Faso	0.046	0.050	0.056	0.060	0.054	0.061	0.069	0.080	0.084	0.124	0.148	0.160	0.177	0.184
Côte d'Ivoire	0.054	0.061	0.076	0.090	0.103	0.123	0.150	0.162	0.177	0.199	0.184	0.219	0.231	0.244

Table 6.13. (*cont.*)

	1950	1955	1960	1965	1970	1975	1980	1985	1990	1995	2000	2005	2010	2015
Gambia	0.060	0.068	0.076	0.090	0.108	0.120	0.139	0.159	0.176	0.135	0.156	0.168	0.175	0.179
Ghana	0.110	0.139	0.163	0.170	0.204	0.167	0.249	0.168	0.184	0.268	0.300	0.314	0.322	0.361
Guinea	0.032	0.038	0.044	0.053	0.060	0.068	0.078	0.089	0.097	0.130	0.138	0.154	0.157	0.174
Guinea-Bissau	0.024	0.026	0.029	0.040	0.047	0.071	0.078	0.080	0.087	0.132	0.140	0.153	0.163	0.203
Liberia	0.083	0.089	0.098	0.109	0.120	0.143	0.112	0.144	0.130	0.137	0.181	0.216	0.270	0.283
Mali	0.043	0.047	0.067	0.070	0.064	0.077	0.090	0.098	0.103	0.142	0.147	0.177	0.188	0.210
Mauritania	0.084	0.090	0.111	0.113	0.121	0.129	0.115	0.121	0.123	0.164	0.178	0.171	0.231	0.223
Niger	0.043	0.044	0.052	0.056	0.059	0.062	0.073	0.078	0.106	0.128	0.134	0.148	0.128	0.197
Nigeria	0.068	0.089	0.111	0.116	0.102	0.108	0.145	0.118	0.132	0.133	0.204	0.215	0.232	0.286
Senegal	0.066	0.072	0.094	0.101	0.115	0.133	0.154	0.178	0.196	0.220	0.229	0.214	0.246	0.282
Sierra Leone	0.050	0.066	0.078	0.097	0.084	0.097	0.111	0.117	0.121	0.095	0.120	0.193	0.206	0.206
Togo	0.049	0.054	0.074	0.080	0.076	0.098	0.127	0.133	0.146	0.175	0.187	0.188	0.224	0.226
East Africa	*0.063*	*0.072*	*0.080*	*0.098*	*0.103*	*0.104*	*0.116*	*0.124*	*0.135*	*0.158*	*0.167*	*0.182*	*0.205*	*0.233*
Burundi	0.055	0.061	0.069	0.086	0.080	0.085	0.095	0.113	0.101	0.125	0.132	0.140	0.153	0.129
Eritrea	0.058	0.064	0.068	0.057	0.062	0.058	0.060	0.062	0.074	0.101	0.104	0.096	0.102	0.107
Ethiopia	0.033	0.039	0.043	0.049	0.055	0.050	0.056	0.060	0.078	0.107	0.118	0.121	0.144	0.170
Kenya	0.082	0.091	0.106	0.140	0.148	0.158	0.177	0.186	0.207	0.233	0.235	0.256	0.272	0.293
Rwanda	0.052	0.058	0.080	0.103	0.111	0.106	0.123	0.134	0.113	0.097	0.137	0.165	0.183	0.224
Seychelles	0.251	0.266	0.282	0.296	0.319	0.331	0.310	0.325	0.341	0.379	0.401	0.453	0.463	0.459
Sudan	0.060	0.076	0.066	0.082	0.074	0.094	0.107	0.118	0.080	0.097	0.099	0.151	0.161	0.176
Tanzania	0.091	0.096	0.112	0.139	0.144	0.148	0.156	0.163	0.171	0.194	0.202	0.221	0.254	0.304

Uganda	0.092	0.100	0.114	0.139	0.124	0.083	0.102	0.101	0.146	0.167	0.174	0.196	0.232	0.257
Southern Africa	*0.108*	*0.119*	*0.128*	*0.142*	*0.154*	*0.160*	*0.169*	*0.180*	*0.201*	*0.270*	*0.266*	*0.272*	*0.284*	*0.320*
Angola	0.036	0.038	0.041	0.050	0.058	0.073	0.082	0.090	0.101	0.114	0.121	0.152	0.190	0.210
Botswana	0.080	0.090	0.098	0.129	0.194	0.233	0.263	0.330	0.384	0.397	0.372	0.390	0.410	0.443
Eswatini	0.075	0.086	0.096	0.124	0.148	0.158	0.188	0.207	0.219	0.223	0.207	0.192	0.200	0.207
Lesotho	0.098	0.107	0.116	0.141	0.145	0.157	0.172	0.182	0.209	0.241	0.229	0.272	0.279	0.288
Madagascar	0.087	0.097	0.108	0.124	0.131	0.130	0.132	0.141	0.147	0.209	0.210	0.217	0.191	0.262
Malawi	0.049	0.057	0.065	0.082	0.086	0.099	0.109	0.118	0.124	0.209	0.215	0.219	0.245	0.270
Mauritius	0.198	0.220	0.237	0.254	0.313	0.337	0.374	0.404	0.428	0.453	0.471	0.488	0.493	0.547
Mozambique	0.041	0.048	0.052	0.061	0.065	0.086	0.086	0.096	0.122	0.168	0.193	0.189	0.205	0.242
Namibia	0.110	0.120	0.129	0.145	0.152	0.164	0.188	0.208	0.330	0.352	0.336	0.339	0.356	0.390
South Africa	0.153	0.167	0.177	0.185	0.198	0.204	0.210	0.222	0.250	0.375	0.367	0.370	0.378	0.430
Zambia	0.114	0.121	0.131	0.171	0.176	0.176	0.185	0.187	0.192	0.235	0.217	0.228	0.256	0.299
Zimbabwe	0.128	0.141	0.147	0.142	0.159	0.169	0.202	0.226	0.254	0.247	0.207	0.185	0.217	0.256
Africa	*0.083*	*0.092*	*0.107*	*0.119*	*0.121*	*0.128*	*0.151*	*0.154*	*0.169*	*0.201*	*0.218*	*0.230*	*0.245*	*0.276*

Ghana based on their achievements in life expectancy (only since the 2010s in Senegal) and civil and political rights (from 1995 onwards in Benin). In addition, Liberia and Nigeria moved closer to Benin and Senegal from the late 2000s onwards. At the bottom of the AHD league appear Guinea, Burkina Faso, Niger, Mali, and Guinea Bissau, joined by Gambia from the 1990s onwards. Performance in schooling confirms the bottom positions of Niger, Burkina Faso, Mali, and Guinea Bissau, and those of Niger and Guinea Bissau (joined by Sierra Leone and Nigeria) in terms of life expectancy. In civil and political liberties, Guinea, Mali, and Guinea Bissau (until 1990) sit at the bottom again – joined by Togo, Mauritania, and Gambia (from 1995) – as are, in terms of material welfare, Guinea and Niger (and Togo, as of 2000). Thus, we find coastal countries at the top, to which Liberia and Nigeria add the feature of being resource abundant and, at the bottom, landlocked and resource-poor countries that are also syndrome victims: Burkina Faso, Mali – which suffered from looting between the late 1960s and the early 1990s – and Niger – a failed state during the 1990s. However, Guinea and Guinea Bissau were also coastal countries (and, the former, resource rich), but both victims of the regulatory syndrome and to state breakdown in the 2000s (in the latter's case). Thus, institutions prevailed over geographic features in conditioning West African countries' AHD performance.

In East Africa, apart from the Seychelles, an exception with the highest levels of AHD and its dimensions by far (headed only by Tanzania in civil and political liberties), Kenya and Tanzania, followed by Uganda, to which Rwanda has been catching up during the last two decades, are at the top in terms of AHD and its dimensions of schooling and civil and political liberties. However, these countries do not lead longevity and material well-being. In the case of life expectancy, it is worth noting the dramatic collapse of Kenya and, to a lesser extent, Uganda and Burundi, in the 1990s, as a consequence of HIV/AIDS, and that of Rwanda, where genocide and pandemics provoked the sharpest fall in life expectancy, which in 1995 was the lowest in Africa since 1950. A process of convergence has taken place in life expectancy during the past decade. At the opposite end of the spectrum are the cases of civil and political rights and, to a lesser extent, material well-being, in which dispersion has increased since 1990. The bottom AHD positions are occupied by Sudan, Burundi, Ethiopia, and Eritrea.[11] These results are confirmed for civil and political rights, schooling (but not for Eritrea), and adjusted income (except Sudan). In the case of life expectancy, the last places correspond to Uganda and Burundi and, until 2010, Rwanda, countries severely hit by HIV/AIDS. It is worth stressing that, contrary to Kenya and Tanzania, both coastal countries, the countries that fared worse in terms of human development were landlocked, resource-poor countries. However, these countries also suffered from institutional difficulties or syndromes. Ethiopia was subjected to strict regulatory controls, Burundi was a breakdown state in the 1960s and from the late 1980s onwards, and was affected by regulatory and redistributive syndromes. Sudan suffered looting and state failure. Rwanda, which experienced a redistributive syndrome between the early 1970s and 1990s, recovered, however, after 2000. Interestingly, Uganda, another landlocked, resource-poor nation, which suffered looting and state breakdown, managed to catch up from the late 1990s onwards.

Lastly, in Southern Africa, Angola and Mozambique, coastal countries severely hit by civil war, state failure, and regulatory and redistributive syndromes, have been at the bottom over time, with the addition of Zimbabwe and Eswatini (former Swaziland) since 2000. Zimbabwe's misfortunes can hardly be attributed to being landlocked, but rather to economic and political mismanagement. Strict regulatory controls (including state ownership of enterprises and protectionism) have existed in Zimbabwe since 1980, accompanied by looting at the turn of the century. Meanwhile, coastal and largely syndrome-free countries (except for South Africa prior to the early 1990s) are found at the top: Mauritius, clearly ahead of the rest, followed by South Africa (which gained considerable momentum from 1995 onwards), Botswana (since 1970), and Namibia (since 1990). Although South Africa and Botswana had been severely hit by HIV/AIDS since 1990, democratisation enabled them to improve their relative AHD positions (Maitpose and Matsheka, 2008). A closer look reveals that the countries at the top in terms of human development also led each of its dimensions (except Namibia in terms of education). Conversely, those countries at the bottom in AHD terms also had the lowest level in all dimensions, except for material well-being in the case of Angola and schooling in the case of Zimbabwe. Mozambique was also at the bottom in terms of schooling and civil and political rights, and Eswatini in schooling and life expectancy.

In the case of South Africa, its high index of human development by African standards conceals wide differences between the White and non-White (Black and Asian descent) population. Thus, for example, in 1950, life expectancy at birth was, on average, 45 years, but this figure conceals the fact that it was 65.7 years among Whites but only 40 years among Blacks (Simkins and van Heyningen, 1989; UN, 2000). The absolute gap, which had been widening during the first half of the twentieth century, narrowed, without closing completely, thereafter.[12] Similar gaps also existed in education and income (Feinstein 2005).

If we now consider the country ranking (Table 6.14), we find that, leaving aside the exceptional cases of the islands of Mauritius and the Seychelles, with low population density, which occupy the top positions from 1950 to 2015, the first quartile consists of Southern African countries – South Africa, Namibia, Botswana (from 1970), and Lesotho, Zambia, and Zimbabwe (until 1970, 1980, and 1990, respectively) – followed by those from the North (all but Libya), plus the exception of Ghana, a West African country. The top AHD countries closely reflect Asongu and Nwachukwu's (2017) typology, according to which middle-income, English common law, oil-poor, non-landlocked, Christian-oriented, and politically stable countries tend to achieve higher human development.

Although it presents a shift from West and Southern to Central and East countries, the lowest quartile has had a very stable composition: most countries at the bottom have remained there throughout the nearly 60 years considered. These include landlocked and resource-poor countries: Burkina Faso, Mali (up to 1990), and Niger, in West Africa; Burundi, in East Africa; and Chad, in Central Africa, plus coastal countries, both resource-rich (Guinea, and Sierra Leone) and resource-poor (Guinea-Bissau in West Africa, and Ethiopia and Eritrea in East Africa). All have undergone episodes of severe economic regulation and redistribution, including looting and/or state breakdown. These bottom countries were joined by landlocked and resource-poor countries – DR Congo (from 1980) and CAR (1970 and 2005–2015) – which had in common failed states and civil conflict, and by Mozambique (up to 1980) and Angola (until 2005), both coastal countries (and only Angola resource abundant) that experienced regulatory syndrome, including looting, and state breakdown, associated with civil war. Therefore, it seems clear that poor institutional setting, rather than geographic traits, is the common denominator of countries at the bottom of the AHD ranking.

How do countries' performance in terms of human development relate to their initial levels? A simple scattered diagram suggests a weak

Table 6.14. *AHD ranking of African countries, 1950–2015*

	1950		1960		1970		1980
Seychelles	0.251	Seychelles	0.282	Mauritius	0.319	Mauritius	0.374
Mauritius	0.198	Mauritius	0.237	Seychelles	0.313	Seychelles	0.310
South Africa	0.153	South Africa	0.177	Ghana	0.204	Botswana	0.263
Egypt	0.129	Ghana	0.163	South Africa	0.198	Ghana	0.249
Zimbabwe	0.128	Zimbabwe	0.147	Botswana	0.194	Tunisia	0.210
Zambia	0.114	Zambia	0.131	Zambia	0.176	South Africa	0.210
Namibia	0.110	Gabon	0.129	Zimbabwe	0.159	Zimbabwe	0.202
Ghana	0.110	Namibia	0.129	Tunisia	0.158	Namibia	0.188
Algeria	0.101	Egypt	0.129	Namibia	0.152	Gabon	0.188
Lesotho	0.098	Tunisia	0.124	Eswatini	0.148	Eswatini	0.188
Uganda	0.092	Congo	0.122	Kenya	0.148	Zambia	0.185
Tanzania	0.091	Lesotho	0.116	Lesotho	0.145	Algeria	0.178
Gabon	0.090	Uganda	0.114	Tanzania	0.144	Kenya	0.177
Congo	0.089	Tanzania	0.112	Egypt	0.144	Egypt	0.176
Madagascar	0.087	Mauritania	0.111	Gabon	0.142	Lesotho	0.172
Mauritania	0.084	Nigeria	0.111	Madagascar	0.131	São Tomé & Principe	0.167
Nigeria		Madagascar	0.108	Algeria	0.127	Morocco	0.161
Liberia	0.083	Kenya	0.106	Uganda	0.124	Libya	0.156
Kenya	0.082	Libya	0.099	Mauritania	0.121	Tanzania	0.156
Botswana	0.080	Botswana	0.098	Morocco	0.121	Senegal	0.154
Eswatini	0.075						

Table 6.14. (cont.)

	1950		1960		1970		1980
Tunisia	0.074	Liberia	0.098	Liberia	0.120	Côte d'Ivoire	0.150
CAR	0.069	Eswatini	0.096	Senegal	0.115	Nigeria	0.145
Nigeria	0.068	Senegal	0.094	Rwanda	0.111	Congo	0.142
Cameroon	0.067	Congo DR	0.092	Cameroon	0.108	Gambia	0.139
Libya	0.066	Morocco	0.089	Gambia	0.108	Cameroon	0.138
Senegal	0.066	Algeria	0.089	Côte d'Ivoire	0.103	Madagascar	0.132
Morocco	0.065	Benin	0.088	São Tomé & Príncipe	0.103	Togo	0.127
Congo DR	0.063	Cameroon	0.087	Libya	0.102	Rwanda	0.123
Sudan	0.060	Equatorial Guinea	0.086	Nigeria	0.102	Mauritania	0.115
Gambia	0.060	Rwanda	0.080	Congo	0.092	Liberia	0.112
Eritrea	0.058	Sierra Leone	0.078	Benin	0.091	Sierra Leone	0.111
São Tomé & Príncipe	0.055	CAR	0.076	Equatorial Guinea	0.086	Malawi	0.109
Burundi	0.055	Gambia	0.076	Malawi	0.086	Benin	0.108
Côte d'Ivoire	0.054	Côte d'Ivoire	0.076	Sierra Leone	0.084	Sudan	0.107
Equatorial Guinea	0.052	Togo	0.074	Congo DR	0.082	CAR	0.104
Rwanda	0.052	São Tomé & Príncipe	0.071	Burundi	0.080	Equatorial Guinea	0.102
Benin	0.052	Togo	0.069	Togo	0.076	Uganda	0.102
Sierra Leone	0.050	Sudan	0.068	Sudan	0.074	Burundi	0.095

1990		2000		2010		2015	
Togo	0.049	Mali	0.067	CAR	0.071	Congo DR	0.091
Malawi	0.049	Sudan	0.066	Mozambique	0.065	Mali	0.090
Burkina Faso	0.046	Malawi	0.065	Mali	0.064	Mozambique	0.086
Niger	0.043	Burkina Faso	0.056	Eritrea	0.062	Angola	0.082
Mali	0.043	Mozambique	0.052	Chad	0.062	Guinea	0.078
Mozambique	0.041	Niger	0.052	Guinea	0.060	Guinea-Bissau	0.078
Chad	0.039	Chad	0.047	Niger	0.059	Niger	0.073
Angola	0.036	Guinea	0.044	Angola	0.058	Burkina Faso	0.069
Ethiopia	0.033	Ethiopia	0.043	Ethiopia	0.055	Chad	0.060
Guinea	0.032	Angola	0.041	Burkina Faso	0.054	Eritrea	0.060
Guinea-Bissau	0.024	Guinea-Bissau	0.029	Guinea-Bissau	0.047	Ethiopia	0.056

1990		2000		2010		2015	
Mauritius	0.428	Mauritius	0.471	Mauritius	0.493	Mauritius	0.547
Botswana	0.384	Seychelles	0.401	Seychelles	0.463	Seychelles	0.459
Seychelles	0.341	Botswana	0.372	Tunisia	0.410	Tunisia	0.457
Namibia	0.330	South Africa	0.367	Botswana	0.378	Botswana	0.443
Zimbabwe	0.254	Namibia	0.336	South Africa	0.356	South Africa	0.430
South Africa	0.250	São Tomé & Principe	0.300	Namibia	0.323	Namibia	0.390
Algeria	0.246	Ghana	0.295	Ghana	0.322	Ghana	0.361
Egypt	0.242	Egypt	0.283	São Tomé & Principe	0.309	São Tomé & Principe	0.349
Gabon	0.235	Gabon	0.271	Gabon	0.305	Gabon	0.343
Eswatini	0.219	Algeria	0.260	Algeria	0.301	Algeria	0.327
Tunisia	0.218	Morocco	0.251	Morocco	0.293	Morocco	0.322

Table 6.14. (*cont.*)

	1990		2000		2010		2015
São Tomé & Príncipe	0.210	Tunisia	0.251	Tunisia	0.285	Tanzania	0.304
Lesotho	0.209	Kenya	0.235	Lesotho	0.279	Zambia	0.299
Kenya	0.207	Senegal	0.229	Kenya	0.272	Kenya	0.293
Morocco	0.203	Lesotho	0.229	Liberia	0.270	Libya	0.290
Senegal	0.196	Benin	0.229	Benin	0.269	Lesotho	0.288
Zambia	0.192	Zambia	0.217	Zambia	0.256	Nigeria	0.286
Congo	0.188	Tanzania	0.217	Tanzania	0.254	Liberia	0.283
Libya	0.185	Libya	0.215	Libya	0.249	Senegal	0.282
Ghana	0.184	Senegal	0.210	Senegal	0.246	Benin	0.275
Cameroon	0.183	Malawi	0.207	Malawi	0.245	Malawi	0.270
Côte d'Ivoire	0.177	Zimbabwe	0.207	Nigeria	0.232	Egypt	0.264
Gambia	0.176	Nigeria	0.204	Uganda	0.232	Madagascar	0.262
Tanzania	0.171	Tanzania	0.202	Mauritania	0.231	Uganda	0.257
Benin	0.155	Cameroon	0.196	Côte d'Ivoire	0.231	Zimbabwe	0.256
Madagascar	0.147	Mozambique	0.193	Togo	0.224	Côte d'Ivoire	0.244
Uganda	0.146	Togo	0.187	Zimbabwe	0.217	Mozambique	0.242
Togo	0.146	Côte d'Ivoire	0.184	Cameroon	0.212	Congo	0.230
Equatorial Guinea	0.141	Congo	0.182	Sierra Leone	0.206	Togo	0.226
Nigeria	0.132	Liberia	0.181	Mozambique	0.205	Rwanda	0.224
CAR	0.131	Mauritania	0.178	Eswatini	0.200	Mauritania	0.223
Liberia	0.130	Uganda	0.174	Congo	0.197	Cameroon	0.222

Malawi	0.124	Equatorial Guinea	0.167	Madagascar	0.191	Mali	0.210
Mauritania	0.123	CAR	0.158	Angola	0.190	Angola	0.210
Mozambique	0.122	Gambia	0.156	Mali	0.188	Eswatini	0.207
Sierra Leone	0.121	Burkina Faso	0.148	Rwanda	0.183	Sierra Leone	0.206
Rwanda	0.113	Mali	0.147	Equatorial Guinea	0.180	Guinea-Bissau	0.203
Congo DR	0.112	Guinea-Bissau	0.140	Burkina Faso	0.177	Niger	0.197
Niger	0.106	Guinea	0.138	Gambia	0.175	Equatorial Guinea	0.196
Mali	0.103	Rwanda	0.137	Guinea-Bissau	0.163	Burkina Faso	0.184
Burundi	0.101	Niger	0.134	Sudan	0.161	Congo DR	0.181
Angola	0.101	Burundi	0.132	CAR	0.158	Gambia	0.179
Guinea	0.097	Angola	0.121	Guinea	0.157	Sudan	0.176
Guinea-Bissau	0.087	Sierra Leone	0.120	Burundi	0.153	Guinea	0.174
Burkina Faso	0.084	Ethiopia	0.118	Ethiopia	0.144	Ethiopia	0.170
Sudan	0.080	Eritrea	0.104	Congo DR	0.141	CAR	0.161
Ethiopia	0.078	Congo DR	0.102	Niger	0.128	Chad	0.144
Eritrea	0.074	Sudan	0.099	Chad	0.116	Burundi	0.129
Chad	0.073	Chad	0.095	Eritrea	0.102	Eritrea	0.107

negative correlation between initial AHD levels and its rate of growth over 1950–1980. A correlation that increases significantly, however, when only the post-1980 period is considered. This suggests that there was a slight tendency to converge in post-1950 Africa, consistent with the persistence observed in the composition of the top and bottom quartiles.

AHD growth is ranked by countries along with its breakdown into its dimensions' contributions over the periods 1950–1980, 1980–2015, and 1950–2015 in Table 6.15. It appears that from 1950–1980, schooling made the main contribution to AHD growth (over half on average), followed by life expectancy, while civil and political liberties and adjusted income had a residual contribution. Meanwhile, in the post-1980 period, civil and political rights and schooling dominated AHD growth, with life expectancy relegated to a minor contribution. If the entire period 1950–2015 is considered, schooling contributed nearly half of AHD growth, and life expectancy and civil and political rights almost a quarter each.

6.7 Concluding Remarks

There has been sustained improvement in human development in Africa since 1880, faster between 1920 and 1960, under colonial rule, but the continent remained in the bottom 10 per cent of world distribution over time. A contrast exists, however, between North and Southern Africa, which moved away from the bottom, and the remaining regions, that remained there.

Although Africa's AHD relative position in the world was lower than in terms of GDP per head, the long-run performance in terms of human development does not confirm the pessimistic assessments of Africa derived from real GDP per head, as AHD doubled per capita GDP growth rate, and thrived during phases of sluggish economic performance (1913–1950 and 1980–2000). Thus, non-income dimensions drove AHD gains. Schooling made the largest single contribution to AHD over time, followed by similar contributions by longevity and political and civil liberties, helping explain the disparities between the behaviour of AHD and per capita income.

Life expectancy gains simultaneous to faltering growth of GDP per head in the 1980s appear to be consistent with an upward shift in the health function, triggered by medical technology improvements, while no movements take place along the function as a consequence of

Table 6.15. *AHD growth and its breakdown by dimensions, 1950–2015*

1950–1980	AHDI	Schooling	Life expectancy	Liberal democracy	Adjusted income
Botswana	4.0	1.1	0.7	1.5	0.7
Guinea-Bissau	4.0	1.8	0.5	1.1	0.5
São Tomé & Príncipe	3.7	2.4	0.5	0.5	0.3
Tunisia	3.5	1.3	0.7	1.3	0.3
Côte d'Ivoire	3.4	1.9	0.9	0.4	0.2
Togo	3.2	1.8	0.8	0.3	0.2
Eswatini	3.0	1.2	0.8	0.4	0.7
Morocco	3.0	1.2	0.6	1.2	0.1
Guinea	3.0	2.2	0.7	-0.2	0.3
Rwanda	2.9	1.4	0.3	1.0	0.2
Libya	2.9	1.8	0.7	-0.5	0.9
Gambia	2.8	1.0	0.9	0.7	0.1
Senegal	2.8	1.5	0.5	0.8	0.0
Angola	2.8	1.9	0.7	0.2	0.0
Ghana	2.7	1.2	0.5	1.1	0.0
Malawi	2.7	1.4	0.4	0.4	0.4
Sierra Leone	2.6	1.4	0.7	0.2	0.2
Kenya	2.6	1.1	0.7	0.6	0.2
Nigeria	2.5	1.2	0.4	0.7	0.2
Mali	2.5	1.3	0.5	0.5	0.2
Benin	2.5	0.9	0.8	0.7	0.0

Table 6.15. (cont.)

1950–1980	AHDI	Schooling	Life expectancy	Liberal democracy	Adjusted income
Mozambique	2.5	1.3	0.5	0.7	0.0
Gabon	2.5	1.2	0.7	0.3	0.3
Cameroon	2.4	1.4	0.7	0.1	0.2
Equatorial Guinea	2.2	1.3	0.5	0.0	0.5
Mauritius	2.1	0.8	0.5	0.7	0.1
Sudan	1.9	1.2	0.5	0.2	0.0
Algeria	1.9	1.0	0.6	0.0	0.2
Lesotho	1.9	0.5	0.7	0.3	0.4
Burundi	1.9	0.7	0.4	0.6	0.3
Ethiopia	1.8	1.2	0.6	-0.3	0.3
Tanzania	1.8	0.3	0.6	0.7	0.2
Niger	1.8	1.1	0.4	0.1	0.1
Namibia	1.8	0.7	0.8	0.2	0.1
Zambia	1.6	0.6	0.6	0.2	0.1
Congo	1.5	1.4	0.8	-0.9	0.2
Zimbabwe	1.5	0.7	0.7	-0.1	0.2
Chad	1.4	1.3	0.8	-0.6	-0.2

	AHDI	Schooling	Life expectancy	Liberal democracy	Adjusted income
CAR	1.4	1.1	0.6	-0.3	0.0
Madagascar	1.4	0.7	0.5	0.2	0.0
Burkina Faso	1.3	0.7	0.6	-0.1	0.2
Congo DR	1.2	1.0	0.3	-0.1	0.0
South Africa	1.0	0.5	0.5	0.0	0.1
Egypt	1.0	0.7	0.6	-0.4	0.2
Mauritania	1.0	0.3	0.8	-0.5	0.4
Liberia	1.0	1.4	0.5	-0.9	0.1
Seychelles	0.7	0.1	0.3	0.0	0.2
Uganda	0.3	0.7	0.4	-0.7	-0.1
Eritrea	0.1	1.2	0.4	-1.7	0.3

1980–2015	AHDI	Schooling	Life expectancy	Liberal democracy	Adjusted income
Ethiopia	3.2	1.0	0.7	1.3	0.2
Mozambique	2.9	0.9	0.4	1.3	0.3
Niger	2.8	1.1	0.8	1.1	-0.1
Burkina Faso	2.8	1.4	0.5	0.8	0.2
Guinea-Bissau	2.7	0.9	0.5	1.3	0.0
Angola	2.7	1.3	0.4	0.8	0.2
Benin	2.7	1.0	0.3	1.3	0.1
Liberia	2.7	0.6	0.4	1.7	-0.1
Uganda	2.6	0.8	0.3	1.3	0.3
Malawi	2.6	0.6	0.6	1.3	0.1
Chad	2.5	1.2	0.1	0.8	0.5
Mali	2.4	0.9	0.6	0.7	0.2

Table 6.15. (*cont.*)

1980–2015	AHDI	Schooling	Life expectancy	Liberal democracy	Adjusted income
Guinea	2.3	0.5	0.5	1.2	0.1
Tunisia	2.2	0.7	0.4	0.9	0.2
São Tomé & Príncipe	2.1	0.9	0.2	1.0	0.0
Namibia	2.1	0.2	0.2	1.6	0.1
South Africa	2.0	0.7	0.0	1.3	0.0
Morocco	2.0	0.9	0.5	0.4	0.2
Congo DR	2.0	0.9	0.4	1.0	-0.3
Madagascar	2.0	0.9	0.5	0.7	-0.2
Nigeria	1.9	1.1	0.3	0.4	0.1
Tanzania	1.9	0.8	0.5	0.4	0.2
Mauritania	1.9	0.6	0.3	0.9	0.1
Equatorial Guinea	1.9	0.3	0.5	0.6	0.5
Sierra Leone	1.8	0.4	0.3	1.0	0.0
Libya	1.8	0.7	0.4	1.0	-0.4
Algeria	1.7	0.8	0.5	0.4	0.0
Senegal	1.7	0.6	0.6	0.5	0.1
Gabon	1.7	0.7	0.3	0.7	0.0
Rwanda	1.7	0.7	0.6	0.2	0.1
Eritrea	1.7	0.8	0.6	0.0	0.2
Togo	1.6	0.6	0.2	1.0	-0.1
Botswana	1.5	1.0	0.1	0.1	0.3

1950–2015	AHDI	Schooling	Life expectancy	Liberal democracy	Adjusted income
Lesotho	1.5	0.4	-0.1	0.9	0.3
Kenya	1.4	0.4	0.1	0.8	0.1
Sudan	1.4	0.8	0.4	0.1	0.1
Côte d'Ivoire	1.4	1.0	-0.1	0.7	-0.1
Congo	1.4	0.4	0.1	0.8	0.1
Zambia	1.4	0.3	0.3	0.7	0.1
Cameroon	1.4	0.6	0.2	0.6	0.0
CAR	1.2	0.9	0.1	0.6	-0.3
Egypt	1.2	0.7	0.5	-0.2	0.1
Seychelles	1.1	0.1	0.2	0.7	0.2
Mauritius	1.1	0.5	0.3	0.1	0.2
Ghana	1.1	0.4	0.3	0.2	0.2
Burundi	0.9	0.9	0.3	-0.2	-0.1
Gambia	0.7	0.9	0.4	-0.7	0.0
Zimbabwe	0.7	0.6	0.0	0.2	-0.1
Eswatini	0.3	0.4	-0.2	-0.1	0.1
Guinea-Bissau	3.3	1.3	0.5	1.2	0.2
São Tomé & Príncipe	2.8	1.6	0.3	0.7	0.1
Tunisia	2.8	1.0	0.5	1.1	0.2
Angola	2.7	1.6	0.5	0.5	0.1
Mozambique	2.7	1.1	0.5	1.0	0.2
Malawi	2.6	1.0	0.5	0.9	0.2

Table 6.15. (cont.)

1950–2015	AHDI	Schooling	Life expectancy	Liberal democracy	Adjusted income
Botswana	2.6	1.0	0.4	0.7	0.5
Guinea	2.6	1.3	0.6	0.5	0.2
Benin	2.6	1.0	0.5	1.0	0.1
Ethiopia	2.5	1.1	0.6	0.6	0.2
Morocco	2.5	1.0	0.5	0.7	0.1
Mali	2.5	1.1	0.5	0.6	0.2
Niger	2.4	1.1	0.6	0.7	0.0
Togo	2.3	1.2	0.5	0.7	0.1
Côte d'Ivoire	2.3	1.4	0.3	0.6	0.0
Libya	2.3	1.2	0.5	0.3	0.2
Rwanda	2.3	1.0	0.4	0.6	0.2
Senegal	2.2	1.0	0.6	0.6	0.0
Nigeria	2.2	1.2	0.3	0.6	0.2
Sierra Leone	2.2	0.9	0.5	0.7	0.1
Burkina Faso	2.1	1.0	0.5	0.4	0.2
Gabon	2.1	1.0	0.5	0.5	0.1
Equatorial Guinea	2.0	0.7	0.5	0.3	0.5
Chad	2.0	1.2	0.4	0.1	0.2
Kenya	2.0	0.7	0.4	0.7	0.1
Namibia	1.9	0.5	0.5	0.9	0.1
Liberia	1.9	0.9	0.4	0.5	0.0

Tanzania	1.8	0.6	0.5	0.6	0.2
Cameroon	1.8	1.0	0.4	0.4	0.1
Ghana	1.8	0.8	0.3	0.6	0.1
Algeria	1.8	0.9	0.6	0.2	0.1
Gambia	1.7	1.0	0.7	0.0	0.1
Madagascar	1.7	0.8	0.5	0.4	-0.1
Sudan	1.7	1.0	0.5	0.1	0.1
Lesotho	1.7	0.5	0.2	0.6	0.3
Congo DR	1.6	1.0	0.4	0.5	-0.2
Uganda	1.6	0.8	0.4	0.4	0.1
South Africa	1.6	0.6	0.2	0.7	0.1
Mauritius	1.6	0.6	0.4	0.4	0.2
Eswatini	1.6	0.8	0.3	0.1	0.4
Mauritania	1.5	0.5	0.5	0.3	0.2
Zambia	1.5	0.5	0.4	0.5	0.1
Congo	1.5	0.9	0.4	0.0	0.1
Burundi	1.3	0.8	0.3	0.1	0.1
CAR	1.3	1.0	0.3	0.2	-0.2
Egypt	1.1	0.7	0.5	-0.3	0.2
Zimbabwe	1.1	0.6	0.3	0.1	0.1
Eritrea	1.0	1.0	0.5	-0.8	0.2
Seychelles	0.9	0.1	0.3	0.4	0.2

stagnant or declining nutrition and poor provision of public services. This would also help resolve the paradox of stagnant or declining height, mostly conditioned by movements along the health function, and shrinking infant mortality (and, consequently, increasing life expectancy at birth), as a result of outward shifts in the function. The downside of the paradox is that poor infant nutrition in the 1980s conditions adult health and places Africa at disadvantage vis-à-vis joining the *second* health transition.

Africa experienced a long-run catching up from the late 1920s onwards, rising from comparatively very low initial levels to above one-third of the *OECD*'s, unlike GDP per head, which fell from over 30 to less than 10 per cent. Schooling was the main driver of human development's catching up over the past hundred years, while life expectancy made a significant contribution in the interwar years, during the early phase of the epidemiological transition, and as of 2010, while civil and political liberties fulfilled a similar function at the time of independence and, in particular, in the 1990s.

A closer look at post-1950 country level reveals that, rather than a divide between coastal and resource-rich nations, at the top, and the landlocked, resource-poor countries, at the bottom, it was the absence of institutional distortions that made the difference in terms of human development success.

On the whole, the evidence with regard to human development in Africa offers mixed results, albeit the continent remains at the bottom of world distribution. It does not support a pessimistic view of the colonial era, and refutes the depiction of Africa's performance from 1960 as one of 'lost decades', since, despite slowdown episodes, AHD improved substantially over the long run.

Postscript

This book has attempted to assess world human development, understood as 'a process of expanding the real freedoms that people enjoy' (Sen, 1999: 3), during the age of globalisation and modern economic growth. The findings suggest substantial gains over the past 150 years that, nonetheless, leave room for improvement. The *Augmented Human Development Index* on which the study draws, shows today's world at half of its maximum potential level. Moreover, the distribution of human development across countries has become more even in relative terms over time, with the gap between developed and developing countries (the *OECD* and the *Rest* in this volume) shrinking, and the middle and the lower deciles achieving more than proportional gains than the top deciles. However, in absolute terms, such differences have increased, with the *OECD* forging ahead and the *Rest* (or, more precisely, part of it) being left behind, and the top decile obtaining the largest absolute gains.

These cautiously optimistic results compare favourably with those for GDP per person, distribution of which became more unequal until late in the twentieth century, with the gap between the *OECD* and the *Rest* widening until 2000, and the top decile faring better over time in absolute and relative terms.

Non-income components of human development account for differences in relation to GDP per head in terms of trends and distribution, despite the fact that rising average incomes facilitate improvements in health and education through social spending and better nutrition, and are correlated with the spread of liberal democracy. Life expectancy at birth has been the main AHD contributor over time, although concentrated during the central decades of the twentieth century (1920s–1970), when the epidemiological transition diffused internationally. New social ideas, ranging from nation-building and liberal principles to human capital formation, fuelled the expansion of mass schooling, which has made a steady contribution to AHD over time. Long-run

241

advances in health and education were more evenly distributed across countries than rises in average incomes, and often occurred at times of sluggish economic growth, as was the case during the globalisation backlash of 1914–1950. Civil and political liberties' contribution to human development has been less steady but led the latter's gains during the last two decades of the twentieth century and contributed to AHD inequality reduction from the 1970s, as authoritarian regimes yielded to liberal democracy.

All in all, historical experience in terms of human development suggests that people's choices have been enlarged over the past one and a half centuries, as individuals slowly tread the long and arduous path to freedom.

Improving human development estimates remains a pressing task. In addition to improving the quality of the crude indicators employed, a major challenge is to compute global inequality, which combines inequality between countries' national averages with inequality within each country. An initial, relatively feasible, but not insignificant step would be to allow for gender differences within countries for each variable of the *AHDI*, something that so far has been rendered impossible by the lack of consistent and comprehensive data.

Policy implications may be derived from this lack of synchrony between human development and real average incomes. Some time ago, Amartya Sen and Jagdish Baghwati debated whether economic policy in India should have multiple objectives or should give exclusive priority to economic growth, on the grounds that the latter will automatically promote access to better health, longer life, improved skills, and deeper knowledge (*New York Times*, 21 August 2013). From the historical evidence offered in this volume, it is possible to suggest that, in a context of civil and political liberties, policy interventions in favour of health and education are, under some conditions, advisable, in order to realise the full potential of economic growth for human development.

What are the challenges ahead? Trying to provide answers is tantamount to entering unsafe territory. The late Angus Maddison used to discuss potential future scenarios that derive from projecting trends for the recent past. Historians know how unpredictable the future is and how risky projections are, so I will not make that mistake. However, it is possible to identify some of the challenges facing human development in the immediate future. In terms of health, a major challenge is that of increasing 'morbidity compression', that is, making the rise in longevity and the decline in morbidity converge. In regions of sub-Saharan Africa, for example, the coexistence of a rise in longevity with high morbidity highlights external medical intervention in a context of malnutrition and exposure to communicable disease. Moreover, this will result in unhealthy adults being unable to benefit from the ongoing second health transition. If this challenge is not addressed, there is a real risk of increasing international inequality in life expectancy, as observed at the turn of the century, somehow replicating the experience of the early decades of the twentieth century.

In terms of education, increasing quality along with the quantity of schooling represents a major challenge in some developing regions, even if an association between increases in quality and quantity is evident for the world on average over the past half a century. Lack of social consensus to fight poor-quality schooling is a problem often linked to uneven access to education, a mechanism that feeds income inequality over time. Again, not addressing this challenge will delay AHD improvement across the board.

Civil and political liberties constitute a most delicate plant, maintenance of which requires more than simple promotion of economic growth. The rise of illiberal democracies in relatively advanced countries and the economic success of authoritarian countries in recent times makes the threat to freedoms real. This revives classical liberals' concern over the conflict between democracy, centred on deciding who rules, and liberty, focused on control over the ruler. Liberal democracy overcame this conflict, but the rise of populism suggests that it may return in the future and thereby hamper the advancement of human development.

Appendix A
The Augmented Human Development Index: Sources and Procedures

The complete dataset is freely accessible at https://frdelpino.es/investi gacion/en/category/01_social-sciences/02_world-economy/03_human-development-world-economy/

Life Expectancy at Birth

Life expectancy is defined as 'the average number of years of life which would remain for males and females reaching the ages specified if they continued to be subjected to the same mortality experienced in the year (s) to which these life expectancies refer' (United Nations, 2000). Most data for the period 1980 to 2015 come from Human Development Reports (UNDP, 2010 and 2016) while the World Bank (World Development Indicators) provides data for 1960–1975 (exceptionally completed with data from UNESCO) and the United Nations' Demographic Yearbook Historical Supplement (United Nations, 2000) for the 1950s. Pre-1950 estimates come mostly from Riley (2005b), Flora (1983), and the OxLAD database for Latin America (Astorga et al., 2003), completed with the national sources listed below. Nonetheless, for most OECD countries (namely, Europe, the European offshoots – Australia, Canada, New Zealand, the United States – plus Israel, Japan, Korea, and Taiwan), the Human Mortality Dataset (2021) www.mortality.org/ (HMD hereafter) has been preferred, completed with the Clio-Infra Dataset www.clio-infra.eu/.

Occasionally, dearth of data has forced me to introduce some assumptions for the period before the epidemiological or health transition that, in developing regions, particularly those of South Asia and sub-Saharan Africa, often started during the interwar years (Omran, 1971; Riley 2005b, 2005c). In particular, I have accepted Riley's (2005a, p. 539) assumption that 'the average of all life expectancy estimates of acceptable quality for countries in a region provides the best available gauge of the pretransition average for the entire region'.

Maximum and minimum values for the life expectancy index were established at 85 and 20 years, respectively. A 'floor' of 25 years has been accepted as the minimum historical value for life expectancy at birth. Such a 'floor' precludes a zero value for the transformed life expectancy index and, consequently, for the *AHDI*.

North Africa

Algeria, 1913–1925, and 1938, Clio-Infra. 1900–1929, inferred from the infant survival rate (*ISR*, that is, 400 – as the maximum infant mortality rate per thousand – minus the country's infant mortality rate (Prados de la Escosura, 2013). Egypt, 1929–1938, from Fargues (1986); 1913, assumed to be as Tunisia's; and 1900, the same as Algeria's. Libya, 1900–1938, assumed to be identical to Egypt's. Morocco, 1900–1938, assumed to be the same as Algeria's, except 1913, the same as Tunisia's. Tunisia, 1900, 1929, assumed to be the same as Algeria. 1913, 1925, Condé (1973), cited in Riley (2005c); 1930s, Clio-Infra.

Central Africa. Estimates for CAR, Chad, Congo, Congo D.R., and Gabon over 1870–1929, and for Cameroon (1870–1913) inferred from heights (Prados de la Escosura, 2013).

West Africa. Figures for 1938 are projected backwards, with estimates inferred from heights and infant survival rates (*ISR*) (Prados de la Escosura, 2013), for Benin, Burkina Faso, Côte d'Ivoire, Gambia, Ghana (but for 1913), Guinea, Guinea-Bissau, Liberia, Mali, Nigeria (except for 1929, from Ayeni 1976), Senegal (except for 1929), and Sierra Leone (except for 1929). Mauritania's and Niger's assumed to identical to Mali's. Togo's assumed to be the same as Benin's, but Benin in 1913, the same as Ghana's.

East Africa. Data for 1938 projected backwards, with estimates inferred from heights and *ISR*, for Burundi, Ethiopia, Rwanda, Somalia, and Tanzania. Djibouti's assumed to be the same as Ethiopia's (Prados de la Escosura, 2013). Riley (2005b) provides estimates of 23.9 years for Kenya and Uganda in the 1930s, so I assigned the minimum historical value of 25 years to these countries over 1870–1929. Sudan's was assumed to be the same as Kenya's.

Southern Africa. Data for 1938 backwards projected backwards, with estimates inferred from heights and *ISR* (Prados de la Escosura, 2013) for Angola, Botswana (1913), Malawi, Mauritius (1870–1913),

Namibia (1870–1880), South Africa (1870), Swaziland (1929), and Zambia. Namibia, 1890–1900, assumed to be the same as for blacks in Cape Colony, from Simkins et al. (1989); 1929–1938, from Notkola et al. (2000), estimated from Northern Namibia's figures adjusted with the ratio all Namibia to Northern Namibia c. 1960. South Africa, 1880–1913, estimates from Simkins et al. (1989). For Zimbabwe, Riley (2005b), following Condé (1973), assigned 26.4 to the 1930s, so I have assigned the minimum goalpost over 1870–1929. Botswana's (except for 1913), Lesotho's, and Swaziland's (except for 1929), were assumed to be identical to Namibia's. Madagascar's, assumed to be the same as Mauritius's and Mozambique's the same as Malawi's. Mauritius, 1930s, Clio-Infra.

Americas

For Latin America, most data come from Arriaga (1968) and the OxLAD database (Astorga *et al.* 2003) (supplemented with the working sheets prepared by Shane and Barbara Hunt, which have been kindly provided by Pablo Astorga). In addition, national sources used are:

Argentina, 1870–1890, Recchini de Lattes and Lattes (1975).

Chile, 1890–1900, assumed to have evolved as Argentina; 1913, 1930s, Clio-Infra; 1950–2005, Díaz, Lüders, and Wagner (2016).

Uruguay, 1870–1900, assumed to have evolved as Argentina; 1900–1938, Ministerio de Salud Pública (2001),

Life expectancy for Colombia, 1870–1900, Cuba, 1870–1900, Panama, 1880–1900, Honduras, 1890–1900, Puerto Rico, 1870–1890, and Venezuela, 1880–1900, has been assumed to evolve as Costa Rica.

Ecuador, 1925–1938, assumed to evolve as Paraguay.

Peru, 1913–1933, assumed to evolve as Bolivia.

Puerto Rico, 1870–1890, assumed to evolve as Costa Rica; 1890, Riley (2005b); 1900–1938, UN (1993).

Jamaica, 1870–1880, assumed to evolve as Costa Rica; 1880–1955, Riley (2005a: 198).

Trinidad-Tobago, 1870–1900, assumed to evolve as Jamaica.

Bahamas and Belize, 1870–1938, assumed to evolve as Jamaica.

Barbados, St. Kitts and Nevis, St. Lucia, St. Vincent and the Grenadines, and Surinam, 1870–1938, assumed to evolve as Trinidad and Tobago.

St. Kitts and Nevis, 1950–1975, assumed to evolve as Surinam.

Canada, 1870–1890, Clio-Infra; 1925–2010, HMD.

USA, 1870–1890, Haines (1994); 1913–1929, Clio-Infra; 1933–2015, HMD.

In the absence of life expectancy estimates for early years, projecting the available figures with infant survival rates (*ISR*) has derived them for Panama, 1900–1929 and Guyana, 1950–1960. Such a procedure was also used to distribute the average life expectancy estimate for Argentina, 1869–1894.

Asia

Most pre-1950 estimates come from Riley (2005b) who claims that the earliest health transition started in the 1870/1890s when mean and median values were 27.5 and 25.1 years, respectively. Lower bound estimates for 1950 or 1940s levels were used for 1938. In the absence of data, pre-1929 life expectancy at birth was assumed to be 25 years.

Bahrain, Oman, Qatar, UAR, and Yemen, 1913–1938, assumed to evolve as Kuwait.

Brunei Darussalam, 1929–1938, assumed to evolve as Malaysia.

Cambodia, 1925–1929, assumed it evolved along China as they had similar levels in 1938; 1938, Siampos (1970), cited in Riley (2005b).

China, 1929, Caldwell et al. (1986), cited in Lavely and Wong (1998); 1930s, Clio-Infra.

Hong Kong SAR, 1900–1938, assumed to evolve as Taiwan.

India, 1880–1938, Clio-Infra; extrapolated to 1870 with Visaria and Visaria (1982); 1900 and 1925, McAlpin (1983).

Indonesia, 1929, Riley (2005b); 1930s, Clio-Infra.

Israel, 1950–1980, Clio-Infra; 1985–2010, HMD.

Japan, 1870, Riley (2005b); 1880, Janetta and Preston (1991); 1890–1900, Johansson and Mosk (1987); 1950–2015, HMD.

Jordan, 1929–1938, assumed to evolve as Syria's.

Korea, 1913–2000, Clio-Infra; 2005–2015, HMD.

Laos, 1929, assumed to evolve as Vietnam.

Lebanon, 1870–1938, assumed to evolve as Cyprus.

Malaysia, 1929–1938, obtained by projecting 1950 level backwards with the infant survival rate.

Nepal, 1925–1933, assumed to evolve as India.

Singapore, 1929–1938, obtained by projecting 1950 level backwards with the infant survival rate.

Sri Lanka, 1890–1913, 1938, Langford and Storey (1993); 1929, Sarkar (1951)

Taiwan, 1890–1938, Cha and Wu (2002). The level assumed for 1890 by Cha and Wu, 25 years, accepted for 1870–1880. 1950, Glass and Grebenik (1967); 1955, Taiwan Official statistics; 1970–2010, HMD.

Thailand, 1938, Vallin (1976).

Turkey, 1870–1900 and 1925–1933 assumed to evolve as Greece; 1913, Pamuk (2018); 1938, Shorter and Macura (1982).

Oceania

Australia, 1870–1900, Whitwell et al. (1997); 1925–2015, HMD.

New Zealand (adjusted for Maori population up to 1950), 1870, Riley (2005b); 1880–1890, Glass and Grebenik (1967); 1950–2010, HMD.

Europe

Albania, 1870–1890, assumed to evolve as Greece; 1900–1933, assumed to evolve as Bulgaria.

Austria, 1870–1929, Clio-Infra; 1950–2010, HMD.

Belgium, 1870–2015, HMD.

Belarus, 1950s, Clio-Infra; 1960–2015, HMD.

Bulgaria, 1870–1890, assumed to evolve as Greece; 1913–1938, Clio-Infra; 1950–2010, HMD.

Croatia, 2005–2015, HMD.

Cyprus, 1870–1880, assumed to be identical to Greece; 1890, Riley (2005b); 1900–1938, Clio-Infra.

Czechoslovakia/Czechia, 1870–1938, Sbr (1962); 1890, Riley (2005b); 1950–2015, HMD.

Denmark, 1870–2015, HMD.

Estonia, 1938–1955, Clio-Infra; 1960–2015, HMD.

Finland, 1870, Kannisto et al. (1999); 1880–2015, HMD.

France, 1870–2015, HMD.

Germany, 1870–1890, Flora (1983); 1950s, Clio-Infra; 1960–2015, HMD.

Greece, 1870–1913, Valaoras (1960), 1933–1980, Clio-Infra; 1985–2015, HMD.

Hungary, 1870–1890, assumed to evolve as Austria; 1950–2015, HMD.

Iceland, 1870–2015, HMD.

Ireland, 1850–1890, assumed to evolve as the UK; 1950–2015, HMD

Italy, 1870, Felice et al. (2016); 1880–2010, HMD.

Latvia and Lithuania, 1925–1955, Clio-Infra; 1960–2010, HMD.

Luxembourg, 1913–1955, Clio-Infra; 1960–2010, HMD.

Netherlands, 1870–2015, HMD.

Norway, 1870–2015, HMD.

Poland, 1870–1913, assuming it evolved as Czechoslovakia; 1950–2010, HMD.

Portugal, 1850–1913, Leite (2005); 1925 (interpolated) and 1933, Valério (2001; I); 1929, Veiga (2005); 1938, United Nations (1993); 1950–2015, HMD.

Romania, 1870–1880, assumed to evolve as Greece, 1890–1890, and along Bulgaria, 1890–1929.

Russia, Pressat (1985) for European Russia, 1870–1913, and European Soviet Union, 1929–1938; 1950s, Clio-Infra; 1960–2015, HMD.

Slovakia, 1925, Clio-Infra; 1929–1938, Sbr (1962); 1950–2015, HMD.

Slovenia, 1950–1980, Clio-Infra; 1985–2015, HMD.

Spain, 1870–1890, Felice et al. (2016); 1900, Dopico and Reher (1998); 1913–2015, HMD.

Sweden, 1870–2010, HMD.

Switzerland, 1870, Flora (1983); 1880–2010, HMD.

Ukraine, 1900, Mazur (1969); 1925–1955, Clio-Infra; 1960–2010, HMD.

United Kingdom, 1850–1900, Floud and Harris (1997); 1925–2015, HMD.

Yugoslavia, assumed to evolve as Greece, 1870–1880, and along Bulgaria, 1890–1929. For 1929 and 1938, life expectancy was estimated by projecting the available figures with infant survival rates for 1950.

Average Years of Education

Education attainment is measured by the average years of total schooling (primary, secondary, and tertiary) for population aged 15 and over. Most figures for 2015 and 2010 derive from the

Human Development Reports 2016 and 2013 (UNDP, 2016, 2013). For 1870–2010, the most comprehensive database is the Clio-Infra dataset www.clio-infra.eu/Indicators/AverageYearsofEducation.html put together by Bas van Leeuwen, Jieli van Leeuwen-Li, and Péter Földvári in 2013, which provides decadal figures (years ending in 0). These figures come from historical reconstructions derived from national statistical offices for the post-1960 period and the authors' own estimates through the perpetual inventory method up to 1950. Clio-Infra database relies on Morrisson and Murtin (2009) dataset for 78 countries at 10-year intervals.

I completed the dataset with estimates for years ending in 5 between 1915 and 2005 from Földvári and van Leeuwen (2014) for Europe, while for the rest of the world have interpolated them on the basis of Barro and Lee's dataset (2013, version 2.2, updated on June 2018) www .barrolee.com/ for population aged 15 and over for 1950–2010, and Lee and Lee's (2016) dataset for population aged 15–64, over 1915–1935 https://barrolee.github.io/BarroLeeDataSet/DataLeeLee.html.

Specifically, for, say, 2005, the formula used is

$$Y_{2005} = ((2 * X_{2005})/(X_{2000} + X_{2010})) * (Y_{2000} + Y_{2010}),$$

where Y represents the Clio-Infra values and X those of Barro and Lee (2013, v. 2.2).

I have assigned the values for 1915, 1930, 1935, and 1940 to my 1913, 1929, 1933, and 1938 benchmarks, respectively.

I have filled missing values for earlier years in Clio-Infra by projecting their levels with Lee and Lee (2016) estimates. This was the case for Barbados, Colombia, and Ecuador (1870); Cyprus and Serbia (1870–1880); Czechia and Romania (1870–1890); Iceland, Poland, Gambia, and Zambia (1870–1913); Haiti and Togo (1870–1925); DR Congo, Lesotho, Liberia, Libya, Swaziland, Afghanistan, Cambodia, and Jordan (1870–1938).

I have also filled Clio-Infra missing values by projecting their levels with Barro and Lee (2013, 2018) for Estonia, Latvia, Lithuania, Ukraine, Burundi, Central African Republic (CAR), Gabon, Armenia, and Nepal (1950–1955); and Moldova, Kazakhstan, Kyrgyzstan, Tajikistan, and Uzbekistan (1950–1965).

Lack of Clio-Infra 1950–2010 estimates for Belize, Albania, Croatia, Malta, Slovenia, Sudan, Bahrain, Brunei Darussalam, Hong Kong, Indonesia, Kuwait, Mongolia, Qatar, Taiwan, United Arab Emirates

(UAE), and Yemen led me to use Barro and Lee's (2013, v. 2.2) figures for these countries. For Belize, Albania, Malta, Sudan, Hong Kong, Kuwait, Taiwan, and Yemen, Barro and Lee's figures for 1950 were projected backwards to 1870 with Lee and Lee's (2016) years of schooling.

Lastly, missing values for some countries before 1950 have been estimated by assuming they evolved as their neighbours.

Africa

Botswana, 1870–1913, and Namibia, 1870–1938, assumed to evolve as Lesotho; pre-1960 Burkina Faso, Chad, and Guinea, as Mali, Niger, and Sierra Leone, respectively; pre-1950 Burundi and Rwanda, as Uganda; pre-1950 CAR, Congo, and Gabon, as Cameroon; pre-1950 Mauritania as Senegal; pre-1950 Tanzania as Kenya; Seychelles, 1870–1913, as Mauritius. Guinea-Bissau, 1870–2010, was assumed to evolve as Guinea.

Americas

Bahamas, 1870–1990, assumed to evolve as Barbados and St. Kitts and Nevis and St. Vincent and the Grenadines, 1870–2005, as Trinidad-Tobago.

Asia

It has been assumed that pre-1929 Lebanon evolved as Cyprus; pre-1950 Laos as Cambodia; and pre-1950 Bahrain, Brunei-Darussalam, Qatar, Saudi Arabia, and United Arab Emirates (UAE) as Kuwait.

Maximum and the minimum values are established at 15 and 0 years, respectively. However, the lowest historical value was set at 0.1 years of education. Such a 'floor' precludes a zero value for the transformed education index and, consequently, for the *HIHD*.

Index of Liberal Democracy

Varieties of Democracy [V-Dem] Coppedge *et al.* (2018) provides the *Liberal Democracy Index* www.v-dem.net/en/, which combines the electoral democracy index and the liberal component index. The electoral democracy index incorporates indices of freedom of association, expression, suffrage, and clean elections. The liberal component index includes indices of equality before the law and individual liberty, judicial constraints on the executive, and legislative constraints on the executive.

The index ranges between 0, low, and 1, high. With regard to other dimensions of human development, I have adopted a 'floor' level that in this case is 0.01.

Missing values for some countries, mostly before 1900, have been estimated by assuming they evolved as their neighbours and, exceptionally, were assigned the same values.

Africa

For most countries in sub-Saharan Africa, except Ethiopia, Liberia, Madagascar, and Tanzania, lacking estimates for 1870–1890, I have assigned the 'floor' value of 0.01. This assumption is consistent with their low values for 1913. In the case of South Africa, I assumed it evolved as the Orange Free State in Polity 2 (Polity 4 database) (Marshall et al., 2018).

Algeria, 1870–1890 assumed to evolve as Tunisia.

Cameroon, 1920–1960, assumed to evolve as Central African Republic.

Americas

Jamaica, 1870–1890, assumed to evolve as Cuba.

The Bahamas and Belize, 1950–2015, assumed to have the same values as Jamaica.

St. Kitts, St. Lucia, and St. Vincent and the Grenadines, 1950–2015, same values as Barbados.

Asia

Brunei Darussalam, same values as Malaysia.

Cambodia and Laos, 1870–1890, assumed to evolve as Vietnam.

Iraq, Jordan, Lebanon, and Syria, 1870–1913, assumed to evolve as Turkey.

Hong Kong and Taiwan, assumed to evolve as China.

Qatar, 1870–1890, assume to evolve as Oman.

Sri Lanka, 1870–1890, assumed to evolve as India.
United Arab Emirates, 1870–1970, assumed to evolve as Qatar.
Yemen, 1870–1890, the 'floor' was accepted, as the value for 1913 was 0.011.

Europe

Albania, 1870–1900, as an Ottoman colony, same values as Turkey.

Belgium, 1870–1890, I assumed it evolved as the average of Vanhanen Index of Democratization (Vanhanen, 2016) and Polity 2 (Marshall et al., 2018).

Czechoslovakia, 1870–1913, as part of Austria-Hungary, I used the average value of Austria and Hungary.

Ireland, 1870–1913, same values as the United Kingdom.

Poland, 1870–1913, same values as Russia.

Per Capita GDP

GDP per head is expressed in 1990 Geary-Khamis dollars. Unless stated below, GDP per head data come from the Maddison Project Database (2018) [MPD2018], completed with Maddison (2006, 2010) and the Maddison Project Database 2013 [MPD2013]] www.rug.nl/ggdc/histor icaldevelopment/maddison/ and, for Latin America since 1950, CEPAL (2009, 2017)www.iterwp.cepal.org/. Conference Board (2016) estimates have been accepted for China since 1950, specifically, the so-called alternative series. Otherwise, for specific countries shown below, per capita GDP levels for (usually) 1950 have been projected backwards with volume indices of real per capita GDP taken from historical national accounts.

I have assumed a lower bound for *per capita* GDP that has been set at G-K 1990 $300, which represents a basic level of physiological subsistence (Sagar and Najam, 1998; Milanovic et al., 2011), below both the World Bank's extreme poverty threshold of G-K 1990 $1 a day per person and Maddison's (2006) G-K 1990 $400 per capita.

Africa

Most pre-1950 estimates come from projecting the 1950 benchmark in the MDP2018 with Prados de la Escosura (2012) estimates. The GDP data set for Africa includes available estimates for the northern region and South Africa. In North Africa, 1870–1950, estimates come from Maddison (2006: 577–580) completed with some interpolations on the basis of my own indirect estimates. For Algeria, I interpolated the levels for 1890 and 1900. For Tunisia, I accepted Maddison estimates for 1913 and interpolated the rest of the benchmarks. In the case of Morocco, I found Maddison's level for 1913 too low relative to Tunisia, and used my own estimates. For Egypt, Maddison figures were also used but re-scaled by accepting Pamuk (2006) level for 1950. In the case of South Africa, I deflated Stadler (1963) nominal GDP estimates for 1913–1950 with Alvaredo and Atkinson (2010) price index, and used population figures from Feinstein (2005: 257–258) to derive per capita GDP. Then, the estimates for 1913 were projected backwards to 1870 with my own indirect estimates.

Further assumptions were needed to fill missing values of GDP per head for some sub-Saharan countries. Following Maddison's approach, I assumed that growth trends for missing countries were similar to those of their neighbours. Thus, in the case of French Equatorial Africa (CAR, Congo, Gabon, and Chad), over 1870–1929, I assumed they grew in the same way as similar countries (coastal or landlocked, resource abundant or scarce) in French West Africa. Similarly, during the same period, Cameroon, Guinea-Bissau, and Togo were assumed to grow at the same rate as similar countries in West French Africa. Liberia was assumed to evolve as Sierra Leone over 1900–1913. I assumed The Gambia (1870–1913) and Sierra Leone (1870–1900) evolved as Ghana. In East Africa, I accepted Uganda's pace of growth for Rwanda and Burundi (1913–1929) while Kenya's pace of growth during 1870–1913 was assumed to be similar to Tanzania's. Ethiopia and Sudan were also assumed to evolve as Egypt over 1870–1913. In southern Africa, Mozambique was assumed to evolve as Angola (1870–1900), and Zambia and Malawi (1913–1929) as Zimbabwe. Lastly, in the cases of Botswana and Lesotho (1913–1938), Namibia (1870–1929), and Swaziland (1870–1938), I accepted the growth rate for South Africa.

Americas

MPD2018 benchmark for 1990 has been projected back and forth with CEPAL (2009) and (2017) for Latin America and the Caribbean over 1950–2015, except in the case of Cuba for 1950–1990. Pre-1950 period, per capita GDP volumes derive from MPD2018, MPD2103, Astorga and Fitzgerald (1998) and MOxLAD database (Astorga *et al.* 2003). Otherwise, national sources have been used.

Argentina, Della Paolera et al. (2003), 1884–1950. I projected the resulting level for 1884 backwards 1875 with Cortés Conde (1997) growth rate and assumed the level of 1870 to be equal to that of 1875.

Brazil, 1870–1950, Goldsmith (1986).

Bolivia, 1870–1950, Herranz-Loncán and Peres Cajías (2016). Figures for 1870 and 1880 interpolated from those for 1850 and 1883.

Chile, 1870–1950, Díaz, Lüders, and Wagner (2016).

Colombia, 1870–1905, Kalmanovitz Krauter and López Rivera (2009) and data kindly provided by Salomon Kalmanovitz in private communication; 1905–1950, GRECO (2002).

Cuba, up to 1902, Santamaría (2005); 1902–1958, Ward and Devereux (2012); 1958–1990, MDP2018; 1990–2015, CEPAL (2017). An important caveat is that neither the MPD2018 benchmark level for 1990 (nor the MPD2013 or Maddison's 2006, 2010) has been accepted. The reason is that, given the lack of PPPs for Cuba in 1990, Maddison (2006: 192) assumed Cuban per capita GDP was 15 per cent below the Latin American average. Since this is an arbitrary assumption, I started from Brundenius and Zimbalist's (1989) estimate of Cuba's GDP per head relative to six major Latin American countries (Argentina, Brazil, Chile, Colombia, Mexico, and Venezuela, LA6) in 1980 (provided in Astorga and Fitzgerald, 1998) and applied this ratio to the average per capita income of LA6 in 1980 Geary-Khamis dollars to derive Cuba's level in 1980. Then, following Maddison (1995: 166), I derived the level for 1990 with the growth rate of real per capita GDP at national prices over 1980–1990 and reflated the result with the US implicit GDP deflator in order to arrive at an estimate of per capita GDP in 1990 at 1990 Geary-Khamis dollars. Interestingly, Cuba's position relative to the US in 1929 and 1955 is very close to the one Ward and Devereux (2012) estimated using a different approach.

Jamaica, 1870–1929, Eisner (1961).

Mexico, 1870–1900, Coatsworth (1989: 41); 1896–1950, INEGI (1995)

Puerto Rico, 1900–1940, Devereux (2019); 1940–1950, Anuario Estadístico de Puerto Rico (1955: 150).

Peru, 1870–1950, Seminario (2015).

Uruguay, 1870–1950, Bértola (2016).

Venezuela, 1870–1950, Batista (1997). I have preferred Batista's well-known estimates to de Corso's (2013, 2018).

Central America (Costa Rica, El Salvador, Guatemala, Honduras, and Nicaragua), I derived the level for 1913 by assuming the growth over 1913–1920 was identical to that of 1920–1925, the latter derived from OxLAD database (Astorga *et al.* 2003).

Caribbean. Bahamas, Barbados, Belize, Guyana, since 1950, Trinidad-Tobago, 1950–1970, and St. Kitts and Nevis, St. Vincent and the Grenadines, from 1990, Maddison (2006, 2010), Conference Board (2016), and Bulmer-Thomas (kindly provided in private communication)

Asia

Middle East (Iran, Iraq, Jordan, Lebanon, Palestine (Israel), Saudi Arabia, Syria, Yemen, and the Gulf (Bahrain, Kuwait, Oman, Qatar, UAE), 1870–1913, Pamuk (2006)

Cambodia and Laos were assumed to evolve as Vietnam, 1870–1938.

Korea, 1870–1913, MPD2013; 1913–1938, Cha and Kim (2006). I obtained the figures for 1880–1900 through log-linear interpolation.

Myanmar, 1880–1890, assumed to evolve as India.

Malaysia, 1870–1913, assumed to evolve along Indonesia.

Philippines, 1890, Bourguignon and Morrisson (2002).

Turkey, MPD2013. 1880, Altug et al. (2008) with 1890–1900 figures log-linearly interpolated.

Taiwan, 1890–1900, assumed to evolve as China's; 1900, Cha and Wu (2002).

For the Middle East, Indochina (Cambodia, Laos, and Vietnam), and Hong Kong, I interpolated log-linearly the values for 1880–1900 and 1935–1938.

Oceania

New Zealand, 1870–1990, kindly provided by Les Oxley in private communication.

Europe

Austria, 1870–1913, Maddison (2010) level for 1913 projected backwards with Schulze (2000) estimates for Imperial Austria under the assumption that real output per head in Modern Austria evolve as Imperial Austria's.

Belgium, 1870–1913, Horlings (1997); 1929–1938, average of GDP estimates of income and expenditure approaches in Buyst (1997), and output in Horlings (1997).

Bulgaria, 1890–1913, Maddison (2010). 1880, interpolated.

Czechoslovakia, 1880, computed with Good (1994) ratio of 1880 GDP per head to the average GDP per head of 1870 and 1890 applied to MPD2018 average levels for 1870 and 1890.

Cyprus, 1913–1950, Apostolides (2011). I assumed the level for 1913 was identical to that for 1921.

France, 1870–1950, Toutain (1997).

Greece, 1870–1938, Kostelenos et al. (2007) moving base series.

Hungary, 1870–1913, Schulze (2000) estimates for Imperial Hungary.

Ireland, 1880–1900, applying the ratio Ireland/UK in 1913 to UK real per capita GDP.

Malta, 1913–1950, Apostolides (2011). I assumed the level for 1913 was identical to that for 1921.

Portugal, 1850–1913, Lains (2006).

Romania, MPD2013. 1880, computed with Good (1994) ratio of 1880 GDP per head to the average GDP per head of 1870 and 1890 applied to MPD2013 average levels for 1870 and 1890.

Russia, 1870–1885, Imperial Russia, Goldsmith (1961), agricultural and industrial output weighted with Gregory (1982) weights for 1883–1887; 1885–1913, Gregory (1982, Table 3.1); 1913–1928, Markevich and Harrison (2011).

Spain, 1870–2015, Prados de la Escosura (2017).

United Kingdom, 1850–1913, MPD2013.

Yugoslavia, 1880, computed with Good (1994) ratio of 1880 GDP per head to the average GDP per head of 1870 and 1890 applied to MPD2018 average levels for 1870 and 1890.

Population

All figures are adjusted to refer to mid-year and to take into account the territorial changes and are derived from UNESCO, www.data.uis .unesco.org/, for 1970–2015, Maddison (2010), and Mitchell (2003a, 2003b, 2003c), completed for Latin America and the Caribbean with CEPAL (2009 and 2017), 1950–2015, and OxLAD database (Astorga et al., 2003), 1900–1938. Otherwise, national sources were used.

Cyprus, 1929–1938, Apostolides (2011).

Spain, 1870–2015, Prados de la Escosura (2017).

Turkey, 1870–1913, Pamuk (2006, 2018).

Algeria and Tunisia, 1870–1950, Fargues (1986).

South Africa, 1870–2000, Feinstein (2005).

Sub-Saharan Africa, 1910–1950 data come from Jan-Pieter Smits (private communication), completed with Banks (2010), for Ethiopia, Liberia, Malawi, and Sierra Leone. Missing observations for sub-Saharan African countries in the late nineteenth century were filled by assuming the average growth rate for countries in the region.

Appendix B
Alternative Indices of Augmented Human Development and Their Drivers

Do the drivers of human development derived with alternative specifications of the augmented index coincide with the *AHDI* drivers? The UNDP HDI inspired *AHDI-undp* provides similar patterns to the *AHDI*. Life expectancy leads during the interwar years and schooling represents the main and steadiest contributor, but exhibits slower growth, and both longevity and education drive long-run human development. *AHDI-zambrano*, which uses Zambrano (2017) transformation of income, also presents a shared leadership of longevity and education and maintains life expectancy's lead in the first half of the twentieth century, but enhances the contribution of per capita income at the expense of life expectancy and, to a lesser extent, of education. In addition, *AHDI-bértola-vecchi* and *AHDI-hmv*, indices that exclude the log transformation of income, provide similar levels to the *AHDI* over time, but the contribution of income increases remarkably and dominates in the long run, becoming the single main driver of human development across the different main phases of its evolution, except for 1914–1950, when life expectancy leads in the *AHDI-bértola-vecchi*, and schooling does so in the *AHDI-hmv*.

If, alternatively, *AHDI-hmv-eei*, that is, Herrero et al.'s (2012) transformation proposal for conventional HDI dimensions is considered, the dominance of the income dimension observed for the *AHDI-hmv* is fully confirmed. Lastly, when *AHDI-bértola-kakwani*, for which I adopt and Bértola and Ocampo's (2012) proposal, is considered, the results for *AHDI-bértola-vecchi* are validated, except for the increase experienced by the contribution of the social dimensions, life expectancy, in particular, which becomes the leading driver of human development in the long run. Thus, unless it is transformed at a declining rate, per capita income, a non-bounded variable, will drive the human development index.

Appendix C
International Inequality

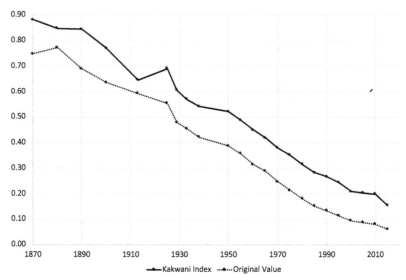

Figure C.1 Pop-weighted inequality in schooling: Kakwani index and original values.

Source: MLD, Table 3.2 and see the text.

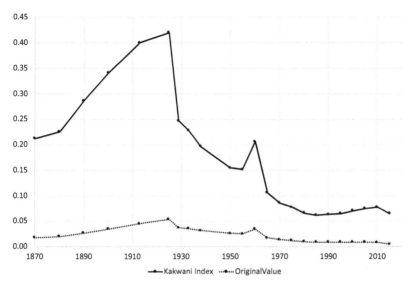

Figure C.2 Pop-weighted inequality in life expectancy: Kakwani index and original values.

Source: MLD, Table 2 and see the text

Table C.1. *International AHD inequality, 1870–2015:*
the contribution of China and India, sub-Saharan Africa, and
Russia (MLD)

	Actual	Excluding China and India	Excluding sub-Saharan Africa	Excluding Russia
1870	0.27	0.27	0.26	0.29
1880	0.30	0.30	0.29	0.32
1890	0.33	0.32	0.31	0.35
1900	0.34	0.32	0.33	0.36
1913	0.29	0.28	0.28	0.32
1925	0.34	0.31	0.33	0.36
1929	0.28	0.30	0.27	0.30
1933	0.25	0.27	0.23	0.27
1938	0.22	0.25	0.21	0.24
1950	0.25	0.24	0.24	0.27
1955	0.22	0.22	0.21	0.24
1960	0.24	0.21	0.23	0.25
1965	0.19	0.20	0.18	0.20
1970	0.19	0.21	0.17	0.20
1975	0.18	0.21	0.17	0.19
1980	0.15	0.19	0.13	0.16
1985	0.14	0.18	0.12	0.15
1990	0.14	0.17	0.12	0.14
1995	0.12	0.16	0.11	0.13
2000	0.11	0.14	0.09	0.11
2005	0.10	0.13	0.09	0.10
2010	0.09	0.12	0.08	0.10
2015	0.09	0.10	0.08	0.09

Table C.2. *International inequality in schooling, 1870–2015: the contribution of China and India, sub-Saharan Africa, and Russia (MLD) (Kakwani Indices)*

	Actual	Excluding China and India	Excluding sub-Saharan Africa	Excluding Russia
1870	0.88	0.82	0.86	0.94
1880	0.85	0.83	0.82	0.91
1890	0.84	0.83	0.80	0.90
1900	0.77	0.82	0.72	0.82
1913	0.65	0.66	0.58	0.70
1925	0.69	0.64	0.62	0.75
1929	0.60	0.61	0.53	0.66
1933	0.57	0.57	0.50	0.62
1938	0.54	0.53	0.47	0.59
1950	0.52	0.54	0.45	0.56
1955	0.49	0.51	0.42	0.51
1960	0.45	0.48	0.39	0.47
1965	0.42	0.45	0.36	0.44
1970	0.38	0.42	0.33	0.39
1975	0.35	0.41	0.30	0.36
1980	0.31	0.36	0.27	0.33
1985	0.28	0.32	0.24	0.29
1990	0.27	0.31	0.24	0.27
1995	0.24	0.29	0.21	0.25
2000	0.21	0.26	0.18	0.21
2005	0.20	0.25	0.17	0.21
2010	0.20	0.24	0.17	0.20
2015	0.15	0.21	0.13	0.15

Table C.3. *International inequality in life expectancy, 1870–2015: the contribution of China and India, sub-Saharan Africa, and Russia (MLD) (Kakwani indices)*

	Actual	Excluding China and India	Excluding sub-Saharan Africa	Excluding Russia
1870	0.21	0.19	0.21	0.23
1880	0.23	0.20	0.23	0.24
1890	0.29	0.23	0.29	0.31
1900	0.34	0.25	0.34	0.37
1913	0.40	0.26	0.40	0.44
1925	0.42	0.25	0.42	0.45
1929	0.25	0.22	0.24	0.27
1933	0.23	0.21	0.21	0.25
1938	0.20	0.17	0.19	0.21
1950	0.15	0.15	0.14	0.16
1955	0.15	0.15	0.14	0.15
1960	0.21	0.14	0.20	0.20
1965	0.11	0.13	0.09	0.10
1970	0.09	0.11	0.07	0.09
1975	0.08	0.10	0.06	0.08
1980	0.07	0.09	0.05	0.07
1985	0.06	0.08	0.04	0.07
1990	0.06	0.08	0.04	0.07
1995	0.06	0.09	0.04	0.07
2000	0.07	0.10	0.04	0.07
2005	0.07	0.10	0.04	0.08
2010	0.08	0.11	0.05	0.08
2015	0.06	0.09	0.04	0.07

Table C.4. *International inequality in civil and political liberties,*
1870–2015: the contribution of China and India, sub-Saharan Africa,
and Russia (MLD)

	Actual	Excluding China and India	Excluding sub-Saharan Africa	Excluding Russia
1870	0.47	0.38	0.45	0.51
1880	0.54	0.47	0.52	0.58
1890	0.58	0.52	0.55	0.60
1900	0.58	0.51	0.57	0.59
1913	0.33	0.39	0.32	0.34
1925	0.55	0.64	0.55	0.48
1929	0.56	0.66	0.56	0.49
1933	0.52	0.66	0.52	0.44
1938	0.54	0.74	0.55	0.46
1950	0.68	0.59	0.69	0.60
1955	0.68	0.56	0.69	0.61
1960	0.71	0.56	0.72	0.65
1965	0.72	0.58	0.74	0.65
1970	0.80	0.66	0.81	0.75
1975	0.77	0.67	0.78	0.72
1980	0.66	0.68	0.67	0.60
1985	0.63	0.65	0.63	0.58
1990	0.54	0.44	0.52	0.55
1995	0.48	0.38	0.47	0.49
2000	0.42	0.30	0.43	0.43
2005	0.39	0.27	0.40	0.39
2010	0.35	0.26	0.37	0.35
2015	0.41	0.26	0.45	0.41

Table C.5 *International inequality in real GDP per head, 1870–2015: the contribution of China and India, sub-Saharan Africa, and Russia (MLD)*

	Actual	Excluding China and India	Excluding sub-Saharan Africa	Excluding Russia
1870	0.18	0.18	0.18	0.20
1880	0.22	0.20	0.22	0.23
1890	0.25	0.21	0.25	0.27
1900	0.30	0.22	0.30	0.32
1913	0.36	0.25	0.35	0.39
1925	0.39	0.28	0.39	0.42
1929	0.41	0.29	0.41	0.45
1933	0.34	0.23	0.33	0.37
1938	0.42	0.25	0.41	0.45
1950	0.57	0.40	0.58	0.61
1955	0.55	0.41	0.55	0.59
1960	0.57	0.41	0.57	0.61
1965	0.58	0.44	0.58	0.62
1970	0.62	0.46	0.62	0.65
1975	0.63	0.47	0.63	0.67
1980	0.62	0.47	0.61	0.67
1985	0.60	0.50	0.57	0.64
1990	0.62	0.56	0.58	0.65
1995	0.58	0.61	0.52	0.60
2000	0.57	0.65	0.50	0.59
2005	0.50	0.62	0.42	0.52
2010	0.42	0.57	0.33	0.43
2015	0.39	0.56	0.28	0.40

Appendix D
Augmented *Human Development Index in World Regions*

Table D.1. *AHDI and its components: Western Europe*
Panel A. Levels

	AHDI	Kakwani index of schooling	Kakwani index of life expectancy	UNDP index of income	Liberal democracy index
1870	0.168	0.097	0.073	0.486	0.229
1880	0.194	0.114	0.086	0.503	0.286
1890	0.213	0.132	0.100	0.524	0.294
1900	0.232	0.149	0.117	0.549	0.305
1913	0.260	0.168	0.149	0.577	0.319
1925	0.301	0.188	0.185	0.587	0.400
1929	0.308	0.196	0.192	0.605	0.397
1933	0.301	0.205	0.215	0.590	0.317
1938	0.300	0.215	0.223	0.614	0.274
1950	0.399	0.231	0.302	0.621	0.583
1955	0.422	0.248	0.332	0.658	0.587
1960	0.448	0.271	0.350	0.688	0.615
1965	0.472	0.303	0.367	0.720	0.617
1970	0.497	0.339	0.379	0.750	0.634
1975	0.526	0.376	0.397	0.770	0.667
1980	0.569	0.414	0.426	0.792	0.751
1985	0.596	0.446	0.452	0.803	0.777
1990	0.622	0.482	0.481	0.824	0.787
1995	0.647	0.512	0.511	0.834	0.801
2000	0.673	0.539	0.554	0.855	0.802
2005	0.696	0.560	0.607	0.865	0.801
2010	0.727	0.584	0.667	0.867	0.827
2015	0.729	0.577	0.718	0.871	0.782

Table D.1. *(cont.) Panel B. AHD Drivers** *(%)*

	Kakwani index of schooling	Kakwani index of life expectancy	UNDP index of income	Liberal democracy index	*AHDI*
1870–1880	0.4	0.4	0.1	0.6	1.5
1880–1890	0.4	0.4	0.1	0.1	0.9
1890–1900	0.3	0.4	0.1	0.1	0.9
1900–1913	0.2	0.5	0.1	0.1	0.9
1913–1929	0.2	0.4	0.1	0.3	1.1
1929–1938	0.3	0.4	0.0	−1.0	−0.3
1938–1950	0.1	0.6	0.0	1.6	2.4
1950–1960	0.4	0.4	0.3	0.1	1.2
1960–1970	0.6	0.2	0.2	0.1	1.1
1970–1980	0.5	0.3	0.1	0.4	1.4
1980–1990	0.4	0.3	0.1	0.1	0.9
1990–2000	0.3	0.4	0.1	0.0	0.8
2000–2010	0.2	0.5	0.0	0.1	0.8
2010–2015	−0.1	0.4	0.0	−0.3	0.0
1870–2015	0.3	0.4	0.1	0.2	1.0

* Dimensions' contribution to *AHDI* growth.

Table D.2. *AHDI and its components: Western offshoots*
Panel A. Levels

	AHDI	Kakwani index of schooling	Kakwani index of Life expectancy	UNDP index of income	Liberal democracy index
1870	0.239	0.168	0.111	0.512	0.342
1880	0.238	0.187	0.090	0.553	0.348
1890	0.265	0.211	0.120	0.565	0.343
1900	0.301	0.234	0.145	0.594	0.404
1913	0.331	0.254	0.176	0.637	0.424
1925	0.382	0.292	0.218	0.662	0.506
1929	0.387	0.306	0.217	0.676	0.498
1933	0.398	0.318	0.241	0.618	0.528
1938	0.415	0.330	0.256	0.666	0.529
1950	0.469	0.374	0.323	0.736	0.544

Table D.2. (*cont.*)

	AHDI	Kakwani index of schooling	Kakwani index of Life expectancy	UNDP index of income	Liberal democracy index
1955	0.490	0.394	0.346	0.756	0.560
1960	0.507	0.421	0.351	0.763	0.587
1965	0.530	0.452	0.358	0.791	0.616
1970	0.556	0.481	0.366	0.810	0.672
1975	0.598	0.532	0.397	0.824	0.734
1980	0.634	0.576	0.423	0.845	0.786
1985	0.660	0.619	0.445	0.862	0.798
1990	0.692	0.686	0.465	0.879	0.815
1995	0.712	0.741	0.480	0.889	0.814
2000	0.731	0.741	0.509	0.914	0.827
2005	0.748	0.795	0.536	0.927	0.794
2010	0.793	0.855	0.582	0.926	0.860
2015	0.776	0.782	0.592	0.936	0.836

Panel B. AHD drivers [*] *(%)*

	Kakwani index of schooling	Kakwani index of life expectancy	UNDP index of income	Liberal democracy index	AHDI
1870–1880	0.3	−0.5	0.2	0.0	0.0
1880–1890	0.3	0.7	0.1	0.0	1.0
1890–1900	0.3	0.5	0.1	0.4	1.3
1900–1913	0.2	0.4	0.1	0.1	0.7
1913–1929	0.3	0.3	0.1	0.3	1.0
1929–1938	0.2	0.5	0.0	0.2	0.8
1938–1950	0.3	0.5	0.2	0.1	1.0
1950–1960	0.3	0.2	0.1	0.2	0.8
1960–1970	0.3	0.1	0.1	0.3	0.9
1970–1980	0.5	0.4	0.1	0.4	1.3
1980–1990	0.4	0.2	0.1	0.1	0.9
1990–2000	0.2	0.2	0.1	0.0	0.5
2000–2010	0.4	0.3	0.0	0.1	0.8
2010–2015	−0.4	0.1	0.1	−0.1	−0.4
2000–2015	0.1	0.3	0.0	0.0	0.4
1870–2015	0.3	0.3	0.1	0.2	0.8

[*] Dimensions' contribution to *AHDI* growth.

Table D.3 *AHDI and its components: Japan*
Panel A. Levels

	AHDI	Kakwani index of schooling	Kakwani index of LIFE EXPECTANCY	UNDP index of Income	Liberal democracy index
1870	0.087	0.025	0.071	0.325	0.100
1880	0.095	0.029	0.075	0.350	0.108
1890	0.116	0.040	0.076	0.376	0.158
1900	0.139	0.058	0.081	0.401	0.199
1913	0.172	0.110	0.090	0.427	0.207
1925	0.191	0.128	0.103	0.477	0.214
1929	0.209	0.148	0.120	0.489	0.219
1933	0.216	0.167	0.128	0.497	0.205
1938	0.223	0.182	0.137	0.520	0.193
1950	0.304	0.221	0.222	0.480	0.362
1955	0.419	0.262	0.291	0.540	0.745
1960	0.465	0.316	0.317	0.599	0.779
1965	0.498	0.339	0.355	0.664	0.771
1970	0.546	0.416	0.386	0.744	0.742
1975	0.575	0.443	0.434	0.769	0.739
1980	0.610	0.492	0.477	0.796	0.740
1985	0.656	0.553	0.527	0.818	0.775
1990	0.675	0.575	0.571	0.851	0.741
1995	0.719	0.650	0.600	0.862	0.797
2000	0.749	0.691	0.681	0.869	0.771
2005	0.779	0.736	0.741	0.877	0.771
2010	0.815	0.773	0.832	0.878	0.781
2015	0.803	0.656	0.993	0.888	0.718

Panel B. AHD Drivers [*] *(%)*

	Kakwani index of schooling	Kakwani index of life expectancy	UNDP index of income	Liberal democracy index	AHDI
1870–1880	0.4	0.1	0.2	0.2	0.9
1880–1890	0.8	0.0	0.2	1.0	2.0
1890–1900	0.9	0.2	0.2	0.6	1.8
1900–1913	1.2	0.2	0.1	0.1	1.6
1913–1929	0.5	0.4	0.2	0.1	1.2

Table D.3 (*cont.*)

	Kakwani index of schooling	Kakwani index of life expectancy	UNDP index of income	Liberal democracy index	AHDI
1929–1938	0.6	0.4	0.2	–0.4	0.7
1938–1950	0.4	1.0	–0.2	1.3	2.6
1950–1960	0.9	0.9	0.6	1.9	4.3
1960–1970	0.7	0.5	0.5	–0.1	1.6
1970–1980	0.4	0.5	0.2	0.0	1.1
1980–1990	0.4	0.4	0.2	0.0	1.0
1990–2000	0.5	0.4	0.1	0.1	1.0
2000–2010	0.3	0.5	0.0	0.0	0.8
2010–2015	–0.8	0.9	0.1	–0.4	–0.3
2000–2015	–0.1	0.6	0.0	–0.1	0.5
1870–2015	0.6	0.5	0.2	0.3	1.5

* Dimensions' contribution to *AHDI* growth.

Table D.4. *AHDI and its components: Eastern Europe*
Panel A. Levels

	AHDI	Kakwani index of Schooling	Kakwani index of life expectancy	UNDP index of income	Liberal democracy index
1870	0.092	0.042	0.047	0.370	0.098
1880	0.097	0.047	0.050	0.396	0.093
1890	0.103	0.054	0.055	0.419	0.090
1900	0.117	0.062	0.073	0.442	0.093
1913	0.135	0.078	0.088	0.462	0.105
1925	0.196	0.099	0.119	0.473	0.265
1929	0.190	0.106	0.135	0.484	0.188
1933	0.191	0.116	0.137	0.457	0.182
1938	0.200	0.128	0.161	0.487	0.157
1950	0.172	0.153	0.238	0.497	0.049
1955	0.190	0.169	0.284	0.525	0.051
1960	0.213	0.190	0.306	0.559	0.063
1965	0.229	0.212	0.330	0.589	0.067
1970	0.237	0.234	0.336	0.616	0.065
1975	0.252	0.264	0.351	0.651	0.067

Table D.4. (*cont.*)

	AHDI	Kakwani index of Schooling	Kakwani index of life expectancy	UNDP index of income	Liberal democracy index
1980	0.261	0.286	0.351	0.664	0.070
1985	0.272	0.316	0.356	0.671	0.072
1990	0.403	0.344	0.364	0.666	0.316
1995	0.456	0.375	0.351	0.621	0.530
2000	0.472	0.407	0.372	0.644	0.511
2005	0.504	0.440	0.383	0.689	0.556
2010	0.530	0.469	0.417	0.716	0.563
2015	0.536	0.483	0.448	0.732	0.521

Panel B. AHD drivers[*] (%)

	Kakwani index of schooling	Kakwani index of life expectancy	UNDP index of income	Liberal democracy index	AHDI
1870–1880	0.3	0.1	0.2	−0.1	0.5
1880–1890	0.3	0.2	0.1	−0.1	0.6
1890–1900	0.4	0.7	0.1	0.1	1.3
1900–1913	0.4	0.4	0.1	0.2	1.1
1913–1929	0.5	0.7	0.1	0.9	2.1
1929–1938	0.5	0.5	0.0	−0.5	0.5
1938–1950	0.4	0.8	0.0	−2.4	−1.2
1950–1960	0.5	0.6	0.3	0.6	2.1
1960–1970	0.5	0.2	0.2	0.1	1.1
1970–1980	0.5	0.1	0.2	0.2	1.0
1980–1990	0.5	0.1	0.0	3.8	4.3
1990–2000	0.4	0.1	−0.1	1.2	1.6
2000–2010	0.4	0.3	0.3	0.2	1.2
2010–2015	0.1	0.4	0.1	−0.4	0.2
1870–2015	0.4	0.4	0.1	0.3	1.2

[*] Dimensions' contribution to *AHDI* growth

Table D.4. *(cont.) Panel C. AHD catching up to the OECD: Dimensions'*
contribution (%)

	Kakwani index of schooling	Kakwani index of life expectancy	UNDP index of income	Liberal democracy index	*AHDI*
1870–1880	–0.1	–0.1	0.0	–0.6	–0.7
1880–1890	–0.1	–0.2	0.0	–0.2	–0.4
1890–1900	0.0	0.3	0.0	–0.2	0.2
1900–1913	0.2	–0.1	0.0	0.1	0.2
1913–1929	0.2	0.3	0.0	0.6	1.0
1929–1938	0.3	0.1	0.0	0.0	0.4
1938–1950	0.1	0.2	–0.1	–3.4	–3.2
1950–1960	0.1	0.2	0.1	0.3	0.7
1960–1970	0.0	0.0	0.0	0.0	0.0
1970–1980	0.0	–0.2	0.1	–0.2	–0.3
1980–1990	0.1	–0.2	–0.1	3.7	3.4
1990–2000	0.1	–0.3	–0.2	1.1	0.9
2000–2010	0.1	–0.1	0.2	0.2	0.4
2010–2015	0.4	0.1	0.1	–0.2	0.4
1870–2015	0.1	0.0	0.0	0.1	0.2

Table D.5. *AHDI and its components: Russia*
Panel A. Levels

	AHDI	Kakwani index of schooling	Kakwani index of Life Expectancy	UNDP index of income	Liberal democracy index
1870	0.069	0.023	0.034	0.330	0.087
1880	0.066	0.025	0.038	0.324	0.060
1890	0.066	0.028	0.044	0.352	0.045
1900	0.070	0.031	0.052	0.404	0.037
1913	0.097	0.050	0.056	0.431	0.073
1925	0.084	0.058	0.105	0.390	0.021
1929	0.089	0.068	0.113	0.427	0.019
1933	0.094	0.089	0.120	0.439	0.017
1938	0.102	0.113	0.128	0.499	0.015
1950	0.127	0.150	0.215	0.544	0.015
1955	0.161	0.190	0.280	0.569	0.022

Table D.5. (*cont.*)

	AHDI	Kakwani index of schooling	Kakwani index of Life Expectancy	UNDP index of income	Liberal democracy index
1960	0.181	0.215	0.331	0.597	0.025
1965	0.189	0.247	0.343	0.623	0.024
1970	0.195	0.278	0.333	0.654	0.024
1975	0.200	0.304	0.326	0.669	0.024
1980	0.216	0.343	0.314	0.677	0.030
1985	0.228	0.371	0.325	0.684	0.033
1990	0.316	0.393	0.339	0.708	0.105
1995	0.377	0.363	0.277	0.629	0.319
2000	0.358	0.364	0.286	0.644	0.244
2005	0.352	0.449	0.286	0.696	0.171
2010	0.385	0.563	0.335	0.725	0.161
2015	0.373	0.597	0.366	0.735	0.121

Panel B. AHD drivers [*] *(%)*

	Kakwani index of schooling	Kakwani index of life expectancy	UNDP index of income	Liberal democracy index	AHDI
1870–1880	0.3	0.3	0.0	−0.9	−0.4
1880–1890	0.2	0.3	0.2	−0.7	0.1
1890–1900	0.2	0.4	0.3	−0.5	0.5
1900–1913	0.9	0.1	0.1	1.3	2.5
1913–1929	0.5	1.1	0.0	−2.1	−0.6
1929–1938	1.4	0.4	0.4	−0.7	1.5
1938–1950	0.6	1.1	0.2	0.0	1.9
1950–1960	0.9	1.1	0.2	1.3	3.5
1960–1970	0.6	0.0	0.2	−0.1	0.8
1970–1980	0.5	−0.1	0.1	0.6	1.0
1980–1990	0.3	0.2	0.1	3.1	3.8
1990–2000	−0.2	−0.4	−0.2	2.1	1.3
2000–2010	1.1	0.4	0.3	−1.0	0.7
2010–2015	0.3	0.5	0.1	−1.4	−0.6
1870–2015	0.6	0.4	0.1	0.1	1.2

[*] Dimensions' contribution to *AHDI* growth.

Table D.5. *(cont.) Panel C. AHD catching up to the OECD: Dimensions'*
contribution (%)

	Kakwani index of schooling	Kakwani index of life expectancy	UNDP index of income	Liberal democracy index	*AHDI*
1870–1880	–0.1	0.1	–0.2	–1.4	–1.6
1880–1890	–0.2	–0.1	0.1	–0.8	–0.9
1890–1900	–0.1	0.0	0.2	–0.7	–0.6
1900–1913	0.7	–0.3	0.0	1.2	1.6
1913–1929	0.1	0.7	–0.1	–2.4	–1.7
1929–1938	1.1	0.0	0.4	–0.2	1.4
1938–1950	0.4	0.5	0.1	–1.0	–0.1
1950–1960	0.4	0.7	0.0	0.9	2.1
1960–1970	0.1	–0.2	0.0	–0.2	–0.3
1970–1980	0.1	–0.5	0.0	0.2	–0.3
1980–1990	–0.1	–0.1	0.0	3.1	2.9
1990–2000	–0.5	–0.7	–0.3	2.0	0.5
2000–2010	0.8	0.0	0.3	–1.1	0.0
2010–2015	0.6	0.2	0.0	–1.2	–0.4
1870–2015	0.2	0.0	0.0	–0.2	0.1

Table D.6. *AHDI and its components: China*
Panel A. Levels

	AHDI	Kakwani index of schooling	Kakwani index of life expectancy	UNDP index of income	Liberal democracy index
1870	0.040	0.026	0.019	0.263	0.020
1880	0.041	0.027	0.019	0.266	0.020
1890	0.041	0.028	0.019	0.263	0.019
1900	0.041	0.030	0.019	0.255	0.020
1913	0.056	0.032	0.019	0.249	0.065
1925	0.049	0.023	0.019	0.252	0.053
1929	0.067	0.034	0.049	0.252	0.049
1933	0.074	0.036	0.058	0.257	0.056
1938	0.076	0.038	0.063	0.252	0.055
1950	0.068	0.044	0.092	0.215	0.024

Table D.6. (*cont.*)

	AHDI	Kakwani index of schooling	Kakwani index of life expectancy	UNDP index of income	Liberal democracy index
1955	0.084	0.052	0.114	0.273	0.030
1960	0.077	0.066	0.069	0.278	0.027
1965	0.108	0.081	0.184	0.322	0.028
1970	0.117	0.099	0.246	0.333	0.023
1975	0.125	0.115	0.279	0.348	0.022
1980	0.165	0.136	0.294	0.376	0.049
1985	0.179	0.156	0.306	0.413	0.052
1990	0.185	0.173	0.322	0.434	0.049
1995	0.212	0.202	0.345	0.494	0.059
2000	0.229	0.227	0.373	0.532	0.061
2005	0.245	0.247	0.396	0.595	0.062
2010	0.268	0.265	0.414	0.664	0.071
2015	0.250	0.263	0.473	0.703	0.045

Panel B. AHD drivers [*] *(%)*

	Kakwani index of schooling	Kakwani index of life expectancy	UNDP index of income	Liberal democracy index	AHDI
1870–1880	0.1	0.0	0.0	0.0	0.2
1880–1890	0.1	0.0	0.0	–0.1	0.0
1890–1900	0.1	0.0	–0.1	0.1	0.2
1900–1913	0.2	0.0	0.0	2.3	2.4
1913–1929	0.1	1.5	0.0	–0.4	1.1
1929–1938	0.3	0.7	0.0	0.3	1.3
1938–1950	0.3	0.8	–0.3	–1.7	–0.9
1950–1960	1.0	–0.7	0.6	0.3	1.2
1960–1970	1.0	3.2	0.5	–0.4	4.2
1970–1980	0.8	0.4	0.3	1.9	3.4
1980–1990	0.6	0.2	0.4	0.0	1.2
1990–2000	0.7	0.4	0.5	0.5	2.1
2000–2010	0.4	0.3	0.6	0.4	1.6
2010–2015	0.0	0.7	0.3	–2.3	–1.4
1870–2015	0.4	0.6	0.2	0.1	1.3

[*] Dimensions' contribution to *AHDI* growth.

Table D.6. *(cont.) Panel C. AHD catching up to the OECD: Dimensions'* contribution (%)

	Kakwani index of schooling	Kakwani index of life expectancy	UNDP index of income	Liberal democracy index	AHDI
1870–1880	-0.3	-0.2	-0.1	-0.4	-1.0
1880–1890	-0.3	-0.4	-0.1	-0.2	-1.1
1890–1900	-0.2	-0.4	-0.2	-0.1	-0.9
1900–1913	-0.1	-0.4	-0.2	2.2	1.5
1913–1929	-0.3	1.1	-0.1	-0.7	0.0
1929–1938	0.0	0.3	0.0	0.8	1.2
1938–1950	0.1	0.2	-0.4	-2.7	-2.9
1950–1960	0.6	-1.1	0.4	-0.1	-0.2
1960–1970	0.5	3.0	0.2	-0.5	3.2
1970–1980	0.3	0.1	0.2	1.5	2.1
1980–1990	0.2	-0.1	0.3	-0.1	0.3
1990–2000	0.4	0.1	0.4	0.5	1.4
2000–2010	0.1	-0.1	0.5	0.3	0.8
2010–2015	0.2	0.4	0.2	-2.0	-1.1
1870–2015	0.1	0.2	0.1	-0.1	0.2

Table D.7. *AHDI and its components: South Asia*
Panel A. Levels

	AHDI	Kakwani index of schooling	Kakwani index of life expectancy	UNDP index of income	Liberal democracy index
1870	0.030	0.002	0.017	0.271	0.074
1880	0.032	0.003	0.019	0.276	0.074
1890	0.035	0.004	0.017	0.286	0.077
1900	0.042	0.007	0.018	0.291	0.082
1913	0.045	0.009	0.018	0.310	0.084
1925	0.060	0.015	0.029	0.316	0.095
1929	0.066	0.018	0.035	0.323	0.096
1933	0.071	0.021	0.042	0.316	0.091
1938	0.082	0.024	0.049	0.309	0.129
1950	0.118	0.030	0.091	0.297	0.242
1955	0.143	0.033	0.094	0.308	0.430

Table D.7. (*cont.*)

	AHDI	Kakwani index of schooling	Kakwani index of life expectancy	UNDP index of income	Liberal democracy index
1960	0.153	0.037	0.110	0.324	0.418
1965	0.169	0.042	0.125	0.330	0.462
1970	0.183	0.052	0.141	0.350	0.436
1975	0.176	0.062	0.157	0.352	0.283
1980	0.211	0.071	0.181	0.362	0.430
1985	0.227	0.081	0.197	0.385	0.434
1990	0.249	0.092	0.210	0.414	0.478
1995	0.270	0.107	0.225	0.438	0.508
2000	0.292	0.130	0.243	0.466	0.491
2005	0.305	0.139	0.260	0.504	0.476
2010	0.323	0.145	0.279	0.553	0.487
2015	0.356	0.190	0.327	0.592	0.438

*Panel B. AHD drivers** *(%)*

	Kakwani index of schooling	Kakwani index of life expectancy	UNDP index of income	Liberal democracy index	AHDI
1870–1880	0.3	0.3	0.0	0.0	0.6
1880–1890	0.8	–0.2	0.1	0.1	0.7
1890–1900	1.6	0.0	0.0	0.2	1.8
1900–1913	0.5	0.0	0.1	0.0	0.6
1913–1929	1.0	1.1	0.1	0.2	2.4
1929–1938	0.8	1.0	–0.1	0.8	2.5
1938–1950	0.5	1.3	–0.1	1.3	3.0
1950–1960	0.6	0.5	0.2	1.4	2.6
1960–1970	0.8	0.6	0.2	0.1	1.8
1970–1980	0.8	0.6	0.1	0.0	1.5
1980–1990	0.7	0.4	0.3	0.3	1.6
1990–2000	0.9	0.4	0.3	0.1	1.6
2000–2010	0.3	0.4	0.4	0.0	1.0
2010–2015	1.4	0.8	0.3	–0.5	2.0
1870–2015	0.7	0.5	0.1	0.3	1.7

* Includes Afghanistan, Bangladesh, India, Nepal, Pakistan, and Sri Lanka.
** Dimensions' contribution to *AHDI* growth.

Table D.7. *(cont.) Panel C. AHD catching up to the OECD: Dimensions'*
contribution (%)

	Kakwani index of schooling	Kakwani index of life expectancy	UNDP index of income	Liberal democracy index	AHDI
1870–1880	–0.2	0.1	–0.1	–0.4	–0.6
1880–1890	0.4	–0.6	0.0	0.0	–0.3
1890–1900	1.3	–0.4	–0.1	–0.1	0.8
1900–1913	0.2	–0.4	0.0	–0.1	–0.2
1913–1929	0.7	0.7	0.0	–0.1	1.3
1929–1938	0.5	0.6	–0.1	1.3	2.3
1938–1950	0.2	0.6	–0.2	0.3	1.0
1950–1960	0.1	0.1	0.0	1.0	1.2
1960–1970	0.3	0.4	0.0	0.0	0.7
1970–1980	0.3	0.3	0.0	–0.4	0.2
1980–1990	0.2	0.1	0.2	0.2	0.7
1990–2000	0.6	0.1	0.2	0.0	0.9
2000–2010	0.0	0.0	0.4	–0.1	0.2
2010–2015	1.7	0.6	0.3	–0.3	2.2
1870–2015	0.4	0.1	0.0	0.1	0.7

Table D.8. *AHDI and its components: East Asia*[*]
Panel A. Levels

	AHDI	Kakwani index of schooling	Kakwani index of life expectancy	UNDP index of income	Liberal democracy index
1870	0.035	0.008	0.019	0.277	0.037
1880	0.036	0.008	0.019	0.301	0.038
1890	0.036	0.008	0.019	0.309	0.036
1900	0.041	0.009	0.020	0.325	0.049
1913	0.048	0.010	0.027	0.344	0.052
1925	0.064	0.019	0.041	0.368	0.059
1929	0.070	0.022	0.048	0.383	0.058
1933	0.079	0.029	0.059	0.375	0.062
1938	0.091	0.034	0.071	0.390	0.071
1950	0.127	0.051	0.102	0.343	0.146
1955	0.149	0.062	0.120	0.372	0.178

Table D.8. (*cont.*)

	AHDI	Kakwani index of schooling	Kakwani index of life expectancy	UNDP index of income	Liberal democracy index
1960	0.154	0.072	0.131	0.386	0.156
1965	0.158	0.088	0.152	0.403	0.114
1970	0.176	0.109	0.173	0.433	0.119
1975	0.185	0.125	0.194	0.468	0.104
1980	0.193	0.148	0.223	0.509	0.083
1985	0.211	0.163	0.253	0.530	0.091
1990	0.270	0.178	0.280	0.576	0.185
1995	0.295	0.199	0.306	0.621	0.201
2000	0.370	0.219	0.334	0.636	0.404
2005	0.392	0.252	0.360	0.666	0.392
2010	0.415	0.284	0.388	0.696	0.389
2015	0.424	0.297	0.384	0.722	0.393

* Excluding Japan.

Panel B. AHD drivers [*] *(%)*

	Kakwani index of schooling	Kakwani index of life expectancy	UNDP index of income	Liberal democracy index	AHDI
1870–1880	0.0	0.0	0.2	0.1	0.3
1880–1890	0.0	0.0	0.1	−0.1	0.0
1890–1900	0.2	0.1	0.1	0.7	1.2
1900–1913	0.3	0.6	0.1	0.1	1.2
1913–1929	1.2	0.9	0.2	0.2	2.4
1929–1938	1.2	1.1	0.0	0.5	2.9
1938–1950	0.8	0.7	−0.3	1.5	2.8
1950–1960	0.8	0.6	0.3	0.2	1.9
1960–1970	1.0	0.7	0.3	−0.7	1.3
1970–1980	0.8	0.6	0.4	−0.9	0.9
1980–1990	0.5	0.6	0.3	2.0	3.4
1990–2000	0.5	0.4	0.2	1.9	3.2
2000–2010	0.6	0.4	0.2	−0.1	1.1
2010–2015	0.2	0.0	0.2	0.0	0.4
1870–2015	0.6	0.5	0.2	0.4	1.7

* Dimensions' contribution to *AHDI* growth.

Table D.8. *(cont.) Panel C. AHD catching up to the OECD: Dimensions'* contribution (%)

	Kakwani index of schooling	Kakwani index of life expectancy	UNDP index of income	Liberal democracy index	AHDI
1870–1880	–0.4	–0.2	0.1	–0.4	–0.9
1880–1890	–0.4	–0.4	0.0	–0.2	–1.0
1890–1900	–0.1	–0.3	0.0	0.5	0.1
1900–1913	0.0	0.2	0.0	0.0	0.3
1913–1929	0.9	0.5	0.1	–0.1	1.3
1929–1938	0.9	0.7	0.0	1.0	2.7
1938–1950	0.6	0.1	–0.4	0.5	0.9
1950–1960	0.4	0.2	0.1	–0.2	0.5
1960–1970	0.5	0.5	0.1	–0.8	0.3
1970–1980	0.3	0.3	0.3	–1.2	–0.4
1980–1990	0.1	0.3	0.2	1.9	2.5
1990–2000	0.2	0.1	0.2	1.9	2.4
2000–2010	0.4	0.0	0.2	–0.2	0.4
2010–2015	0.5	–0.3	0.1	0.3	0.6
1870–2015	0.3	0.1	0.1	0.2	0.7

Table D.9. *AHDI and its components: Middle East*[*]
Panel A. Levels

	AHDI	Kakwani index of schooling	Kakwani index of life expectancy	UNDP index of income	Liberal democracy index
1870	0.038	0.006	0.023	0.322	0.043
1880	0.037	0.007	0.024	0.330	0.033
1890	0.038	0.008	0.026	0.347	0.027
1900	0.041	0.010	0.028	0.360	0.028
1913	0.051	0.011	0.030	0.377	0.054
1925	0.060	0.013	0.033	0.374	0.079
1929	0.068	0.016	0.044	0.397	0.078
1933	0.074	0.018	0.049	0.410	0.084
1938	0.084	0.020	0.065	0.436	0.086
1950	0.124	0.028	0.121	0.469	0.147
1955	0.140	0.035	0.132	0.497	0.166

Table D.9. (*cont.*)

	AHDI	Kakwani index of schooling	Kakwani index of life expectancy	UNDP index of income	Liberal democracy index
1960	0.132	0.044	0.141	0.524	0.092
1965	0.166	0.054	0.161	0.556	0.160
1970	0.198	0.066	0.184	0.601	0.212
1975	0.221	0.080	0.209	0.649	0.218
1980	0.200	0.100	0.229	0.651	0.109
1985	0.238	0.125	0.253	0.639	0.159
1990	0.263	0.144	0.283	0.633	0.186
1995	0.289	0.166	0.317	0.645	0.206
2000	0.319	0.192	0.347	0.657	0.237
2005	0.342	0.217	0.364	0.678	0.255
2010	0.354	0.249	0.384	0.691	0.239
2015	0.349	0.271	0.420	0.691	0.188

* Including Turkey.

Panel B. AHD drivers * *(%)*

	Kakwani index of schooling	Kakwani index of life expectancy	UNDP index of income	Liberal democracy index	AHDI
1870–1880	0.4	0.1	0.1	−0.7	−0.1
1880–1890	0.3	0.2	0.1	−0.5	0.1
1890–1900	0.3	0.2	0.1	0.1	0.7
1900–1913	0.3	0.1	0.1	1.2	1.7
1913–1929	0.6	0.6	0.1	0.6	1.8
1929–1938	0.7	1.1	0.3	0.3	2.3
1938–1950	0.7	1.3	0.2	1.1	3.3
1950–1960	1.1	0.4	0.3	−1.2	0.6
1960–1970	1.0	0.7	0.3	2.1	4.1
1970–1980	1.0	0.5	0.2	−1.7	0.1
1980–1990	0.9	0.5	−0.1	1.3	2.7
1990–2000	0.7	0.5	0.1	0.6	1.9
2000–2010	0.6	0.3	0.1	0.0	1.0
2010–2015	0.4	0.4	0.0	−1.2	−0.3
1870–2015	0.6	0.5	0.1	0.3	1.5

* Dimensions' contribution to *AHDI* growth.

Table D.9. *(cont.) Panel C. AHD catching up to the OECD: Dimensions'*
contribution (%)

	Kakwani index of schooling	Kakwani index of life expectancy	UNDP index of income	Liberal democracy index	*AHDI*
1870–1880	0.0	−0.1	−0.1	−1.1	−1.3
1880–1890	−0.1	−0.2	0.0	−0.6	−0.9
1890–1900	0.0	−0.2	0.0	−0.1	−0.3
1900–1913	0.0	−0.3	0.0	1.1	0.8
1913–1929	0.2	0.2	0.0	0.3	0.7
1929–1938	0.4	0.7	0.3	0.8	2.1
1938–1950	0.5	0.7	0.0	0.1	1.3
1950–1960	0.7	0.0	0.1	−1.5	−0.8
1960–1970	0.5	0.5	0.1	2.0	3.0
1970–1980	0.6	0.2	0.1	−2.0	−1.2
1980–1990	0.5	0.2	−0.2	1.3	1.8
1990–2000	0.4	0.2	0.0	0.5	1.2
2000–2010	0.4	−0.1	0.1	−0.1	0.3
2010–2015	0.7	0.2	0.0	−1.0	−0.1
1870–2015	0.3	0.1	0.0	0.0	0.5

Table D.10. *AHDI and its components: Sub-Saharan Africa*
Panel A. Levels

	AHDI	Kakwani index of schooling	Kakwani index of life expectancy	UNDP index of income	Liberal democracy index
1870	0.027	0.005	0.021	0.280	0.020
1880	0.028	0.005	0.021	0.286	0.020
1890	0.029	0.005	0.022	0.292	0.020
1900	0.035	0.006	0.024	0.296	0.038
1913	0.041	0.006	0.026	0.310	0.055
1925	0.047	0.009	0.028	0.313	0.066
1929	0.051	0.010	0.034	0.313	0.067
1933	0.054	0.011	0.036	0.300	0.068
1938	0.061	0.013	0.049	0.325	0.067
1950	0.077	0.019	0.072	0.343	0.075
1955	0.089	0.024	0.083	0.362	0.087

Table D.10. (*cont.*)

	AHDI	Kakwani index of schooling	Kakwani index of life expectancy	UNDP index of income	Liberal democracy index
1960	0.104	0.030	0.089	0.372	0.118
1965	0.116	0.034	0.100	0.390	0.133
1970	0.117	0.041	0.112	0.408	0.099
1975	0.121	0.047	0.123	0.413	0.089
1980	0.143	0.055	0.137	0.414	0.133
1985	0.139	0.067	0.144	0.396	0.098
1990	0.153	0.081	0.148	0.394	0.117
1995	0.186	0.096	0.148	0.381	0.221
2000	0.202	0.105	0.148	0.392	0.274
2005	0.214	0.117	0.155	0.416	0.280
2010	0.230	0.132	0.169	0.443	0.282
2015	0.266	0.157	0.220	0.460	0.316

Panel B. AHD drivers [*] *(%)*

	Kakwani index of schooling	Kakwani index of life expectancy	UNDP index of income	Liberal democracy index	AHDI
1870–1880	0.1	0.1	0.1	0.0	0.3
1880–1890	0.1	0.1	0.0	0.0	0.3
1890–1900	0.2	0.2	0.0	1.6	2.0
1900–1913	0.2	0.2	0.1	0.7	1.2
1913–1929	0.6	0.4	0.0	0.3	1.4
1929–1938	0.8	1.0	0.1	0.0	2.0
1938–1950	0.8	0.8	0.1	0.2	1.9
1950–1960	1.1	0.5	0.2	1.1	3.0
1960–1970	0.8	0.6	0.2	−0.4	1.2
1970–1980	0.7	0.5	0.0	0.7	2.0
1980–1990	1.0	0.2	−0.1	−0.3	0.7
1990–2000	0.6	0.0	0.0	2.1	2.8
2000–2010	0.6	0.3	0.3	0.1	1.3
2010–2015	0.8	1.3	0.2	0.6	2.9
1870-2015	0.6	0.4	0.1	0.5	1.6

[*] Dimensions' contribution to *AHDI* growth.

Table D.10. *(cont.) Panel C. AHD catching up to the OECD: Dimensions'* contribution (%)

	Kakwani index of schooling	Kakwani index of life expectancy	UNDP index of income	Liberal democracy index	*AHDI*
1870–1880	−0.3	−0.1	−0.1	−0.4	−0.9
1880–1890	−0.3	−0.3	−0.1	−0.1	−0.8
1890–1900	−0.2	−0.2	−0.1	1.4	0.9
1900–1913	0.0	−0.2	0.0	0.6	0.3
1913–1929	0.3	0.0	−0.1	0.0	0.3
1929–1938	0.6	0.6	0.1	0.5	1.8
1938–1950	0.5	0.2	0.0	−0.7	0.0
1950–1960	0.7	0.1	0.0	0.7	1.5
1960–1970	0.3	0.3	0.0	−0.6	0.1
1970–1980	0.3	0.2	−0.1	0.4	0.7
1980–1990	0.6	−0.1	−0.2	−0.4	−0.2
1990–2000	0.3	−0.3	−0.1	2.1	2.0
2000–2010	0.3	−0.1	0.3	0.0	0.5
2010–2015	1.1	1.1	0.1	0.8	3.2
1870–2015	0.3	0.0	0.0	0.3	0.5

Appendix E
Latin America

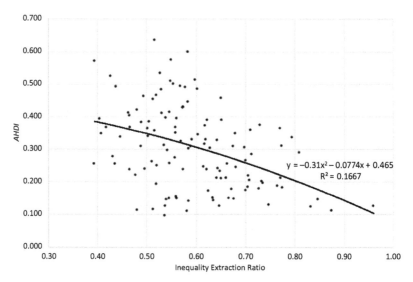

Figure E.1 *AHDI* and IER in Latin American countries, 1950–2010.
Sources: IER, Prados de la Escosura (2007a), updated with Székely (2001) and Székely and Mendoza and (2015) inequality estimates for 1980–2010; *AHDI*, see the text.

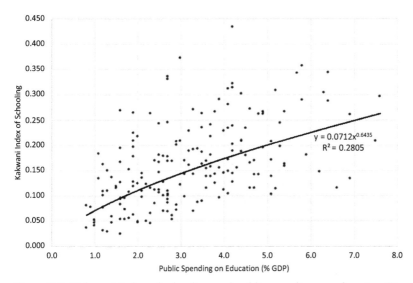

Figure E.2 Kakwani Index of schooling and public spending on education (% GDP) in Latin American countries, 1954–2010.

Sources: Public spending on education, Frankema (2009), completed for 2010 with Arroyo Abad and Lindert (2017); Kakwani index of schooling, see the text.

Notes

Introduction

1 On attempts to provide alternative well-being measures, cf. Adelman and Morris (1967), Beckerman (1966), Beckerman and Bacon (1966), Ehrlich (1969), Hicks and Streeten (1981), Morris (1979), Streeten *et al.* (1981), McGranahan *et al.* (1985), and Ram (1982). For negative and positive assessment of composite indices, cf. Ravallion (2012a) and Krishnakumar (2018).

2 Reactions to well-being indices have always been critical. For example, Morris's (1979) Physical Quality of Life Index [PQLI], an unweighted average of normalised indices of infant mortality, life expectancy, and literacy, was seriously questioned on the basis of the high collinearity between its first two components (Hopkins, 1991). For historical applications, cf. Federico and Toniolo (1991) and Domínguez and Guijarro (2000). Mazumdar (1999) widened the PQLI index to include other social dimensions in an attempt to measure the quality of life.

3 Alternatives include the welfare economics approach, which values various dimensions of quality of life in monetary terms (cf. Nordhaus and Tobin, 1972; Becker et al., 2005; Jones and Klenow, 2016; Gallardo Albarrán, 2017), and Subjective Well-Being (SWB), which places life satisfaction at its centre (Easterlin, 1974, Kahneman and Deaton, 2010; Veenhoven and Vengust, 2013; Clark, 2018).

4 For critical assessment of the capabilities approach, cf. Dean (2009). A different view of capabilities is offered by Nussbaum (2011: 19), who distinguishes two purposes in the capabilities approach, 'as a theory of basic social justice' (her own approach), and 'for comparative quality-of-life assessment' (Sen's approach). Good surveys of the theory and practice of the concept of capabilities are provided by Robeyns (2005, 2006, 2011).

5 That is, positive freedom, 'freedom to', and negative freedom, 'freedom from' (Berlin, 1958).

Chapter 1

1 The *AHDI* improves on the 'hybrid' historical index of human development (*HIHD*) (Prados de la Escosura, 2015b), which only considers the first three dimensions and uses literacy and enrolment rather than years of schooling as proxies for education.

2 Cf. Riley (2001) and Benavot and Riddle (1988).

3 The *Human Development Report 2014* (UNDP, 2014) represented a change with respect to the *Human Development Report 2010* (UNDP, 2010) in which the unweighted average was geometric. Previously, education attainment was proxied by rates of total (primary, secondary, and tertiary) enrolment and adult literacy combined in index form as a weighted arithmetic average (two-thirds literacy and one-third enrolment). Mean years of schooling were used instead of enrolment only once before, in the *Human Development Report 1994* (UNDP, 1994).

4 The previous 2010 goalposts were 83.2 and 20 years for life expectancy, 13.2 and 20.6 years as maxima for mean years of schooling and expected years of schooling, respectively, with 0 as the minima. In the case of GNI per capita, 108,211 and 163 PPP dollars were the maximum and minimum goalposts: UNDP (2010: 216).

5 The upper limit was set on the basis of Kahneman and Deaton (2010: 16491), finding that 'there is no improvement … in … emotional well-being' as per capita income exceeds 75,000$. The lower limit was supposed to represent a subsistence minimum (UNDP, 2014, Technical Notes: 2).

6 I will not consider, however, the concern about combining stocks (life expectancy and schooling years) and flows (per capita income) in the *HDI*, discussed extensively by Aturupane *et al.* (1994: 246) and Klugman *et al.* (2011: 259).

7 Sagar and Najam (1998: 254), chose a minimum value for per capita income of $300.

8 Four benchmark estimates for 1990, 2000, 2006, and 2016 from Murray *et al.* (2017) are pooled in Figure 1.1. Canning (2012) reports a similar finding.

9 The decline in age-specific disability as life expectancy at birth increases is compatible, however, with years lost to disability (YLD) rising with life expectancy because YLD tend to be concentrated at the end of life (Salomon *et al.*, 2012). Perhaps then, the view that while longevity increases, periods of ill health can be longer, but are lived in better health and less disability, due to advances in medical technology (Manton, 1982), qualifies Fries' morbidity compression hypothesis (Fries, 1980; Fries *et al.*, 2011; Lindgren, 2016). Nonetheless, Cutler

et al. (2014) and Chernew *et al.* (2016) find that the reduction in disabled life expectancy runs parallel to the increase in healthy life expectancy, suggesting a compression of morbidity for the U.S. between 1990 and 2010. A note of historical caution is warranted, as evidence for a stable association between death and ill health prior to 1990 is scant and inconclusive (Riley, 1990; Howse, 2006; Bleakley, 2007, 2010; Cutler *et al.*, 2010).

10 The measure of quality-adjusted years of education used here is derived as the product of normalised indices (namely, expressed relative to its maximum value) of cognitive skills (as a measure of quality), provided by Altinok *et al.* (2018), and years of schooling (as a measure of quantity) is each country's average over 1965–2015. A word of caution is needed, though, as no evidence that the relationship between quality-adjusted years of education and quantity of education exists prior to 1965.

11 Kakwani (1993: 313–315), drawing on Atkinson (1970), uses an achievement function,

$$f(x, Mo, M) = \left((M - Mo)^{1-\varepsilon} - (M - x^{1-\varepsilon}) \right) / \left((M - Mo)^{1-\varepsilon} \right), \text{for } 0 < \varepsilon < 1,$$

$$[1.4]$$

ε being an inequality-aversion parameter, and opts for $\varepsilon = 1$, which satisfies all the axioms of the improvement index, that is, the difference between the values of the achievement index between two periods, while it does not satisfy them for $0 < \varepsilon < 1$. The UNDP social dimensions' transformation represents a particular case, for $\varepsilon = 0$, which yields equation [1.1].

12 This reasoning ignores the interpretation of per capita income in terms of capabilities.

13 Zambrano's (2014: 863–864) original notation has been changed to match that of equation [1.1].

14 Zambrano's (2017) proposal does not seem to me a less discretional, more intuitive, and simpler option. Kakwani (1993: 324) considers the logarithm of GDP per head an adequate measure of economic welfare in the absence of income distribution information.

15 As Herrero *et al.* (2012) establish a maximum level for the inequality-adjusted income of GEKS $2011 60,000, over a maximum unadjusted income of GEKS $2011 75,000, I applied their ratio (60/75) to the maximum income in G-K $1990 47,000, obtaining a maximum inequality-adjusted income of $37,600. Global income inequality comes from van Zanden *et al.* (2014. 294), completed with Lakner and Milanovic (2016: 229), and Milanovic (2020: 10), for the post-2000 years.

16 Zambrano (2017: 536) uses a value of 0.5 as an example and I have used this here.

17 The income dimension was adjusted for inequality in the early stages of the *HDI*, but this was then abandoned because of the lack of reliable data across countries, while no attempt was made to compute inequality for the social dimensions (UNDP, 1993). Cf. Hicks (1997).

18 Cf. Klugman *et al.* (2011: 280–282), and Herrero *et al.* (2012: 256–258), for critical assessments of the UNDP attempt. Herrero *et al.* (2012: 257) noted, in particular, that since the available data on longevity and education are unrelated to the social and economic stratification behind income inequality, the inequality-adjusted *HDI* is difficult to interpret. They introduced, nonetheless, an inequality adjustment of income (an egalitarian equivalent income) that can be interpreted as a 'capability measure that transforms income into material wellbeing'. Bértola *et al.* (2011) attempted to include inequality in the three dimensions of human development for a group of Latin American and Western European countries over the long run.

19 At least, directly, since it could be argued that functionings in health and education also imply capabilities. Security is also an important dimension that deserve to be included (I owe this remark to Ewout Frankema). However, the inclusion of civil and political rights in the *AHDI* partially offsets this.

20 Cf. Knutsen *et al.* (2019). Vanhanen's Index is comparable, though less comprehensive, to the 'Electoral Democracy' component of the *Liberal Democracy Index* (LDI), and Polity 2, although includes also negative freedom elements as the 'Liberal' component of the LDI, is much less comprehensive than the LDI. Polity2 (Marshall *et al.*, 2018) and the Index of Democratisation (Vanhanen, 2016) can be depicted, according to Földvári (2017: 760), as *de jure* and *de facto* measures of political institutions.

21 PCA is a statistical technique for transforming a large set of variables into a smaller set of uncorrelated variables that accounts for most of the variation in the original variables. The principal components are linear combinations of the original variables with characteristic vectors of the correlation matrix of original variables as weights. The first principal component captures the largest proportion of the variation in the original set of variables. See Ram (1982) for a pioneering use of PCA to computing the Physical Index of Quality of Life. Also, cf. Ogwang (1994), Ogwang and Abdou (2003), and Lai (2000).

22 Ravallion (2012b) recommends keeping the arithmetic average and using Chakravarty's (2003) proposal to reduce substitutability.

23 Interestingly, a similar argument about hidden (and questionable) trade-offs had already been used by Ravallion (1997) to criticise arithmetic aggregation. He claimed the implicit monetary valuation of an extra year of life expectancy rises dramatically with income as, by construction, the UNDP *HDI* implicitly values life relatively less in poor than in rich countries. It is worth stressing that the logarithmic transformation of income is about five times more important than the geometric average in explaining the trade-off between life expectancy and income across countries (Zambrano, 2017: 522). This point had actually already been made by Ravallion himself long before, when he argued that the striking trade-off between per capita income and longevity arises 'from the fact that the marginal effect on the *HDI* of longer life is a constant', while at the same time 'the marginal effect of extra income falls very sharply as income increases' (Ravallion, 1997: 633).

24 Interestingly, in their utility approach to welfare, Jones and Klenow (2016: 2439) also find the 'implied value of life ... substantially lower in poor countries'.

25 Whether a social welfare approach is appropriate to assess human development appears to be the issue at stake. Canning (2012: 1786) provides a clarifying illustration by comparing two metrics for health status, QALY and DALY. QALY (quality-adjusted life years) uses a utilitarian social welfare function in which health is valued in terms of individuals' willingness to trade them off. Alternatively, DALY (disability-adjusted life years) depends on adjustments for disability based on objective criteria. In the capabilities approach, well-being is measured by the objective size of the choice set, and not by the utility of the choices, as a healthy lifespan represents a constraint on individuals' choice.

26 Herrero *et al.*'s (2012) view is at odds with the characterisation of the index as purely ordinal (Vecchi *et al.*, 2017: 467).

27 Note that due to dearth of data, this specification differs from that in the UNDP (2010) *HDI*, which measures education as the unweighted geometric average of expected years of schooling and mean years of schooling. Nonetheless, making a virtue out of necessity, I could argue along with Herrero *et al.* (2012: 249–250), that using one single indicator for education facilitates the interpretation of the human development index.

28 This is due to the lack of historical estimates of per capita GNI.

29 The 2010 goalposts (UNDP, 2010) were used in the 'hybrid' historical index of human development in Prados de la Escosura (2015b).

30 G-K 1990$ $47,000 corresponds to GEKS $2011 75,000, that is, the maximum set in UNDP (2014). In the case of the minimum, $100, I have

retained this without adjusting it for price variation, as a higher 'floor' has been introduced for countries' per capita income.

31 Sagar and Najam (1998: 254); Milanovic *et al.* (2011: 262).

32 These results largely confirm those of Klasen (2018: 9), who emphasises the stability of country ranking via alternate use of the arithmetic and geometric aggregation.

33 Note that *Zambrano* specification shares with *UNDP* specification the transformation of all dimensions except that for income, in which equation [1.6] is used in the *Zambrano* specification.

34 Note that as the *Bértola-Vecchi* specification employs the UNDP transformation of social dimensions, it actually follows Bértola and Ocampo (2012: 43), Relative Index RI1.

35 The *HMV* specification only partially follows Herrero *et al.* (2012), since it is not adjusted for income for inequality.

36 Note that the *Bértola-Kakwani* specification actually follows Bértola *et al.* (2011) and Bértola and Ocampo (2012) very closely, Relative Index RI2.

Chapter 2

1 See, for example, Oulton (2012). However, there are strong opposite views. Cf. Szreter (1997).

2 The rate of growth of human development falls to 1.2 when all dimensions, income included, are considered (Table 2.1, Panel B).

3 I owe this remark to Nick Crafts. No doubt there is a trade-off between the impact of disasters (wars, depressions) in the short run and benefits (for the survivors) in the medium or long run, the latter being the focus here.

4 The drivers of human development in the *AHDI* largely coincide with those derived from alternative specifications of the *augmented* index of human development (see Chapter 1) that, nonetheless, allocate more weight to the contribution of income when no log transformation is used (Appendix B).

5 If instead of the Kakwani index the original values of life expectancy at birth are used, the association is also positive but flattens out as the share of social transfers in GDP approaches 10 per cent.

6 This depiction is more restricted than Riley's (2005b), which associates the 'health transition' with persistent gains in survival and dates its beginnings in Denmark in the 1770s, way before the germ theory of disease was designed and accepted. However, even with this broad definition, only a handful of countries had started it before the 1870s, 8 out of a sample of 119 countries (Riley, 2005b: 745).

7 Riley (2001: 19), disagrees and considers that unchecked or ineffectively checked disease rather than infectious disease was the main cause of death

in pre-transition societies. In Omran (1971, 1998), the epidemiological transition is a very comprehensive concept, including health and parts of the demographic transitions. The narrower concept used here overlaps Omran's second and third stages in Western societies, that is, the ages of 'receding pandemics' and 'degenerative and man-made diseases'.

8 Later, the introduction of sulphonamides and, then, penicillin represented a major leap forwards in the reduction of maternal mortality (Loudon, 2000).

9 However, the decline of the female–male mortality ratio predated mass vaccination (Harris, 2008).

10 (Lipset, 1959: 80) sustained that 'the factors subsumed under economic development [industrialisation, urbanisation, wealth, and education] carry with it the political correlate of democracy'.

11 Mukand and Rodrik's (2020) 'illiberal' democracy brings back to the conflict Classical liberals observed between democracy, which focuses on who exercises the power, and liberty, which sets the limits of power (Rodríguez Braun, 2010).

12 Namely, the breakdown of Austria-Hungary and Russia's empires, the rise of fascism and Nazism in the interwar period and their defeat in World War II, the subsequent demise of colonial empires and the Cold War, and the collapse of the Soviet Union.

Chapter 3

1 Since in the present state of the art it is not possible to derive measures of within-country inequality for the well-being dimensions considered over such a large country sample and long time span, I will focus on international inequality, on the basis of national averages for each dimension.

2 Relative inequality depends on the ratio of countries to the mean, and absolute inequality measures the absolute distance between countries. Consider, for example, GDP per head in two countries, country A, $1,000 and country B, $10,000. If GDP per head is doubled in both countries, the absolute difference between country B and country A will widen, from 9,000 (= 10,000 − 1,000) to 18,000 (=20,000 − 2,000), but in relative terms the difference will not change, and country B will continue to be ten times richer than country A. Cf. Ravallion (2004: 23–24).

3 The determinant role played by China and India in the international income distribution is a recurrent feature in later studies, cf. Firebaugh (1999), Bourguignon and Morrisson (2002), Milanovic (2005), and Sala-i-Martin (2006).

4 Dowrick and Akmal (2005) found, however, that inequality increased slightly between 1980 and 1993. In a thorough survey, Anand and Segal

(2008) express an agnostic view regarding the direction of change in global inequality over 1970–2000. Liberati (2015) confirmed Milanovic's finding and pointed out a moderate decline in global inequality since the beginning of the twenty-first century.

5 For example, if all countries double their income, relative inequality will remain the same, but absolute inequality will widen. Cf. Anand and Segal (2015) and Atkinson and Brandolini (2010).

6 Morrison and Murtin (2013) use Bourguignon and Morrisson's transnational units or 'large' countries (32 rather than 33, in their case).

7 Goesling and Firebaugh (2004) also hypothesised an inverted U-shape evolution of health inequality over the past two centuries, starting from low levels that would have increased since the late nineteenth century and peaked in the interwar years, to decline during the second half of the twentieth century.

8 Morrisson and Murtin (2005) used a slightly modified version of the UNDP *HDI*. More recently, Auke Rijpma (2017) has constructed a comprehensive well-being index for the past two centuries on the basis of a wide range of indicators (income, health, education, political institutions, freedom, inequality, and personal security) and using a latent variable model. This composite index shows more intense improvement and stronger convergence over time than GDP per head. Also, Koen Decancq *et al.* (2009), using a flexible index of multidimensional well-being, showed a decline in unweighted inequality from 1975–2000.

9 This conclusion was disputed by Eric Neumayer (2003), who rejected Hobijn and Franses's (2001) 'achievement indices' to assess inequality and, using the original values of a set of social variables (life expectancy, infant survival, education enrolment, literacy, and telephone and television availability), restated the view of a reduction in inequality between 1960 and 2000.

10 The attempt by Clio Infra www.clio-infra.eu/ to provide inequality measures for education and income falls short of the amount of data required in my estimates.

11 This assertion only applies in the context of perfectly decomposable entropy indices, such as MLD or Theil T (Milanovic, 2005: 25).

12 It could also be argued that the dispersion in social dimensions tends to be significantly lower than in the case of income; in other words, the longevity or education gap between the rich and the poor is less than proportional to their income gap.

13 Data sources and procedures are provided in Appendix A.

14 Martínez (2016) found that education was its main driver in the UNDP *HDI* that, as discussed, excludes the freedom dimension.

15 The absolute inequality measure is derived as the mean value times the relative inequality measure. Cf. Anand and Segal (2015: 967).

Chapter 4

1 Advanced countries here largely coincide with the membership of the Organisation for Economic Co-operation and Development (*OECD*) up to 1994: Western Europe, its 'Western Offshoots', and Japan. Western Europe includes Austria, Belgium, Denmark, Finland, France, Germany, Greece, Ireland, Italy, the Netherlands, Norway, Portugal, Spain, Sweden, Switzerland, and the United Kingdom. 'Western Offshoots' consists of Australia, Canada, New Zealand, and the United States (Maddison, 1995: 23). Three *OECD* members, therefore, are excluded. Iceland and Luxemburg are omitted due to lack of augmented human development estimates, and Turkey is included within the Middle East in order to reduce heterogeneity within the group.

Chapter 5

1 The term "Latin America" is used in an extensive way here, and includes Brazil and the Caribbean.

2 The IER measures the distance from a country's inequality level to the inequality possibility frontier, namely, 'the maximum Gini that is achievable at a given level of mean income provided that all population but an infinitesimally small elite live at the subsistence minimum' (Milanovic, 2011: 501). IER is equal to G / G^*, where G and G^* are observed and maximum feasible Gini. And G^* $(\mu) = (\alpha - 1) / \alpha$, where α is the ratio between the mean income (μ) and the subsistence minimum (s) set equal to G-K $300.

3 That is, using a linear transformation of the variables and GDP per head (previously transformed in logs) that are subsequently combined into the *HDI* as an arithmetic average.

4 Cf. Hatton (2011) on the case of Britain. For a comprehensive discussion of height as a measure of well-being, cf. Harris (2021).

Chapter 6

1 It has been argued that physical well-being was even higher under colonial rule than in the early post-independence years, in spite of the unprecedented expansion of investment in public health and education after 1960 (Moradi, Austin, and Baten, 2013).

2 As well as long-term consequences on the levels of trust in medicine nowadays (Lowes and Montero, 2021). For a recent negative assessment of the impact of colonialism on heights, cf. Baten and Maravall (2021).

3 It goes beyond Prados de la Escosura's (2013) study of Africa's human development in which the Historical Index of Human Development (HIHD) used only the conventional three dimensions (longevity, education, and material living standard), leaving freedom aside.

4 Population-weighted averages of human development are provided for these five regions whose composition is defined according the African Development Bank criteria.

5 As Morten Jerven put it (2009: 77), 'with the exception of some resource-rich enclaves, a few island states, and South Africa, the income of one African economy is not meaningfully different from another'. James Riley (2005a) stresses a similar point with regards to life expectancy and suggests that, in the absence of reliable estimates for a country, the best choice is using its neighbours'.

6 'Syndromes' are also described by these authors as 'dysfunctional political-economy configurations'. It should be noted that in Collier and O'Connell (2008) typology countries are not characterised by their growth outcomes, but rather by their institutional settings and policies.

7 State-led industrialisation would occur behind high trade barriers and financed through the taxation of exports (Collier and O'Connell 2008: 90). These authors also distinguish between 'hard' and 'soft' regulatory controls.

8 An extreme form of a redistributive syndrome is looting by which is meant 'a situation in which assets, whether private or public, are stripped outside the context of the rule of law and due process' (Collier and O'Connell 2008: 89, 91–92).

9 Anticipated redistribution occurs when an elite group anticipates a loss of power, and unsustainable spending happens when a country fails to transform temporary income into permanent income (Collier and O'Connell 2008: 94–95).

10 It could be argued that DR Congo is a resource-abundant economy. However, it is not according to Collier and O'Connell definition, who consider a country land abundant when the value of the 'rents' contained in the exports of primary commodities is above 10 per cent of GDP.

11 No data are available for Somalia, Djibouti, and South Sudan – here included in Sudan – but presumably they would have also been in this group.

12 In 1980, life expectancy at birth had increased for Blacks up to 57 years while that of Whites to 69.7 (United Nations 2000).

References

Acemoglu, D. and S. Johnson (2007), "Disease and Development: The Effects of Life Expectancy on Economic Growth", *Journal of Political Economy* 115: 925–985.

Acemoglu, D., S. Johnson, and J.A. Robinson (2002), "Reversal of Fortune: Geography and Institutions in the Making of the Modern World Income Distribution", *Quarterly Journal of Economics* 117(4): 1231–1294.

Acemoglu, D., S. Johnson, J.A. Robinson, and P. Yared (2008), "Income and Democracy", *American Economic Review* 98: 808–842.

Acemoglu, D., S. Johnson, J. A. Robinson, and P. Yared (2009), "Reevaluating the Modernization Hypothesis", *Journal of Monetary Economics* 56: 1043–1058.

Acemoglu, D. and J.A. Robinson (2006), *Economic Origins of Dictatorship and Democracy*, New York: Cambridge University Press.

(2010), "Why Is Africa Poor?", *Economic History of Developing Regions* 25(1), 21–50

Adelman, I. and C.T. Morris (1967), *Society, Politics and Economic Development, Baltimore*, MD: Johns Hopkins University Press.

Aghion, P., X. Jaravel, T. Persson, and D. Rouzet (2019), "Education and Military Rivalry", *Journal of the European Economic Association* 17 (2): 376–412.

Agyei-Mensah, S. (2001), "Twelve Years of HIV/AIDS in Ghana: Puzzles of Interpretation", *Canadian Journal of African Studies/Revue Canadienne des Études Africaines* 35(3): 441–472.

Akachi, Y. and D. Canning (2010), "Health Trends in Sub-Saharan Africa: Conflicting Evidence from Infant Mortality Rates and Adult Heights", *Economics and Human Biology* 8: 273–288.

Akyeampong, E., R.H. Bates, N. Nunn, and J.A. Robinson (eds.) (2014), *Africa's Development in Historical Perspective*, Cambridge: Cambridge University Press.

Alesina, A., P. Giuliano, and B. Reich (2020), Nation-Building and Education: Theory and Evidence, NBER Working Paper No. 18839 (revised).

Alesina, A., B. Reich, and A. Riboni (2020), Nation-Building, Nationalism, and Wars, CEPR Discussion Paper 15561.

Alkire, S. (2002), "Dimensions of Human Development", *World Development*, 30: 181–205.

Altinok, N., N. Angrist, and H.A. Patrinos (2018), Global Data Set on Education Quality (1965–2015), World Bank Policy Research Working Paper 8314.

Altug, S., A. Filiztekin, and S. Pamuk (2008), "Sources of Long-Term Growth for Turkey, 1880–2005," *European Review of Economic History* 12: 393–430.

Alvaredo, F., and A.B. Atkinson (2010), Colonial Rule, Apartheid and Natural Resources: Top Incomes in South Africa 1903–2005, OxCarre Research paper 46/2010.

Anand, S. and A. Sen (2000), "The Income Component of the Human Development Index", *Journal of Human Development* 1: 83–106.

Anand, S. and P. Segal (2008), "What Do We Know about Global Income Inequality?", *Journal of Economic Literature* 46(1): 57–94.

(2015), "The Global Distribution of Income", in A. Atkinson and F. Bourguignon (eds.), *Handbook of Income Distribution*, Vol. 2A, Amsterdam: Elsevier, pp. 937–979.

Anand, S. (2018), Recasting Human Development Measures, UNDP Human Development Report Discussion Paper.

Ansell, B. and J. Lindvall (2013), "The Political Origins of Primary Education Systems:Ideology, Institutions, and Interdenominational Conflict in an Era of Nation-Building", *American Political Science Review* 107(3): 505–522.

Anuario Estadístico de Puerto Rico (1955), San Juan: Bureau of Economics and Statistics, Division of Statistics, Section of Economic Indices.

Apostolides, A. (2011), "The Growth of Two Small Economies in the Great Depression: GDP Estimation for Cyprus and Malta during the Interwar Period (1921–1938)", MPRA Paper 30276, http://mpra.ub.uni-muenchen.de/30276/

Arriaga, E. E. (1968). *New Life Tables for Latin American Populations in the Nineteenth and Twentieth Centuries*. Population Monographs Series No. 3, Institute of International Studies, University of California Berkeley.

Arroyo Abad, L. (2015), "The Limits of the *Estado Docente*: Education and Political Participation in Peru, 1876-1940", *Revista de Historia Económica/Journal of Iberian and Latin American Economic History* 34(1): 81–109.

Arroyo Abad, L. and P.H. Lindert (2017), "Fiscal Redistribution in Latin America since the Nineteenth Century", in L. Bértola and J.G. Williamson (eds.), *Has Latin American Inequality Changed Direction?*, Springer, pp. 243–281.

Asongu, S.A. and J.C. Nwachukwu (2017), "The Comparative Inclusive Human Development of Globalisation in Africa", *Social Indicators Research* 134: 1027–1050.

Astorga, P. (2017), "Real Wages and Skill Premiums in Latin America, 1900–2011", *Revista de Historia Económica/Journal of Iberian and Latin American Economic History* 35(3): 319–353.

Astorga, P. and E.V.K. Fitzgerald (1998). "Statistical Appendix", in R. Thorp, *Progress, Poverty and Exclusion: An Economic History of Latin America in the 20th Century*. Washington, DC: Inter-American Development Bank, pp. 307–365.

Astorga, P., A. R. Bergés, and E. V. K. FitzGerald (2003), *The Oxford Latin American Economic History Database* [OxLAD, now MOXLAD], Oxford: Latin American Centre, University of Oxford, available at: http://moxlad.fcs.edu.uy/

Astorga, P., A.R. Bergés, and E. V. K. FitzGerald (2005), "The Standard of Living in Latin America during the Twentieth Century", *Economic History Review* 58(4): 765–796.

Atkinson, A.B. (1970), "On the Measurement of Inequality", *Journal of Economic Theory* 2: 244–263.

Atkinson, A.B. and A. Brandolini (2010), "On Analysing the World Distribution of Income", *World Bank Economic Review* 24(1): 1–37.

Aturupane, H., P. Glewwe, and P. Isenman (1994), "Poverty, Human Development, and Growth: An Emerging Consensus?", *American Economic Review*, 84(2): 244–249.

Ayeni, O. (1976); "Retrospective Estimates of Mortality from the Nigerian Medical Censuses of 1930–1932: A Research Note", *Nigerian Journal of Economic and Social Studies* 18: 461–469.

Bandiera, O., M. Mohnen, I. Rasul, and M. Viarengo (2018), "Nation-Building through Compulsory Schooling During the Age of Mass Migration", *Economic Journal* 129: 62–109.

Banks, A.S. (2010), Cross-National Time-Series Data Archive www.databanksinternational.com/

Baptista, A. (1997), *Bases cuantitativas de la economía venezolana, 1830–1995*, Caracas: Fundación Polar.

Barro, R. and J.W. Lee (2013), "A New Data Set of Educational Attainment in the World, 1950–2010", *Journal of Development Economics* 104: 184–198 (Updated dataset v 2.1, February 2016) www.barrolee.com/

Baten, J. and L. Maravall (2021), "The Influence of Colonialism on Africa's Welfare: An Anthropometric Study", *Journal of Comparative Economics* 49: 751–775.

Bates, R.H., J.H. Coatsworth, and J.G. Williamson (2007), "Lost Decades: Post Independence in Latin America and Africa", *Journal of Economic History* 67(4): 917–943.

Becker, G. S., T.J. Philipson, and R.R. Soares (2005), "The Quantity and Quality of Life and the Evolution of World Inequality", *American Economic Review* 95(1): 277–291.

Beckerman, W. (1976), *An Introduction to National Income Analysis*. 2nd ed., London: Weidenfeld and Nicholson.

(1993), "Is Economic Growth Still Desirable?", in A. Szirmai, B. van Ark, and D. Pilat (eds.), *Explaining Economic Growth. Essays in Honour of Angus Maddison*, Amsterdam: North Holland, pp. 77–100.

Beckerman, W. and R. Bacon (1966), "International Comparisons of Income Levels: A Suggested New Measure", *Economic Journal* 76: 516–536.

Benavot, A. and P. Riddle (1988), "The Expansion of Primary Education, 1870–1940: Trends and Issues", *Sociology of Education* 61: 191–210.

Berdine, G., V. Geloso, and B. Powell (2018), "Cuban Infant Mortality and Longevity: Health Care or Repression?", *Health Policy and Planning* 33: 755–757.

Berlin, I. (1958), *Two Concepts of Liberty*, Oxford: Clarendon Press.

Berry, A., F. Bourguignon, and C. Morrisson (1983), "Changes in the World Distribution between 1950 and 1977", *Economic Journal* 93(37): 331–350

Bértola, L. (2016), El PBI de Uruguay, 1870–2015: Una reconstrucción, Universidad de la República PHES Documento Online N° 48.

Bértola, L. and J.A. Ocampo (2012), *The Economic Development of Latin America since Independence*, Oxford: Oxford University Press.

Bértola, L., M. Hernández, J. Rodríguez, and S. Siniscalchi (2011), A Century of Human Development and Inequality: A Comparative Perspective, HIPOD Working Paper

Bleakley, H. (2007), "Disease and Development: Evidence from Hookworm Eradication in the American South", *Quarterly Journal of Economics* 122: 73–117.

(2010), "Malaria Eradication in the Americas: A Retrospective Analysis of Childhood Exposure", *American Economic Journal: Applied Economics* 2: 1–45.

Bleynat, I., A.E. Challú, and P. Segal (2021), "Inequality, Living Standards, and Growth: Two Centuries of Economic Development in Mexico", *Economic History Review* 74(3): 584–610.

Boix, C. (2003), *Democracy and Redistribution*, New York: Cambridge University Press.

(2011), "Democracy, Development, and the International System", *American Political Science Review* 105(4): 809–828.

Bolt, J. and L. Gardner (2020), "How Africans Shaped British Colonial Institutions: Evidence from Local Taxation", *Journal of Economic History* 80(4): 1189–1223.

Booth, J.A. (1974), "Rural Violence in Colombia: 1948–1963", *Western Political Quarterly* 27(4): 657–679.

Borrescio-Higa, F., C.G. Bozzoli, and F. Droller (2019), "Early Life Environment and Adult Height: The Case of Chile", *Economics and Human Biology* 33: 134–143.

Botana, N. and E. Gallo (1997), *De la República Posible a la República Verdadera: 1880–1910*, Buenos Aires: Ariel.

Bourguignon, F. and C. Morrisson (2002), "Inequality among World Citizens", *American Economic Review* 92(4): 727–744, dataset available at: www.delta.ens.fr/xix

Bowden, S. and P. Mosley (2012), Politics, Public Expenditure and the Evolution of Poverty in Africa 1920–2009, Sheffield Economic Research Paper Series 2012-003

Bowden, S., B. Chiripanhura, and P. Mosley (2008), "Measuring and Explaining Poverty in Six African Countries: A Long-Period Approach", *Journal of International Development* 20: 1049–1079.

Brainerd, E. (2010a), Human Development in Eastern Europe and the CIS since 1990, UNDP Human Development Reports Research Paper 16.

(2010b), "Reassessing the Standard of Living in the Soviet Union: An Analysis Using Archival and Anthropometric Data", *Journal of Economic History* 70: 83–117.

Brainerd, E. and D.M. Cutler (2005), "Autopsy on an Empire: Understanding Mortality in Russia and the Former Soviet Union", *Journal of Economic Perspectives* 19: 107–130.

Branisa, B., J. Peres-Cajías, and N. Caspa (2020), "The Biological Standard of Living in La Paz (Bolivia), 1880s–1920s: Persistent Stagnation and Inequality", *Economics and Human Biology* 37, 100849.

Brieba, D. (2018), "State Capacity and Health Outcomes: Comparing Argentina's and Chile's Reduction of Infant and Maternal Mortality, 1960–2013", *World Development* 101: 37–53.

Broadberry, S. and L. Gardner (2016), "Economic Development in Africa and Europe: Reciprocal Comparisons", *Revista de Historia Económica/ Journal of Iberian and Latin American Economic History* 34(1): 11–37.

(2022), "Economic Growth in Sub-Saharan Africa, 1885–2008: Evidence from Eight Countries", *Explorations in Economic History* 83: 101424.

Broadberry, S.N. and J. Wallis (2017), Growing, Shrinking and Long Run Economic Performance: Historical Perspectives on Economic Development, CEPR Discussion Papers 11973.

Brundenius, C. and A. Zimbalist (1989), *The Cuban Economy: Measurement and Analysis of Socialist Performance*. Baltimore: Johns Hopkins

Bulmer-Thomas, V. (2003), *The Economic History of Latin America since Independence*, Cambridge: Cambridge University Press, 2 vols., 2nd ed.

Bunce, V.(1990), "The Struggle for Liberal Democracy in Eastern Europe", *World Policy Journal* 7(3): 395–430

Buyst, E. (1997), "New GNP Estimates for the Belgian Economy during the Interwar Period", *Review of Income and Wealth* 43: 357–375.

Caldwell, J., M. Bracher, G. Santow, and P. Caldwell (1986), "Population Trends in China—A Perspective Provided by the 1982 Census", in C. Li (ed.), *A Census of One Billion People*, Hong Kong: Republic of China Population Census Office, pp. 352–392.

Canning, D. (2012), "Progress in Health around the World", *Journal of Development Studies* 48(12):1784–1798.

Cardona, C. and D. Bishai (2018), "The Slowing Pace of Life Expectancy Gains since 1950", *BMC Public Health* 18:151 doi.org/10.1186/s12889-018-5058-9

Castañeda Garza, D. and E. Bengtsson (2020), Income Inequality in Mexico 1895–1940: Industrialization, Revolution, Institutions, Lund Papers in Economic History 212.

CEPAL (Comisión Económica para América Latina y el Caribe) (2009), "América Latina y el Caribe. Series históricas de estadísticas económicas 1950–2008", *Cuadernos Estadísticos* 37, available at: www.eclac.cl/deype/cuaderno37/index.htm

(2017), Economic Indicators and Statistics. Total Annual Gross Domestic Product (GDP) Per Capita at Constant Prices in Dollars, available at: http://interwp.cepal.org/

Cha, M.S. and N. N. Kim (2006), Korea's First Industrial Revolution, 1911–40, Naksungdae Institute of Economic Research [NIER] Working Papers Series 3, available at: www.naksung.re.kr/papers/wp2006-3.pdf

Cha, M.S. and T.M. Wu (2002), *Colonial Transition to Modern Economic Growth in Korea and Taiwan*, Unpublished manuscript.

Chakravarty, S.R. (2003), "A Generalized Human Development Index", *Review of Development Economics* 7: 99–114.

(2011), "A Reconsideration of the Tradeoffs in the New Human Development Index", *Journal of Economic Inequality* 9: 471–474.

Chernew, M., D.M. Cutler, K. Gosh, and M.B. Landrum (2016), Understanding the Improvement in Disability Free Life Expectancy in the U.S. Elderly Population, NBER Working Paper Series 22306.

Clark, A.E. (2018), "Four Decades of the Economics of Happiness: Where Next?", *Review of Income and Wealth* 64(2): 245–269.

Clark, R. (2011), "World Health Inequality: Convergence, Divergence, and Development", *Social Science & Medicine* 72(4): 617–624.

Clio-Infra Dataset, www.clio-infra.eu/

Coatsworth, J.H. (1989), "The Decline of the Mexican Economy, 1800–1860", in R. Liehr (ed.). *América Latina en la época de Simón Bolívar. La formación de las economías nacionales y los intereses económicos europeos 1800–1850.* Berlin: Colloquium, pp. 27–53.

(2005), "Structures, Endowments, and Institutions in the Economic History of Latin America", *Latin American Research Review* 40(3): 126–144.

(2008), "Inequality, Institutions and Economic Growth in Latin America", *Journal of Latin American Studies* 40: 545–569.

Cogneau, D. and L. Rouanet (2011), "Living Conditions in Côte d'Ivoire, Ghana and Western Africa 1925–1985: What Do Survey Data on Height Stature Tell Us?", *Economic History of Developing Regions* 26(2): 55-82.

Cogneau, D. and Moradi, A. (2014), "Borders That Divide: Education and Religion in Ghana and Togo since Colonial Times", *Journal of Economic History* 74(3): 693–728.

Collier, P. (2000), "Ethnicity, Politics, and Economic Performance", *Economics and Politics* 12: 225–245.

Collier, P. and W. Gunning (1999a), "Explaining African Economic Performance", *Journal of Economic Literature* 37(1): 64–111.

(1999b), "Why Has Africa Grown Slowly?", *Journal of Economic Perspectives* 13(3): 3–22.

Collier, P. and O'Connell, S.A. (2008), "Opportunities and Choices", in B.J. Ndulu, S.A. O'Connell, J.P. Azam, *et al.* (eds.), *The Political Economy of Economic Growth in Africa, 1960–2000.* Cambridge: Cambridge University Press, 2 vols., I, pp. 76–136.

Collier, R.B. (1999), *Paths towards Democracy*, Cambridge: Cambridge University Press.

Conference Board, Total Economy Database, May 2016, www.conference-board.org/data/economydatabase/

Condé, J. (1973), *Some Demographic Aspects of Human Resources in Africa*, Paris: OECD Development Centre.

Coppedge, M., J. Gerring, C.H. Knutsen, *et al.* (2018), V-Dem [Country-Year/Country-Date] Dataset v8, Varieties of Democracy (V-Dem) Project, available at: https://doi.org/10.23696/vdemcy18 (Accessed on 4 May 2019).

Corso, G. de (2013), "El crecimiento económico de Venezuela, desde la oligarquía conservadora hasta la revolución bolivariana: 1830–2012. Una visión cuantitativa", *Revista de Historia Económica/Journal of Iberian and Latin American Economic History*, 31(3): 321–357.

(2018), "El PIB y la población de Venezuela desde el periodo tardo colonial hasta 2014", *Tiempo & Economía* 5(1): 9–39.

Cortés Conde, R. (1997), *La economía argentina en el largo plazo*. Buenos Aires: Editorial Sudamericana/Universidad de San Andrés.

Coyle, D. (2014), *GDP: A Brief but Affectionate History*, Princeton, NJ: Princeton University Press.

Crafts N.F. R. (1997a), "The Human Development Index and Changes in the Standard of Living: Some Historical Comparisons", *European Review of Economic History* 1(3): 299–322.

(1997b), "Some Dimensions of the 'Quality of Life' during the British Industrial Revolution", *Economic History Review* 50(4): 617–639.

Cutler, D. and Miller, G. (2005), "The Role of Public Health Improvements in Health Advance: The Twentieth Century United States", *Demography* 42(1): 1–22.

Cutler, D., W. Fung, M. Kremer, M. Singhal, and T. Vogl (2010), "Early-Life Malaria Exposure and Adult Outcomes: Evidence from Malaria Eradication in India", *American Economic Journal: Applied Economics* 2: 72–94.

Cutler, D.M., A. Deaton, and A. Lleras-Muney (2006), "The Determinants of Mortality", *Journal of Economic Perspectives* 20: 97–120.

Cutler, D.M., K. Ghosh, and M.B. Landrum (2014), "Evidence for Significant Compression of Morbidity in the Elderly U.S. Population", in D.A. Wise (ed.), *Discoveries in the Economics of Aging*, Chicago: University of Chicago Press, pp. 21–51.

Darden, K. and H. Mylonas (2015), "Threats to Territorial integrity, National Mass Schooling, and Linguistic Commonality", *Comparative Political Studies* 49(11): 1446–1479.

Dasgupta, P. (1990), "Well-Being and the Extent of Its Realization in Poor Countries", *Economic Journal* 100(400): 1–32.

Dasgupta, P. and M. Weale (1992), "On Measuring the Quality of Life", *World Development* 20: 119–131.

Deaton, A. (2006), Global Patterns of Income and Health: Facts, Interpretations, and Policies, NBER Working Papers 12735.

(2013), *The Great Escape. Health, Wealth, and the Origins of Inequality*, Princeton, NJ: Princeton University Press.

Decancq, K., A. Decoster, and E. Schokkaert (2009), "The Evolution of World Inequality in Well-Being", *World Development* 37(1): 11–25.

Dean, H. (2009), "Critiquing Capabilities: The Distractions of a Beguiling Concept", *Critical Social Policy* 29(2): 261–273.

Della Paolera, G., A. M. Taylor, and C. G. Bozolli (2003). "Historical Statistics", in G. Della Paolera and A. M. Taylor (eds.). *A New Economic History of Argentina*. New York: Cambridge University Press (with CD-ROM), pp. 376–385.

Desai, M. (1991), "Human Development: Concept and Measurement", *European Economic Review* 35: 350–357.

Desowitz, R.S. (1991), *The Malaria Capers: More Tales of Parasites and People, Research and Reality*, New York: W.W. Norton.

Devereux, J. (2010), The Health of the Revolution: Explaining the Cuban Healthcare Paradox, Queens College, CUNY, Unpublished manuscript.

(2019), "Arrested Development? Puerto Rico in an American Century", *Journal of Economic History* 79(3): 708–735.

(2021), "The Absolution of History: Cuban Living Standards after 60 Years of Revolutionary Rule", *Revista de Historia Económica/ Journal of Iberian and Latin American Economic History* 39(1): 5–36.

Díaz-Briquets, S. (1981) "Determinants of Mortality Transition in Developing Countries before and after the Second World War: Some Evidence from Cuba", *Population Studies* 35(3): 399–411.

Díaz, J., R. Lüders, and G. Wagner (2016), *Chile 1810–2010. La República en cifras. Historical Statistics*, Santiago: Ediciones Universidad Católica de Chile, available at: http://cliolab.economia.uc.cl/BD.html

Domínguez, R. and M. Guijarro (2000), "Evolución de las disparidades espaciales del bienestar en España, 1860–1930: El Índice Físico de Calidad de Vida", *Revista de Historia Económica* 18(1): 109–137.

Dopico, F. and D.S. Reher (1998), *El declive de la mortalidad en España, 1860–1930*, Asociación de Demografía Histórica, Monografía No. 1.

Dowrick, S. and M. Akmal (2005), "Contradictory Trends in Global Income Inequality: A Tale of Two Biases", *Review of Income and Wealth* 51(2): 201–230.

Dowrick, S., Y. Dunlop, and J. Quiggin (2003), "Social Indicators and Comparisons of Living Standards", *Journal of Development Economics* 70: 501–529.

Dréze, J. and A.K. Sen (2002), *India: Development and Participation*, Delhi: Oxford University Press.

Dutton, J. Jr.(1979), "Changes in Soviet Mortality Patterns, 1959–77", *Population and Development Review* 5: 267–291.

Easterlin, R.A. (1974), "Does Economic Growth Improve Human Lot?", in P.A. David and M.W. Reder (eds.), *Nations and Households in Economic Growth: Essays in Honor of Moses Abramovitz*, New York: Academic Press, pp. 89–125.

(1999), "How Beneficient Is the Market? A Look at the Modern History of Mortality", *European Review of Economic History* 3(3): 257–294.

Easterly, W. and R. Levine (1997), "Africa's Growth Tragedy: Policies and Ethnic Divisions", *Quarterly Journal of Economics* 112(4): 1203–1250.

Easterly, W. (2001), "The Lost Decades: Developing Countries' Stagnation in Spite of Policy Reform 1980–1998", *Journal of Economic Growth* 6: 135–157.

Edwards, R.D. (2011), "Changes in World Inequality in Length of Life: 1970–2000", *Population and Development Review* 37(3): 499–528.

Eggleston, K.N. and V. Fuchs (2012), "The New Demographic Transition: Most Gains in Life Expectancy Now Realized Late in Life", *Journal of Economic Perspectives* 26: 137–156.

Ehrlich, E. (1969), "Dynamic International Comparisons of National Incomes Expressed in Terms of Physical Indicators", *Osteuropa Wirtschaft* 14(1): 1–25.

Eisner, G. (1961). *Jamaica, 1830–1930: A Study in Economic Growth.* Manchester: Manchester University Press.

Engerman, S.L. (1997), "The Standard of Living Debate in International Perspective. Measure and Indicators", in R.H. Steckel and R. Floud (eds.), *Health and Welfare during Industrialization*, Chicago: University of Chicago Press, pp. 17–45.

Engerman, S.L. and K.L. Sokoloff (2002), Factor Endowments, Inequality, and Paths of Development among New World Economies, NBER Working Paper No. 9259.

Engerman, S.L., E.V. Mariscal, and K.L- Sokoloff (2009), "The Evolution of Schooling in the Americas, 1800–1925", in D. Eltis, F.D. Lewis and K.L. Sokoloff (eds.), *Human Capital and Institutions: A Long-Run View*, New York: Cambridge University Press, pp. 93–142.

Fargues, P. (1986), "Un siècle de transition démographique en Afrique méditerranéenne 1885–1985", *Population* 41(2), 205–232.

Faye, M.L., J.W: McArthur, J.D. Sachs, and T. Snow (2004), "The Challenges Facing Landlocked Developing Countries", *Journal of Human Development* 5(1):31–68.

Federico, G. and G. Toniolo (1991), "Italy", in R. Sylla and G. Toniolo (eds.), *Patterns of European Industrialization. The Nineteenth Century*, London: Routledge, pp. 197–217.

Feinstein, C.H. (2005), *An Economic History of South Africa: Conquest, Discrimination and Development*, Cambridge: Cambridge University Press.

Felice, E., J. Pujol Andreu, and C. d'Ippoliti (2016), "GDP and Life Expectancy in Italy and Spain over the Long Run: A Time-Series

Approach", *Demographic Research* 35: 813–866, available at: www .demographic-research.org/Volumes/Vol35/28/

Fenske, J. (2013), "Does Land Abundance Explain African Institutions?", *Economic Journal* 123: 1363–1390.

Ferreira, F. and Robalino (2011), "Social Protection in Latin America", in J.A. Ocampo and J. Ros (eds.), *The Oxford Handbook of Latin American Economics*, Oxford: Oxford University Press, pp. 836–862.

Firebaugh, G. (1999), "Empirics of World Income Inequality", *American Journal of Sociology* 104(6): 1597–1630.

Fleurbaey, M. (2009), "Beyond GDP: The Quest for a Measure of Social Welfare", *Journal of Economic Literature* 47(4): 1029–1075.

(2015), "Beyond Income and Wealth", *Review of Income and Wealth*, 61 (2): 199–219.

Flora, P. (1983), *State, Economy, and Society in Western Europe 1815–1975. A Data Handbook in Two Volumes*, Frankfurt: Campus.

Floud, R. and B Harris (1997), "Health, Height, and Welfare: Britain, 1700–1980", in R.H. Steckel and R. Floud (eds.), *Health and Welfare during Industrialization*, Chicago: University of Chicago Press, pp. 91–126.

Fogel, R.W. (2004), *The Escape from Hunger and Premature Death, 1700–2010: Europe, American and the Third World*, New York: Cambridge University Press.

(2009), "Biotechnology and the Burden of Age-Related Diseases", in D. Eltis, F.D. Lewis, and K.L. Sokoloff (eds.), *Human Capital and Institutions: A Long-Run View*, New York: Cambridge University Press, pp. 11–26.

Földvári, P. (2017), "De Facto Versus de Jure Political Institutions in the Long-Run: A Multivariate Analysis, 1820–2000", *Social Indicators Research*, 130: 759–777.

Földvári, P. and B. van Leeuwen (2014), "Educational and Income Inequality in Europe, ca. 1870–2000", *Cliometrica* 8: 271–300.

Fosu, A.K. and G. Mwabu (2010), Human Development in Africa, UNDP Human Development Research Paper 2010/08

Frankema, E. (2009), "The Expansion of Mass Education in Twentieth Century Latin America: A Global Perspective", *Revista de Historia Económica/Journal of Iberian and Latin American Economic History* 27(3): 359–396.

(2012), "The Origins of Formal Education in Sub-Saharan Africa. Was British Rule More Benign?", *European Review of Economic History* 16 (4): 335–355.

(2021), Why Africa Is Not That Poor?, African Economic History Working Paper Series 61.

Frankema, E. and M. van Waijenburg (2012), "Structural Impediments to African Growth? New Evidence from Real Wages in British Africa, 1880–1965", *Journal of Economic History* 72(4): 895–926.

Franken, D. (2019), "Anthropometric History of Brazil, 1850–1950: Insights from Military and Passport Records", *Revista de Historia Económica/Journal of Iberian and Latin American Economic History* 37(2): 377–408.

Fries, J.F. (1980), "Aging, Natural Death, and the Compression of Morbidity", *New England Journal of Medicine* 303(3): 130–135.

Fries, J.F., B. Bruce, and E. Chakravarty (2011), "Compression of Morbidity 1980–2011: A Focused Review of Paradigms and Progress", *Journal of Aging Research,* available at: http://dx.doi.org/10.4061/2011/261702 (Accessed on 22 April 2019)

Fuentes-Vásquez, M.J. (2019), "Educational Disparities in Colombia, 1904–58: New Evidence from a Regional Level Approach", *Revista de Historia Económica/Journal of Iberian and Latin American Economic History* 37(3): 443–478.

Gallardo Albarrán, D. (2017), Missed Opportunities? The Development of Human Welfare in Western Europe, 1913–1950, Groningen Growth and Development Centre Research Memorandum 166.

Gellner, E. (1983), *Nations and Nationalism,* Ithaca, NY: Cornell University Press.

Gerry, C.J., Y. Raskina, and D. Tsyplakova (2018), "Convergence or Divergence? Life Expectancy Patterns in Post-communist Countries, 1959–2010", *Social Indicators Research* 140: 309–332.

Glass, D.V. and E. Grebenik (1967), "World Population, 1800–1950", in H.J. Habakkuk and M. Postan (eds.), *Cambridge Economic History of Europe, Vol. VI. The Industrial Revolutions and After: Incomes, Population, and Technological Change,* Cambridge: Cambridge University Press, I, pp. 56–138.

Goda, T. and A. Torres García (2017), "The Rising Tide of Absolute Global Income Inequality during 1850–2010: Is It Driven by Inequality Within or Between Countries?", *Social Indicators Research* 130: 1051–1072

Goesling, B. and D.P. Baker (2008), "Three Faces of International Inequality", *Research in Social Stratification and Mobility* 26: 183–198.

Goesling, B. and G. Firebaugh (2004), "The Trend in International Health Inequality", *Population and Development Review* 30(1): 131–146.

Goldsmith, R. W. (1961), "The Economic Growth of Tsarist Russia: 1860–1913", *Economic Development and Cultural Change,* 9: 441–475.

(1986), *Desenvolvimento financeiro sob um século de inflação.* Rio de Janeiro: Harper & Row do Brasil.

Gómez-León, M. (2021), "The Kuznets Curve in Brazil, 1850–2010", *Revista de Historia Económica/Journal of Iberian and Latin American Economic History* 39(1): 37–61.

Good, D.F. (1994), "The Economic Lag of Central and Eastern Europe: Income Estimates for the Habsburg Successor States, 1870–1910", *Journal of Economic History* 54: 869–891.

Gormely, P. J. (1995), "The Human Development Index in 1994: Impact of Income on Country Rank", *Journal of Economic and Social Measurement* 21(4): 253–267.

GRECO (Grupo de Estudios de Crecimiento Económico) (2002), *El Crecimiento económico colombiano en el Siglo XX*. Bogotá: Banco de la República–Fondo de Cultura Económica.

Gregory, P. (1982), *Russian National Income*, Cambridge: Cambridge University Press.

Grynspan, R. and L.F. López-Calva (2011), "Multidimensional Poverty in Latin America: Concept, Measurement, and Policy", in J.A. Ocampo and J. Ros (eds.), *The Oxford Handbook of Latin American Economics*, Oxford: Oxford University Press, pp. 715–740.

Haber, S. (ed.) (1997). *How Latin America Fell Behind? Essays on the Economic Histories of Brazil and Mexico, 1800–1914*. Stanford: Stanford University Press.

Haines, M. (1994), Estimated Life Tables for the United States, 1850–1900, National Bureau of Economic Research Working Paper Series on Historical Factors in Long Run Growth 15.

Hansen, C.W. (2013), "Life Expectancy and Human Capital: Evidence from the International Epidemiological Transition", *Journal of Health Economics* 32: 1142–1152

Hansen, C.W. and H. Strulik (2017), "Life Expectancy and Education: Evidence from the Cardiovascular Revolution", *Journal of Economic Growth* 22: 421–450.

Hanushek, E.A. and L. Woessmann (2012), "Schooling, Educational Achievement, and the Latin American Growth Puzzle", *Journal of Development Economics* 99: 497–512.

Harris, B. (2008), "Gender, Health and Welfare in England and Wales since Industrialisation", *Research in Economic History* 26: 157–204.

(2021), "Anthropometric History and the Measurement of Wellbeing", *Vienna Yearbook of Population Research* 19: 1–33.

Hatton, T.J. (2011), How Have Europeans Grown so Tall?, CEPR Discussion Paper 8490.

Hatton, T.J. and B.E. Brey (2010), "Long Run Trends in the Heights of European Men, 19th–20th Centuries", *Economics and Human Biology* 8: 405–413.

Hayek, F.A. (1944), *The Road to Serfdom*, London: Routledge.

Heckman, J.J. and C.O. Corbin (2016), "Capabilities and Skills", *Journal of Human Development and Capabilities* 17(3): 342–359.

Heldring, L. and J.A. Robinson (2018), "Colonialism and Development in Africa", in C. Lancaster and N. van de Walle (eds.), *The Oxford Handbook of the Politics of Development*, Oxford: Oxford University Press, pp. 295–327.

Herranz-Loncán, A. and J.A. Peres-Cajías (2016), "Tracking the Reversal of Fortune in the Americas. Bolivian GDP per Capita Since the Mid-Nineteenth Century", *Cliometrica* 10(1): 99–112.

Herranz-Loncán, A. and P. Astorga (2021), "Latin America: Stalled Catching-Up", in S. Broadberry and K. Fukao (eds.), *The Cambridge Economic History of the Modern World. Vol. II. 1870 to the Present*, Cambridge: Cambridge University Press, II, pp. 251–275.

Herrero, C., R. Martínez, and A. Villar (2012), "A Newer Human Development Index", *Journal of Human Development and Capabilities* 13: 247–268.

Heston, A. (1994), "A Brief Review of Some Problems in Using National Accounts Data in Level of Output Comparisons and Growth Studies", *Journal of Development Economics* 44: 29–52.

Hicks, D.A. (1997), "The Inequality-Adjusted Human Development Index: A Constructive Proposal", *World Development* 25(8): 1283–1298.

Hicks, N. and P. Streeten (1979), "Indicators of Development: The Search for a Basic Needs Yardstick", *World Development* 7: 567–580.

Hobijn, B. and P.H. Franses (2001), "Are Living Standards Converging?", *Structural Change and Economic Dynamics* 12: 171–200.

Hofman, A. and P. Valderrama (2021), "Long Run Economic Growth Performance in Latin America 1820–2016", *Journal of Economic Surveys* 35(3): 833–869.

Hopkins, M. (1991), "Human Development Revisited: A New UNDP Report", *World Development* 19(10): 1469–1473.

Horlings, E. (1997), *The Contribution of the Service Sector to Gross Domestic Product in Belgium, 1835–1990*, Universiteit Utrecht, Unpublished manuscript.

Howse, K. (2006) Increasing Life Expectancy and the Compression of Morbidity: A Critical Review of the Debate, Oxford Institute of Ageing Working Paper 226.

Human Mortality Database (2021), University of California; Berkeley (USA); and Max Planck Institute for Demographic Research (Germany), available at: www.mortality.org and www.humanmortality.de

Huntington, S. P. (1991), *The Third Wave: Democratization in the Late Twentieth Century*, Norman: University of Oklahoma Press

INEGI (1995). *Estadísticas históricas de México*, Mexico DF: INEGI.

Ivanov, A. and M. Peleah (2010), From Centrally Planned Development to Human Development, UNDP Human Development Reports Research Paper 38.

Jannetta, A.B. and S.H. Preston (1991), "Two Centuries of Mortality Change in Central Japan: The Evidence from a Temple Death Register", *Population Studies* 45: 417–436.

Jaramillo-Echeverri, J., A. Meisel-Roca, and M.T. Ramírez-Giraldo (2019), "More Than 100 years of Improvements in Living Standards: The Case of Colombia", *Cliometrica* 13: 323–366.

Jayachandran, S., A. Lleras-Muney, and K.V. Smith (2010), "Modern Medicine and the Twentieth Century Decline in Mortality: Evidence on the Impact of Sulfa Drugs", *American Economic Journal: Applied Economics* 2: 118–146.

Jerven, M. (2009), "The Relativity of Poverty and Income: How Reliable Are African Economic Statistics?", *African Affairs* 109(434): 77–96.

(2010), "African Growth Recurring: An Economic History Perspective on African Growth Episodes, 1690–2010", *Economic History of Developing Regions* 25(2): 127–154.

Johansson, S.R. and C. Mosk (1987), "Exposure, Resistance and Life Expectancy: Disease and Death during the Economic Development of Japan, 1900–1960", *Population Studies* 41: 207–235.

Jones, C.I. and P.J. Klenow (2016), "Beyond GDP? Welfare across Countries and Time", *American Economic Review* 106(9): 2426–2457

Juif, D. and E. Frankema (2018), "From Coercion to Compensation: Institutional Responses to Labour Scarcity in the Central African Copperbelt", *Journal of Institutional Economics* 14(2): 313–343.

Kahneman, D., and A. Deaton (2010), "High Income Improves Evaluation of Life but Not Emotional Well-Being", *Proceedings of the National Academy of Sciences of the United States of America* 107(38): 16489–16493.

Kakwani, N. (1993), "Performance in Living Standards. An International Comparison", *Journal of Development Economics* 41: 307–336.

Kalmanovitz Krauter, S. and E. López Rivera (2009), *Las cuentas nacionales de Colombia en el siglo XIX*. Bogotá: Universidad de Bogotá Jorge Tadeo Lozano.

Kannisto, V., M. Nieminen, and O. Turpeinen (1999), "Finnish Life Tables since 1751", *Demographic Research* 1, available at: www.demographic-research.org/Volumes/Vol1/1

Kelley, A.C. (1991), "The Human Development Index: 'Handle with Care'", *Population and Development Review* 17(2): 315–324.

Klasen, S. (2018), Human Development Indices and Indicators: A Critical Evaluation, UNDP Human Development Report Background Paper.

Klasing, M.J. and P. Milionis (2020), "The International Epidemiological Transition and the Education Gender Gap", *Journal of Economic Growth* 25: 37–86.

Klugman, J., F. Rodríguez, and H.-J. Choi (2011), "The HDI 2010: New Controversies, Old Critiques", *Journal of Economic Inequality* 9: 249–288.

Knutsen, C.H., J. Teorell, T. Wig, *et al.* (2019), "Introducing the Historical Varieties of Democracy Dataset: Political Institutions in the Long 19th Century", *Journal of Peace Research* 56(3): 440–451.

Korzeniewicz, R.P. and T.P. Moran (1997), "World Economic Trends in the Distribution of Income, 1965–1992", *American Journal of Sociology* 102(4): 1000–1039

Kostelenos, G. and Associates (2007), Gross Domestic Product, 1830–1939 *(in Greek)*, Athens: Centre of Planning and Economic Research (KEPE).

Krishnakumar, J. (2018) "Trade-Offs in a Multidimensional Human Development Index", *Social Indicators Research* 138(3): 991–1022.

Lai, D. (2000), "Temporal Analysis of Human Development Indicators: Principal Component Approach", *Social Indicators Research* 51(3): 331–366.

Lains, P. (2006), "Growth in a Protected Environment: Portugal, 1850–1950", *Research in Economic History* 24: 121–163.

Lakner, Ch. and B. Milanovic (2016), "Global Income Distribution: From the Fall of the Berlin Wall to the Great Recession", *World Bank Economic Review* 30(2): 203–232.

Langford, C. and P. Storey (1993), "Sex Differentials in Mortality Early in the Twentieth Century: Sri Lanka and India Compared", *Population and Development Review* 19: 263–282.

Lavely, W. and R. B. Wong (1998), "Revising the Malthusian Narrative: The Comparative Study of Population Dynamics in Late Imperial China", *Journal of Asian Studies* 57: 714–748.

Lee, J.-W. and H. Lee (2016), "Human Capital in the Long Run", *Journal of Development Economics* 122: 147–169). Dataset available at: www .barrolee.com/Lee_Lee_LRdata.htm

Leite, Joaquim da Costa (2005), "População e crescimento económico", in P. Lains and A. Ferreira da Silva (eds.), *História Económica de Portugal 1700–2000 Vol. II O Século XIX*, Lisboa: Imprensa de Ciências Sociais, pp. 43–81.

Lewis, W.A. (1954), "Economic Development with Unlimited Supplies of Labour", *Manchester School* 22(2): 139–191.

(1955), *Theory of Economic Growth*, London: George Allen & Unwin.

Liberati, P. (2015), "The World Distribution of Income and Its Inequality, 1970–2009", *Review of Income and Wealth* 61(2): 248–273.

Lindert, P.H. (1994), "The Rise of Social Spending, 1880–1930", *Explorations in Economic History* 31(1): 1–37.

(2004), *Growing Public. Social Spending and Economic Growth since the Eighteenth Century*, Cambridge: Cambridge University Press.

(2010), "The Unequal Lag In Latin American Schooling since 1900: Follow the Money", *Revista de Historia Económica/Journal of Iberian and Latin American Economic History* 28(2): 375–405.

(2017), The Rise and Future of Progressive Redistribution, Tulane University, CEQ Institute Working Paper 73.

Lindgren, B. (2016), The Rise in Life Expectancy, Health Trends among the Elderly, and the Demand for Care. A Selected Literature Review, NBER Working Paper 22521

Lipset, S.M. (1959), "Some Social Requisites of Democracy: Economic Development and Political Legitimacy", *American Political Science Review* 53(1): 69–105

Llorca-Jaña, M., D. Clarke, J. Navarrete-Montalvo, R. Araya-Valenzuela, and M. Allende (2020), "New Anthropometric Evidence on Living Standards in Nineteenth-Century Chile", *Economics and Human Biology* 36, 100819.

Llorca-Jaña, M., J. Navarrete-Montalvo, R. Araya-Valenzuela, F. Droller, M. Allende, and J. Rivas (2021), "Height in Twentieth-Century Chilean Men: Growth with Divergence", *Cliometrica* 15: 135–166.

López-Alonso, M. And R. Vélez-Grajales (2017), "Using Heights to Trace Living Standards and Inequality in Mexico Since 1850", in L. Bértola and J.G. Williamson (eds.), *Has Latin American Inequality Changed Direction?*, Springer, pp. 65–87.

Loudon, I. (2000), "Maternal Mortality in the Past and Its Relevance to Developing Countries Today", *American Journal of Clinical Nutrition* 72(1) (supplement): 241S–246S.

Lowes, S. and E. Montero (2021), "The Legacy of Colonial Medicine in Central Africa", *American Economic Review* 111(4): 1294–1314

Mackenbach, J.P. (2013), "Political Conditions and Life Expectancy in Europe, 1900–2008", *Social Science & Medicine* 82: 134–146.

Maddison, A. (1995), *Monitoring the World Economy, 1820–1992*, Paris: OECD Development Centre.

(2006), *The World Economy*, Paris: OECD Development Centre.

(2010), "Statistics on World Population, GDP and per Capita GDP, 1–2008 AD", horizontal file, available at: www.ggdc.net/maddison/

Maddison Project Database (2013, 2018), www.ggdc.net/maddison/maddison-project/home.htm

Maitpose, G.S. and T.C. Matsheka (2008), "The Indigenous Developmental State and Growth in Botswana", in B.J. Ndulu, S.A. O'Connell, J.P. Azam, *et al.* (eds.), *The Political Economy of Economic Growth in Africa, 1960–2000*, Cambridge: Cambridge University Press, 2 vols., II, pp. 511–546.

Mandle, J.R. (1970), "The Decline of Mortality in British Guiana, 1911–1960", *Demography* 7(3): 301–315.

Manton, K.G. (1982), "Changing Concepts of Morbidity and Mortality in the Elderly Population", *Milbank Memorial Fund Quarterly/Health and Society* 60: 183–244.

Manzano, D. (2017), *Bringing Down the Educational Wall: Political Regimes, Ideology, and the Expansion of Education*, Cambridge: Cambridge University Press.

Markevich, A. and M. Harrison (2011), "Russia's Real National Income: The Great War, Civil War, and Recovery, 1913 to 1928", *Journal of Economic History* 71: 672–703.

Marshall, M.G., T.R. Gurr, an K. Jaggers (2018), *Polity IV Project. Political Regime Characteristics and Transitions, 1800–2017*, Vienna, VA: Center for Systemic Peace, available at: www.systemicpeace.org/inscrdata.html (Accessed on 14 February 2019).

Martínez, R. (2012), "Inequality and the New Human Development Index", *Applied Economics Letters* 19(6): 533–535.

(2016), "Inequality Decomposition and Human Development", *Journal of Human Development and Capabilities* 17(3): 415–425.

Marx, K. and F. Engels (1846, 1932), *The German Ideology*, D. Riazanov (ed.), Moscow: Marx-Engels Institute.

Masood, E. (2016), *The Great Invention: The Story of GDP and the Making (and Unmaking) of the Modern World*, New York: Pegasus.

Mathers, C. D., R. Sadana, J.A. Salomon, C.J.L. Murray, and A.D. Lopez (2001), "Healthy Life Expectancy in 191 Countries", *Lancet* 357: 1685–1691.

Mazumdar, K. (1999), "Measuring the Well-Beings of the Developing Countries: Achievement and Improvement Indices", *Social Indicators Research* 47(1): 1–60.

Mazur, D. P. (1969), "Expectancy of Life at Birth in 36 Nationalities of the Soviet Union: 1958–60", *Population Studies* 23: 225–246.

McAlpin, M.B. (1983), "Famines, Epidemics, and Population Growth: The Case of India", *Journal of Interdisciplinary History* 14: 352–366.

McGranahan, D.V., P. Pizarro, and C. Richard (1985), *Measurement and Analysis of Socio-Economic Development*, Geneva: United Nations Research Institute for Social Development [UNRISD].

McKeown, T. and R.G. Record (1962), "Reasons for the Decline of Mortality in England and Wales during the Nineteenth Century", *Population Studies* 16: 94–122.

McKeown, T., R.G. Record, and R.D. Turner (1975), "An Interpretation of the Decline of Mortality in England and Wales during the Twentieth Century", *Population Studies* 29: 391–422.

Meisel-Roca, A., M.T. Ramírez-Giraldo, and D. Santos-Cárdenas (2019), "Socio-economic Determinants and Spatial Convergence of Biological Well-Being: The Case of Colombia, 1920–1990", *Revista de Historia Económica/Journal of Iberian and Latin American Economic History* 37(2): 297–338.

Meng, X., N. Qian, and P. Yared (2015), "The Institutional Causes of China's Great Famine, 1959–1961", *Review of Economic Studies* 82: 1568–1611

Mesa-Lago, C. (2005), "Problemas sociales y económicos en Cuba durante la crisis y la recuperación", *Revista de la CEPAL* 86: 183–205

Meyer, J.W., F.O. Ramirez, and Y.N. Soysal (1992), "World Expansion of Mass Education, 1870–1980", *Sociology of Education* 65: 128–149

Michalopoulos, S. and E. Papaioannou (2020), "Historical Legacies and African Development", *Journal of Economic Literature* 58(1): 53–128.

Milanovic, B. (2005), *Worlds Apart:. Measuring International and Global Inequality*, Princeton, NJ: Princeton University Press.

  (2016), *Global Inequality: A New Approach for the Age of Globalization*, Cambridge, MA: Belknap Press of Harvard University Press.

  (2020), After the Financial Crisis: the Evolution of the Global Income Distribution between 2008 and 2013, MPRA Paper No. 101560, available at: https://mpra.ub.uni-muenchen.de/101560/ (Accessed on 7 July 2020).

Milanovic, B., P.H. Lindert, and J.G. Williamson (2011), "Pre-Industrial Inequality", *Economic Journal* 121: 255–272.

Ministerio de Salud Pública (2001), *Tablas de Mortalidad del Uruguay por sexo y edad / 1908 – 1999*, Montevideo: Ministerio de Salud Pública, Dirección General de la Salud, Departamento de Estadística.

Mitchell, B. R. (2003a), *International Historical Statistics: Africa, Asia, and Oceania 1750–2000*, New York: Palgrave Macmillan.

  (2003b), *International Historical Statistics: The Americas, 1750–2000*, New York: Palgrave Macmillan.

  (2003c) *International Historical Statistics: Europe 1750–2000*, New York: Palgrave Macmillan.

Moradi, A. (2008), "Confronting Colonial Legacies. Lessons from Human Development in Ghana and Kenya 1880–2000", *Journal of International Development* 20: 1007–1021.

(2009), "Towards an Objective Account of Nutrition and Health in Colonial Kenya: A Study of Stature in African Army Recruits and Civilians, 1880–1980", *Journal of Economic History* 69(3): 720–755

(2010), "Nutritional Status and Economic Development in Sub-Saharan Africa, 1950–1980", *Economics and Human Biology* 8: 16–29.

Moradi, A. and J. Baten (2005), "Inequality in Sub-Saharan Africa: New Data and New Insights from Anthropometric Estimates", *World Development* 33(8): 1233–1265.

Moradi, A., G. Austin, and J. Baten (2013), Heights and Development in a Cash-Crop Colony: Living Standards in Ghana, 1870–1980, ERSA Working Paper 325.

Morris, M.D. (1979), *Measuring the Condition of the World's Poor: The Physical Quality of Life Index*, New York: Pergamon.

Morrisson, C. and F. Murtin (2005), *The World Distribution of Human Capital, Life Expectancy and Income: A Multi-dimensional Approach*, Unpublished manuscript.

(2009), "The Century of Education", *Journal of Human Capital* 3(1): 1–42.

(2013), "The Kuznets Curve of Human Capital Inequality: 1870–2010", *Journal of Income Inequality* 11(3): 283–301.

Mukand, S.W. and D. Rodrik (2020), "The Political Economy of Liberal Democracy", *Economic Journal* 130: 765–792.

Murray, C.J.L. and A.D. Lopez (1997), "Regional Patterns of Disability-Free Life Expectancy and Disability-Adjusted Life Expectancy: Global Burden of Disease Study", *Lancet* 349: 1347–1352.

Murray, C.J.L. et al. (2017), "Global, Regional, and National Disability-Adjusted Life-Years (DALYs) for 333 Diseases and Injuries and Healthy Life Expectancy (HALE) for 195 Countries and Territories, 1990–2016: A Systematic Analysis for the Global Burden of Disease Study 2016", *Lancet* 390: 1260–1344.

Narizny, K. (2012), "Anglo-American Primacy and the Global Spread of Democracy: An International Genealogy", *World Politics* 64(2): 341–372.

Ndulu, B.J., S.A. O'Connell, J.P. Azam, *et al.* (eds.) (2008), *The Political Economy of Economic Growth in Africa, 1960–2000*, Cambridge: Cambridge University Press, 2 vols. and CD-ROM.

Neumayer, E. (2003), "Beyond Income: Convergence in Living Standards, Big Time", *Structural Change and Economic Dynamics* 14: 275–296

Newland, C. (1991), "La educación elemental en Hispanoamérica: desde la independencia hasta la centralización de los sistemas educativos nacionales", *Hispanic American Historical Review* 71(2): 335–364.

(1994), "The *Estado Docente* and Its Expansion: Spanish American Elemetary Education, 1900–1950", *Journal of Latin American Studies* 26: 449–467.

Nguefack-Tsague, G., S. Klasen, and W. Zucchini (2011), "On Weighting the Components of the Human Development Index: A Statistical Justification", *Journal of Human Development and Capabilities* 12(2): 183–202.

Niño-Zarazúa, M., L. Roope, and F. Tarp (2017), "Global Inequality: Relatively Lower, Absolutely Higher", *Review of Income and Wealth* 63(4): 661–684.

Noble, M.D. (2016), Illuminating Democracy: Trends, Predictors, and Outcomes of Liberal Democracy 1972–2013, University of North Carolina. Unpublished Ph.D. Dissertation.

Noman, A. and J. Stiglitz (2015), "Economics and Policy. Some Lessons from Africa's Experience", in C. Monga and J.Y. Lin (eds.), *The Oxford Handbook of Africa and Economics*, Oxford: Oxford University Press, 2 vols., II, pp. 830–848.

Noorbakhsh, F. (2006), International Convergence or Higher Inequality in Human Development? Evidence for 1975 to 2002, UNU-WIDER Research Paper No. 2006/15

Nordhaus, W.D. (2000), "New Directions in National Economic Accounting", *American Economic Review* 90(2): 259–263.

Nordhaus, W.D., and J. Tobin (1972), "Is Growth Obsolete?", in *National Bureau of Economic Research, Economic Growth: Fiftieth Anniversary Colloquium V*, New York: Columbia University Press, pp. 1–80.

Notkola, V., I.M. Timaeus, and H. Siiskonen, H. (2000), "Mortality Transition in the Ovamboland Region of Namibia, 1930–1990", *Population Studies* 54(2): 153–167.

Nussbaum, M.C. (2011), *Creating Capabilities: The Human Development Approach*, Cambridge, MA: Harvard University Press

Núñez, J. and G. Pérez (2015), "Trends in Physical Stature across Socioeconomic Groups of Chilean Boys, 1880–1997", *Economics and Human Biology* 16: 100–114.

Nunn, N. (2008), "The Long Term Effects of Africa's Slave Trades", *Quarterly Journal of Economics* 123: 139–176.

Nunn, N. and L. Wantchekon (2011), "The Slave Trade and the Origins of Mistrust in Africa", *American Economic Review* 101(7): 3221–3252.

Ocampo, J.A. and J. Ros (2011), "Shifting Paradigm in Latin America's Economic Development", in J.A. Ocampo and J. Ros (eds.), *The Oxford Handbook of Latin American Economics*, Oxford: Oxford University Press, pp. 3–25.

OECD (2011), *How's Life. Measuring Wellbeing*. Paris: OECD Publishing, available at : http://dx.doi.org/10.1787/9789264121164-en

Ogwang, T. (1994), "The Choice of Principal Variables for Computing the Human Development Index", *World Development* 22(12): 2011–2014.

Ogwang, T. and A. Abdou (2003), "The Choice of Principal Variables for Computing Some Measures of Human Well-Being", *Social Indicators Research* 64: 139–152

Omran, A.R. (1971), "The Epidemiological Transition: A Theory of Epidemiology of Population Change", *Milbank Memorial Fund Quarterly* 49(4): 509–538.

Omran, A. R. (1998), "The Epidemiologic Transition Theory Revisited Thirty Years Later", *World Health Statistics Quarterly* 53 (2,3,4): 99–119. available at: https://apps.who.int/iris/handle/10665/330604

Oulton, P. (2012), Hooray for GDP! LSE Centre for Economic Performance Occasional Paper 30.

Paglayan, A.S. (2021), "The Non-Democratic Roots of Mass Education: Evidence from 200 Years", *American Political Science Review* 115(1): 179–198.

Palacios, M. (1995), *Entre la legitimidad y la violencia. Colombia 1875–1994*, Bogotá: Norma.

Palma, N. and J. Reis (2021), "Can Autocracy Promote Literacy? Evidence from a Cultural Alignment Success Story", *Journal of Economic Behavior and Organization* 1865: 412–436.

Pamuk, Ş. (2006), "Estimating Economic Growth in the Middle East since 1820", *Journal of Economic History* 66(3): 809–828.

(2018), *Uneven Centuries: Economic Development of Turkey since 1820*, Princeton, NJ: Princeton University Press.

Prados de la Escosura, L. (2007a), "Inequality and Poverty in Latin America: A Long-Run Exploration", in T.J. Hatton, K.H. O'Rourke, and A.M. Taylor (eds.), *The New Comparative Economic History*, Cambridge, MA: MIT Press, pp. 291–315.

(2007b), "When Did Latin America Fall Behind?", in S. Edwards, G. Esquivel, and G. Marquez (eds.), *The Decline of Latin American Economies: Growth, Institutions, and Crisis*, Chicago: NBER/University of Chicago Press, pp. 15–57.

(2012), "Output per Head in Pre-independence Sub-Saharan Africa: Quantitative Conjectures", *Economic History of Developing Regions* 27(2): 1–35.

(2013), "Human Development in Africa: A Long-Run Perspective", *Explorations in Economic History* 50: 161–178.

(2015a), "Human Development as Positive Freedom: Latin America in Historical Perspective", *Journal of Human Development and Capabilities* 16(3): 342–373.

(2015b), "World Human Development: 1870–2007", *Review of Income and Wealth* 61(2): 220–247.

(2017), *Spanish Economic Growth, 1850–2015*, London: Palgrave-Macmillan.

Prados de la Escosura, L. and M.S. Cha (2021), "Living Standards, Inequality, and Human Development", in S. Broadberry and K. Fukao (eds.), *The Cambridge Economic History of the Modern World. Vol. II. 1870 to the Present*, Cambridge: Cambridge University Press, II, pp. 442–470.

Prebisch, R. (1950), *The Economic Development of Latin America and Its Principal Problems*, Lake Success, New York: United Nations.

Pressat, R. (1985), "Historical Perspectives on the Population of the Soviet Union", *Population and Development Review* 11: 315–334.

Preston, S. (1975), "The Changing Relationship between Mortality and the Level of Economic Development", *Population Studies* 29(2): 231–248.

Ram, R. (1980), "Physical Quality of Life Index and Inter-country Inequality", *Economic Letters* 5: 195–199.

(1982), "Composite Indices of Physical Quality of Life, Basic Needs Fulfilment, And Income. A 'Principal Component'", *Representation', Journal of Development Economics* 11: 227–247.

(1992), "International Inequalities in Human Development and Real Income", *Economic Letters* 38: 351–354.

(2006), "State of the Life Span Revolution between 1980 and 2000", *Journal of Development Economics* 80: 518–526.

Ravallion, M. (1997), "Good and Bad Growth: The Human Development Reports", *World Development* 25(5): 631–638.

(2004), "Competing Concepts of Inequality in the Globalization Debate", in S.M. Collins and C. Graham (eds.), *Brookings Trade Forum: Globalization, Poverty, and Inequality*, Washington, DC: Brookings Institution Press, pp. 1–23.

(2012a), "Mashup Indices of Development", *World Bank Research Observer* 27(1): 1–32.

(2012b), "Troubling Tradeoffs in the Human Development Index", *Journal of Development Economics* 99: 201–209.

Ravallion, M. and Chen (2017), Welfare-Consistent Global Poverty Measures, World Bank Policy Research Working Paper 8170.

Recchini de Lattes, Z. and A. E. Lattes (eds.) (1975), *La población de Argentina*, Buenos Aires: Instituto Nacional de Estadística y Censos.

Reimers, F. (2006), "Education and Social Progress", in V. Bulmer-Thomas, J.H. Coatsworth, and R. Cortés Conde (eds.), *The Cambridge Economic History of Latin America. Vol. II. The Long Twentieth Century*, New York: Cambridge University Press, II, pp. 427–480.

Rijpma, A. (2017), What Can't Money Buy? Wellbeing and GDP since 1820, CGEH Working Paper Series 78

Riley, J.C. (1990), "The Risk of Being Sick: Morbidity Trends in Four Countries", *Population and Development Review* 16: 403–432.

(2001), *Rising Life Expectancy: A Global History*, New York: Cambridge University Press.

(2005a), *Poverty and Life Expectancy. The Jamaica Paradox*, New York: Cambridge University Press.

(2005b), "The Timing and Pace of Health Transitions around the World", *Population and Development Review* 31: 741–764.

(2005c), "Bibliography of Works Providing Estimates of Life Expectancy at Birth and Estimates of the Beginning Period of Health Transitions in Countries with a Population in 2000 of at Least 400,000", available at: www.lifetable.de/RileyBib.htm

Robeyns, I. (2005), "The Capability Approach: A Theoretical Survey", *Journal of Human Development* 6(1): 93–117

(2006), "The Capability Approach in Practice", *Journal of Political Philosophy* 14(3): 352–376.

(2011), "The Capability Approach", in E.N. Zalta (ed.), *The Stanford Encyclopedia of Philosophy*, available at: https://plato.stanford.edu/archives/sum2011/entries/capability-approach/

Robinson, J.A. and S. Henn (2021), Africa's Latent Assets, CEPR Discussion Paper 15963.

Rodríguez Braun, C. (2010), "On Liberty's Liberty", *Independent Review* 14(4): 599–612.

Rodríguez Weber, J.E. (2016), Estimación de desigualdad de ingreso y otras variables relacionadas para Chile entre 860 y 1970. Metodología y resultados obtenidos, Universidad de la República PHES Documento de Trabajo 44.

Sachs, J.D. and A.M. Warner (1997), "Sources of Slow Growth in African Economies", *Journal of African Economies* 6(3): 335–376.

Sagar, A .D. and A. Najam (1998), "The Human Development Index: A Critical Review", *Ecological Economics* 25: 249–264

Sala-i-Martin, X. (2006), "The World Distribution of Income: Falling Poverty ... and Convergence, Period", *Quarterly Journal of Economics* 121(2): 351–397.

Salomon, J.A., H. Wang, M.K. Freeman, T., *et al.* (2012), "Healthy Life Expectancy for 187 Countries, 1990–2010: A Systematic Analysis for the Global Burden Disease Study 2010", *Lancet* 380: 2144–2162.

Salvatore, R. (2019), "The Biological Wellbeing of the Working-Poor: The Height of Prisoners in Buenos Aires Province, Argentina, 1885–1939", *Economics and Human Biology* 34: 92–102.

Salvatore, R.D., J.H. Coatsworth, and A.E. Challú (eds.) (2010), *Living Standards in Latin American History: Height, Welfare and Development, 1750–2000*. Cambridge, MA: Harvard University Press.

Santamaría, A. (2005), "Las cuentas nacionales de Cuba, 1690–2005", Centro de Estudios Históricos, Centro Superior de Investigaciones Científicas (mimeo)

Sarkar, N.K. (1951), "A Note on Abridged Life Tables for Ceylon, 1900–1947", *Population Studies* 4: 439–443.

Sbr, V. (1962), "Population Development and Population Policy in Czechoslovakia", *Population Studies* 16: 147–159.

Schultz, T.P. (1998), "Inequality in the Distribution of Personal Income in the World: How It Is Changing and Why", *Journal of Population Economics* 11: 307–344.

Schulze, M.S. (2000), "Patterns of Growth and Stagnation in the Late Nineteenth Century Habsburg Economy", *European Review of Economic History* 4: 311–340.

Seminario, B. (2015), *El desarrollo de la economía peruana en la era moderna. Precios, población, demanda y producción desde 1700*, Lima: Universidad del Pacífico.

Sen, A. (1981), "Public Action and the Quality of Life in Developing Countries", *Oxford Bulletin of Economics and Statistics* 43: 287–319.

(1984), "The Living Standard", *Oxford Economic Papers* 36: 74–90.

(1999), *Development as Freedom*, Oxford: Oxford University Press.

(2020), "Human Development and Mahbub ul Haq", in *UNDP, Human Development Report 2020. The Next Frontier. Human Development and the Anthropocene*, New York: UNDP, p. xi

Shkolnikov, V., M. McKee, and D.A. Leon (2001), "Changes in Life Expectancy in Russia in the Mid-1990s", *Lancet* 357: 917–921.

Shorter, F.C. and M. Macura (1982), *Trends in Fertility and Mortality in Turkey 1935–1975*, Washington, DC: National Academy Press.

Siampos, G.S. (1970), "The Population of Cambodia, 1945–1980", *Milbank Memorial Fund Quarterly* 48: 317–360.

Simkins, Ch. And E. van Heyningen (1989), "Mortality and Migration in the Cape Colony, 1891–1904", *International Journal of African Historical Studies* 22(1): 79–111.

Singer, H.W. (1950), "The Distribution of Gains between Investing and Borrowing Countries", *American Economic Review (Papers and Proceedings)* 40: 473–485.

Srinivasan, T.N. (1994), "Human Development: A New Paradigm or Reinvention of the Wheel?", *American Economic Review*, 84(2): 238–243.

Stadler, J. J. (1963), "The Gross Domestic Product of South Africa 1911–1959", *South African Journal of Economics* 31(3): 185–208

Steckel, R.H. (2009), "Extending the Reach of Anthropometric History to the Distant Past", in D. Eltis, F.D. Lewis, and K.L. Sokoloff (eds.), *Human Capital and Institutions: A Long-Run View*, New York: Cambridge University Press, pp. 27–45.

Stiglitz, J.E., A. Sen, and J.P. Fitoussi (2009), *Report by the Commission on the Measurement of Economic Performance and Social Progress*, available at: http://ec.europa.eu/eurostat/documents/118025/118123/Fitoussi+Commission+report

Stillman, S. (2006), "Health and Nutrition in Eastern Europe and the Former Soviet Union during the Decade of Transition: A Review of the Literature", *Economics and Human Biology* 4: 104–146.

Stolnitz, G.J. (1955), "A Century of International Mortality Trends", *Population Studies* 9: 24–55.

Stolper, W. and P. Samuelson (1941), "Protection and Real Wages", *Review of Economic Studies* 9(1): 58–73.

Streeten, P., S. Burki, M. ul Haq, N. Hicks, and F. Stewart (1981), *First Things First: Meeting Basic Human Needs in Developing Countries*, New York: Oxford University Press.

Syrquin, M. (2016), ""A Review Essay on GDP: A Brief but Affectionate History by Diane Coyle", *Journal of Economic Literature* 254(2): 573–588.

Székely, M. (2001), The 1990s in Latin America: Another Decade of Persistent Inequality, but with Somewhat Lower Poverty, Inter-American Development Bank Research Department Working Paper 454.

Székely, M. and P. Mendoza (2015), "Is the Decline in Inequality in Latin America Here to Stay?", *Journal of Human Development and Capabilities* 16(3): 397–419.

(2017), "Declining Inequality in Latin America: Structural Shift or Temporary Phenomenon?", *Oxford Development Studies* 45(2): 204–221.

Szreter, S. (1997), "Economic Growth, Disruption, Deprivation, Disease, and Death: On the Importance of the Politics of Public Health for Development", *Population and Development Review* 23 (4): 693–728.

Teng, Y. (2019), "Educational Inequality and Its Determinants: Evidence for Women in Nine Latin American Countries, 1950s–1990s", *Revista de Historia Económica/Journal of Iberian and Latin American Economic History* 37(3): 409–441.

Theil, H. (1967), *Economics and Information Theory*, Amsterdam: North Holland.

(1979), "Components of the Change in Regional inequality", *Economic Letters* 4: 191–193.

(1989), "The Development of International Inequality 1960–1985", *Journal of Econometrics* 42: 145–155.

Ticchi, D. and A. Vindigni (2008), War and Endogenous Democracy, IZA Discussion Paper 3397.

Toutain, J.C. (1997), "Le produit intérieur brut de la France, 1789–1990", *Économies et Sociétés. Histoire Économique Quantitative* 11: 5–136.

United Nations (1954), *Report on International Definition and Measurement of Standards and Levels of Living*, New York: United Nations.

(1993), *Demographic Yearbook 1991 Special Issue: Population Ageing and the Situation of Elderly Persons*, New York: United Nations.

(2000), *Demographic Yearbook Historical Supplement 1948–1997*, New York: United Nations.

United Nations Development Programme (1990–2020), *Human Development Report*, New York: Oxford University Press.

Urquiola, M. (2011), "Education", in J.A. Ocampo and J. Ros (eds.), *The Oxford Handbook of Latin American Economics*, Oxford: Oxford University Press, pp. 813–835.

Valaoras, V. (1960), "A Reconstruction of the Demographic History of Modern Greece", *Miliband Memorial Fund Quarterly* 38: 114–139.

Valério, N. (2001), *Estatísticas Históricas Portuguesas*, Lisboa: Instituto Nacional de Estatística, 2 vols.

Vallin, J. (1976), "La population de la Thaïlande", *Population* 31: 153–175.

Vanhanen, T. (2016), Measures of Democracy 1810–2014. FSD1289, Version 7.0 (2016-05-30). Finnish Social Science Data Archive, available at: http://urn.fi/urn:nbn:fi:fsd:T-FSD1289 (Accessed on 11 May 2019)

Vecchi, G., N. Amendola, and G. Gabbuti (2017), "Human Development", in G. Vecchi (ed.), *Measuring Wellbeing. A History of Italian Living Standards* Oxford: Oxford University Press, pp. 454–491.

Veenhoven, R. and F. Vengust (2013), "The Easterlin Illusion: Economic Growth Does Go with Greater Happiness", *International Journal of Happiness and Development* 1(4), 311–343

Veiga, T. Rodrigues (2005), "A transição demográfica", in P. Lains and A. Ferreira da Silva (eds.), *História Económica de Portugal 1700–2000*, Lisboa: Imprensa de Ciências Sociais, III O Século XX, pp. 37–63.

Visaria, L. and P. Visaria (1982), "Population (1757–1947)", in D. Kumar (with M. Desai) (ed.), *Cambridge Economic History of India*, Cambridge: Cambridge University Press, II, pp. 463–532.

Ward, M. and J. Devereux (2012), "The Road Not Taken: Pre-Revolutionary Cuban Living Standards in Comparative Perspective", *Journal of Economic History* 72(1): 104–132.

Whitwell, G., Ch. de Souza, and S. Nicholas (1997), "Height, Health, and Economic Growth in Australia", in R.H. Steckel and R. Floud (eds.), *Health and Welfare during Industrialization*, Chicago: University of Chicago Press, pp. 379–422.

Williamson, J.G. (1997), "Globalization and Inequality, Past and Present", *World Bank Research Observer* 12(2): 117–135.

(2010), "Five Centuries of Latin American Income Inequality", *Revista de Historia Económica/Journal of Iberian and Latin American Economic History* 28(2): 227–252.

World Bank (2020), "World Development Indicators Database", Washington, DC: World Bank, available at: http://data.worldbank.org/data-catalog

Zambrano, E. (2014), "An Axiomatization of the Human Development Index", *Social Choice Welfare* 42: 853–872.

(2017), "The 'Troubling Tradeoffs' Paradox and a Resolution", *Review of Income and Wealth* 63(3): 520–541.

Zanden, J.L. van, J. Baten, P. Foldvári, and B. van Leeuwen (2014), "The Changing Shape of Global Inequality 1820–2000: Exploring a New Dataset", *Review of Income and Wealth* 60(2): 279–297.

Zwart, P. de (2011a), Real Wages at the Cape of Good Hope: A Long-Term Perspective, 1652–1912. CGEH Working Paper Series no. 13, available at: www.cgeh.nl/working-paper-series/

(2011b), "South African Living Standards in Global Perspective, 1835–1910", *Economic History of Developing Regions* 26(1): 49–74.

Index

Acemoglu, 15, 57, 62, 136, 184
achievement, 1–4, 14–15, 24, 36, 68,
    149
  function, 19, 290
  index, 290, 295, *See* functionings
agency, 3–4, 9, 25, 28, 134, 179, 217
antibiotics, 59, 140, 153
Argentina
  civil liberties, 175–6
  country ranking 41, 48, 51–3,
    157–73, 175
  health 155, 176
  heights 138
  historical index 142–4, 149
  infant mortality 139
  nation building schooling 61, 141,
    154, 176
  per capita GDP 255
Asia, 41, 60, 135, 225, 247, 251–6
  East Asia 100–1, 103, 111, 117–25,
    127–33, 279
  South Asia 100–1, 103, 117–25,
    127–33, 244, 277
Australia, 48, 51, 99, 244, 248, 296
authoritarian
  countries, 60–1, 243
  experiences, 9, 134
  ideologies, 7, 92, 95
  regime, 6–7, 92, 95, 107, 242
  rule, 64

Baghwati, 242
basic needs, 2–3, 25, 134, 179
Bértola, 135, 141–4, 255
  indices, 21–5, 33–6, 259, 291, 293
Botswana, 49–50, 53–4, 223–9, 233–8,
    245–6, 251–4
Brazil, 138, 142–3, 149, 181, 255, 296
  country ranking, 48–9, 52–3,
    159–62, 164–74

Britain, 25, 57, 185, 296, *See* United
    Kingdom

Canada, 48, 51, 99, 244, 247, 296
capabilities, 14–15, 22–5, 27–8, 65,
    290–1
  approach, 1–4, 36, 68, 288, 292
capitalism, 57
cardiovascular, 16, 59, 62, 130
Chile, 138–43, 149, 154–5, 175–7,
    246, 255
  country ranking, 41, 48, 52–3,
    157–73, 179
China, 100–1, 117–25, 127–33, 275
  Great Leap Forward, 56, 71, 105,
    110
  inequality, 66, 75–7, 262–6, 294
  country ranking, 41, 49, 54–5
  sources, 29, 247, 252–3, 256
civil and political liberties, 3–9, 29, 56,
    107–9, 122–31, 242–3
  Africa, 200, 206–9, 211–20, 224,
    232, 240
  inequality, 72–7, 81, 87–8, 90–4,
    115–16, 265
  Latin America, 152–3, 156–7,
    164–82, *See* freedom
Colombia, 139, 142–3, 149, 154–5,
    180
  country ranking, 48, 52–3, 159–74
  sources, 256, 250, 255
colonial, 5, 185–6, 294, 296
  era, 8, 136, 184, 198, 240
  rule, 8, 59, 110, 125, 189, 232
consumption, 2, 132, 138, 186
Crafts, 25, 293
Cuba, 41, 140, 143–4, 175, 178–9
  country ranking, 48, 53–4,
    157–74
  sources, 246, 252, 254–5

death, 14, 17, 58–9, 130, 139, 182,
    290–3
Deaton, 1, 16, 20, 59, 288–9
democracy, 61–2, 252, 294
    liberal, 6–7, 21–2, 25, 29, 61–4,
        241–3
    index, 28–31, 35, 38–9, 56, 267–85,
        291
    Africa, 188–9, 195–204, 206–7,
        210–20, 233–8
    inequality, 74, 87–8, 92, 95
    Latin America, 145–6, 151, 158
    OECD and the Rest, 104–7, 111,
        119, 124, 129–33,
    See democratisation
democratisation, 56, 61–3, 122, 141–3,
    225, 291, *See* democracy
disability, 17, 289, 292
disease, 17, 61, 138–40, 177, 243,
    293–4
    cardiovascular and respiratory, 16,
        59, 62, 130
    chronic, 58
    germ theory, 58, 140, 153, 293
    infectious, 8, 16, 58–9, 125, 182–3,
        186
    Global Burden of, 17
drugs, 7–9, 57–9, 64, 125, 179, 182

Easterlin, 57, 59, 288
Eastern Europe, 41, 56, 74, 91, 107,
    117–35, 271
economic growth, 1–3, 6, 40–1, 57–8,
    102, 241–3
    Africa, 184
    Latin America, 135, 137–8, 140,
        142, 146, 182
education, 1–9, 13–18, 23–36, 40,
    56–64, 241–3, 259, 287–9
    Africa, 185–6, 213–15, 225–6
    inequality, 67, 69–71, 74, 77, 90, 93
    Latin America, 137, 139–43, 146,
        153–6, 175–9, 181–2
    OECD and the Rest, 107–9, 117,
        122, 125, 129–31, 136
    years, 143, 249–51, 290, *See*
        schooling
Egypt, 49–54, 217–21, 229–30, 235–9,
    245, 254
Engerman, 1, 136, 141

epidemiological transition, 6–8, 57–64,
    73–4, 91–5, 241–4, 294
    Africa, 248
    Latin America, 176–8, 182
    OECD and the Rest, 105, 129, 133,
    See health transition

famine, 71, 105, 119, 125
Fogel, 16, 58
food, 138
freedom, 1–9, 24–9, 36, 56, 241–3,
    252, 295–7
    civil and political freedoms, 64,
        109–10, 117, 126
    Africa, 220
    Latin America, 144, 151, 156, 176,
        178–9, 181–2
    OECD and the Rest, 109–10, 117,
        122, 126, 130–1, 133–4
    negative, 3, 25, 288, 291
    positive, 3, 25, 288, *See* civil and
        political liberties
functionings, 2–3, 24, 291, *See*
    achievement

Gini, 22, 24, 66, 296
globalisation, 1–3, 37, 67, 86, 94, 241
    backlash, 6–7, 40, 64, 146, 182, 242
Golden Age, 41, 81, 84–6, 88, 115,
    130–1
government, 25, 57, 60–1, 139, 144
    activism, 8, 59, 109
    intervention, *See* public
Great Leap Forward, 56, 71, 77, 105,
    110, 119, 125
growth incidence curve, 5, 65, 79,
    82–90

Harris, 249, 294, 296
Hatton, 15, 296
health, 1–9, 13–23, 33–41, 57–8,
    63–73, 241–2, 289–96
    Africa, 184–6, 198, 232, 240
    health function, 57–8, 198, 232,
        240
    Latin America, 137–40, 143–6,
        153–5, 157, 177–9, 181–3
    OECD and the Rest, 125, 132, 134
    public, 59, 137–40, 143, 153, 182,
        296

health (cont.)
  transition, 6, 58–62, 73–4, 91–5,
    243–4, 247, 293
    Africa, 186, 200, 240
    Latin America, 157
    OECD and the Rest, 105, 113, *See*
      epidemiological transition
height, 2, 8, 15, 245, 296
  Africa, 185–6, 198, 240
  Latin America, 138–40, 176–7, 179,
    181–3
Herrero, 15–16, 20–4, 28, 33–5, 259,
  290–3
HIV/AIDS, 68, 220, 224–5
hygiene, 143

income
  egalitarian equivalent, 22–4, 35–6,
    291
income per capita, *See* GDP per capita
independence, 5, 8, 135, 140
  Africa, 8, 77, 184–6, 208–14, 240,
    296
  Latin America, 175, 178
India, 49, 53–4, 75, 242–56, 262–6,
  278, 294
inequality, 2–7, 22–5, 35–6, 62–95,
  242–3, 260–6, 290–5
  Africa, 185, 187, 193
  Latin America, 136, 138, 140–1,
    143, 165, 177
  OECD and the Rest, 102–3, 110–15,
    132
  absolute, 4, 65–7, 77–82, 294–5
  relative, 4, 6, 65–6, 78–83, 94, 294–5
  Extraction Ratio, 7, 149, 286, 296
infant mortality, 2, 59, 69, 125, 288
  Africa, 186, 198, 240, 245
  Latin America, 139–40, 177, 182,
    See infant survival
infant survival, 8, 139, 177, 183, 186,
    245–9, 295, *See* infant mortality
interwar, 8, 32, 40–1, 244, 259, 294–5
  Africa, 192, 240
  inequality,
    74, 77
  Latin America, 156–7, 175, 177,
    180–2
  OECD and the Rest, 110, 116, 122,
    125–6

Jamaica, 140, 158, 175, 178, 246, 252,
  255
  ranking, 48, 52, 159–74
Japan, 41, 99–101, 110–19, 244–7,
  270, 280, 296
  ranking, 48, 51

Kakwani, 4, 18–23, 29–30, 33–6, 259,
  290–3
  index, 20, 38–9, 56–8, 60, 70,
    267–87
    Africa, 188–9, 194–220
    inequality, 70–1, 73, 84–7, 90–1,
      260–1
    Latin America, 142–3, 145–6, 150–8
    OECD and the Rest, 104–7, 111,
      113–14, 117–18, 121–3, 129–39
Kuznets, 68, 93

life expectancy, 27, 104–7, 109–12,
  117–19, 122–6, 129–33
  Africa, 188–9, 190–206, 208–20,
    224–5, 232–9
  Latin America, 145–6, 151–3,
    155–82, *See* life expectancy at
    birth
  healthy, 17, 290
  inequality, 65–9, 71–80, 84–95,
    112–16
Life expectancy at birth, 57–64, 67–73,
  91, 130, 241, 289
  index, 2–6, 13–22, 28–9, 244–7, 293–7
  Latin America, 130, 140–4, 150,
    177–9, 182
  Africa, 8, 198, 226, 240, *See* life
    expectancy
life satisfaction, 1–2, 288
Lindert, 15, 58, 61, 71, 141, 154–5, 287
literacy, 2, 15, 67, 141–2, 288–9, 295
living standard, 2–3, 2–3, 9, 14, 63, 69,
  297
  Africa, 185
  Latin America, 135, 138, 142, 181
longevity, 3–6, 14–16, 23–7, 30–3, 243,
  259, 289–97
  Africa, 196, 200–2, 209–12, 215–19,
    226, 232
  inequality, 68, 73–4, 94
  Latin America, 142, 151–3, 157,
    175–83

OECD and the Rest, 105–10, 116–19, 122, 125, 130, 133, *See* life expectancy
lost decades, 8, 184, 240

Maddison, 20, 29, 242, 253–8, 296
Project Database, 20, 29, 253
market, 2, 40, 57, 132, 137, 146, 184
medical, 6, 57, 140, 179, 186, 243
innovation, 60
knowledge, 6–7, 9, 58–9, 64, 95, 177
technology, 20, 73, 198, 232, 289
Mexico, 138, 142, 149, 157, 180–1, 255
ranking, 48–9, 53, 159–74
Milanovic, 16, 66–70, 136, 149, 233, 290–6
modernisation, 62
morbidity, 6, 17, 58–9, 186, 198, 242
compression, 17, 242, 289–90
Morrisson, 15, 295
mortality, 28, 56–60, 130–2, 139–43, 177–8, 186, 244, *See* life expectancy, infant mortality
maternal, 8, 59, 139, 182, 294

nation-building, 6–7, 61, 64, 141, 157, 175–6, 241
natural resources, 136, 142
Nussbaum, 288
nutrition, 6–9, 58–9, 138–40, 177–86, 198, 240–3

per capita GDP, 4–5, 8, 19–20, 28–9, 40, 253–7
Africa, 189, 232
inequality, 65, 68, 76, 79, 89–90, 92–3
OECD and the Rest, 114, 116, 155, *See* per capita income
per capita income, 5–6, 14–16, 20–7, 30–6, 41, 255, 289–93
Africa, 185, 192, 204, 232
inequality, 65, 67, 70–1, 74, 77, 90–4
Latin America, 137, 141–2, 146, 149, 155, 158, 182
OECD and the Rest, 102, *See* per capita GDP
Physical Quality of Life Index, 2, 68, 288, 291

population, 4, 13, 25, 28–30, 59–61, 248–58, 296–7
Africa, 186, 225–6
inequality, 65–6, 69–72, 74–6, 78–82, 90, 93, 95
Latin America, 141, 181–2
OECD and the Rest, 109, 112–16
poverty, 137, 149, 253
Preston, 19, 57, 247
Curve, 19–20
public instruction, 61, *See* education
purchasing power parity, 14–15, 29

quality of life, 2, 17, 288

Ravallion, 26–7, 137, 288, 291–2, 294
redistribution, 6, 60, 62, 64, 141, 217, 226, 297
Riley, 28, 57–9, 140, 178, 244–8, 289–97
Russia, 56, 75–7, 100–1, 249–57, 273, 294
inequality, 262–6
OECD and the Rest, 117–24, 126–33
ranking, 48–9, 53–4

sanitation, 7, 140, 143, 183, 186
Schooling, 3–8, 23–7, 57, 60–5, 241–3, 259
years of, 13–18, 20–2, 28–9, 33–5, 249–51, 289–92
Kakwani index of years of, 21–2, 30–5, 38–9, 56, 267–85, 287
Africa, 188–9, 194–205, 208–20, 224–5, 232–40
inequality, 65–7, 71–85, 90, 93–4, 260, 263
Latin America, 140–2, 145–6, 150, 152–8, 164–82
OECD and the Rest, 104–7, 109–11, 113–18, 121–2, 135–6, 129–33, *See* education
Sen, 1–3, 14, 57, 68, 132, 241–2, 288
sewerage, 138, 143, 180
social spending, 9, 57, 137, 142–3, 154, 182, 241
socialism, 56, 59, 74, 91–2, 107, 119, 129–32, *See* socialist
socialist, 9, 41, 91, 95, 126, 130–4

socialist (cont.)
  state, 144, 179, *See* socialism
South Asia, 41, 100–3, 117–25,
  127–33, 244, 277
Soviet Union, 6, 92, 95, 131–2, 249,
  294, *See* Russia
state-led industrialisation, 137, 141–2,
  182, 217, 297
Sub-Saharan Africa, 29, 59, 243–4,
  252, 258, 283
  Africa, 184, 186, 190, 193, 198, 204
  inequality, 68, 74–7, 91, 103, 262–6
  OECD and the Rest, 107, 111,
    117–24, 126–31, 133
sulphonamides, 59, 140, 294

UNDP, 2–3, 13–16, 20–8, 33–9, 63,
  259, 267–95
  Africa, 188–9, 194–204, 210–20
  Latin America, 132–3, 145–6, 158
  OECD and the Rest, 104–7, 111,
    129–33
  sources, 244, 250
United Kingdom, 20, 48–51, 249, 253,
  257, 296, *See* Britain
United Nations Development
  Programme, 2, 13, *See* UNDP
United States, 99, 135, 142, 244, 296,
  See U.S.

urbanisation, 7, 139, 141–2, 182, 186,
  294
U.S., 61, 137, 290, *See* United States
utility, 2, 15, 292

vaccines, 59
Vecchi, 21–2, 24–5, 33–5, 259, 292–3

wages, 136, 139, 181
Washington Consensus, 184
water supply, 7, 139–40, 143, 180,
  183
welfare state, 137, 139, 181
well-being, 1–4, 14, 25–6, 37–40, 57,
  62, 288–96
  Africa, 219–20, 224
  inequality, 65, 67–71, 74–5, 83,
    90–2, 94
  Latin America, 135–40, 142–3, 146,
    149, 178
  OECD and the Rest, 131
Western Europe, 6, 25, 41, 58, 267,
  291, 296
  OECD and the Rest, 99, 110,
    115–19, 130, 135
World Bank, 28, 244, 253

Zambrano, 21–4, 27, 33–5, 259,
  290–3

Lightning Source UK Ltd.
Milton Keynes UK
UKHW022157131222
413895UK00010B/76